THE ART OF INTERIOR DESIGN

DESIGN WITH A FORWARD EMPHASIS
Private residence in Maryland
Architect-designer: Hugh Newell Jacobsen
Photograph: Courtesy of Hugh Newell Jacobsen
With the passage of time subtle change occurs in all forms of art. Interior design and architecture continue to emphasize space. Today there is a new consciousness of vertical space, oblique views, the play of light, muted color, texture, and expressive character.

THE ART OF INTERIOR DESIGN

Second Edition

VICTORIA KLOSS BALL

A Wiley-Interscience Publication

JOHN WILEY & SONS

New York · Chichester · Brisbane · Toronto · Singapore

Library of Congress Cataloging in Publication Data:

Ball, Victoria Kloss.
   The art of interior design.

   "A Wiley-Interscience publication."
   Bibliography: p.
   Includes index.
   1. Interior decoration. I. Title.

NK2110.B33 1982   729   82-2556
ISBN 0-471-09679-2   AACR2

Printed in the United States of America

10 9 8 7 6 5 4 3 2 1

To the many students of
interior design
who have dedicated themselves
to the hard but rewarding task
of making our surroundings
more beautiful

PREFACE

It has been said with some justice that the twentieth century drowns in the sea of specialists' babel. This book introduces one of those specialized languages. However, if learned correctly, it is one that intercommunicates because it speaks about things that are meaningful to all people: this is the language of art.

The following pages venture to make a suitable beginning to the study of the art of interior design. First, it must be understood that interior design is a part of all the professions concerned with the environmental arts. To study or present it without indicating the interrelations between these varied professional arts and their disciplines is sheer folly and actually, today, impossible.

Interior design, nevertheless, has its own terrain. Its program relates to the environment within a building, always with a consideration of intended use, the occupants, and the structure, planning, and design character of the building itself.

The word *art* encompasses the whole concept—the fulfillment of functional, meaningful, and sensuous demands. *Design* is a more particular word. It represents selection and organization for a purpose, in this case to fulfill the expectations of interior design as an art form. Design is the route, the means, the way of accomplishing an art.

The purport of this text therefore is to lay down whatever precepts there are for the attainment of good interior design and to present these precepts in as liberal a manner as possible. Such training as this book may be able to give is a matter of words, of limited illustrations, and of suggestions for reader participation. It is an attempt to say the unsayable, to find pertinent illustrations of the highest quality, and to pose problems that will lead to good thinking and ultimately to good creation.

To state this in another manner, this book attempts training for sensitivity. The author thinks that it is the privilege of the arts to clarify on an intuitive level the difficult and ill-understood phenomena of life. To do this the designer must become a master of the art of harnessing sensations and perceptions. While dealing with this subtle material in an ordered way, the designer must be able to handle it in a liberal fashion so that the needs of a changing yet constant world are fulfilled. The chapters that follow offer specific training within an open-ended focus. A liberal interpretation of the arts is a state of mind. It leads to a vision that stimulates creativity in its best sense.

What the designer does will accomplish more than what I may say here, but I sincerely hope he or she will do better because of what has been said in this book.

VICTORIA KLOSS BALL

Cleveland, Ohio
August 1982

ACKNOWLEDGMENTS

A book is the work of many persons, and it is my pleasure and privilege to acknowledge the contributions of those who have shared in making this one. Although I must take the responsibility for its contents, the merits it may contain are largely due to expertise generously given by others. I regret that only a few of these numerous helpers can be listed. As in all life it is the anonymous givers who are in large part responsible for the success of an enterprise. Well aware of their aid, I extend to them my gratitude.

First I say thank you to those friends in the academic field who urged a revision of an earlier text. Chief advocates were Mary L. Shipley, Professor of Interior Design at Arizona State University at Tempe, and Martha M. Caldwell, Associate Professor, the University of Vermont at Burlington. Mary Shipley is remembered as the principal assistant in the compilation of the former edition.

My prime indebtedness is one of longlasting and personal gratitude to William Dudley Hunt, Jr., FAIA, Architecture Editor at John Wiley & Sons, Inc. His patience, kindness, and good judgment have inspired me to put my best effort into this work.

The representatives of many professional organizations have shared their time and knowledge for various sections of this book. Louise P. Galyon (and previously Blanche R. Bellamy) of the Munsell Color Company have been generous in providing instructional aids. For the updating on lighting I am especially indebted to Howard Haynes of the Illuminating Engineering Society and also to the Institute of Electrical and Electronics Engineers and the Lighting Institute, the General Electric Company. The American Society for Testing and Materials provided information on synthetics. Physicist Arthur H. Benade has been helpful with some of the technical sections.

The Federation of Societies for Coatings Technology has provided current information on the Color-Matching Aptitude Test. The Color Association of the United States (formerly the Textile Color Card Association) has been cooperative. The American Optical Corporation provided information on the American Optical Society Pseudo-Isochromatic Color Test (the A O Test). Fred Billmeyer, Jr., Rensselaer Polytechnic Institute, and C. James Bartleson, Eastman Kodak Research Laboratories, provided information on the Inter-Society Color Council Comparative List of Color Terms.

The help of museums of art is always necessary when one is working in any art-related field. Those who granted permission to use photographs of objects in their collections have been noted in the captions that accompany the pictures and are gratefully acknowledged here. The Cleveland Museum of Art, through the generosity of its Director, Sherman E. Lee, has helped this text immeasurably. Dorothy G. Shepherd, Curator of Textiles and Islamic Art at the Cleveland Museum has not only assisted in locating material in these fields, but she has also been most generous in providing photographs of the architectural work of her late husband Ernst Payer, A.I.A., for this publication. Delbert R. Gutridge, Registrar of the Museum, has been gracious in locating illustrations for our use.

Gary A. Dayton of the Charles Burchfield Center in Buffalo has guided us to the proper sources for Burchfield information and for the Thoreau quotation used in this connection. F. Frederick Bernaski, Chief Registrar of the Kennedy Galleries, New York, generously supplied a photograph of the Burchfield painting reproduced in this book.

The American Craft Council, the Walters Art Gallery, the Metropolitan Museum, The Museum of Modern Art, and the Albright-Knox Gallery were all helpful, as were the magazines *Interior Design* and *Architectural Record*.

Commercial firms, only a very limited number of which could be represented, have also contributed to this book. Much of the advance that can be noted in designing for interiors is due to the generally excellent work done by the design industry.

Without the creativity of architects, designers, and artists and the excellent photographs provided by individual photographers this book would have been all words and no substance. I have tried to select illustrations that are the best examples and the most representative of contemporary trends. It is my regret that much material has had to be excluded solely on the grounds of space limitation.

I wish to acknowledge my debt to the teaching of the late Thomas Munro, Curator of Education at the Cleveland Museum of Art and Professor of Art at Case Western Reserve University, Cleveland, Ohio. Whatever there is of logic in my thinking about art is due to his teaching. His was, in my opinion, one of the great creative minds in the field of aesthetics.

Three draftsmen assisted in the present work. The diagrams that were held over from the earlier version are derived from the work of Algirdas Liutkus, architect. Mary L. Shipley drew figures 5.8, 8.1, 10.7, 10.9, 11.14, and 11.15. The remaining work, with the exception of the plans of specific houses that were provided by their architects, was done by Gordana P. Ukmar, architect. Each of these draftsmen is to be thanked not only for the precise rendering but also for the intelligent interpretation of my rough ideas.

Of the persons indispensable to the fruition of this work, my assistant, Virginia Benade, ranks very important. In addition to her untiring effort with respect to the physical tasks related to the preparation of the manuscript, her editorial and research expertise was constantly called into use in the interest of better form and more accurate detail. And, may I say, she and Gordana Ukmar provided the necessary point of view of the younger generation of readers. This volume would never have happened without them both.

I appreciate the tireless work of the John Wiley & Sons staff, to whom goes the credit for the finished form of this book.

And so to each I say thank you. For better or worse, this is your book. My sincere hope is that you and the leaders in the architectural and interior design fields will undertake to keep it pertinent and up-to-date in the years ahead.

V.K.B.

CONTENTS

THE
ART OF
INTERIOR
DESIGN

1

GOOD ART: THE PROBLEMS WE FACE

Why should you think that beauty which is the most precious thing in the world lies like a stone on the beach for the careless passer-by to pick up idly?

Beauty is something wonderful and strange that the artist fashions out of the chaos of the world in the torment of his soul. And when he has made it, it is not given to all to know it. To recognise it you must repeat the adventure of the artist. It is a melody that he sings to you and to hear it again in your heart you want knowledge and sensitiveness and imagination.

W. Somerset Maugham, *The Moon and Sixpence*

Love is a flower
　　Forever blooming
Life is a fountain
　　Forever leaping
Upward to catch the golden sunlight,
　　Striving to reach the azure heaven.
Failing, falling,
Ever returning
　　To kiss the earth that the flower might live.

Eugene O'Neill, *The Fountain*

Design in an Industrial Age

One belief given currency today is that good designing of interiors is easy and that making a living at interior design is primarily a matter of merchandising done by anyone possessing a modicum of taste and a good money sense. Although both of these are necessary, neither is enough. The techniques involved in solving today's design problems are

1

difficult and multiple: the necessary artistry is not easy to acquire; mastery of the requisite knowledge and skills is hard; and the problems involved in coordinating the wishes and efforts of many persons is formidable. From all this concerted endeavor should come a good work of art, which is the basic reason for the entire enterprise.

Because historicity relates to the subject, let us briefly consider how interior design as a profession came into being. In the sixteenth century in Europe some men whom we now would call interior designers were engaged as muralists, creators of wall and ceiling treatments. They often worked with a team of subordinate painters and sculptors. Their names are associated with work in large churches and palaces. When living (for a few) became more opulent, the designer's duties included the procurement of all equipment,

Figure 1.1. The Seagram Building, New York, 1956–1958.
Architects: Mies van der Rohe and Philip Johnson
Photograph: Ezra Stoller © ESTO
The Seagram is one of the finest examples of the high-rise structural steel building. Its curtain walls are of bronze and tinted glass.

furniture, and floor covering, and they took care of window treatment as well as adornment of surfaces. Since that time and with the shift in wealth from the few to the many, designers have continued working with large houses and in addition have added many new types of buildings such as offices, stores, schools, museums, restaurants (Figures 1.1, 1.2, and 1.3), and theaters. Usually firms have found it advisable to specialize among these.

The builder and the architect historically antedated the designer of the interior. A landscape planner was needed when it became advisable to include the grounds in the total concept. The patron and three other principals were thus involved in creating important environments. When the four groups worked to one purpose, complete and unified production resulted. Sometimes they did not: in the early eighteenth century in France, exteriors might be in the classical style and interiors in the rococo. This need not result in inferior art, but it always means fractionated art. Although our society is commercialized, it is also heterogeneous and individualized. One of the problems of the designer is to understand the production as a whole (Figures 1.4, 1.5, 1.6, and 1.7) and thus fit his or her segment into the larger concept of the aesthetic culture.

Creating unity is one thing; avoiding monotony another (see Figures 8.2 and 8.3). This is the designer's bane from an increasingly industrialized, computerized, systematized, indeed, a robotized market. Do not forget, however, that the very success of such a creature as Artoo-Detoo owes much to the fact that its creator was able to humanize robots. The artist–designer should do no less.

Beauty, the Principal Goal of Interior Design

We are willing to spend time, effort, and money on interior design because we wish beautiful surroundings. The love of beauty is fundamental. The search for one means of its gratification is the goal of our present study. The word beauty, which means so much to all, is difficult to define. It is easier to describe how we feel when we call something beautiful. We respond to a beautiful object with an intense, enjoyable, and enduring interest.

Figure 1.2. Four Seasons Restaurant, Seagram Building, New York, 1956–1958.
Architect: Philip Johnson
Interior designed by Philip Johnson
Photograph: Joseph Molitor Photo
A feeling of ample space is engendered by the high ceiling and the sparsity of
the furnishings and their architectonic arrangement. The directional light
cast by the incandescent ceiling lamps gives a shimmering quality to the draperies made of fine metal chains and the brass and wire sculpture by Richard
Lippold suspended over the bar. The other materials also contribute to the
aura of twentieth-century elegance. The plants, which are changed with the
seasons, and the lines of the draperies soften any too-rigid effect.

Such a benefit is a worthy value in a world
that would otherwise be distasteful or boring.

This tendency to describe beauty in terms
of feelings suggests that beauty is an experience, a special kind of interactivity between
ourselves and our environment. To understand the interdependence of the object appreciated and the person appreciating, it may

be helpful to study a sequence that psycholo-
gists use to illustrate all human experience.
The formula is:

W (world or environment) → S (stimulus)
→ O (our organism with its sense recep-
tors, brain, and muscles) → R (response)
W (world)

Figure 1.3. A view of the bar, Four Seasons Restaurant, Seagram Building, New York, 1956–1958.
Architect: Philip Johnson
Interior designed by Philip Johnson
Photograph: Joseph Molitor Photo

Let us say that a bell rings. This occurs because someone pushed a button. This creates the stimulus that our ears receive. An impulse is sent along the nervous system to the brain, which may interpret the sound as a doorbell. The brain might in turn instigate a physical response transmitted through the muscles; this response could be that of going to the door. Or the brain may interpret the sound as that of a neighbor's bell, in which

case the response might be an attitude of disappointment.

In the experience we call beauty, the W (world) may or may not be physically present as the source of S (stimulus). In a totally imaginative experience of beauty the world is remote. We summon beautiful thoughts and images from a rich mental storehouse. In the experience of beauty the R (response) factor does not always result in overt action. When it does, such action is only an indirect result of the experience. The response can begin and end in the brain. For this reason many writers describe the experience of beauty as contemplative.

The conceptual nature of our reaction to beauty does not mean that the aesthetic experience is passive. The simplest response to beauty is more than a mere sensation. It involves mental activity, the nature of which

depends on the particular experience. We call this experience a perception because it involves an immediate judgment.[1] Because beauty evokes a contemplative response at the same tme that it is experienced actively, it ranks high in any scale of human good. Enjoyment through beauty does no intrinsic

[1]Ralph Barton Perry, *Realms of Value*, Cambridge, Mass.: Harvard University Press, 1954, p. 344.

Figure 1.4. The School House, Boston, Massachusetts, restoration and conversion of a nineteenth-century schoolhouse into an apartment condominium.
Architects: Graham Gund Associates, Inc.
Design team: Peter E. Madsen, David T. Perry, Jane R. Harrington, and Leonard J. Bertaux
Photograph: © Steve Rosenthal
This is a neoclassic brick building originally constructed in 1891. When its primary function was destroyed by the encroachment of the city, it was redesigned as a twenty-one-apartment condominium. The spirit of the past has been preserved skillfully in the orderly simplicity of the interior spaces and furnishings. The work signifies the best of preservation thought whereby fine monuments of our heritage are conserved and placed at the service of contemporary living.

harm. It neither destroys the beautiful object nor interferes with the pleasure or interest of other persons.

The response to beauty is immediate, is frequently emotional, and may be called irrational in the sense that it is often difficult to understand our reasons for considering something beautiful. It is equally difficult at times to persuade someone else to see beauty where we do. This intuitive reaction to beauty is good. Beauty flashes upon our consciousness with a singleness and surety that enables us to forget the *why* in enjoyment of the *is*.

Rationalism requires close attention, an attitude of objectivity, and an analytical method applied for a comparatively long time for one to arrive at any logical conclusion. The quality of ingenuous pleasure unfortunately is lost in the process—a fact that we are inclined to resent. For most losses there are compensating gains. It is sometimes necessary to tear apart in learning how to create.

It is important for designers to create for others as well as for themselves. In the final analysis commissions depend on satisfaction given. It must be understood that the experience of beauty is complex and can be awakened in several ways. Actually emotions, whether aroused by beauty or other things, seldom stem from simple causes but rather from those that are complicated and only vaguely understood. An analysis of the intri-

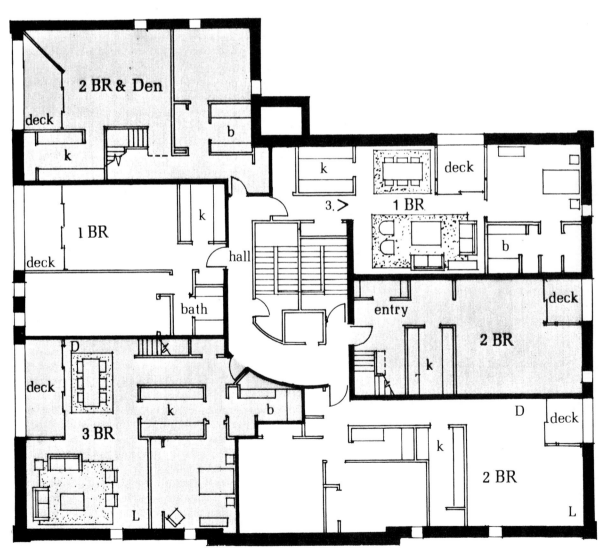

Figure 1.5. Plan of the third floor, the School House, Boston, Massachusetts.
Architects: Graham Gund Associates, Inc.
Plan: Courtesy of Graham Gund Associates

Figure 1.6. A dining room at the School House, Boston, Massachusetts.
Architects: Graham Gund Associates, Inc.
Design team: Peter E. Madsen, David T. Perry, Jane R. Harrington, and Leonard
J. Bertaux
Photograph: © Steve Rosenthal

Figure 1.7. A living room at the School House, Boston, Massachusetts.
Architects: Graham Gund Associates, Inc.
Design team: Peter E. Madsen, David T. Perry, Jane R. Harrington, and Leonard
J. Bertaux
Photograph: © Steve Rosenthal

cate nature of beauty will help us to design environments that will measure up to our own ideals and may please others as well.

Beauty, even though it is quickly sensed, elicits a response derived from a number of more basic or elementary ones—a developed response. Reactions are basic or primary when they are the simplest answer to a stimulus. Giving attention is thus basic. This is the set for all that follows. In some way a beautiful thing must first attract our notice, as advertisers well know.

Having looked at a color we may say that it makes us feel gay, or we may call it by its particular name. These are secondary responses because they depend on the initial focus. If we evaluate the color as harmonious with its surroundings, we are reacting in a more complicated way. If we say that the color is beautiful we are judging it worthy in a revelation that depends on many simpler responses. But can we be certain that someone else will call it beautiful? Not unless we know more about how that person will react to that color in more fundamental ways.

The idea that beauty is caused only by sensuous stimulation is another fallacy that our analysis will destroy. The experience of beauty, although it may not require the conscious use of the higher brain centers, can arise from the stimulation of many areas of the brain. Such areas range from the parts concerned with simple sensuous material to those that are taxed with more meaningful matter. A child may enjoy the redness of a ball; an adult's feeling for the red in the flag may rest on a multitude of associations. This too is good. It gives the instrument of beauty many strings. Which will play the richer tune? Who can say? It is a pity nevertheless if the expanding capabilities should make us deaf to a broken first string. The initial strand is sensuous experience, which is fundamental and universal.

In an attempt to learn why the same object may not seem beautiful to everyone, our analysis returns us to the 0 factor—the human organism. In physical makeup and in respect to accumulated experience no two persons are exactly alike. At any particular moment the physical, mental, and emotional status of two individuals who are looking at the same object may be very different. We ourselves change from time to time. There-

fore, the experience of beauty is a dynamic rather than a static phenomenon. This is one reason for our pleasure in its search.

The Relation of Beauty and Art

Beauty can be found everywhere. We often see it in nature and we frequently meet it in the works of human beings. Whenever we say that something is artistic we usually imply that someone has made something beautiful. The process involved in this accomplishment is one of organization, which means selection and arrangement of materials to create a new form. In the most comprehensive sense in which we use the word, this is art. Art involves the organization of energies to gain a result. When we speak of art, our meaning ordinarily is more restricted. We are thinking of something that was made to be beautiful. Art, as we shall use the term, is the organization of means to gain the kind of effect that we call beauty.

The Relation Between Art and Science

This book deals primarily with the art of interior design. In the process it makes some use of science. Science observes, measures, and tabulates phenomena. From this data it deduces laws of cause and effect. Science considers that truth has been reached when, through reproducing causes, it can achieve predictable effects. Actually this is little different from what the artist is doing. The variance between the artist and the scientist is in a sense one of degree—the degree to which the personal ability of the artist is essential to the success of the end product. When people learn the exact way to organize means to gain ends, when reproduction of the end product can be accomplished by rule, then we have science rather than art.

Just as the creative scientist frequently proceeds by conjecture and is spiritual kin to the creative artist, so too, the wise artist makes all possible use of the precision of science. This is especially true today when the interior designer deals with colors, light, and materials that are highly standardized. In the complex field of art, however, there is much that will remain indeterminate. Beyond the recipes there is the need for the particular artist to bring his or her ability to bear on a specific problem.

Three Purposes for Creation

When we make something, we usually have a purpose in mind. In reviewing human endeavor we find that its aims have been threefold. The earliest was probably the intention to make something of practical use. People fashioned spearheads and with them killed for defense and food. They molded clay pots and built storage places for their grain. They carved wheels and harnessed water. They built stools, beds, and houses, and thereby made living more comfortable and safe. If we use the term *art* in its broadest sense of useful skill, these are functional art forms because the primary purpose that motivated their creation was utilitarian.

In addition to its practical use an artifact may carry a message. One of the three reasons for creating art is to say something. Communication, suggestion, expression, interpretation, explanation, exposition—all are words used to denote various ways of revealing the hidden aspects of things. We shall use the term *expression* (Figures 1.8 and 1.9) in this regard. The art involved is that of organizing details that are known in such a way that they will illuminate the unknown. Thus expressive art implies a sensitivity on the part of the artist not to one type of phenomenon but to at least two types. It involves a recognition of likenesses between things that may be totally unlike in kind. For instance, we say that a chemist explains the nature of a substance in writing a formula showing a certain causal relation between the atoms by means of signs. By the same token an oriental artist can express the infinite by a few deft brush strokes.

When likenesses of this sort are well established in a culture they become symbols. Language is the great symbolic art. Any such art is highly significant and useful because it simplifies our many-sided existence. It indicates parallels and hence the possibility of unity out of variety, order from chaos.

The third purpose of art creation is for intensifying perceptual experience, for enhancing immediate discriminatory pleasure. This is without any thought for either use or meaning. This reason for art we shall call design. Design then is the basic structural framework of art without which nothing else can succeed.

The Complete Aesthetic Form

The three purposes just outlined enter in varying degrees into the creation of all art. Insofar as we comprehend and appreciate the fulfillment of these aims, we shall find aesthetic form to be compounded of its functional, expressive, and design aspects. All three points of view are important in considering interior design as an art form.

This text sets down directives for a well-designed interior. If this designing is to seem beautiful to persons of mature sensibilities, it must fly in echelon, flanked by thought for the purposes of the interior spaces and for the necessity to express these in terms of human values.

What Can an Interior Design Say?

The surroundings we create reveal more than our abilities as artists of visual design and the expressions that are related to the separate visual qualities. They become an exposition of character in a very special kind of way.

Character is related to a personal set of values. It shows that to which we allocate top drawer space in life's bureau of accounts. When character is shaped to capitalize on the best qualities in a civilization, its possessor may be called cultured. Some interiors seem to have been created by designers with such culture.

The fields of relative values have often been classified as the good, the true, and the beautiful. It is the fundamental purpose of education to inculcate standards of excellence in these. The value cabinet of life is larger than its subdivisions and thus represents a transcendent worth that for want of a better word may be called the right. This is not just the ethically right, nor the scientifically right, nor the aesthetically right. Yet if it neglects any of these it is never perfection.

This kind of equity frequently eludes those who focus too narrowly in filing material in one of the small pigeonholes of existence. To discover this kind of rightness is really to acquire wisdom. The first of its servants is knowledge, not of one kind of thing but of many. Knowledge, which can only be attained through the exercise of judgment, requires perspicuity—that ability to see through a sit-

Figure 1.8. Thorncrown Chapel, Eureka Springs, Arkansas, 1980.
Architect: E. Fay Jones
Photograph: © Hursley & Lark; Greg Hursley, photographer
This beautiful sanctuary, known affectionately as the Wayfarers' Chapel, was
built by architect E. Fay Jones on James Reed's Arkansas property. Providing the
chapel was Mr. Reed's response to the apparent enjoyment of the many
who paused close to a nearby road to enjoy the beauty of the Ozark Mountains
from this location. The chapel is an expression of the union of worship and
nature. Made on a foundation of local fieldstone and using standard-sized
linked pine lumber for its modular frame with spaces filled with glass, it seems
to grow from rather than to be placed on its forest setting. The diamond-shaped
voids in the roof allow a force of moving light to play over the powerfully
suggestive succession of crosses.

Figure 1.9. Interior, Thorncrown Chapel, Eureka Springs, Arkansas, 1980.
Architect: E. Fay Jones
Photograph: © Hursley & Lark; Christopher Lark, photographer

uation and winnow the chaff from the wheat, the false from the true. Also needed is sensitivity, which depends on circumspection, the ability to see around a situation and to reflect on its many facets. The third personage in the retinue of wisdom is imagination, that farseeing friend who envisages the finished product and who knows the best way to effect it.

Education attempts to convey knowledge directly, but sensitivity and imagination can only be taught indirectly. It is the supreme responsibility of the arts to develop these qualities. Those who possess them are potential artists. A work of art is brought into being fundamentally by a way of life. Moreover, once created, it shapes life.

What Is Taste?

Taste, a word often unjustly derided, is indeed a possession very much to be desired. Taste, when we imply distinction and grace in its use, is the ability to make wisdom explicit through art. It is, therefore, a preeminent art. Living is the most complex of arts and the one to which the general term *good taste* is frequently applied. Although each specific art is meaningful to the person of taste, it becomes the particular prerogative of an art like interior design to express taste because of its close association with life.

Since there is no art that can be learned by rule, there is no book written that can go further than the kindergarten in giving answers to questions of taste. Decisions of taste, however trivial their manifestations, must be based on a scale of values. These decisions are most difficult when standards of excellence in several arts seem to conflict. When and where is a painting vulgar? When should one use clever but destructive wit? What is the line of demarcation between conventionality and pedantry, self-expression and eccentricity? Reaction to such issues can be called the real measure of taste.

Of What Value Is Taste?

Persons of cultured tastes have developed a certain finesse of action that speaks in every detail of their daily life. This kind of taste is such a real thing that it can be counted on to function in a very definite

way. That is the reason that when employment is considered taste is actually a marketable commodity.

Beyond its economic value it possesses a social worth. One characteristic of taste is its awareness of and respect for the various influences on a culture. Creative artists and scientists are not the sole producers of a civilization. Pilots cannot steer a ship that harbors a mutinous crew. There must be directives from both the helm and the hold. Leaders learn from keen observation of the world.

However necessary both parties are in a boat race, a coxswain cannot reach the oarsmen without a megaphone. This interpreter in the artistic world is the person of taste. Taste is the creative force that can alter the common mind to adjust to new levels of culture.

Acquisition of Taste

Taste is acquired. No one is born with it. Nevertheless, one of the earmarks of its possession is the naturalness with which it is worn. Although the timid person who is fearful of following personal preferences has not gained taste, neither has the opinionated person who prescribes for less-enlightened friends from a quickly read docket.

Taste is worn naturally when it comes from inner convictions. It is like a finely tailored cloak that can be disregarded because it fits so well. Wearer and garment seem fused, and it is certain that each gives assurance to the other. This kind of confidence results from personal integrity that acknowledges other values lying deeper than surface appearance. Taste also recognizes that appearance is one important way to make these values manifest.

In its gratification by expression, taste has something of the inner compulsion of the evangelist. It also has a soupçon of the good actor in its makeup, a little of that skill in presentation that makes the offering seem attractive. A dull taste may be less desirable than a poor one because it cannot project its hidden meaning.

Through breadth of understanding, taste possesses that true sophistication that not only sees excellence in the familiar, but likewise in the new; it recognizes old friends in unaccustomed raiment.

Taste is at once simple and difficult to acquire. It is so simple that it involves nothing more than the willingness and ability to observe and to think about what has been observed. Simplicity of this sort is always deceptive. It has been aptly said that simplicity is never simple. It is difficult because its reflections are not only about things but also about relations between things. The preparation for this can never be narrow, quick, or effortless.

Students who cannot recognize the fact that taste in creating attractive surroundings depends on many apparently irrelevant factors (for instance, the kinds of books that are read, the music that is listened to, the friends that are chosen, the kind of character that is evolved) can never master the difficult side of designing, and their lessons will forever be half learned.

How Can a House Teach Taste?

We all strive to improve our taste and inculcate excellent standards in the next generation. Although the instruments and musicians of old may be lost, we hope that their music will live on.

Taste is first born of preference. Our preferences are almost subconsciously acquired. They come from indirect messages so transmitted through the complex telegraphic network of existence that they become largely emotional in character.

Artistic preferences come from music a child hears soon after birth. Needless to say our earliest impressions and thus our earliest preferences are formed at home. Training in sensitivity and imagination may thus be taught by the house itself. A house tells us a great deal about the culture of its occupants. And what it tells us it teaches its children.

What are some ways in which a house can influence? Honesty, or the esteem for integrity, is of a piece with the honest use of materials. Genuineness is learned from objects that are unostentatious. Graciousness is acquired in a house that is designed not just to put friends at ease, but to make them realize their value. Love can be taught by a well-cared for home. Courage can be learned from a cheerful emotional tone. Spirituality becomes easy to one whose house provides a

sanctuary for those qualities which, like flowers, are most ephemeral and most eternal in worth. Openmindedness can be taught by a house that has come to terms with time.

Examples of what we have just been discussing can be found in public as well as private buildings.

Conscious Training for Taste

Taste is also born of discernment, which is a rational process that seeks to determine the values in a situation. It is on this conscious intellectual level that taste can be improved. The undertaking is as difficult, however, as the proverbial task of lifting oneself by one's bootstraps. It is hard to operate on a member that must function in performing the act.

There are a few guideposts that have seemed helpful. Start as students of this fast-moving, changing world. If it becomes boring for one second—look out. That is the sign of stalemate. Seek excellence in the pattern of today. It is exhilarating to find that it is always there.

The integrity of personal taste must be respected. If our taste and that of the best of the surrounding culture are homogeneous, we fortunately inherit good taste in our culture. If we move to another culture, respect for our basic preferences is still essential. The past is the only firm ground on which we are able to build the future.

In formal training the curriculum must be broad as well as specialized. It must seek to understand our civilization, and this certainly requires a knowledge of its history, its philosophy, and its science. It also requires specialized study in the arts, not only to appreciate artistic excellence but likewise to obtain that fullest comprehension of the relations between the physical and the human experiential world.

Skill

The production of any art that touches closely the lives of people requires great skill. Skill is proficiency in accomplishment. It is competence. It is the executor in interior design where taste is the director. Manual skill requires good sense organs and muscular coordination. It requires a mind able to learn the necessary manipulation, and it needs persistency in working toward that end.

Few interior designers can master all of the skills required in the execution of their plans. But each must learn what is known as organizational skill, the ability to accomplish through the instrumentality of others.

Style

Style is another word with several meanings. Unlike *taste*, most of them are felicitous in nature. In that beloved little book with which every freshman English student should be familiar, E. B. White defines style as "that which is distinguished and distinguishing."[2] We like this definition as well as his statement that there is no satisfactory explanation of style. It is and always will remain a mystery. There are, however, some pointers about its achievement. And, when they relate to interior design, we shall not hesitate to assert them as we progress.

[2]William Strunk, Jr., *The Elements of Style*, 3rd ed., with Revisions, an Introduction, and a Chapter on Writing by E. B. White, New York: Macmillan, 1979.

2

COORDINATING INTERIOR DESIGN WITH BUILDING STRUCTURE

Something was wrong in our set-up, we were off the true some-where, if we could behave like that. My reaction had nothing to do with the ethics of the occasion; it was the discord that worried me. It jarred as I believe the first misfire, indicating a fault in some smoothly running machine, must jar on the ears of an engineer.

Laurens Van Der Post, *Venture to the Interior*[1]

The Importance of Structure

Interior design implements and qualifies spaces so that they serve the many uses for which they are intended. The plan and space potential with which the interior designer deals are directly dependent on the structure of the building. This close relation suggests that interior treatment is most congruous when it seems part of the whole program (Figure 2.1). The designer should be capable of appreciating the vision behind the creation of the spaces. A disjointed exterior and interior suggest some malfunctioning in aesthetic handling. There should be some overall compatibility in choices and arrangements This does not necessarily impose a slavish restriction in the realm of style.

For centuries it has been accepted as a requirement for good art that a medium (a material, a process, a tool) should express its unique character in its finished form. This precept has not always been followed throughout the long history of art. Indeed, its fracture has at times created some of the most engaging art. The art of the theater, for instance, is partially built on a world of make believe. However, whenever the medium is not respected it partakes in something of the nature of sham.

Our pragmatic modern world frowns on any form of artistic deception. Looked at from a puritanical point of view, camouflage in any guise smacks of dishonesty; considered as a sincere wish to improve imaginatively on a situation, it is not. Torroja says in his *Philosophy of Structures*: "Though it is sinful to lie, it is not always reprehensible to hide the whole truth."[2] This probably best sums up the situation.

[1]New York: William Morrow & Company, Inc., 1952, p. 141.

[2]Eduardo Torroja, *Philosophy of Structures*, Berkeley and Los Angeles: University of California Press, 1958, p. 270.

15

Figure 2.1. Exterior–interior: a unity. Home of Mr. and Mrs. Robert A. Little,
Pepper Pike, Ohio.
Architect: Robert A. Little
Photographer: Lionel Freedman
In this charming home, the exterior and interior seem part of a comprehensive
whole.

Problem Solving

At this stage the serious student should
begin to work on a simple problem in designing an interior that can be carried through
several stages of development. This may be a
house interior or a single element of a large
complex such as an office or a classroom. The
exterior of the building should be specified
because it will enter into the manner of the
solutions.

Modern Building Construction

THE LOGIC OF STRUCTURE

Everyone can understand the logic of structure in building. Its primary purposes are to
enclose space, to make feasible passage
through space, and occasionally to create desired conditions in space by restricting natural forces (e.g., in pools or terraces). To do

all this a structure must be capable of standing erect and supporting its own weight. In
addition, it must be able to carry a superimposed load. It should withstand elemental
stresses such as wind or snow. It must resist
chemical enemies such as fire and corrosion,
physical ones such as soil erosion, and ani-
mate, such as termites. What are some of the
ways of building that are designed to do
these things?

Economic considerations can be expected to
play an important role in any building program. The solution in a particular situation
is usually one that is financially advantageous. For this, materials, trained people,
and tools must be readily available. For instance, in early American building the Swedes
of New Jersey and Delaware built log houses
because they were knowledgeable about this
manner of construction in their homeland.
The English in New England, although for-

est wood was equally available, built in post-and-beam construction because this was a building type of their native country. A structural system suited to a skyscraper might be wasteful if used for a house. Therefore, suitability of method to purpose is the first law of good construction.

STRUCTURAL SYSTEMS

Structures can be divided into two basic systems, one that stands and supports its load on the principle of compressive strength and the other that achieves the same result using tensile strength. The first performs because it can hold up loads from beneath; the second can hang up loads between supports

(Figure 2.2). Various construction materials are classified according to their ability to do these tasks. There are four principal classes of materials to be considered: masonry, wood, metals, and combinations such as reinforced concrete.

Masonry. Solid masonry of small units—stone, brick, and concrete blocks or hollow tile—is one of the oldest types of construction. Solid masonry is said to be load bearing because it is designed to carry superimposed loads. Although masonry is strong in compressive strength, walls must be thick and spans small to be effective. Therefore, solid masonry walls are seldom used today, except for details such as fireplace partitions.

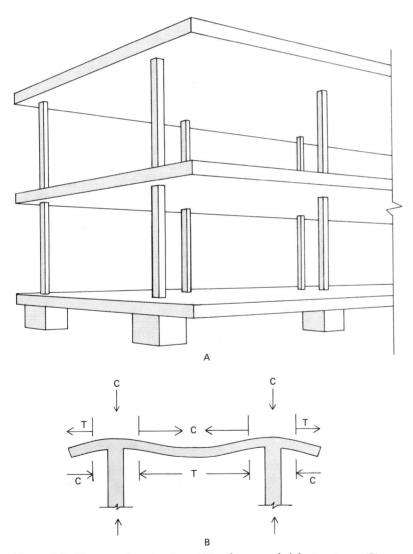

Figure 2.2. Compression–tension. (A) column and slab structure; (B) compression–tension diagram.

One of the practical advantages of masonry is its easy maintenance. It needs no protective coating. It does, however, require some engineering to consider problems of moisture removal. Looking at the beautiful solid brick walls of such old buildings as Jefferson's Monticello in Virginia, one notices the so-called weep holes allowed for this purpose.

One means of using masonry economically is through the forms of the arch, the vault, and the dome. Here additional strength is secured by dispersing the lateral as well as the downward stresses of the superimposed loading. Again, either buttressing, as in Gothic structure, or thick walls must be considered. Although masonry is seldom used for load bearing in contemporary building, it is frequently used as a facing because of its inherent appealing warmth.

Wood. Wood is one of the earliest building materials and, like stone, it is friendly. It is strong in both tension and compression (across the grain). American builders are accustomed to the techniques required in wood positioning, and wood is easily handled. Although it requires protection from sun drying, moisture, and termites, it is durable. It is a good thermal insulator because of its porosity. It is lively enough to withstand vibrations and is readily available in long slender members.

The chief disadvantages of wood are its inflammability and the fact that it does not have the same properties in all direction (i.e., it is not isotropic). It will shrink more tangentially than with the lengthwise grain. Uneven shrinkage of wood leads to warping, splitting, and to the possible cracking of materials that are bonded to it.

Through manipulation into laminated wood and impregnated wood, greater strength is attained. Thus wood is entering into the category of precision engineering materials. In laminated wood thin layers are compressed and glued to form a homogeneous substance. In plywood the alternate layers are bonded in opposed grains. Impregnated wood has its pores filled with a plastic that gives it greater hardness.

It is important to understand contemporary practice in wood framing because it is so commonly used in house construction. This framing is largely rectangular, in which vertical members attached to a concrete base support horizontal lintels. These structural members carry the weight of floors, walls, ceilings, and roof. They must also carry furnishings and people. Don't forget the last because when people are moving, especially in rhythmic motion such as dancing, the vibration increases the stresses. Operating machinery will do the same.

In early European and American timber work the vertical supports were large wood posts into which horizontal beams were tenoned. This framework was very strong and the individual members could be widely spaced. Many contemporary buildings use this same principle, generally with a framework of steel that has great strength per unit of thickness (Figures 2.3 and 2.4).

Frequently a 4- or 6-foot module is employed, or, in the case of very tall buildings, the module will have a much wider span (Figure 2.5). Originally the module was a Greek or Roman unit of architectural measure derived from the diameter of a building's columns. Such a unit helps to standardize the rest of the building.

The framing structure of wood is now, as formerly, often left exposed, and the comprehension of the work that it is doing becomes part of the aesthetic enjoyment derived from viewing the building. It is the kind of pleasure to be gained from watching the muscular stress of an athlete. Possibly it is the sort of pleasure that comes from contemplating the figure underneath the clothes, and it is one reason we favor today's garments that can reveal rather than hide this interplay.

In the early 1800s when America was expanding westward with phenomenal speed, a type of skeletal wood framing known as *Western* or *platform framing* was inaugurated in Chicago (Figure 2.6). This makes use of smaller pieces of wood employed at more frequent intervals, thus distributing stresses more evenly and making the whole system necessary to the support.

Wood buildings are anchored to a base of concrete. This concrete base is often incorporated with the basement wall that is widened at the bottom into a footing that spreads the load.[3] Cinders and drainage tile are placed

---

[3]Cubic footage cost of building a basement must be compared with the land costs involved when spreading over the ground. Where land values are high it may be more economical to place service features in a basement. It is more pleasurable, however, to have them located on the first floor.

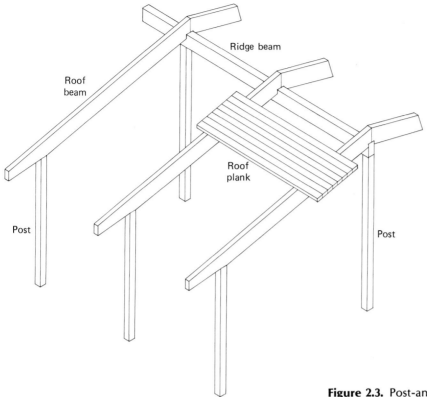

Figure 2.3. Post-and-beam construction.

Figure 2.4. Post-and-beam construction: wood. Model made by students of the Department of Architecture and Art, Case Western Reserve University, Cleveland, Ohio.
Photograph: courtesy of G. Ukmar, photographer

outside the foundation walls to keep them watertight. Waterproofing of joints and outer surfaces is essential. Sills are placed on top of foundation walls. Their purpose is to hold the framing to the foundation.

In platform framing the studs are upright framing members placed 16 inches on center (measured from center to center, abbreviated o.c.). Sixteen inches is one of the common modules or units of measure for woodwork. Studs are 2″ × 4″ pieces of lumber placed so that the broad side is at right angles to the wall. The studs are multiplied at the corners and at openings and are frequently interbraced for greater strength. It is there-fore economical of lumber to plan for relatively few openings.

The wood joists are the horizontal members that support the floors. Larger horizontal members are known as beams. Sometimes the cross supports are supplemented by steel or concrete beams where it is necessary to bear a heavy load or to span a long distance. Wood joists for residences vary from 2″ × 6″ to 3″ × 14″. They are, like the studs, 16″ o.c.

Additional rigidity can be given to wood-framed walls by an outer covering of composition board or by diagonal wood bracing. Waterproofing is added to the exterior of this.

Figure 2.5. Medusa Portland Cement Company, Cleveland, Ohio.
Architect: Ernst Payer
Photograph: Hube Henry, Hedrich-Blessing
The elegance of this building of steel, aluminum, and concrete is in part due to the wide spacing between the posts, which creates a spacious, quiet, modular rhythm. Its construction uses the lift slab method whereby slabs for the upper floors are poured at ground level and lifted into position. According to the architect, the advantages of this type of construction are economy—through avoiding the need for scaffolding—and a freedom of shape design. With concrete slab construction, curved shapes are generally possible without excessive costs—the wire reinforcing inside the slab is adjusted to correspond to the stresses.

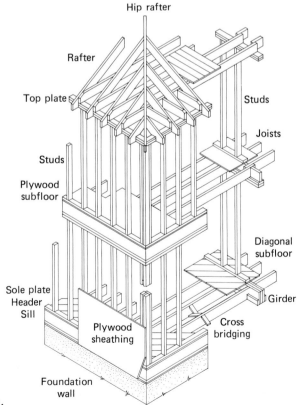

Figure 2.6. Western or platform frame construction.

20

A skeletal wood frame, rather monotonous in appearance, must have a covering for aesthetic as well as functional reasons. This added skin should be appraised both for its artistic validity and for outside and inside compatibility.

Steel and Other Metals. For tall buildings or large spans, steel or metal alloys provide structural strength. Steel is isotropic, elastic, of great and calculable strength, and for most purposes fire resistant. With this it has the disadvantage of a high rate of heat conductivity in all but paper-thin layers, a potential for oxidizing if not properly treated, and a high cost if fabricated in small amounts. (Rolled steel in standard sizes is the only practical solution to this problem.)

Inasmuch as steel has strength in all directions for compression and especially for tension, it can be used both for rigid vertical and horizontal framing members. Because of the necessity to make it rustproof and because it does not have the lovely porosity of natural materials, it is usually not exposed to view. Its aesthetic quality when planned for in the total form may offer a particular challenge that has a character of its own. Exposed steel beam trusses are of this nature.

Concrete and Reinforced Concrete. Concrete is a mixture of a cementing material and an aggregate such as gravel or sand, that sets to a hard monolith. Concrete alone is a very old material skillfully used by Roman builders. It has many advantages including the capability of being shaped into almost any form. It is fairly inexpensive provided it is used where its manipulation is understood and where labor is relatively cheap. It is fireproof, isotropic, and an excellent material for sound and heat insulation. However, concrete, like stone, is strong in compression but weak in tension.

To increase its tensile strength concrete is frequently combined with steel to form a composition in which steel bands under tension are embedded in the concrete (i.e., ferroconcrete). It has been found advantageous either to prestress or posttension this steel before the conditioning of the matrix. This provides the greatest capabilities: concrete furnishes the compressive strength and steel the tensile.

The most sensational use of ferroconcrete is seen in monolithic structures in which fantastic biomorphic shapes span unbelievable spaces (Figures 2.7 and 2.8). Such build-

Figure 2.7. Dulles International Airport terminal building, Chantilly, Virginia, 1963.
Architect: Eero Saarinen
Photograph: Joseph Molitor Photo
Certainly one of the world's most beautiful airports, the Dulles terminal, with its restrained, curved roof of wire and concrete, expresses, in the words of its creator, "the movement and excitement of travel by air."

Figure 2.8. Interior, Dulles International Airport terminal building, Chantilly, Virginia, 1963.
Architect: Eero Saarinen
Photograph: Joseph Molitor Photo
The interior at Dulles is noteworthy for its clearly indicated routing. With the two upper stories for departures and the lower for arrivals, passenger progression is shortened to 150 feet across the building.

ings are unusual largely because of the expensive forms needed for their execution.

Reinforced concrete is more customarily found in horizontal members such as floors and roofs. In lift-slab construction, entire floors can be formed on the ground and then lifted into position. Smaller members such as blocks and tiles may be prefabricated; they are frequently used to provide the desirable qualities of lightness with strength. Concrete alone can be used to protect steel structural members from rust and corrosion.

ROOF STRUCTURE

Roofs are the lids to buildings and as such merit consideration apart from foundations and walls. They must either bear or drain off water and snow. Gutters and downspouts are part of much roof equipment.

Roofs may be curved or straight in silhouette, slanting or flat in direction, continuous with or broken from walls in extension. Curved roofs are descendents of the arch, the vault, and the dome. They originated in lands where small building units such as stone and brick were the most available building materials. The curved form is seen today as an economical, functional, and graceful shape that can be made from various plastic materials (Figure 2.9).

Straight-line roofs have various contours and pitches. Every break in the profile necessitates carefully applied flashings to make the roof watertight. The traditional straight-line roof used in northern European countries is the gabled roof. The common types of gable are: the hip, which slants from the ridge pole on four slopes: the gambrel, which has two distinct slopes on its long axis; the jerkin, which has two slopes on each of the four sides; and the shed, which has one slope. Rafters are the sloping supporting structural

Figure 2.9. A unique architectural conception. Residence of Peter Kurt Woerner, Guilford, Connecticut.
Architect: Peter Kurt Woerner
Photograph: © Robert Perron 1976
This unusual house (see also Color Plate 7) is built on a granite ridge above the tidal marsh facing Long Island Sound. The main arches are constructed from laminated 2″ × 12″ planks of Douglas fir. The structure is covered with a thin sheet of plywood that acts like a stressed skin. Mr. Woerner feels that such a marsh, teeming with life from the tides, provides a never ending source of interest and study; the pure arc form best signifies this rising from and returning to the earth.

members of such roofs, and purlins are the horizontal ones that are parallel to the sides of the building. Wood trusses and tie beams often give added rigidity to gabled roofs.

The final finish on all roofs is dependent on their pitch. Steep roofs generally are covered with small overlapping pieces. Wood or aslphalt shingles are customary. Slate, metal shingles, and tile can be placed safely on roofs that are not too steep. As the roof pitch becomes low, small unit shingles are not practical because of the tendency of water to back up under them. Asbestos and metal-rolled roofing are frequently used in this situation. These finishes are seldom employed on roofs whose pitches are so steep that they are visible. They may be used on nearly flat roofs if great strength is not required. Canvas-rolled roofing is seen frequently on small decks.

When the roof is flat and the span is large, the basic structural support is made of such materials as wood, concrete, or metal. Upon this base a built-up roof is placed for water-tightness. This is a lamination of tar and roofing felt topped with gravel or marble chips. Such roofs can stand up against the snows of northern winters and can be built to carry off excess water by means of properly located drainage systems.

It should be mentioned that one form of roof made pratical through the use of new structural potentials is the cantilevered roof that projects from its support like a flag from a flagpole. This has certain size limitations but with the use of some additional bracing can project large roof spans with consequent appearance of weightlessness.

PLUMBING AND WIRING

Any habitation today that is not equipped with a hot and cold water supply under pressure is considered substandard. Central heating and air conditioning are also normal. Electricity for multiple uses is not even questioned. It is obvious, therefore, that the building must carry an enormous network of ducts and wires that are hidden within its entrails. Extra space must be reserved for this organism, and it is common sense to plan so that it can be as compact as possible. In the laying of this ductwork the building is protected by codes and sanitary ordinances that specify sizes, construction, and types of fitting. If not correctly installed, the skeleton and skin may have to be incised for alteration. Our forefathers purchased more enclosed space for their dollars, but their buildings consisted of bones and skin without any organic flow.

OPENINGS

The doors and windows of a building are its natural contacts with the outside world. Necessary and desirable, they are also weak links in a structure because they are breaks in its continuity. If they are not fitted tightly an unwelcome transfer of air occurs. If they are not well braced they will sag. It costs money in time and materials to cut holes in a wall and then to fill them satisfactorily.

For these reasons we arrive at the idea that it is wise structural planning to have as few openings as possible and to have them extend between already existing supports. This is not always feasible. Planning factors may suggest other solutions. This line of reasoning means that several large openings that fit into the building module are better than many small ones that break into a wall. Such a commensurate solution also introduces a rhythm that can be exceedingly important in determining the entire design (Figures 2.10 and 2.11).

Windows and glass doors are escape routes for heat unless precautions are taken to install them so that they are weathertight. Double glazing (see the subsection on climate control in this chapter) is recommended for heat conservation.

Contemporary planning eliminates most interior doors except where privacy (bedrooms and baths) or protection (storage and closets) make them necessary.

Doors and the framing of doors and windows are made of wood, steel, or lightweight alloys. Wood or composition board doors are of solid or hollow-core construction. Sliding glass partitions fit into the building framework and provide for the maximum of air and light with the minimum of upkeep. However, many other types such as reversible and rotating frames are designed for this purpose.

Sectional division of openings provides for directed ventilation. In the jalousie, in which the panes are not framed, the visual effect of solid glass is achieved with the maximum ventilation. The hopper opening that pivots horizontally provides ventilation with little draft, although it can usurp valuable indoor space when open. The traditional casement window requires external space, and the sash window limits the size of the opening. Louvered doors permit the passage of air without visibility.

Screen and storm sash come with most door and window systems. In old installations this extra equipment was hinged to the exterior trim. Progress is in the direction of either easy demounting or of total unit incorporation. Screens, for instance, may roll into the sill when not needed, and double glazing takes away the need for a storm sash.

STAIRS

A flight of stairs is composed of treads, frequently 10 inches wide, and risers, about 7½ inches high. This provides a safe, comfortable incline of about 36 degrees from the horizontal. A stringer or finishing strip is usually provided along the side. Minimum head room should be at least 6 feet 8 inches. For safety there should be a balustrade, and the individual balusters should not be too widely spaced. A common stair width is 3 feet.

Spiral stairways are economical of floor space. Care must be taken to ensure that the individual wedge-shaped treads are not too narrow. Narrow wedge sections are dangerous. Modern architects frequently use the open stair (Figure 2.12), which consists of a tread and no solid riser. Each tread in such a flight should extend far enough under the tread above to ensure safety from tripping.

Stairs are usually supported by a wall. Some stairs are freestanding (Figure 2.13) and are supported by their own rigidity or by suspended or attached supports. Ramps are

Figure 2.10. The Grossman house, near Denver, Colorado.
Architect: Theodor A. Grossman, Jr.
Photographer: Theodor Grossman
This architect's home uses post-and-beam construction on a broad modular
unit to create an interior spaciousness of unique charm. Its wide glass openings
make possible an enjoyment of the outdoors as an integral part of living.

Figure 2.11. Interior, the Grossman house, near Denver, Colorado.
Architect: Theodor A. Grossman, Jr.
Photographer: Theodor Grossman

Figure 2.12. Open stairs and sculptured wall, Medusa Portland Cement Company, Cleveland, Ohio.
Architect: Ernst Payer
Sculptured wall by William M. McVey
Photograph: Hube Henry, Hedrich-Blessing
The open stair in this large entrance hall to a corporate headquarters building conveys an impression of lightness and space. The adjacent sculptured wall, washed by light, provides textural interest.

occasionally used in place of stairs. They should be inclined less steeply than a stairway.

CHIMNEY AND FIREPLACE

All buildings that have fuel-burning heating equipment require chimneys. An open fireplace (Figure 2.14) may be considered a luxury in today's interior, but what price emotional warmth? The chimney, for one reason or another, is probably here for a long stay.

A fire requires oxygen from a fresh supply of air. It must have some avenue for harmful gases to escape. These two necessities are met by the chimney flue. This is a tile pipe that extends from a chamber above the fire to the outdoors. This small chamber is known as the smoke chamber. It is isolated from the main fire by a smoke shelf designed to prevent gusts of wind from coming down the chimney and causing smoke to back up in the room. Below the smoke shelf is a damper that can be opened and closed to either cause or shut off an upward draft of air. There must be a separate flue for each fireplace or fuel-burning furnace. Who has not seen pictures

Figure 2.13. A superb art collection. The home of Mr. and Mrs. Bernard J. Reis, New York City.

Photograph: Courtesy of Mrs. Bernard J. Reis

The stairway is an interesting closed form leading from the living room to the upper floors. The entire house is enriched by the Reis collection of art, beautifully displayed against the light walls. The visible objects are: on low room divider—A Khmer stone Buddha; on lower stair wall—multiple small paintings by Ad Reinhardt and an oil painting by Barbara Reis Poe; on upper stair wall—a 1967 Mark Rothko painting in grey and black; and at left rear in front of window—a 1920 Jacques Lipchitz sculpture, "The Harpist."

Figure 2.14. Residence of Mr. and Mrs. Robert A. Little, Pepper Pike, Ohio.
Architect: Robert A. Little
Photographer: Lionel Freedman
Embers on the hearth add to the emotional warmth of homes of all periods, as shown by this interesting contemporary fireplace.

A

Masonry

Exterior wall

Flue

Ashpit door

Hearth

B

Figure 2.15. Fireplace construction with wood trim. (A) elevation; (B) plan.

of the many-tiled flues, known as chimney pots, that project like sentinels above the roofs of English Tudor houses? These flues must be higher than any surrounding house-top so that no swirling air currents will enter.

Chimneys (Figure 2.15) could be vulnerable spots in the fire armor of a construction. To reduce fire hazards they are completely separated from the rest of the structure. No part of the building holds up a chimney, and it supports no part of the building load. The chimney rests on its own spread footing. The space between the framing and the chimney is filled with fireproof insulating material. Chimneys made of prefabricated sections are now available.

Crickets are just one of the living things that love a hearth. A hearth consists of the inner hearth on which the fire is built plus the front hearth, which is in reality an area of fireproof floor material surrounding the essential hearth. If the inner hearth is elevated, there may be no need for a front hearth. The inner hearth is surmounted by the fire chamber with its damper. Medium-sized fire chambers are about 36 inches wide, 30 inches high, and 18 inches deep. Most fire chambers have slanting sides and a sloping top for heat reflection. Some hearths are of open structure and have neither sides nor back.

JOINTING

Every joint in a structure, like every opening, is a potential weakness; a chain can be no stronger than its links.

The system of jointing should fulfill certain requirements. It should be uncomplicated, inexpensive, strong, and weathertight. Wood structures are customarily nailed together. Wood dowels are found in place of iron nails in some early American homes. Major structural parts were often mortised and tenoned together (see Chapter 10, Construction of Wood Furniture).

In experimenting with new building materials the building industry is studying jointing. Some builders find that modifications of the older methods of fitting parts into parts are good. The use of synthetic adhesives for plywood construction suggests possibilities for the future. A continuous structure without joints would be ideal. Steel structures with welded joints are a step in this direction.

Monolithic concrete is in this respect excellent. The famous architect Mies van der Rohe did not hide the joinings of the separate parts of his buildings. They were executed with such precision and nicety that they became objects for admiration.

REFINEMENTS ON BASIC STRUCTURE

Climate Control. The objective of air conditioning is the maintenance of fresh, clean air that is free from objectionable odors and possesses desirable humidity and temperature. Because of today's problems of fuel conservation, the ultimate aim is to secure these results as economically as possible. There are two methods of accomplishing climate control: the first is to plan a building so that it will further this end; the second is to use mechanical equipment for this purpose. Let us consider them in this order.

A building should be well insulated. Insulation prevents the transfer of heat. A building should be weathertight, and insulation should be provided for exterior walls and for those adjacent to unheated areas. Insulation materials depend on any of three different methods of preventing heat loss. The insulating material itself may be a poor conductor. Wood and glass fiber are of this nature. The material may be in a finely divided state so that the minute air pockets separating the particles will prevent heat transfer. Or the material may be reflective and turn back heat, as a paper-thin layer of metal foil does. Reflective materials also can act as vapor barriers to prevent moisture condensation within the walls or seepage from the ground.

Double-glazed windows are insulated because of the small air pockets between the panes. This air space has been dehydrated and sealed. Traverse draperies provide additional insulation against heat loss, especially if they are made of a material such as wool that has good insulating properties. Some materials are manufactured with heat-reflecting backing. It is noteworthy that as early as the 1600s in England, winter frames covered with a taut insulating fabric were often placed in drafty windows.[4]

Once we have stopped up the escape hatches for heat, we begin to think about heating the interior in cold weather. Natural heat sources

[4]Peter Thornton and Maurice Tomlin, "Ham House," *Furniture History* 15, 59 (1980).

should be used whenever possible. This is where solar heating planned into the building is important because the sun is the great source of free heat. Radiant energy in the band known as infrared carries the most intense heat. These heat waves easily travel through double-glazed windows. Not all radiant energy waves carry such intense heat. The rays of low heat intensity that may be present in the heated air of a room are not sufficiently strong to escape outward through those very same windows, hence large double-glazed windows, if properly oriented to catch all of the infrared rays of the sun, become channels for trapping heat.

How can a structure be planned to secure the benefits of solar radiation (a program sometimes known as solar-assist; see Figure 2.16)? Large windows should face the sun. In the northern hemisphere this means south. Inasmuch as the sun rides about 60 degrees above the horizon in the summer and 30 in the winter, windows with projecting eaves can be designed to permit the sun to miss a room in the first instance and to sweep across it in the second. When a building is only one room in width, it is possible to receive the benefit of a low winter sun in all rooms. Eaves can be designed composed of individual lattices that will be as effective in regulating the flow of radiant energy as a solid eave would be. A heavy concrete floor is an aid to solar heating because it acts as a storage reservoir for heat.

There are a few problems with solar heating: Northern windows are useless for this purpose. Therefore, in those orientations it is not wise to open large areas to glass. Moreover, in the summer the rising and especially the setting sun hangs low in the horizon for a long period. Windows in the east and the west will let in much unwanted heat and cannot be sufficiently protected by eaves or awnings. Blue tinted heat-resistant glass is effective.

In its present state of development, solar heat is only used as a partial heating system. It must be supplemented in most climates by mechanical heating equipment that is classified according to the source of heat (i.e., the fuel) that it uses. This may be wood, coal, gas, electricity, natural organic products such as peat and animal refuse, and in some experimental work the inner heat reserves of the earth itself. Each source necessitates its own mechanical equipment that should be carefully installed and maintained. All furnaces and all mechanical climate-control machinery today comes in comparatively neat packages that can be operated with the maximum of safety and the minimum of manual regulation and labor. In large installations this apparatus may be provided as a coordinated *system*, a new name added to the commercial vocabulary.

Whereas the furnace type does not greatly influence the type of building structure, the channels for heat transmission do have some relevance to plans. For instance, hot-air and

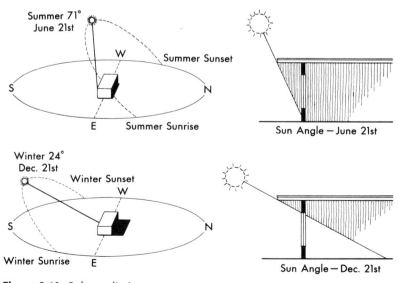

Figure 2.16. Solar radiation.

hot-water heating systems are economical, but are most effective in a compact building with a basement. Both may be used in larger areas if the heat is forced through the pipes. Heat conveyed by steam is used in many large installations.

One of the newer types of heat transmitting systems (the principle, however, was used by the Romans) is known as radiant heating. In this system large portions of the room surface are heated to relatively low temperatures rather than small portions being heated to relatively high temperatures. This heat is usually transmitted by hot water or steam and occasionally by electric conduits that flow through coils in the floor, ceiling, or baseboard. By heating large areas in an insulated space the heat radiates from hot surfaces to cooler ones until an equilibrium is established. All objects and persons in the space share this even temperature.

Radiant heating has many obvious advantages. In the first place, no heating apparatus is markedly visible. Also there is no dirt thrown up on the wall in the path of rising air currents. When the floor is a heated panel it becomes a warmer, safer place for children to play. Room temperatures are evenly distributed and there should be no drafts. This system is well suited to the building without a basement. The saving incurred by not digging a basement may offset the installation costs of the panel heating. It is very economical to operate.

Summer cooling is also the task of climate control. The building itself can help this project. Good insulation is as important to summer cooling as it is to winter heating because it prevents heat passage. Old masonry and adobe houses are deliciously cool in summer.

Planting provides evaporative cooling. Trees shading the south side of a house should be deciduous so that they will not screen winter solar heat. Make southern terraces of medium lightness in tone. A light terrace will reflect heat, whereas a dark one will absorb and hold it. Light-toned roofing is advisable to reflect heat. Solar windows should have properly designed overhangs. Screens that have small reflective metal openings are of value in turning back the sun's rays.

The use of convection currents through ventilation is a desirable way to cool air. A building should be opened toward the prevailing cool breezes, and there should be an opposite and somewhat higher opening for the escape of warm air.

Forced mechanical ventilation is frequently included in a ventilating system. Fans are the usual method of accomplishing this. They may be blow fans that stir up the existing air or exhaust fans that pull the hot air out of a space. Exhaust fans are customarily used in kitchens and baths. Many spaces are equipped with exhaust fans at ceiling level. These pull the air from a ventilator placed near ground level up into an attic or upper air chamber. Air chambers close to the roof should always be equipped with louvred ventilators that are located at opposite ends of the space. Such openings not only serve to create a wash of moving air and thus prevent pockets of warm air; they also carry off the moisture that accumulates with trapped warm air. Breathing vents are useful to prevent moisture damage in insulated walls.

When temperatures soar, the climate control afforded by the building may be supplemented by mechanical cooling. This machinery operates on the same principle as refrigerated food storage units. The cost of mechanical air cooling is moderate when the building is properly planned and when the system is used only in severe heat.

Fresh air intakes are necessary, and cleansing the incoming air is good. Air may be introduced through a fine mesh filter or through a water spray. Electrostatic cleansers are often used in industry.

It is important to give air the proper moisture content. Air can take on moisture from passing over a spray. Cooking vapors, baths, and washing add moisture to the atmosphere of a small house. The problem is more liable to be that of dehumidifying the indoor air. All moisture-producing apparatus such as driers should be vented. Chemicals of an absorbent nature can be used in attic and basement spaces. Cooling the air and removing the moisture at the place where it is cooled is a part of summer air conditioning and a principle of some mechanized dehumidifiers.

Climate control today affords more than just winter heat. Its equitable environment makes possible the use of many fragile materials that were heretofore prohibitive in upkeep. It should also aid our comfort and health. Without it the rapid growth of the sun belt probably never would have occurred.

Sound Conditioning. Small quarters, open plans, thin walls, and much use of glass has made it necessary to pay careful attention to sound conditioning. This is not a problem that can be solved simply by hanging a sound-absorbing ceiling. For large installations and critical situations an acoustical engineer should be consulted. Basic principles, however, can be understood by all concerned.

Sounds are caused by the vibrations of some elastic mechanical object which passes these vibrations on, either to another object or to the surrounding air, whence it comes to the listener's ears. In the air these vibrations set up longitudinal motions (compressions and rarefactions) which, to make them easier to visualize, are usually illustrated as transverse waves like those of the sea. Sound is transmitted most easily from one material to another when both are of similar elasticity and density. Flexible but inelastic, porous, dense materials absorb sound; rigid, nonporous materials reflect sound.

Undesirable sound is called noise. Noise is sound that is too intense, out of place, or of poor quality. These three conditions are closely interconnected. Sound from a neighbor's radio when it intrudes into our sleeping quarters is misplaced. We may tolerate the intense noise caused by our own children at play. The hum of many typewriters is unpleasant noise.

We know that sound that is too loud can inflict bodily damage, fray the nerves, and create emotional disturbances. Too little sound can be depressing. A gauge for the ideal tolerance level is that at which an average whisper can be heard 4 feet away.

The sound level in and around a building can be controlled by isolation and construction. It is suggested, rather unrealistically, that 200 feet should separate a dwelling from a busy street. Foliage produces enough isolation to be somewhat useful against noise. Ventilating and heating machinery should run quietly. However, if machinery is attached to the frame of a building, even the most sophisticasted system of rubber isolation mountings will only partially prevent noise vibrations from entering the building. In a properly planned building such machinery should be installed on a solid foundation at ground level rather than overhead and well away from parts of the building where noise would be especially troublesome.

In addition to exerting some control on the intensity of sound, a structure should facilitate the creation of good quality sound. This is done by providing conditions that will accurately render the loudness, pitch, and timbre of the sound. Loudness correlates with the magnitude of the to-and-fro oscillation of the vibrating sound source. Pitch is mainly governed by the number of repetitions this vibration makes each second. Timbre is the human response to the detailed shape of the vibration: its symmetry, its jaggedness, or the number of subsidiary motions that make up each of its repetitions.

Sound qualities can be impaired by the way sound is reflected from the surfaces of a room. Sound waves bounce off surfaces like a rubber ball. Each time they bounce, some of the impetus is absorbed. Finally the vibrations are stilled. The time required for this to happen is called the time of reverberation. Its length has a great effect on the quality of the sound. If it is too long, successive sounds overlap, producing confusion. If the time of reverberation is too short, the room "feels dead," and the ear does not get a chance to savor the value of the sounds that come to it. Soft draperies, pile carpets, cloak closets, and porous ceilings are useful in absorbing sound, whereas things like furniture, statuary, and recessed openings serve to diffuse it. The amount and placement of sound-absorbing material in relation to reflective and diffusing material regulates the reverberation time and the way in which the sound is diffused.

The sound quality is impaired if the reflected waves coincide in certain rhythms with the incident waves. To prevent this the walls of rooms intended for musical uses are sometimes not parallel. Sound may be directed toward a live wall (sound reflective) and sent back to a dead wall (sound absorptive). Flexible treatment, afforded by soft traverse draperies, may be required when audiences vary in size. This is due to the fact that people with their clothing constitute absorptive factors in a space. The placement of speakers in radio and record transmission is in the interest of securing the binaural reception of sound that was of good quality at its source.

INTERIOR FLOORS, WALLS, CEILINGS

Added materials such as carpets, rugs, shades, curtains, and pictures may be used in interiors, and they too should be related to the interior finishes that in turn are suited to the architecture. In today's world interior finishes for floors are often of some natural substance such as stone, slate, brick, wood, or a composite such as concrete. The first three are laid over a concrete base. Concrete or reinforced concrete flooring is used in slabs or poured into forms. It may be integral with its support. In one-story construction it rests on a properly drained and insulated bed.

Widely spaced posts, beams, and rafters are often left exposed on the inside of a structure as well as on the outside. Any rigid and suitable material may form the walls between the supports. When the framework is Western or platform, the traditional interior wall finish is plaster applied to wood or metal lath. Wood fiber or gypsum boards are frequently substituted; this is known as drywall construction. Because of cost, solid wood paneling has unfortunately almost gone out of existence. Ceilings may be treated in manners similar to walls. Sometimes an exterior material is carried to the inside partitions to indicate continuity.

Additional surfacing materials may be added to introduce economy in upkeep, comfort in use, and desired appearance. These fall into the following categories: *aggregates* such as chipped marble in concrete; *tiles* such as asphalt, ceramic, cork, rubber, synthetic, and acoustical; *thin materials* such as wallpapers, wall fabrics, and wood veneers; and *linoleum*.

The Beauty of Structures

This chapter has sidestepped an immediate discussion of interior design to consider the structural means of creating interiors. Although this diversion is necessary from a practical point of view, it is also hoped that it has added to our appreciation of the many beautiful buildings that have been created in the modern idiom. The truly masterful creators have exploited their structural knowledge in a logical and consistent manner and while so doing have had keen regard for the visual and expressive factors that the structural design made possible. Others, less great, have used similar means to create mediocre buildings.

The Relation Between Building Structure and Interior Design

For all of us who deal with these structures, a sensitive comprehension of relations existing between them and the smallest sector of the finished form needs to exist. This is a matter of material compatibility, shape, color and texture accord, and even more—organizational correspondence.

We suggest five types of buildings, although there could easily be more and there are many that combine several types of construction in one situation. Buildings similar to these, with their interior treatments, are carried through the entire text.

Stone structures
Post-and-beam wood structures
Western- or platform-frame structures
Steel-and-glass structures
Monolithic ferroconcrete structures

3

FUNCTIONAL PLANNING OF INTERIORS

The ways we live today are different from the ways people lived in other times, and this perforce alters the premise from which the architects begin designing, and thus affects the ultimate solution.

Katherine M. Ford and Thomas H. Creighton, *The American House Today*[1]

Functional Types Today

It is not within the possibilities of this text to analyze the functional planning of interiors for all building types, of which there are about two score. Functional types of spaces number more than this since many crossovers occur—kitchen planning, for instance, appearing within several larger categories. Specialized books must be consulted in regard to the needs of new species. For some of them a vast new field known as contract design now exists. Its purpose is to plan and install interiors where there may be many duplicate units and in which special legal requirements such as fireproofing and safety guarantees are factors. Such multiple installations of potentially interchangeable units makes frequent use of what is known as systems (e.g., a ceiling panel system, a sound-absorbing system, a storage system).

The Dwelling: A Basic Type

In this chapter we give our first attention to the dwelling unit. It constitutes the focus of much interior designing; many designers are particularly happy with this individualized work, and its problems are among the most complex encountered. Human habitations are regarded as the basic artifacts in any civilization. While we focus our attention on this type we note how frequently its planning techniques are fundamental to all good work concerned with space arranging.

A dwelling is intended to provide the best possible environment for living, usually for group living. Its first requirement is to provide for the physical well-being of the occupants. Essentially a house must provide space in which to exist. This enclosed space is currently very expensive and frequently is not extensive. Careful planning often is required to make it at all adequate.

What should this space provide? First it must provide shelter. It should ensure safety from unnecessary physical hazards. This is the negative side of its function. In any building designed for human occupancy we expect positive provisions for light, sanitation, and climate control. We may plan for optimal sound conditions. The disposition of spaces should facilitate the sort of work that goes on within. In a house this goes under the prosaic name of housekeeping—a more suitable term would be peoplekeeping. In other words, a house is one of the few building types that come into existence for the principal purpose of benefiting its inhabitants. The work pursued in most others is generally extrinsic to the welfare of the laborers who engage in it (e.g., in an office or a factory). It has been customary to think of a house as charged with the responsibility of nurturing the young, caring for the old, and of helping the interdependent sexes. We must admit that changing mores are altering this picture. Nevertheless, these purposes are all included in the work of familykeeping. The space of the house must provide for this many-faceted task.

People are also extroverts. Buildings must accommodate some of their social activities. As a social artifact, a dwelling can help a household gain from and contribute to the rich treasure of friendship.

The character of the American household has changed radically during the last few decades. Not only has the average family grown smaller with the years, but any one individual household changes its character during its lifetime. The beginning nucleus usually increases in size. Eventually there comes a time when the household is again diminished, and the home that was bursting at its seams is suddenly empty.

Planning Techniques

Structure relates to the material mass of a building. The plan dictates the way in which its spaces function. It arranges the interior so that it will serve the purposes—both physical and psychological—for which it was created.

COST

The economy of the late twentieth century regulates both structure and planning. Today's building costs soar. To economize, the following suggestions are made:

Seek a structural system in keeping with the money available. For instance, prefabrication may be the economical order of the day.
Select a location that relates to the building cost. It is sound economy to restrict costs so that they are compatible with the median levels in a community.

Where land values are high, plan for a compact building. A rambling one will cost more because it has more square feet of wall and roof per cubic feet of interior.
Consider carefully good planning techniques.

THE SITE AND THE COMMUNITY

Complete planning for a building includes thought for its site and for the community in which it is to be located. The latter, through its zoning laws and character, becomes one of the dictators of the form. Indeed, the neighborhood is one of the assets being purchased. There is much to be gained through good zoning laws. They should be intelligent, wisely permissive rather than foolishly restrictive, and their standards should be maintained.

The site itself is important, influencing the character of whatever is placed on it. A tall, formal building seems incongruous among low rolling hills. The values obtained from land ownership are significant, but they are also expensive. In a metropolitan environment, private outdoor space and building isolation are luxuries that may be justified economically because they can improve the appearance of both the building and the community. It is a generous as well as a canny custom to reserve some of our property to please the passerby.

SPACE LIMITATIONS

Since private possession of space is expensive, waste space is taboo. What is waste space? A family room? A living or "great" room? An executive suite? A museum or library foyer? The question often arises. The parlor of our great-grandparents, which was opened only on formal occasions, we label waste space. A careful study of the society of their days will show how useful this reserved space was in their lives. Space is only wasted if it serves no important physical or psychological function.

The modern planner first eliminates unusable space. If unused because it is uncomfortable it should be ruled out. Unfinished space is expensive unless usable for storage.

The modern builder considers the structural economy of space essential. A structure with space economy provided through such means as steel supports and longer internal spans really gains interior space. Built-in furniture can often be planned in the interest of space conservation.

Mechanized economy in space use must be considered. The good planner will use the most compact machinery units.

Flexible and multiple use of space is part of the program. Flexible partitions, multipurpose furniture, changeable furniture arrangements, the provision for ample storage—these help make space available for several uses. A small space is in general more useful if it is not cut up into too many rooms.

Space saving is closely related to energy saving. There is a correlation between the size of enclosed space, the function for which it is intended, and the energy required to maintain it so that it can function. A neat adjustment of these factors must be considered. Service, whether human or mechanical, costs money. A big house certainly requires energy to service, but a small house is not always easy to maintain. It is the planner's job to adjust the procurable space to needs so that service cost is kept low. This is saving space through work conditioning.

PLANNING FOR FUNCTIONS

Next we come to grips with the real problem, the one for which the space was bought. What are the various activities that it must accommodate? These break down into two categories: the major activities that are the reason for the building's existence and the service activities that are for the purpose of expediting the major ones. Functions may fall into both categories. For instance, gardening can augment the food supplies as well as be an enjoyable avocation. Here is a suggested list:

Major Activities

1. Private.
   a. Sleeping and dressing.
   b. Personal cleanliness and sanitation.
   c. Care of infants, the sick, and the infirm.
   d. Intellectual: reading and writing.
   e. Hobbies or creative interests.
2. Social.
   a. Dining.
   b. Recreation: music, television, entertaining, and conversation.
   c. Provision for house guests.

Service Activities

1. Housework.
   a. Food preparation and service.
   b. Laundry.

c. Housecleaning.
   d. Operation of utilities, heat, water, and so forth.
   e. Care of grounds.
   f. Car servicing.
   g. Productive industry, sewing, and so forth.
2. Storage.
3. Communication within and to the house.
   a. Entrances and exits.
   b. Circulation.
   c. Audio communication: telephones, security systems.

This kind of analysis gives us a first intimation of the orientation of the various areas. The space that is most pleasantly located would be assigned logically to the major activities and probably to social affairs because they are shared by the greatest number of persons. Service areas are planned to be as attractive as possible, but they are not usually those with the best view, breeze, or sun.

The picture now may look somewhat chaotic, like this:

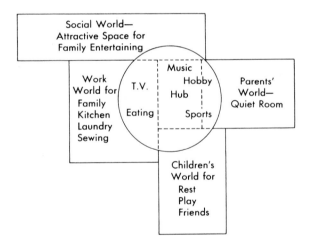

PLANNING FOR COORDINATION AND CIRCULATION

A building is filled with people going places and doing things. This involves good coordination and circulation between spaces. Coordination and circulation are dependent on each other.

Flexibility in the use of space and equipment is considered first. If two activities make similar space and equipment demands and do not usurp the same time, they may be coordinated in use. A dining space adjacent to a living area makes it possible to collapse dining furniture and to use the entire space for entertainment. Two classrooms with a folding partition between can be thrown together as a study room or lecture hall.

Coordination planning also involves an analysis of persons as they engage in their activities.

	Social World	Adult Private World
Main Entrance		
Children's and Service Entrance	Service Area	Children's Play Indoors
	Children's Play Outdoors	Children's Sleeping
	Adult Hobbies	

If anyone's activities involve several locations, these locations should be placed to expedite travel between them. If meal preparation and reception at a door is on the agenda, stove and door should not be too far apart.

In a house good coordination planning means that the functioning spaces are so interrelated that the engineer or manager or coordinator can control the activities. Where the mother does most of the work, the planning for good coordination may result in organization of the sort seen in Figure 3.3. The plan may be very unorthodox.

Related to the coordination of spaces is the consideration of circulation through them. The first bugaboo here is ambiguity. It should be perfectly obvious on entering a building just where one is expected to go first, second, third (Figure 3.4). This problem of sequential ordering of spaces is so important that in planning within large buildings such as hospitals an important aspect of contract work for such installations involves what is known as signage, the proper making and placing of signs to indicate clearly the various routes of traffic.

Circulation routes should not only be evident, they should be planned to be as direct as possible. They should not interfere with areas allocated to other functional groups. If a circulation route must be part of a room space, let it cross the short end, thus leaving a large pocket for major uses.

One example of partial abrogation of this rule is seen in the planning of commercial showroom displays, in museum arrangements (Figure 3.5), and often in the arrangements in merchandising centers (Figure 3.6). Here, although major direction is predetermined, variety and unexpected deviations from this pattern are in the order of good routing. People are expected to loiter, to turn left or right at will, and to find numerous exhibits to tempt the eye. The straight path and monotony are out.

This introduces another idea. A good piece of architectural planning in respect to travel will evolve its visual pleasures in time. However short and direct, a circulation route should offer an interesting visual as well as physical trip. The corollary to this, of course, is that the interior of a well-planned building always presents a pleasingly designed space to view. It is unfortunate, for instance, if a door is too closely faced by a wall unless there is a glimpse of an interesting scene beyond. Conversely, there is occasional need in planning to shut off private areas from social or public ones, a need that varies with people and circumstance. Instead of posting a sign, *DO NOT ENTER*, the building plan can carry the message. No obvious circulation route should lead to the secluded area; its entrance

Figure 3.3. A plan with children's activities in mind. Residence of Mr. and Mrs. Charles Hickox, Pepper Pike, Ohio.
Architect: Robert A. Little
Photograph: Courtesy House and Garden. Copyright © 1955 by The Condé Nast Publications Inc.
A gracious home has solved the problem of associating children's activities and the amenities of family and social life by coordination around a central service area, left. The children's bedroom area is to the right.

Figure 3.4. Circulation planning.

Figure 3.5. A museum gallery arrangement. Installation at the Cleveland
Museum of Art, Cleveland, Ohio. Exhibition: 1976 Year in Review.
Designer: William E. Ward
Photograph by Nicholas Hlobeczy, courtesy The Cleveland Museum of Art
Museum arrangements for special exhibitions are planned so that the viewer
will have an interesting walk-through space.

Figure 3.6. New merchandising patterns. Many retail stores have designed their spaces to rotate the basic planning grid by approximately 45 degrees in relation to the building space. This directs traffic at angles that can open up circulation patterns and vistas.

should not be conspicuous, and a sliding door may suggest a barricade. A different level can also provide a separation.

As a summary of planning techniques, let us think of them as the first step in space designing. A good plan should have such simplicity and logic that it will result in well-designed spaces that are suited to use, effectively coordinated, and giving definite instructions for physical and visual journeys. In addition, a plan is capable of expressing certain qualities. It can provide an expression of formality, graciousness, hospitality, or even a certain aloofness.

PSYCHOLOGICAL PLANNING

A real estate agent reports that many prospective buyers, after endless review of available houses, often exclaim, "This is my home." Why? Probably for seldom-recognized and little-understood reasons.

Obviously the more public a building the less attention it can pay to the needs of distinct personalities. Here the planner must develop that sixth sense that appraises group personality. Some psychological planning is always possible and desirable, differing only in degree in various instances. A business office, for example, should be designed so that in addition to its obvious response to overt requirements it becomes a pleasant place in which to work. Occasionally in respect to this commandment we find office suites in which the executive offices are too extravagant and the typists' are too meager. Probably neither should be overdone, but it is certain that the establishment quarters must have some legitimate right to a space that will help the company's public image, and the many workers will do better if their allocated space allows the mind some variation, release, and inspiration.

There are practically no buildings that can be divorced from the need for psychological planning. Even churches, synagogues, and temples are not immune. Some congregations feel happiest with an interior that partakes of a refuge; others prefer to reach for the stars.

Planning that most private sanctuary, a home, is a similar matter. Here individual personality planning is vitally important. Each of us has a unique contribution to make to life, and we each make individual requests of a house. These should be assembled and should become of importance equal to the list of functions previously made. At this stage, neglect the obvious and concentrate on private dreams. And, as a good psychologist, interpret their hidden meanings.

We wish to be esteemed by our friends. It may be essential that the house bolster our pride. We may have a special need to feel wanted, protected, and sheltered. This is another kind of house. Stimulation for creativ-

ity? Still another. A planner must be both sensitive and self-effacing to create for psychological functions.

Representing a Final Plan

At this point it is possible to make a plan of a proposed area. First learn the rudiments of architectural symbolic language (Figure 3.7). A plan is simply a horizontal slice cut through a building at a particular level and represented in a definite scale on paper. The meaning of ¼" = 1' is that ¼ inch on the graph represents 1 foot on the building. The plan may be a simple one in which the wall thicknesses and relevant measures are indicated by a solid line. Or it may be more detailed to indicate materials, construction, and built-in features.

An adequate type of floor plan may be made in the following manner. Take all inside measurements of a room at floor or window level. Reducing these measures to a suitable scale, draw a section of the room. Walls extend outside these measures and for a simple drawing are filled in with a heavy black line. Load-bearing walls can be made 8 inches

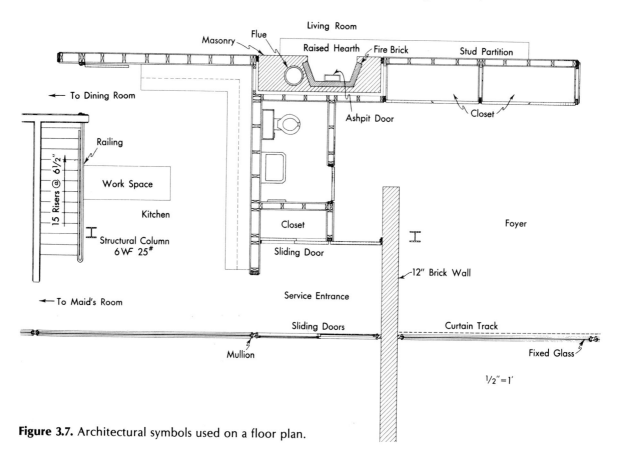

Figure 3.7. Architectural symbols used on a floor plan.

thick and screen walls the actual thickness of the material.

Windows are indicated by very fine lines. A double-hung window may be symbolized by four lines, two for the outer and inner edges of the sill, two for the double sash. Other types of windows are drawn with very thin lines according to the spacing of the sash. Door openings and casement windows should have their swing indicated by an arc and a straight line perpendicular to it. Fireplaces and built-in equipment are shown in cross section. It is wise to include electrical outlets on a complete floor plan, with line and dot signs for their switches (see Figure 6.25). A line of dashes indicates a construction above the plan level such as an archway.

Most architectural plans have their dimensions indicated. The letters and figures for these are consistent throughout. If the room size alone is given, the dimensions are placed just below the room name. If the plan is carried out in greater detail, the dimensions are grouped and are indicated on lines terminated by arrows abutting on projections of the lines between which the measures are taken.

Furniture to be placed in the plan may be measured and indicated in the same way. It is well to cut out small-scaled patterns—called plan templates—of the pieces of furniture to be used (Figure 3.8). These can be shifted around on the floor plan until the most satisfactory arrangement is reached.

Final Planning

Service Areas
Kitchen 9′ × 12′

	Width	Depth	Height
Refrigerator	Variable	30″	68″
Range	Variable	24″	36″
Sink with built-in dishwasher	Variable	24″	36″
Separate dishwasher	25″	25″	36″
Counter with knee space for sitting			30″
Linear counter space with cabinets above and below	96 to 108″		

The controlling location for service tasks in a house should be near the kitchen, the garage, and the tools. When the family performs its own work, place these centers not too far apart. To the degree that a house is serviced by persons outside the family, an isolation of specialized work areas is desirable.

Household work areas can be pleasant. In the kitchen an outdoor view is appreciated and a glimpse of the living room is not amiss. A hearth fire either in the living room or in the kitchen is heartening. The television may be the modern substitute. The tool room and garage can be equally inviting. Too frequently in the past the first was found near a furnace room in the basement and the dark cold garage was located at the rear of the lot. Bringing the basement rooms upstairs and placing them adjacent to the space well designed for car service has been a planning step forward.

There should be a direct circulation route from the kitchen to the dining area even if it is only across a counter. It is a good idea to plan a chlidren's play area, even a family room, the wash room, the entrance doors, the laundry, and the sewing areas close to the kitchen—the hub of the universe! From the tool space and garage there should be direct communication with the yard, the play areas, the utility area, and the family entrance with its nearby cleanup room.

In arranging equipment in any service area, observe production-line technique: the material should move in the direction of its processing with as little crisscrossing as possible and preferably with no interference by traffic going to and from other areas.

In the food-processing center the equipment is best placed in a shape that approximates the letter U (Figure 3.9). Variations of this into one or two straight lines or into an elbow-shaped L may be necessary because of the architecture. Allow at least 3 feet of empty floor space in a U formation and 4 to 5 feet in an area where the space between the counters is used for passage.

The island kitchen where the work units are concentrated in the center is used by many planners. This can free window walls and living areas. Production-line sequence of equipment is as important here as in any other planning arrangement. In most of these layouts, what is known as a work triangle is created between the refrigerator, sink, and stove. Enough space between these centers should be provided so that the worker can reach them easily but will not grow dizzy making too many turns in a restricted area.

In sequence from the outer door, the first unit is a storage center containing the refrigerator, closets for canned and perishable

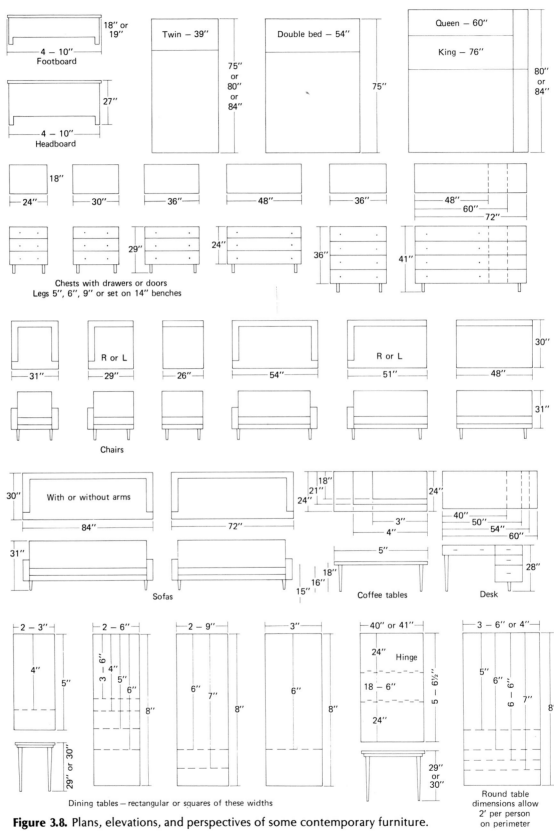

Figure 3.8. Plans, elevations, and perspectives of some contemporary furniture.

Plan of grand piano

28¼ – 35

17 – 19

27½ – 34¼

24¾ – 26

16

19

|— 16 – 23½ —| |— 18½ – 32¼ —| |— 18 – 27 —| |— 19½ – 32¼ —|

Pianos				Height with lid raised
	Depth	Width	Height	
Concert grand	9'8"	5'4"	3'3"	6'1"
Music room grand	7'	5'	3'4"	6'1"
Parlor grand	6'3"	4'10"	3'4"	5'10"
Baby grand	4'5"	4'7"	3'	4'4"
Spinet	2'1"	4'10"	3'4"	–
Studio	2'1"	4'9"	3'10"	–

H 1 – 8,
1 – 7
or 1 – 6

Bench

14
16

|— 3 – 0 —|

Elevation

Spinet piano – Plan

W 16
D 20
H 35

W 26
D 23½
H 32
SH 18½

W 46, 75, 100
D 35
H 25
SH 16

W 32½
D 32¼
H 33⅜
SH 15

W 32
D 31½
H 30

W 30
D 30
H 30
SH 17

W 21¾
D 32¼
H 32¼
SH 17½

W 30¾
D 27½
H 28½
SH 16

W 24½
D 20½
H 27¼
SH 17½

W 40
D 34
H 35½

W 25½
D 20
H 16
Ottoman

W 19½
D 21½
H 29¼
SH 18

W 18
D 22¼
H 31½
SH 17¾

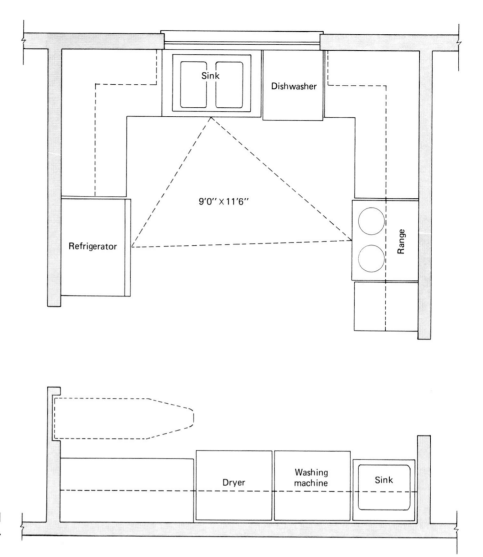

9'0" × 11'6"

Figure 3.9. Plan of a U-shaped kitchen with a laundry center.

goods, and a work top for receiving, sorting, and cleaning supplies. Adjacent is a food-preparation center with cabinets for the required utensils. The sink is in this vicinity because water is so essential to all food work.

The sink becomes the nucleus of the kitchen cleaning center. It is often located below a window for air and view. In many small houses this sink is used for water for house cleaning. In some houses an extra sink and faucet is placed in the cleaning supplies storage space.

The cooking center is next in order. This should include the range and space for storage of the utensils used at the range. Last there should be a serving center, because many foods go directly from the range to the serving dish. In some contemporary plans, the different units of the range are dissoci-

ated—the grills are sunk in the counter top and the oven is separately located in a wall unit. When the counter top is used as a pass-through shelf to the dining space, the cooking grills should not be located where they will conflict with the passage. The oven should not be located where it would be difficult to lift pans onto a serving counter space.

Many kitchen areas include a small informal spot for eating. These are variously known as breakfast rooms, lunch or snack bars, or dinettes. The best location for this space is between the cooking center and the dining room. It functions more pleasantly if it is on an outside wall. When located near the dining room, it is a useful baffle for kitchen noise and sights. It can be well used as a space for setting out extra utensils and special courses such as a salad or dessert. Storage of dining equipment may be in this place. One end of this space is often used for a pass-through shelf.

As dining in the modern house often is in several different areas, the kitchen work areas must be planned so that they will be located convenient to all of these spots. Some juggling and even some compromise may be required to effect this.

Laundry 8′ × 9′

	Width	Depth	Height
Washer	34″	25″	36″
Dryer	31″	28″	36″
Ironing board	5′	1′4″	2′6″
Sorting shelves	4′6″	1′6″	36″

(Equipment may need a clearance from the wall)

In the days before heated basements (just to reminisce!) the laundry had to be near the kitchen stove. From there it graduated to the basement. Soiled clothes were sent from the second floor to the cellar and were brought up a flight of stairs to the drying yard whence they might descend again for ironing before they retraced their steps to the wardrobes and the linen closet. Mechanical dryers can eliminate the backyard trip, and good planning can do away with most of the other steps. There is no reason that a laundry need be in the basement. It should be near the kitchen and should not be far from the bedrooms, baths, and dining areas where soiled items come from and to which clean ones are returned.

Laundry equipment should be in the following order. First comes the receiving center with its chute and hamper and sorting shelves. Next one encounters the washer, dryer, and drying lines. Last is the ironing and storage center with racks for hanging clothes fresh from the dryer and shelf space for folding and stacking clean articles. Sewing equipment for repairs might also be located here. Do not forget that an auxiliary small tub is desirable for hand laundry.

Utility Room 4′ × 6′ Minimum

The utility room is the modern counterpart of the furnace room. It usually houses the air conditioning units and the hot water heater and may contain the garbage- and rubbish-disposal units.

Storage
Average Sizes of Some Common Storage Areas

	Width	Depth	Height
Closet in bedroom (per person)	4′	2′6″	6′-8′
Bookshelves	Variable	10″-12″	10″-12″ (between shelves)

A house without adequate provision for storage is no more efficient than the nomad's tent in providing for the needs of our twentieth-century household. Civilization began when it became possible to keep the treasures of the past and to store for the future. Storage both of supplies and of sources of knowledge facilitated the advancement of learning.

The modern dwelling needs reserve space for many types of articles. In the first place it needs closets that free space for multiple use. Card tables and chairs may be brought out for a card party at the same time that collapsible furniture is put away to make room for large gatherings. A list of occasional-use furnishings should be made.

Every household stores some supplies and movable equipment used to service its present possessions. Mops and the vacuum cleaner, for example, are such servicing equipment.

Some storage is planned merely in the interest of providing the best kind of care for a family's soilable possessions. Silverware is placed in chests that are compartmentalized and lined with a tarnishproof felt.

Some space is planned to help a household provide for its future. Almost all seasonal equipment may be so considered. In addition, a household gives thought to other foreseeable needs. The old-time vegetable cellar may be gone, but the large-size freezer is with us.

All of the types of articles so far considered have supplied some physical need in the lives of the household. There is also call for storage of articles that fulfill an emotional one. Our modern civilization is apt to deplore the preservation of belongings for sentimental reasons. We have adopted this attitude from the necessity for space saving and because the nineteenth century seems to have overindulged in romantic preservation of keepsakes. The value of this kind of article to a household bears no relevance to its intrinsic worth. Such mementos may vary from a child's broken toy to the rosepoint lace on grandmother's wedding gown. To criticize the storage of such articles within the household vaults is to criticize all attempts to revive the past and to establish continuity with it. Inasmuch as the animals alone are forced to live only in the present, we would be foolish to limit ourselves to the immediacy of a similar existence. A proportional relation between past, present, and future is more desirable. Rightly used, the modern counterpart of the attic may give our children the key to rich experience.

We store many articles in the household that help create a more varied and satisfying personal life. The token to which we have just referred may serve this end in a purely associational way. Other objects such as filing cabinets or projection equipment are more practically useful. This motley grouping of articles for family interests should have storage space.

Some vehicles such as automobiles, bicycles, and snowmobiles help the household take flight in a physical as well as a mental manner. These too, must be stored.

It is extremely difficult to classify storage needs. This does not mean that the equivalent of the old-time attic that could embrace everything is the best solution to our requirements. Storage requirements are somewhat specialized. Indeed, in offices storage systems designed for specialized uses have wide distribution.

Various storage needs can be satisfied with space at different cost levels. Structural costs may be low. Walls can be nonloadbearing. Air conditioning requirements of various storage spaces may differ. Storage space for summer furniture needs no heat. Storage for outer wraps in use does. Humidity control is essential for many articles.

The location of the storage space is important. It should be near where the article is used. When articles are necessary in several places it may be advisable to duplicate facilities. This might be true for storage of children's toys and for cleaning supplies.

The frequency of use of the articles will be a certain clue to the location of their storage. Things for occasional use can certainly be placed farthest from the usual household activities. Articles for quick emergency use

should be most accessible. Concealed locations are important for some valuables.

Within the allocated space, storage should be planned so that the article is readily accessible and the space is easily cleaned. Storage that is too high or too low for reach should be avoided for all but infrequently used articles. Storage that is too deep is also inefficient. It should be unnecessary to remove one set of articles to reach another set. In the kitchen, for instance, narrow storage space with sliding doors at counter level would be valuable.

Planned storage gives thought to the size of the article to be stored. It is uneconomical to plan a full room-height closet and a 5-foot-high garment pole to hang jackets, shirtwaists, skirts, and trousers. The Bibliography in this book has references giving tables of standard sizes of everything from washcloths to phonograph records to trays. In storage that is really designed well the spaces should be tailored to the needs.

Sleeping and Dressing
Average Sizes of Bedrooms

Small bunk room for a child	8′ × 8′
Single bedroom	8′3″ × 12′
Double bedroom	12′ × 14′

The area primarily devoted to sleeping and dressing frequently must serve other functions. The bathroom, a private sitting room, and a work area are often part of this private apartment. With careful planning, provision can be made for these activities within very limited space.

The sleeping quarters are best located on the quiet side of the building away from street and service. Many prefer an elevation above the ground floor for these areas. Early risers speak for an eastern location; late risers are not so committed.

The several sleeping rooms are usually grouped. Sometimes one reserved for guests is isolated from the family bedrooms. This gives the visitor a feeling of greater privacy. Since the guest room may be flexible in its uses, locating it near the main living quarters permits other activities when it is not occupied by a house guest.

In the complex of bedrooms, the relation of the rooms of parents and children must be

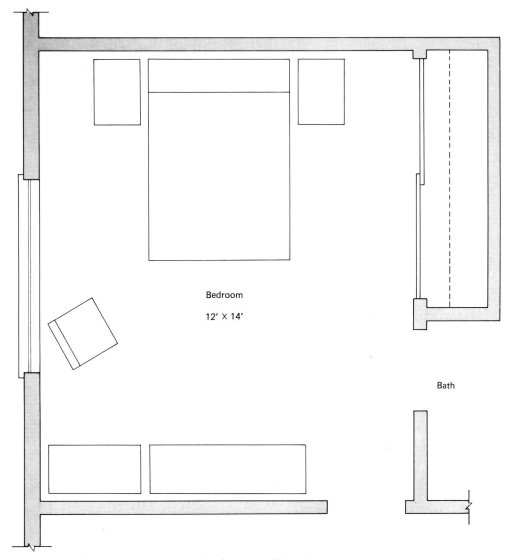

Bedroom

12' X 14'

Bath

Figure 3.10. Plan of an average-size bedroom with furniture arrangement.

considered carefully. When the children are very young, the parents' room should be close by. As the children grow older, greater isolation is desirable. This flexible sort of arrangement sometimes can be accomplished by the addition of doors to what were previously open passageways. A parents' room should be placed nearer the main artery than the young child's. Thus the parents are aware of the child's whereabouts and are in a position to be guardians.

In planning the master bedroom there are divided opinions arising from divergent reasoning. If the dressing area is considered a very private sanctum, it should be least accessible. When, however, it serves for the convenience of others, it is placed close to the main hall. It is always adjacent to a bath. The sleeping compartment certainly should be the most remote of the entire bedroom grouping. Unless complete air conditioning is supplied, it is placed advisedly where it will benefit from cross ventilation. On the other hand, space too near windows often results in too much glare. Moreover, the window area is frequently reserved for a seating arrangement because of the light and view. With complete air conditioning the expedient of planning sleeping cubicles grouped near the center of the house and equipped for the best sleep conditions has been sensibly suggested.

Beds are the major articles of furnishing. It is convenient to have a small table adjacent to the bed. Many bed headboards include provision for this shelf space in addition to accommodations for light, a clock, and perhaps a radio. A bed with such a headboard requires extra length. A low, so-called slipper chair is a convenience in dressing. A chest for clothes storage and a dressing table and bench are often included. Extras such as comfortable chairs and a desk with its chair may be added. A full-length mirror is desirable. A low folding rack for use for luggage certainly should be available. Some of this equipment may be built into the house and need not be provided as separate pieces.

Children's bedrooms should be equipped with furniture suited to children. As childhood is a temporary thing, such furniture may be inexpensively produced or be flexible enough in use and permanent enough in structure to survive the growing and changing years. Closets with rod grooves at differ-

ent heights, temporary wall finishes such as tackboard, double bunk beds that can collapse into single, movable partitions isolating the bed sections from the larger play sections now and subdividing the space into separate rooms later, temporary storage shelves built at child height—these are all aids.

In the arrangement of bedroom furniture, the bed should be placed away from the wall for ease in servicing. The remaining furniture will be placed to perform its functions. For example, mirrors should be where the light will fall on the face of the person in front of them; easy chairs should command views and light.

Although flexibility and attendant multiple use of bedroom space may at times be necessary, it should not be forgotten that the bedroom is the most private of our castles. When the private areas of the home are made too public, the mind is robbed of an inner retreat.

In contemporary planning a bedroom area is frequently integrated with its own private yard. The private porch or balcony is reappearing as an adaptation of this idea.

Baths

Average Sizes of Bathrooms

Two-fixture lavatories (wash basin, toilet)	2'6" × 6'3" or 3' × 8'6"
Three-fixture bathroom (wash basin, toilet, tub)	5' × 8'
Three-fixture bathroom (wash basin, toilet, square tub)	7'2" × 7'6"
Three-fixture bathroom (wash basin, toilet, shower)	5' × 7'6"

Sizes of Bathroom Fixtures

Shower	3' × 3'
Tub, rectangular	2'6" × 5'
Tub, square	38" × 39"
Wash basin	21" × 30"
Toilet	21" × 31"
(allowances must be made for clearances)	

Figure 3.11. Bath with garden. Home of the architect, Moreland Hills, Ohio.
Architect: Ernst Payer
Photographer: C. W. Ackerman
This unusual bathroom has a sunken tub with Persian blue tile and a small indoor garden. The sliding glass doors at the left lead to a diminutive private patio garden. The ceramic sculpture of mother and child is Norwegian. The water outlet was designed by sculptor William M. McVey.

Perhaps no feature of our houses has undergone more change during the short period of its existence than the bath with plumbing. The most noticeable recent change has been in the increased number of separate baths provided. The equivalent of two bathrooms is now found in most houses of 1000 square footage. Many now have two and one-half (wash basin, toilet) baths. The priva-room, a combination bath and dressing room for each person, is a probability in the future.

The greatest expense in building baths is in the plumbing. Therefore, baths should be grouped around central plumbing whenever possible. This has led to the compartment bath. A compartment bath should be carefully planned if it is to function well.

The functional relation of the bath areas to other areas of the house varies with the household. The first requirement is that the principal bathrooms be near the bedrooms. It is becoming rather common to find two baths with entrances into the master bedroom. One is completely isolated from other rooms. The other may adjoin a children's room or even a guest room and be accessible from the hall.

A bath area intended for use by the sportsman, the gardener, and the children during the day should be located near the service or family entrance to the house. This bath is also useful to the helpers of a family.

If there is only one first-floor lavatory, place it so that it is accessible to the rear yard, the kitchen, and the living rooms. A position off a back corridor may be the solution. A bath should not be exposed to view from the main living areas or corridors. Nevertheless, its position should be immediately apparent.

Private Recreation Areas

The pendulum always swings back. The modern house planner is thinking in terms of two recreation areas. They may not be the erstwhile parlor and living room or even the living room and sun room combinations of the more recent past, but the separation of functions and spaces exists.

The less formal of these twin areas should be planned around the family's leisure pursuits. For small children this is play suited to their age. For the older years the recreational interests are as varied as personalities. Although the accent today is on creativity usually of an active kind, this may easily be overemphasized. The relaxed pace of James Whitcomb Riley's little boy who played aimlessly with summer at "noon time and June time down along the river" has been found to be psychologically sound. Therefore, spaces intended for recreation need not be filled with specific equipment.

A general family recreation zone may well be the one from which the more specialized areas stem. If a household does not center around children and if its unscheduled activities are on the quiet side, a family space is often planned adjacent to the master bedroom suite. A library or study is frequently flanked by a more public living room on one side and is accessible to a bedroom on the other. Where children and more active enterprises are in the picture, the family areas (in a servantless house) are usually integrated with the service rooms. Such an area may be adjacent to the children's bedrooms and be within easy access of the kitchen.

Highly specialized equipment frequently necessitates the reservation of some space in addition to this general household room. Photographers and gardeners, for instance, preempt space that cannot be easily varied in use.

Outdoor space should be planned so that some of it can be used for leisure interests. Children's leisure is all the time. Therefore, a part of the lot may be devoted to their play. Pave some of the space for their wheeled toys. If their sandboxes and swings are covered and raised above such pavement, they will be more useful after rains. Built-up seats may open for storage of some of the children's outdoor tools and provide places off the ground for them to sit.

Food Service and Eating
Average Sizes of Dining Rooms

Dining table and space for four seated persons	10'10" × 10'10"
Dining table and space for six to eight seated persons	10'6" × 12'8"
Dining alcove with chairs for four	10' × 10'
Passage space between edge of dining table and a wall or large piece of furniture	3'6"
Allowance for seating	2' × 1'6"
Dining table for two	2' × 2'6"
Dining table for four	3' × 3'
Dining table for six	3'6" × 5'6"
Dining table for eight	3'6" × 8'

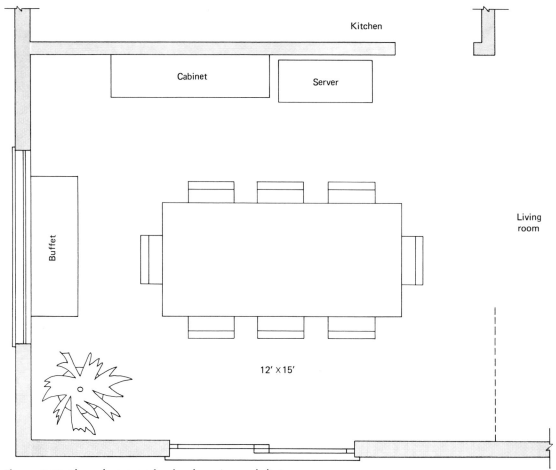

Figure 3.12. Plan of an area for food service and dining.

Figure 3.13. (*opposite*) Plan of a living area of average size.

In addition to a table and seats, a complete dining assemblage includes a service shelf that can be used for extra utensils and for buffet equipment. Near or in the dining room there should be space for storage of dining paraphernalia. Much of this equipment is built in today.

The dining table is customarily situated in the center of the room. Sometimes a table is placed along a window wall or at right angles to it. This kind of arrangement is less formal and makes the room seem larger. The service shelf should be near the kitchen, and it is helpful if it is equipped with warming grilles. A space for quick meals frequently is located between the kitchen and the more formal dining area. It then can supplement a service shelf.

Sometimes a dining room is used as a TV room. This requires a different arrangement of both tables and chairs so that everyone can face the screen. Small tables or long narrow tables with seats along the walls are one answer.

Social Areas
Average Sizes of Living Rooms

Minimum	13′ × 13′
Average	13′ × 17′
Medium	17′ × 23′

The social life of households is diversified. Some have many guests, others few. The social life of some households is largely at home. For others the church, the theater, or the club is the important center. Some can plan

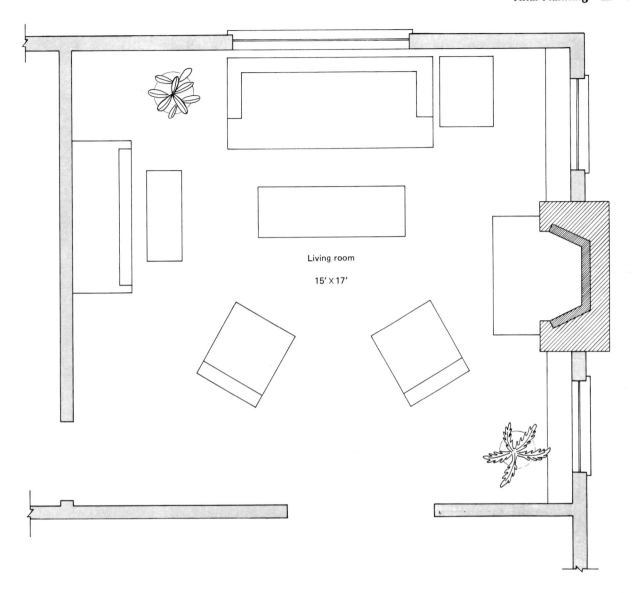

Living room

15' X 17'

for activities suited to one age group. Most must regard the needs of several generations. Some conditions seem constant, and these give qualities of universality to the solutions.

The locations of the social areas should take advantage of the best physical situations. Whether to locate social space completely away from the street is an individual problem. For shut-ins and many others such a sheltered area is not desirable. It is likely that several locations are possible. This creates variety and allows some group separation.

The main living room is the core to which all others relate. This area is far from the seldom-used parlor of the last century. Nevertheless, it should be planned so that it is easily kept neat and attractive. This factor is

so important to some people that appearance may be overemphasized at the expense of functional qualities. The family pride or personal self-esteem that is at the root of this is basically a good thing if not carried to excess.

The house must be planned to facilitate the ready-for-guests tidiness of a main social space at the same time that it is usable for general activities. In the first place, it should be kept as free of traffic lanes as possible. Second, provision must be made for sufficient and convenient facilities for wraps so that the living room chairs will not function as temporary depositories. Adequate places should be present for laying down magazines, papers, or smoking paraphernalia without knocking over ornaments or disarranging the room.

Outdoor living spaces are a distinct advantage, substituting for and enlarging indoor ones. The principal outdoor area is often adjacent to the living room. It is no longer the "front porch," but it may be a breezeway connecting the house with the garage. It could be an interior court or patio, a balcony or a roof. Many modern planners prefer this area to be detached from the house as an open or enclosed terrace.

The sizes of living areas are dictated by the sizes of furniture groups. Seating furniture for family and several guests is basic. Built-in window seats and ledges can take care of numerous guests. The younger crowd prefers stools and cushions. Too much paraphernalia impedes stand-up parties. It is needless to say that provision for adequate lighting is a vital part of the initial consideration. Low tables for accessories complete the list of necessities.

The placement of seating furniture in the social areas is dictated by the size of the space as well as by the immediate use. When conversation is intended, the chairs should occupy no more than a conversational unit space. This is about 13 to 15 feet square. The unit should be held together by a compact arrangement and by the use of decorative equipment such as carpet or wall treatment, which makes it cohesive. If possible, such a conversational unit should have a central focal point such as a hearth, window, or table. Contemporary living rooms are frequently planned so that a conversational group can congregate around the hearth and the view at the same time.

Too rigid or straight-line planning of seating furniture is seldom entirely satisfactory. Therefore built-in seats are functional when they can be supplemented by chairs arranged to break the rigidity of row seating.

Figure 3.14. Apartment in New York City.
Interior designer: Virginia Whitmore Kelly
Photograph: courtesy of Interiors, *copyright 1957, Whitney Publications, Inc.,*
Ben Schnall, photographer
In this living area in an older apartment that has been given a contemporary feeling, the placement of the piano was a prime consideration. The admonitions considered in the accompanying text have been observed carefully.

When a social area is large, it frequently houses several seating groups. Sometimes these groups are isolated; many times they must be integrated. This can be accomplished best if some of the furnishings are selected to be pivotal. A person seated on a chair adjacent to a secondary group should be able to turn it in either direction. The so-called pull-up chair answers this requirement. Benches, chairs without arms, and stools make better pivotal pieces than large stationary pieces do. Objects large in size or with high backs and arms can act as barricades. Thus they isolate rather than unite groupings. Such isolation occasionally is required, and a chair carefully selected with this in mind becomes a room divider. A seat backed by a table or desk is very effective for this purpose.

The seating groups in social areas are not always arranged solely to further conversation. Households desire various kinds of social relaxation. Therefore, provision frequently must be made for music centers, reading centers, television centers, and game centers. In each case the necessary equipment should be provided and arranged to function well and to provide flexibility of use.

The placement of large musical instruments must be considered from several points of view (Figure 3.14). First comes provision for good-quality sound. This was considered in Chapter 2 in the discussion of sound conditioning. Further, such instruments should be placed where air conditions are favorable to the instrument. Do not place them too close to an outside wall unless it is well insulated. Neither should they be close to a radiator. Instruments placed in southern window exposures must be protected carefully from radiant heat.

If the instrument requires a player, the conditions must be physically and psychologically good for a performance. Adequate light is essential. Some pianists do not like to be positioned with their backs to the audience. Many prefer that the instrument separate them from the rest of the room. Grand pianos should be placed with their bass strings parallel to a wall both from the standpoint of opening the piano toward space and of using the graceful curve of the treble side decoratively. Some rooms are sufficiently large to warrant a diagonal placing of the instrument.

A special word about video. It is located frequently near some center of focal interest such as a fireplace. Then the seating can be arranged so that it faces both interesting points. If chairs flank a fireplace, the television may be placed at the opposite end of the room to obtain the necessary focal distance from the screen. This should be approximately equivalent in feet to the diameter of the tube in inches. The image is best seen at eye level, or 4 feet from the floor for a seated viewer.

Many times the television is in a compartment of the wall that can swing out for greater visibility and then go back into a closed space when not in use (Figures 3.15a and b; Figure 3.16). In planning for this, remember that the depth necessary for the tube encasement varies from 1 foot to 2 feet 10 inches. Often other equipment for modern entertainment such as the projection screen and the record player are mounted in a similar manner. A turntable mounting will allow pivoting to a family room nearby. Multiple sets may be the only answer in video households.

Circulation and Communication Areas

Sizes of Circulation Areas

	Minimum	Average
Width of hall (two persons)	3'	4'
Entrance hall	4'6" × 4'6"	5' × 7'

The first communication area is the public social entrance. This should be the most accessible approach. It should be easier for the guest to reach this door than to reach any other, otherwise the law of least resistance goes into effect! Many of our friends arrive in cars. Therefore, a social entrance should be adjacent to an adequate parking zone. If possible, an entrance court that combines parking facilities, walkway, and main doorway is desirable. It is pleasant to experience a short walk before reaching the entrance door. This provides a visual perspective, but it may be a disadvantage in inclement weather.

The social entrance opens on the main artery. It should be readily accessible from the kitchen, living room, and cloak room. When the circulation thoroughfare cuts across functioning areas, its positioning should not interfere unduly with their purposes.

Social routing is first to a reception area, a cloak and "powder" room, the major social

(a) (b)

Figure 3.15. Television installation: A residence in Shaker Heights, Ohio.
(A) closed, (B) open.
Architect: Ernst Payer
Photographer: C. W. Ackerman
This is typical of the custom-designed installation that an architect or interior
designer may be called upon to plan. The heavy television set sits on a ply-
wood platform fastened to a turntable that rests on a drawer. The drawer
slides on double extension guides with nylon rollers.

space, and the dining areas. Some provision
should be made for shielding the living and
dining areas from the view of one entering
the main door. This protects the living space
from the weather and isolates the caller who
comes on some momentary errand.

The routes leading to the private areas of
the building can be separate from the social
corridors if they are not intended for use by
a guest. Complete isolation is seldom practical, although some is always advisable. In
occasional houses the bedrooms open into the
family room. Again the caution should be
made that two antithetical functions cannot
occupy the same space at the same time. A
corridor is not so much useless space. If
strewn with children's toys and family effects, it becomes a hazardous area to use as a
hall.

A service entrance should be clearly indicated and easily reached from the street but
should not be accessible as a social entrance.

The path to the service entrance should not
cut across any outdoor living area. It should
lead directly to all of the main service areas
of the house.

Circulation passages need little equipment.
A shelf or table for the temporary placement
of packages and mail is a help. A waterproof
flooring near the door and facilities for handling rainy weather togs are good. A stool,
chair, or bench may prove useful.

Drawing Wall Elevations

A plan represents the floor of a room. The
walls can be drawn in a similar manner using
vertical rather than horizontal measures.
These wall drawings are called room elevations (Figure 3.17). The ceiling can also be
represented but in general is seldom needed.
Elevation drawings show how each wall of a
room would appear if all the light rays coming
from the wall to our eyes were parallel. Thus

we would see only the front face of all objects that are parallel to a wall. No depth is represented, just as no height was represented on the floor plan. This sort of drawing is known in technical language as a type of orthographic projection.

If an object is not parallel to a wall, its rendering in elevation is slightly irregular. The location of the four corners of the object are transferred from the floor plan by right-angle extension to the base of the wall. From these points verticals are erected to represent the four sides and horizontals are drawn to represent the heights.

Elevation templates of furniture, corresponding to plan templates, are helpful in

making such drawings. Elevation drawings are useful to the designer because they give accurate measures of heights, just as the plan gives width and depth.

A Grid to Represent a Room in Three Dimensions

If we want to obtain a greater sense of reality than is secured through elevation and plan, we can make a perspective drawing. A perspective view of a room represents the room as it actually appears to the eye. There are many methods of making a perspective drawing. One of the simplest and most practical ways to do it is described below. This

Figure 3.16. Placement of audio equipment. Home of the architect, Moreland Hills, Ohio.
Architect: Ernst Payer
Photographer: C. W. Ackerman
In this installation, two loudspeakers are placed 16 feet center to center above a curved light cove (only one shows in this picture). A 20-inch speaker is set into the top of the storage wall to the left of the portrait, directing sound at a 30-degree angle against the low ceiling and toward the living room. The volume of all the speakers is individually controlled from the stereo set housed in the cabinet that stands against the storage wall.

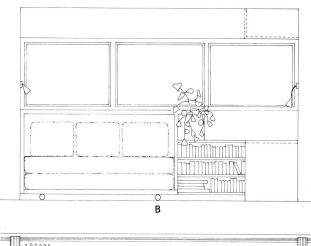

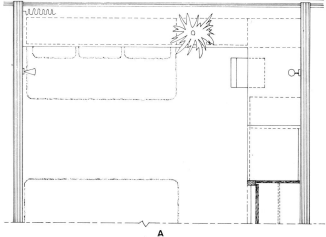

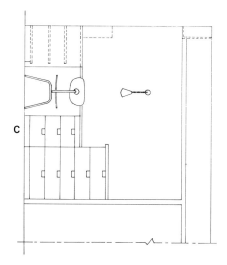

Figure 3.17. Plan of a room with wall elevations.

method will give a basic perspective grid for a particular room. Over this we can place tracing paper and suggest many alternative arrangements of furnishings.

1. Draw a floor plan of the room to scale.
2. Decide which three walls of the room you wish to represent. Call them wall A, B, and C in order.
3. Draw a cross or an arrow on the floor plan to indicate your position. This is usually about one to one and one-half times the width of B and is measured from wall B. It is also a foot or so nearer wall A than wall C. It is placed off-center because that makes a more interesting drawing. This is known as the *station point*, or SP.
4. To whatever scale desired (frequently ½″ = 1′ on 15″ × 20″ illustration board, or ¼″ = 1′ on smaller cardboards), draw wall B in vertical projection. Mark it off in 1 foot squares. This is known as the *true height wall*, or THW.

It is placed near the center of the cardboard. The height of most rooms is 8 or 9 feet.

5. Draw a horizon line or HL 5 feet above the floor line on THW. The HL represents the height of your eyes in viewing this wall. If the HL is higher you will see more of the tops of objects.
6. On the HL place a dot in a position corresponding to your position from the side walls on the floor plan (the same number of feet from wall A as the SP was from it on the floor plan). This is called the *central vanishing point*, or CVP, because it is the place where all lines parallel to walls A and C appear to converge.
7. Place one end of a ruler successively on the corners of the THW and the other on the CVP. Extend lines from the THW to represent floor and ceiling lines of walls A and C.
8. Extend the base line of the THW and mark at 1 foot intervals.
9. Measure on the horizon line from the CVP the distance the SP was taken from wall B (see

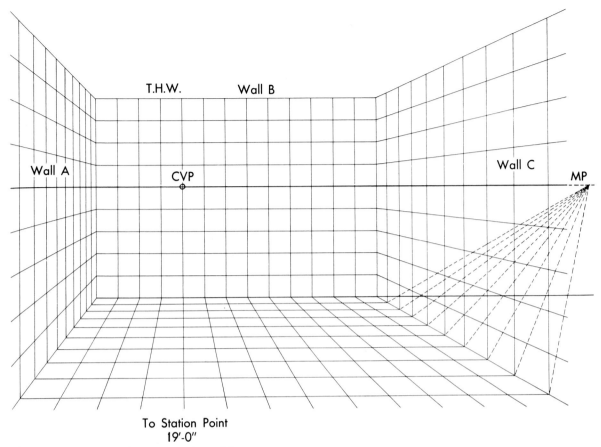

Figure 3.18. A one-point perspective grid.

In Figure 3.18, the following labels appear: T.H.W., Wall B, Wall A, CVP, Wall C, MP, To Station Point 19'-0"

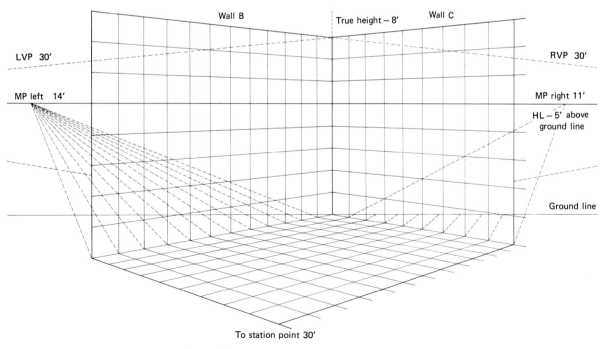

Figure 3.19. A two-point perspective grid.

In Figure 3.19, the following labels appear: Wall B, True height – 8', Wall C, LVP 30', RVP 30', MP left 14', MP right 11', HL – 5' above ground line, Ground line, To station point 30'

point 3, p. 56). This marks the *measuring point*, or MP.

10. Place one end of the ruler on the MP and the other on the 1 foot marks on the base extension of the THW. Put dots where the ruler successively crosses the floor line of wall C.

11. From these dots draw horizontal lines to intersect the floor line of wall A. These lines mark off the feet of the floor plan as they recede into the distance.

12. Draw vertical lines on walls A and C from the ends of each of these floor lines. These lines mark off the feet on the walls.

13. Place one end of the ruler on the CVP and the other end on the foot markings of height and breadth of the THW. This will finish the grid by marking off the walls A and C and the floor into sections representing foot squares the way they look in perspective.

14. A similar two-point perspective grid (Figure 3.19) can be made by placing on a horizon line the right and left vanishing points 30 feet and the right and left measuring points 11 feet and 14 feet, respectively, from the corners of the room. This corner of the room is used as a true height wall. All lines parallel to the right wall vanish in the LVP and all lines parallel to the left wall vanish in the RVP.

Drawing from the Grid

The drawing of furniture in a room from a grid can be done in the following manner.

1. Draw the furniture on the room plan. Know the heights of all pieces or draw them in elevation.
2. Place a piece of tracing paper over the perspective grid.
3. Draw in the walls and floor of the room only.
4. Consider the furniture that is parallel to the walls of the room first.
   a. Draw the base of this furniture on the perspective grid according to its position on the floor plan. Each division on the perspective grid corresponds to one square foot on the floor plan.
   b. Extend vertical lines from the base of the furniture to represent the sides of the furniture.
   c. Measure the height of the furniture on the side walls following this procedure. Draw a horizontal line through any corner on the base of the piece to the side wall. Measure the height on the side wall from the point where this base extension crosses the side wall. Project the height back to the furniture by drawing a horizontal extension line

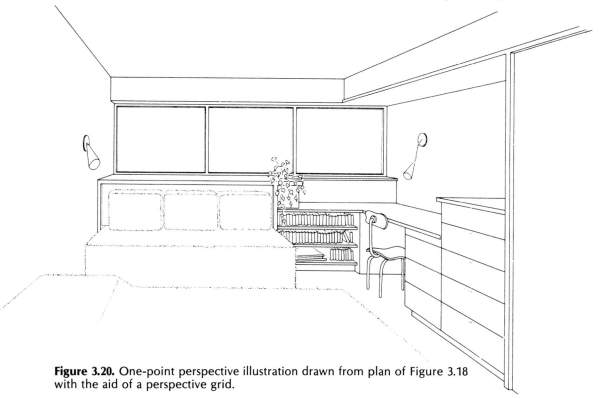

Figure 3.20. One-point perspective illustration drawn from plan of Figure 3.18 with the aid of a perspective grid.

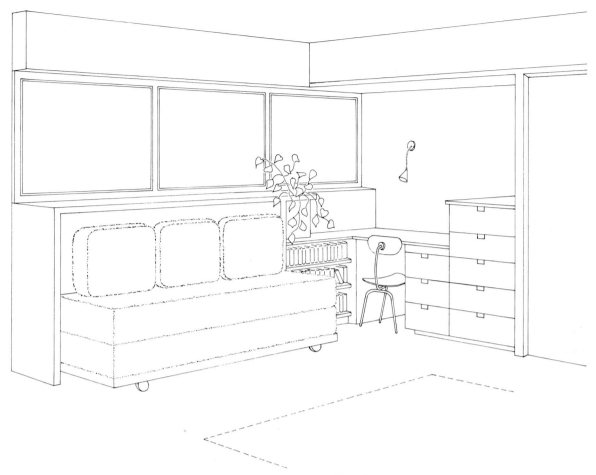

Figure 3.21. Two-point perspective illustration drawn from plan of Figure 3.19 with the aid of a perspective grid.

from this height point to the corresponding side line of the furniture.

d. All lines parallel to the THW on the plan are drawn on the perspective parallel to the THW horizontal lines.

e. All lines parallel to the side walls on the plan are drawn on the perspective through the CVP.

5. Consider the furniture not parallel to the walls of the room next.

a. Draw the base of this furniture on the perspective grid according to its position on the floor plan.

b. Extend vertical lines from the base of the furniture to represent the sides of the furniture.

c. Measure the height of each vertical through each corner on the base of the piece to the side wall. Measure the height on the side wall from the point where this base extension crosses the side wall. Project the height back to its corner vertical by drawing an extension line from the wall height through the VP back to the corresponding side line of the furniture. Connect the height points for the top of the piece of furniture.

All mechanical drawing occasionally may look distorted. Once such drawing is mastered one is advised to take some license and do freehand drawing. An artist's impression is thus more readily obtained.

4

DESIGN ORGANIZATION

*Now there is nothing different in principle here from what
is done in furnishing a room, when the householder sees to
it that tables, chairs, rugs, lamps, color of walls, and spacing of
the pictures on them are so selected and arranged that they
do not clash but form an ensemble. Otherwise there is confusion—confusion that is, in perception.*

*Vision cannot then complete itself. It is broken up into a suc-
cession of disconnected acts, now seeing this, now that, and
no mere succession in a series. When masses are balanced, colors harmonized, and lines and planes meet and intersect
fittingly, perception will be serial in order to grasp the whole,
and each sequential act builds up and reinforces what went
before. Even at first glance there is the sense of qualitative unity.
There is form.*

John Dewey, *Art as Experience*[1]

The Materials of Art

After a consideration of structure and
planning—topics germane to all art but matters that require much skill and learning in
the art of architecture and interior design—
we turn to the necessary and challenging
subject of design. Design is that aspect of art
through which fundamental ends are
achieved. The goal is to create beauty in interiors through the agency of a good design.
We must remember that such design, if it
denies good structure and good planning, will
always offend the sensitive and knowledgeable artist. However, high standards of structure and planning alone cannot ensure beauty.
The sense of beauty is indeed very strange,

and something of empathy, something of
psychology, and something of pure logic enters the picture at this point.

If our goal is the creation of beautiful interiors through the agency of good design,
what plan for accomplishment can we adopt?
At this point we grasp the how rather than
the why of our problem. From here we must
begin to learn our trade.

In the first place, what are our building
blocks? There is no limit to the material
from which art can be made. Art consists of

[1]New York, G. P. Putnam's Sons. Copyright © 1934. Reprinted by permission of the publisher.

the reorganizing of the materials of this world. Therefore, it is made from real things such as wood, stone, plaster, paint, textiles. These materials, together with the tools and processes often used in fabrication, are frequently called the media (singular: medium) of art. Art is also made from the psychological materials of experience such as sensations, strivings, frustrations, emotions, and rationalizations.

Different arts specialize in the use of certain kinds of material. Music uses sounds; literature uses language and ideas. Interior design primarily uses the sensation of sight. A student of interior design needs good eyes and a concern for appearances as working equipment.

Although the visual sensation is most important to the interior designer, other senses are significant. Through the tactile sense we gain pleasure from touching such things as china and fine wood. Through the kinesthetic sense (the sense of muscular tension) we enjoy actual or imaginary movement through space. It is by means of this sense that interior design becomes a time–space art.

The remaining senses can make indirect contributions to a beautiful interior. Oriental civilizations make use of incense and perfume. To the occidental mind this may seem mannered. Nevertheless, probably the most instantly recalled remembrances of our childhood are of such ephemeral things as the spicy canning odors on an early fall day or those of the cedar wood in an old hideaway attic.

The sense of sound (Figure 4.1) can also contribute to the total beauty of an interior. The best of musical art is within our reach if we merely turn the dial with discretion. Lesser sound effects can also play their part, but the intoning of the clock has vanished, and with the modern stove we have lost the sensuous appeal of the crackling wood fire. Where is our imagination? Can't we enrich our modern buildings with pleasant sounds? The cheerful melodies of the door chimes, the clang of the brass dinner gong, the rustle of draperies touched in passing—these may be the essence of a home that our children will remember. Whatever it is, make the sounds of a building pleasant—they will be remembered after visual images have failed.

Materials of the Visual Sensation

Although other sensations may be used in our enjoyment of beautiful interiors, the visual sensation contributes most. In designing an interior we must think of the wall, floors, and furnishings in terms of their visual properties. First we are conscious of space. Like a clean canvas to a painter, what a delightful exacting claim an empty space makes! Modern design in particular regards it as a sacred trust never to be destroyed in subsequent handling.

However, the artist feels the need to qualify this space by the shapes that will define it. He or she further qualifies these shapes by means of color and visual texture. The enveloping of space as it is defined by parameters together with shapes and their modifications by color and visual texture become the ingredients of the visual world. We call them the *components*, or elements, of visual design.[2]

To take a specific example, consider a rectangular space containing an eighteenth-century Chippendale chair and another that was made during the reign of the English Queen Anne. The Chippendale chair has a shape composed of certain masses. It has a line similar to but color and texture different from the Queen Anne chair. If we wish to describe these two chairs more accurately, we need objective quality terms. These basic names specifying quality in respect to which one example of a component may differ from another example of the same component may be called *attributes* or characteristics.

Hue is an attribute of color. We can compare the mahogany and the walnut chairs in terms of their hues. If we give each hue a specific name such as red or brown, we pinpoint one of its color traits. Each component can be specified in terms of attribute traits; a square, for instance, is a shape trait. *Traits* are concrete designations of components characterized in terms of attributes.

The Tests of a Good Visual Design

What are the tests of a good visual design? These are incorporated in our definition of design—organization to enhance perceptual

[2]Thomas Munro, *The Arts and Their Interrelations*, New York: Liberal Arts Press, 1949. This section on components, attributes, and traits is largely derived from Munro's discussion.

Figure 4.1. An audio-visual sense. Watercolor, "Autumnal Fantasy," 37″ × 52½″.
Artist: Charles E. Burchfield
Photograph: Courtesy of Kennedy Galleries, Inc., New York
The notable American painter Charles Burchfield (1893–1967) possessed a keen
synesthetic sensibility and used it to suggest one kind of sensation through
the forms of another. As Gary A. Dayton of the Burchfield Center in Buffalo
writes in his article "Sound-Eyes" (*Link*, Vol. 15, No. 2—Cleveland Institute of
Art magazine), "Even his most quiescent, static works emit to the sensitive
viewer elements not only of movement but of ceaseless, subtle sound." He was
an outstanding exponent of Thoreau's statement "All sensitivity is one, though
it takes many forms."

experience. An experience is something isolated from its background. It stands stark and alone; therefore it has a *unity* of effect. An aesthetic experience should be an enhanced experience, having an intense perceptual effect. Although not deeply intellectual, it is suffused with meanings that are more than mere sensations. The conscious faculties of the mind are engaged. It is in this way that a design holds one's interest. This is the revelation that lies behind "art for art's sake."

Beginning of a Design

Making a good design is really very simple.

All you do is pick some traits that say what you want, give them the proper lieutenants to help carry the cause, and possibly provide a stiff opposition to build up some tension. But never let in a host of Pygmies that will only dissipate your reserve. Simple?

There are a few questions to think about. How to choose compatible visual traits, colors that seem harmonious with shapes, textures that are on friendly terms with both? Will these visual qualities be at cross purposes with the meaning of the total form? *Unity*— how is it made from the many? How are all these qualities meshed? This is problem number one.

Creation involves *organization*—the *choice* and *arrangement* of details for a particular end (Figures 4.2, 4.3, 4.4, and 4.5). Choice or selection comes first. Why are certain qualities to be chosen and others rejected? Each visual trait is selected because it promotes a specific effect. Therefore, begin with the essence of things wished for, the ultimate effect.

Compile or think about a list of words that would characterize the particular kind of effect desired in an interior space. A list is necessary because one word rarely does the job. These words should not be so generalized that they are ambiguous. They may deal with a feeling for one of the components. We may wish the interior to appear spacious, or colorful, or sturdy. The words may suggest an emotion—quiet, restful, exciting. They may be intellectual in their connotations—elegant, quaint. We could find ourselves in semantic deep water if we tried to define these further.

Our list may be refined into two compilations: a list of active conditions and a list of more passive ones. Some words may seem to bridge both sets (*dramatic* and *cool* may be joined by *formal*). The artist must choose the list that is most important. The opposing one will then act as a necessary foil.

When a most important classification has been chosen, the designer then translates it into terms of a few component traits to which the list words are related. These traits are the embryo of a design. The design begins to be unified through the selection of one dominant effect and its translation into visual traits.

It is not important for the artist to be able to name visual traits. Names are merely a great aid to standardization and specification. Nor do many artists actually set down a list of desired effects. This sort of thing becomes something felt rather than expressed. It is, however, extremely important to the artist to be able to make nice discriminations of visual qualities and to have strong feelings about them. This is the beginning of sensitivity and hence of good art. With such awareness the nuances between an interior that is timid and one that is reserved, one that is pretentious and one that is distinguished, emerge.

Further Organization of a Design
GENERAL CONSIDERATION

Even a novice knows that substantial shapes, friendly yellows, and informal textures produce an aura of cheerful comfort. Helpful clients frequently crystallize their thoughts to this extent before going to a designer. Much remains to be done before these suggestions emerge as a well-designed interior. Like the ingredients in a cake, they must be in proper measure and properly combined. The qualities of the ingredients are thereby altered and enhanced and emerge as a good cake. The purpose of organization is to progress step by step to build up the meaning of the original traits. This is a matter of the choice of additional traits and also a matter of placement (relation of details to the paramount visual component—space). These two considerations cannot be separated entirely. Principles that govern selection are also relevant to the arrangement. In learning, although not usually in creation, these principles must be studied consecutively.

ENHANCEMENT OF VISUAL QUALITIES

Because they are part of a design, the qualities of visual ingredients are altered. The company that a brick fireplace keeps in association with walls, floors, and furnishings will make it seem redder or greyer, rougher or smoother, larger or smaller, and ultimately more or less important. By their friends you will know them.

The modification of visual qualities occurs in accordance with relatively definite laws that can often be demonstrated if the evidence is kept very simple. It is obvious that there are only two possible ways of handling a visual quality in context. One is to repeat it and another is to vary it. A third manipulation might be called contrast. Contrast is merely extreme variation.

Repetition, variation, and *contrast* (Figure 4.6) in correct proportions can accentuate forces. Repetition makes a strong statement. If a design begins with the texture of mahogany, this same wood can be repeated in a room. Two pieces will probably attract more attention than one and will augment the impact of this kind of wood. If a designer uses only

Figure 4.2. A beautiful and dignified Virginian home.
Architect: Avery C. Faulkner, FAIA.
General contractor: James G. Davis Co.
Photograph: © Norman McGrath
This home is outstanding for the manner in which it preserves the stateliness and charm of traditional Virginian architecture within the contemporary idiom. The dominant straight lines of the building, the reasoned proportions, and the considered textural handling are important factors.

Figure 4.3. Interior, a beautiful and dignified Virginian home.
Architect: Avery C. Faulkner, FAIA.
General contractor: James G. Davis Co.
Interior designer: Ethel Pilson Warren
Photograph: © Norman McGrath

Figure 4.4. A vacation home in northern Ohio.
"Smultron Backen," home of Mr. and Mrs. Wallace
G. Nesbit.
Designers and builders: Mr. and Mrs. Wallace G. Nesbit.
Photograph: G. C. Ball
The dominant curved lines of this house, done as a
reminder of Scandinavia, create a wonderful, cheerful,
homelike quality.

Figure 4.5. Interior, a vacation home in northern Ohio.
Designers and builders: Mr. and Mrs. Wallace G. Nesbit.
Artist: Rolf Anderson
Photographer: G. C. Ball

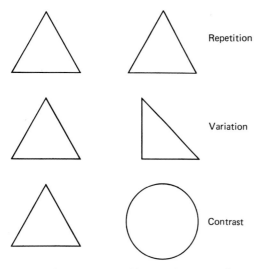

Repetition

Variation

Contrast

Figure 4.6. Diagram: Repetition, variation, and contrast.

straight lines and repeated color, however, the space will cease to be interesting. Monotonous repetition destroys rather than heightens an original effect. Like a bore.

Skillful bewitchery is turned on when the designer presents the same idea in slightly different form. Mark Antony knew, to his undoing, the dangerous allure of "infinite variety." In using variation in traits the designer must be very careful. Differences can destroy if they are not ordered carefully. There are only two times when visual differences support one another. About these Shakespeare speaks so well that one is awed by his perceptive sagacity. "She makes hungry where most she satisfies" (*Antony and Cleopatra*, act 2, scene 2).

When visual differences have their qualities brought into that kind of sequential order in which the eye is carried from a lesser amount to a greater of the same quality, the total effect is magnified. By placing qualities into such a progressive sequence the variations build on one another and the whole is greater than the sum of the parts. This truth appears in many texts under different names such as progressive rhythm, dynamic symmetry, and cumulative propulsion (for further discussion of rhythm see the next section of this chapter).

The second way to regiment differences to heighten an effect is through skillful use of contrast (Figure 4.7). A contrasting material should possess some similarity to the oppos-

ing matter or the design will seem chaotic. If a detail is to strengthen through its dissimilarity, it should have more traits that are unlike its opponent than those that correspond.

At this point in our thinking all of the visual qualities in a design must be organized so that they assume relative importance. Only through group action along with the dominance of some qualities can the enhanced unity of all be gained. Some call this the principle of dominance or relative order. This estimation of quantitative relations is a matter of proportion or relative measure (for further discussion see Chapter 5, Pleasing Proportions).

Quantities can seem changed by environment, but the total complex will seem unaltered if the same proportional relations are maintained. Thus the sensation of constancy can be established in a fluctuating world. One may plan for a large house and find a small one. By adjusting relative sizes, colors, and textures the illusion of spaciousness can be secured.

VISUAL QUALITIES AND THEIR SPATIAL ALIGNMENT

Directional Movement. Because visual art is fundamentally spatial, the positioning of details in a design is important. From this arises a curious circumstance that must be understood thoroughly. The artist endows every object with a certain visual or vital force that is almost biological in character. This may be altered through the company an object keeps. The vital force is capable of directing the eye because of an object's positioning. The placement of objects thus becomes for the artist an alignment of visual forces. If these are unordered, it can cause almost physical discomfort. The artist feels constrained to control vision so that the viewer looks where and when the design intends.

The visual force of a detail is not only the sum of its characteristics; it is also the power of that object to direct the eye—its positional force. And some of you have already guessed that this is the equivalent of its spatial force, its power in space because of spatial interactions.

Actual movement of details such as candle flames and reflections introduces the element of change or motion in art. However, this sort of movement is relatively unimpor-

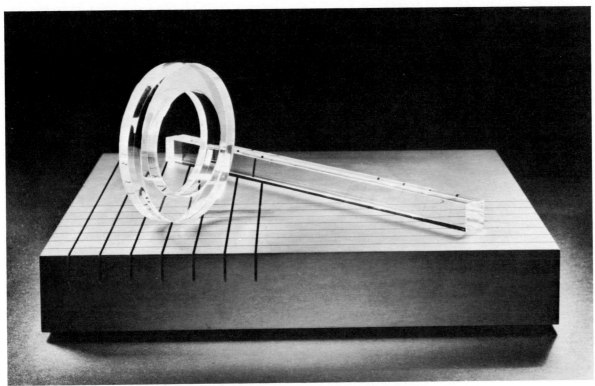

Figure 4.7. Skillful use of contrast. Steuben Glass, "Passage: Unity of Opposites,"
H. 5¾", W. 12".
Artist: Peter Aldridge
Photograph: Courtesy of Steuben Glass
With forms that are almost symbols of the twentieth century—the circle and
the oblong—the artist succinctly illustrates the oneness of our civilization.

tant compared with the kind of activity that has been described as inherent in the form itself. This evolving pattern of formal energy begins with the alignment of visual forces. Sequences are established. Oppositions that create excitement and tensions are likewise introduced. All are further carried out as the eye evaluates the visual forces in space and so organizes the field into up and down, left and right, foreground and background (Figure 4.8).

Change and movement accomplished by means of visual forces must be directed if chaos is to be avoided. This directive is assigned to a principle called *rhythm*. Its first duty is to cause ordered movement that may be of several kinds. One variety is based on quantitative repetition similar to the repetitive measure in music. Metric activity in both visual and audio arts occurs because of alternation between accent and background. This kind of rhythmic repetition is the counterpart of the natural pulsations of the universe and should be used in the manner in which it serves in nature—as a background on which to project more directed rhythms. For instance, if repetitive rhythm becomes too insistent, as when the head thumps in illness, it becomes annoying and can block out more vital patterns of activity.

In music, variations occur superimposed on repetitive rhythms. In the spatial arts, regulated movement due to variation is induced by bidding the eye along a path of lesser to greater forces. This is done by repeating an underlying relationship between the units that is similar to the underlying ratio of all organic growth (what John Dewey called "ordered variation in change"). Because a geometric demonstration of the rhythmic principle relates the phenomenon to the spatial component, it is discussed further in Chapter 5. Such a relation between parts is sometimes called *dynamic* or *progressive rhythm* because it unifies a design by binding details into sequences. It enhances trait quali-

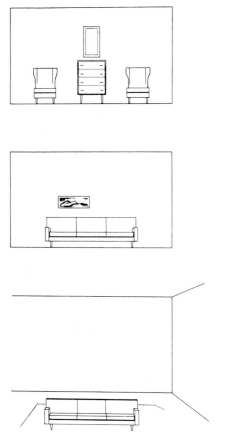

Figure 4.8. Artists can control our vision by compelling us to look up and down, left and right, back and forth.

ties thereby. It moves the eye in planned directions.

Choice. Because details in a design such as a chair or a picture owe their visual force both to their traits and to their placement, the same detail may participate in several alignments. Thus a greyed red chair may be in a color path that will carry the eye to a picture that has bright red areas. The same chair may have a shape that will function in some shape sequence. Or it might be placed in a textural arrangement. These alignments can move the eye to different areas and in different directions. Thus there could be several visual routes out from the chair. Such multiplicity of choice is a characteristic of life's experience and thus is a necessity in creating vitality (Figures 4.9 and 4.10). The details of a design are constantly realigning themselves. It is interesting to discover new activity of this sort, and continuing perceptual enjoyment is gained thereby. This principle of interlocking or integrating a detail in several

themes is also a great help toward unifying a design.

Rest. Rest is as important to a design as it is to life. Visual rest occurs from the equalizing of forces and the balancing of tensions. The equilibrium of a space, like that of the human body, goes beyond the bilateral. We wish to feel anchored to the ground. Because of this we react favorably to ground pull or stability in the lower section of a room. This is one reason that rhythms knitting groups of furnishings into triangular shapes broadened at the base seem so very satisfactory. (We shall later, however, need to come to terms with the fact that the twentieth century can possess weightlessness. This introduces a new idea into all of our thinking about art and what it must portray.)

In physical science balance is obtained by equal forces exerting equal thrusts because of their placement equidistant from a pivot or center of balance. Unequal forces must be adjusted in relation to this center so that equilibrium is obtained. This is the basic principle of the level and the seesaw.

When equal forces exert equal pressure at equal distances, the resulting equilibrium has often been called *bisymmetrical*, *formal*, or *obvious balance*. Symmetry is used in the sense of an analogy or likeness of measures. It is comparatively easy to gain bisymmetry in interior design. All that is necessary is to have enough money to buy two of every article and then to place one of each kind equidistant from the center.

More than this is needed to create interesting bisymmetry. It is necessary to have the internal structure of the arrangement rhythmic in just the same way that the internal formation of the entire space must be both moving and stabilized. Two identical objects can be balanced interestingly on either side of a central object. The relation of each object to the central object constitutes a measure or meter that is balanced because of repetition in reverse position. Examine this meter closely. Check on the horizontal and vertical spacing as well as on the color and textural qualities that effect this balance (Figure 4.11). The introduction of a dynamic internal rhythm will bring interest.

When unequal forces attract equal attention because of their placement, the resulting equilibrium has been called *asymmetrical, in-*

Figure 4.9. A choice of visual routes: I.
Artist: Hiroshige (1797–1858)
Photographer: G. C. Ball
This Japanese print illustrates well one principle of good design—vitality. Starting or returning to the chickadee as the center of interest, how many tonal and spatial routes direct the eye through the picture? And always back to the theme song, the bird itself.

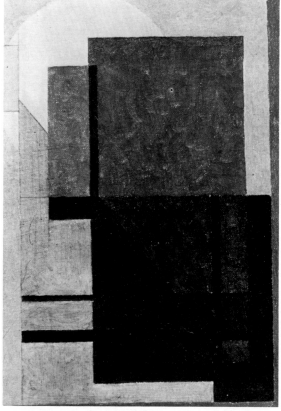

Figure 4.10. A choice of visual routes: II.
Photographer: G. C. Ball
In a design made by a student, the same principle is demonstrated as in Figure 4.9, here with mostly straight lines and flat areas. In the original, hue differences (in tones of blue, black, and yellow) accentuate tonal differences. Proportional relations are skillfully managed to lead the eye to the round yellow contrasting shape in the upper left corner.

formal, or *occult balance.* This kind of balance may be illustrated by the human form in action: the center of balance is still a vertical line descending earthward between the two legs, but the body is not equally disposed on two sides of this line. The muscles in such a body position are more tensed than when the body is at rest and all tensions are equalized. Asymmetry causes a more alive situation than bisymmetry.

Sometimes it seems desirable to have both bisymmetry and asymmetry in the same arrangement. In this case it is best to plan first for the formal balance; because it is so stately and restful it might be given the greater prominence. The composition can then be enlivened with informal arrangements.

Integration of Change and Rest. Relative centers of interest are important in the alignment of forces. Dominance suggests that various locations in a room may be accorded first, second, or third prominence. What is to be background, what foreground? In the foreground, what locations are of greatest importance? Centers of interest or focal points in a room are the spots where the greatest forces of attraction converge. They are the locations where the dominant effect has been given most emphatic statement, the climaxes to which the eye is moved.

If all of the details in a room moved in the same direction and supported the same climax, the room would seem unbalanced. The room also would lack interest because there

Figure 4.11. Beyond the rules. A well-landscaped garden and fountain.
Designer: Lawrence Halprin
Photograph: Courtesy of House and Garden, copyright 1958, The Condé Nast
Publications, Inc.
Notice this charming oasis. It appears balanced and yet, within a circular steel
cage, unequal elements contend for attention. The weight of the dark bowl is
lost in the similar value of the pool into which its water plays. The much smaller
white basin gains attention through contrast with the dark pines of its setting
and by its slightly more vigorous shape. The eye equates these forces and
enjoys the resulting tension, movement, and rest. There are no rules that cover
this sort of artistry, but there are guidelines that, when they are learned and
assimilated, are observable in results.

Figure 4.12. Outpatient lobby, Anna Jacques Hospital, Newburyport,
Massachusetts.
Architect: Gary Lahey, Payette Associates, Inc.
Photographer: Nick Wheeler
This recent addition to a private general hospital is outstanding not only in its
planning in respect to needs, but also in respect to its visual design. Done in
the contemporary idiom, its clearly expressed and functional arrangement of
space, its warm, brown-dominated color scheme, and its natural textures have
met with universal approval from all who have observed or used it. This is
rational designing at its very best.

Figure 4.13. A designer's studio.
Interior designer: Ray W. Clarke
Photographer: Ralph J. Meyers
Here in a studio apartment the designer has managed to include in a small space
objects of personal use and meaning. The order is not regular. However, the
small-patterned draperies and davenport balance the visual activity of the
books and the drawing table. The large wicker chair echoes and softens the
textural activity of the pattern. It is a skillfully organized melange.

would be no tensions. The artist should integrate the various thematic forces so that they cooperate in building some climaxes and oppose one another in creating others.

Climaxes at centers of interest ultimately must be balanced. Asymmetrical balance is frequently used for this. A principal focal point may be opposed by two secondary ones. A center of interest containing much visual activity may oppose a large area of little activity. Sometimes an interior may burst its bonds and look outside for a stabilizing factor. A Georgian building looks inward. A contemporary one usually looks outward.

Many Types of Design Organization

Good design may be of many different types. One basis of classification of design types is with respect to their definiteness or indefiniteness. In a definite design, the organization is more clearly seen. This can be accomplished by devices that are dependent basically on the idea of limitation, regularity, and clean-cut separations. The number of component traits chosen must be limited. Their thematic development should be accomplished largely by repetition rather than variation. They may be clarified by means of isolation and by sharp contrast, their placement clearly defined on either side of a central axis. This kind of definite design we frequently call a formal design (Figure 4.12). A design characterized by expansiveness, irregularity, and merging of divisions would be an informal design (Figure 4.13). There are many degrees of both types. With such freedom of choice we should be able to create for every taste.

Difficulty of Attaining Good Design

A good design is not easily attained. It is easy to obtain unity when an object is so simple that it is indivisible. It is easy to intensify an effect by repeating it. It is possible to interest the attention by something lively and unique. It is natural to please through agreeable sensations.

As the design organization becomes more complicated, trouble frequently begins. Methods that were effective at undeveloped levels often grow to be at loggerheads. Unity can be secured at the expense of intensity, perceptual interest, and pleasure. Any one of the conditions of a good design can be exploited at the sacrifice of others. A good design is a remarkable accomplishment involving the organization of many factors into a new and lovely thing.

Outline of Design Considerations

1. Setting of a goal.
   a. Design for one enhanced perceptual effect.
   b. Test words: unity, intensity, vitality.
2. Selection of principal visual qualities (dominant and subordinate) to gain effect.
   a. Ingredients.
      Visual components: space, shape, color, texture.
      Attributes: basic characteristics of a component.
      Traits: specific examples of component attributes.
   b. Choice of initial traits for their expressive quality.
3. Further organization.
   a. Enhancement of visual qualities through skillful proportional use of repetition, variation, contrast.
   b. Visual qualities and their spatial alignment.
   c. Traits as visual forces.
   d. Evolving pattern of activity.
      Opposing forces (tension).
      Directed movement, grouping, and growth (rhythm).
   e. Overall stability (balance).
      Bisymmetry.
      Asymmetry.
   f. Integration of movement with stability.
      Positions to be regarded
      Visual axis (center of balance).
      Center of interest (climax of attention).
4. Types of design.
   a. Definite and indefinite.
   b. Inward- and outward-looking.

5

SPACE AND SHAPE IN INTERIORS

*Taking possession of space is the first gesture of living things,
of men and of animals, of plants and of clouds, a fundamental
manifestation of equilibrium and of duration. The occupation of
space is the first proof of existence.*

Le Corbusier, *New World of Space*[1]

*We reject all esthetic speculation, all doctrine, all formalism.
Architecture is the will of an epoch transplanted into space;
living, changing, new.
Not yesterday, not tomorrow, only today can be given form.
Only this kind of building will be creative.*

Mies Van Der Rohe, quoted by Philip Johnson in *Mies Van Der Rohe*[2]

Space

In the writings of those men who are the acknowledged great architects of the twentieth century, it is strange that the Europeans such as Mies van der Rohe and Le Corbusier should be the ones to talk about space in the abstract and the Americans such as Louis Sullivan and Frank Lloyd Wright to speak more often of the capabilities and needs of people in relation to space. Space has become such a byword in modern architecture and so much, both sense and nonsense, has been written about it that it becomes urgent to try to understand what the word *space* implies.

Space as boundless extension can be lonesome and cruel or companionable and restful. Space has gained in importance in our civilization because it is a diminishing quantity, at least in any usable location. Possibly the world would be better if every human could inherit four acres, but it is unlikely that this will happen. Therefore, we exalt the importance of space.

Space can be magnificent only when it is defined—by horizon, clouds, mountains, or the frame of a building. In architecture the spaces of the Pantheon, the cathedrals, the Guggenheim Museum and the East Wing of the National Gallery are glorious. The cramped quarters of a slum or prison are destructive

[1]From *New World of Space*, by Le Corbusier. Reprinted by permission of Harcourt Brace Jovanovich, Inc.

[2]Mies Van Der Rohe, as quoted by Philip Johnson, in *Mies Van Der Rohe*, The Museum of Modern Art, third edition, revised, copyright © 1978 by The Museum of Modern Art; second edition, revised, copyright © 1953; first edition, copyright © 1947, renewed 1975. All rights reserved.

to the human spirit. What are designers able to do about handling the spaces that have been entrusted to their care to make them the servant of human beings?

The Relation of Space to Shape

From the artist's point of view, what is space, what is shape? Space and shape are the components basic to interior design. It might be well to remind ourselves that the word *shape* originated in the Anglo-Saxon *sceap*, a creation. It would be impossible to create art were it not for shapes that are measurable configurations existing in space. It is the mind—perception—that differentiates between space and shape, equating the first with background or void and the second with the foreground presence. Visual design depends on this fundamental distinction, further qualified by colors and textures.

As soon as we perceive a configuration as a shape or occupied space we can place it in a certain category of shapes. A dot is a simple location in space. When a dot projects itself along a path it becomes a line. A line that bites its tail is an area: an enclosed two-dimensional space.

Every area in reality has three dimensions because even the thickness of the paper on which it may be drawn has depth. If we regard only the exterior of a substance that has length and breadth we are speaking of its surface. A surface is explained in geometry as a magnitude that has length and breadth only. When a surface is without depressions we allude to it as a plane surface, or a plane. A volume is a three-dimensional shape. Volume is occupied space as measured by cubic (three-dimensional) units. Volume can be divided further into mass, which is its solid matter, and space, or vacancy. In the visual world, mass and space are perceptual qualities only. But take care not to bump your shins on a physical mass!

Attributes of Shape

For the artist, space and shape are real. They have aesthetic qualities that are derived from the combination of their attribute traits. A shape attribute is a basic way in which one shape can differ from another. How might the space in one room differ from that of another? One room could have large dimensions and the other small. The two rooms might have the same proportions but differ in positive size. A thick line is different in size from a thin line of the same length. Size is the first attribute of shape.

Shapes can differ from one another in direction. Direction is estimated in relation to the horizontal, which is parallel to the apparent horizon. The vertical is at right angles to the horizontal, and the oblique is at acute angles to the horizontal. Obviously there are many different kinds of oblique directions. Direction is the second attribute of shape.

The character of any particular detail is a composite of all the attribute traits that it possesses. By its very definition we see a shape as one object or configuration. We must therefore describe its character in terms of the attribute traits it possesses plus any change that has occurred in these traits within its boundaries. Thus the character of a shape is the sum of its size, of its direction, and of any change in its direction in relation to its measure (Figure 5.1).

It would be possible but very labored to describe all shapes scientifically in terms of their sizes, directions, and changes of direction. We do this frequently in general terms expressive of the shape character when we describe things as jagged, sinuous, angular, bulbous, or graceful. These are not scientific words, but when thoughtfully used they make valuable contributions to the language of art.

Choosing Dominant Shape Traits

The first step in planning a room design is to choose dominant shape traits. This involves preliminary thinking about the architectural shape character, about many practi-

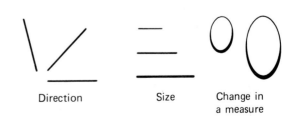

Figure 5.1. Shape attributes. Any shape can differ from another in its direction and size, and can change direction and/or size within a measure.

cal things such as the physical strength of certain kinds of shape, and eventually about the expressive message that shapes can convey.

What is the room shape? Is it large or small? Does it open to a larger space or is it enclosed? Does it have horizontal or vertical emphasis? The room is a shape with which all furnishing shapes must come to terms.

What are some practical considerations relative to the shapes of masses? Modern techniques have reduced the size of furniture without impairing its strength and comfort. We are accustomed to thinking of the strength of wood as lying parallel to the straight grain. Contemporary bent metal and plywood provide strength with curvature. Furniture legs joined with wedges are stronger for being diagonal in direction. Low horizontality in furniture may not be suited to the human anatomy. When you deal with a shape as a physical artifact, you must analyze its practicality.

Our choice of dominant shape traits is largely dictated by their expressive power. Size is relative to the size of the surroundings and only in relation to these is it significant in conveying an expressive message. In many cases relatively large size creates an impression of greater strength and small size an impression of weakness.

Directions derive their expressive quality from the imaginary projection of the human body in directional positions. The horizontal suggests the greatest stability as well as the greatest movement along earthbound space. Direction is modified toward greater activity in the diagonal and to a lesser extent in the vertical. Seldom is the diagonal suitable as the dominant directional emphasis in a room. Greater mental activity and therefore increased dynamics is suggested when a shape changes its direction frequently and when

the degree of change is great. Thus the feelings aroused by a particular kind of shape are modified by its direction and change of direction within a measure.

Although an object may be defined by its size and direction, what we frequently notice is its outline. A room can be analyzed in character by observation of the outline of furnishings, the linear pattern on walls and floor, and the imaginary lines that exist between objects because of their relative positions. A line is a most economical means of expression. It says so much in such a little space.

Table 5.1 illustrates some of the messages that a straight line suggests. They range from intimations of simple physical and emotional states to suggestions of a complex character quality. It is easily seen that our final decision about whether we like or dislike straight lines in a room comes as a result of much that we read into them.

Many shapes have curved outlines. It is more difficult to appraise their statements because there are so many varieties of curves. As compared to the suggestions made by straight lines, all curves veer in the direction of flexibility, weakness, indirection, informality, frivolity, and grace.

Using Shapes as Visual Forces

After selecting the dominant shapes for our space we must study shape forces and their uses. The intrinsic force of a shape is, first, *larger size*. A large object or any grouping of smaller objects seen as an entity will attract our attention. Because one use of forces is to regulate emphases, there are times when the design of a room will be improved by making some of its accents larger. It may tax our ingenuity to accomplish this. A too-small picture may be hung on a larger

TABLE 5.1
The Straight Line

		Modification of These Feelings by the Line's Directional Orientation		
Feelings Generated by a Straight Line		Vertical	Horizontal	Diagonal
Physical response:	Rigidity, strength, stiffness	Less stable	Most stable	Least stable
Simple emotional response:	Directness, positiveness, forcefulness	Spirited	Calm	Energetic
Complex intellectual response (e.g., character meaning):	Formality, dignity	Austere, spiritual	Earthy	Youthful

cloth backdrop. A stencil border placed on the wall surrounding a small picture may serve the same purpose.

The *diagonal direction* is the greatest attention-getter. Its oblique position—because it suggests instability, movement, and change—commands more attention than the more stable vertical and horizontal positions. Sometimes a drapery that is tied back into a moderate diagonal loop may create just the needed emphasis at a window.

Shapes that *change their direction* frequently and abruptly attract much attention. Pattern activity attracts the eye. From this point of view a straight line lacks attraction because it lacks variety. Because a straight line is relatively unobtrusive it is especially useful in a small room. By the same line of reasoning, curves should be used with caution in small areas.

The Meaning and Importance of Proportion

We have discussed space and shapes in art from the standpoint of their choice as visual forces. This is the merest beginning. The success or failure of a work of art depends on how the eye perceives the total spatial configuration. This involves the spaces as well as the shapes that are within the total span of vision.

Here quantitative relations impinge, and these are a matter of *proportion*. Proportion is the wedding of space and number. Most art students expect to dislike mathematics. Mathematics (numbers and their relationships) involves truths that engage the intellectual faculties. In the visual world the artist may prefer to learn these through perception. Mathematics, however, has much to offer art. It can show connections that exist between abstract relations and visual configurations in space. Inasmuch as the interior designer is dealing with large areas and often with expensive materials, some forethought about quantitative choices is not amiss.

The basic numerical aspect of the relation of space and number is called a ratio. In mathematics a ratio is the quotient of one quantity divided by another of the same kind. It is equivalent to a fraction in arithmetic. The simplest spatial demonstration of such an association would be two lines, one of which might be five times as long as the other. Their ratio would be one to five, or 1/5.

Mathematics says that pairs of things have a proportional relationship when the ratios between them are equal. Thus the sequence 2:4:8:16 is in proportion, each pair of numbers possessing a ratio of 1/2. This particular sequence also expresses an *extreme–mean* or *xm* proportion. In any *xm* sequence of four numbers, the ratio between neighboring pairs is constant and the two end numbers when multiplied together give the same result as when the two intermediate numbers are multiplied. In general, two quantities are proportionate when they possess some regular ratio linkage. All things in life that change or grow in an orderly fashion are governed by ratios and proportions. It is this metric recurrence that produces rhythms in the physical world and in good design.

Pleasing Proportions

It would certainly be convenient if we could point to one or several sets of spatial proportions and say that they were most liked. However, it is not possible to do so. As a matter of fact, experiments have shown that there is very little concensus of opinion on this matter. About all that can be said is that persons who have similar tastes seem to prefer the same kind of proportional relations. Apparently everyone is pleased to sense some clear quantitative analogies. Among those who might be said to have a developed aesthetic taste there is a preference for related measures that are subtle in addition to being understandable.

One ratio that exists between sizes of two things and that can be expressed in numbers is called in many art textbooks static symmetry. An illustration of such a ratio would be a picture frame that is twice as high as it is broad or that has four units in height to three in width. Nature uses such proportions in crystalline growth.

Static ratios help unify a design by introducing a common unit of measure. They intensify a design when this measure is repeated in proportion. When such a proportion is in sequence (where the internal numbers of an *xm* ratio are the same number, e.g., 1:2::2:4::4:8), there is an interlocking or integrating of the series by an identical number link. Proportions of this last sort do impel the mind's eye onward by the very rhythm of the sequence. However, such a sequence soon grows too large or too small for our mental agility, and we tend to drop it before going far. The internal cohesive force of any such proportion is probably greater, for this reason, than its rhythmic propulsion onwards. Nevertheless, unification, intensification, integration, propulsion, can all be furthered by static proportions.

There are degrees of subtlety in numerical proportions depending on their initial ratios. In general, this initial relation is obvious, and there is a sort of naïveté introduced into a pattern through its use. Folk art frequently employs recognizable ratios, which are in part responsible for its ingenuous appeal. The mechanical nature of numerical divisions has something in common with the mechanization of our machine world. Early modern art frequently used the equilateral figures of geometry, and it may have been for this reason.

We have been describing the simple case in which a numerical ratio of measures exists between two things, in this case two shapes. Such a ratio can likewise exist between two positions in space or two points on a line. The ratio must of course be made with reference to some external point or points. In

mathematics, a line whose path can be traced by an equation (equality of relations) that can be applied to every point on it is a regular curve. When a series of positions bear an equal size relation to a controlling position (called the center), a circle or a sphere results.

A *parabola* is a curve any point of which maintains its distance from a fixed point equal to its perpendicular distance from a given line (Figure 5.2). Notice the order brought about by the constant ratio.

$$\frac{PF}{MP} = \frac{1}{1} = \frac{P_1F_1}{M_1P_1} = \frac{P_2F_2}{M_2P_2} \cdots$$

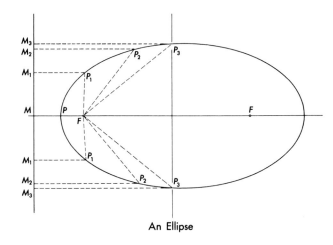

An Ellipse

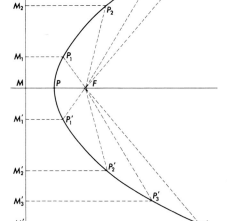

A Parabola

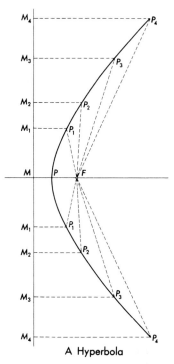

A Hyperbola

Figure 5.2. Order brought about by constant ratios.

An *ellipse* is a curve any point of which maintains a constant ratio of less than one between its distance from a fixed point and a given line.

$$\frac{PF}{MP} \approx \frac{4}{5} = \frac{P_1F_1}{M^1P^1} = \frac{P_2F_2}{M^2P^2} \cdots$$

A *hyperbola* is curve any point of which maintains a constant ratio greater than one between its distance from a fixed point and a given line.

$$\frac{PF}{MP} \approx \frac{3}{2} = \frac{P_1F_1}{M^1P^1} = \frac{P_2F_2}{M^2P^2} \cdots$$

These are only a few of the many curves that can be plotted by reference to some regimented relations or ratios. The graphs made by engineers frequently are beautiful tracts because ratios of resistance to stresses must be systematically ordered and an equality of force must result. Curves become more complex as their points move in three dimensions. There are cycloid, catenary, and spiral curves. It is not an accident that a suspension bridge or a thin convex concrete slab roof assumes the shape that is seen. It is the order inherent in its construction that creates the beauty of a mathematical curve. It indicates the vitality inherent in such a curve because the points of the line maintain a constant ratio but a continuously changing measure in relation to the reference points.

The symmetry that we have been examining is that based on whole-number ratios. An even more intriguing set of proportions is not arithmetical in nature. It is completely geometric and can only be approximated in numbers.[3] This system has been frequently called dynamic symmetry. Dynamic symmetry is a designing tool that was supposedly perfected by the Greeks.

Builders before the Greeks learned to construct a right-angled corner by a practical expedient known as cording. A rope was divided by knots into twelve equal divisions. This rope was so laid on the ground that four knots made one side, three knots the other side, and the five remaining knots thus

[3]If you wish the answer to this paradox we suggest a further exploration into the enticing reasoning of modern mathematics and a study of so-called irrational numbers. In the figures of dynamic symmetry, unity (the square), when divided by the geometric space that has been added to it, results in an irrational number.

formed the hypotenuse of a right-angled triangle. Further extensions of this technique could be used to coordinate a whole building. Design resulted and architecture began.

It is useful to study a few of the geometric tools that come from a study of right-angled triangles. Let us begin with a square, here lettered BDGH. The base of this square is bisected at C. Drawing a diagonal of half the square from C to G, it may be used as a radius to draw the semicircle AEGH. The top and base lines of the square are then extended and are terminated by perpendicular lines at AEFJ. In this process the rectangles ADGJ and BEFH are formed (Figure 5.3). Each of these is called an *xm* rectangle because the ratio of its short side to its long side equals that of its long side to the sum of its short plus its long side. The large rectangle AEFJ is called a root 5 rectangle because the ratio between its two sides is that of one to the square root of five.

A more detailed construction of the *xm* rectangle is also shown (Figure 5.4). BH, the diagonal of half of the square ACHJ, is used as the radius of a circle that cuts the base line at D. The rectangle ADFJ, made by erecting a perpendicular to AC at D and by prolonging it to meet the extension of JH at F, is an *xm* rectangle. Moreover, the rectangle CDFH is an *xm* rectangle. If the square CDEK is taken from this rectangle, the rectangle KEFH is an *xm* rectangle. An *xm* rectangle will remain every time an end square is removed. As the path of these squares turns about the so-called eye of the rectangle (the intersection of the diagonal AF with the diagonal HD of the reciprocal or same-proportioned rectangle CDFH), we can see why the *xm* rectangle has sometimes been called the rectangle of the whirling square. From the illustration it can also be seen how this rectangle contains a continuous *xm* proportion in which the short division of a side is to the long division as the latter is to the whole side (repetition of proportion). These *xm* ratios also hold for the corresponding areas.

The quality of onward propulsion found in all continuously progressive *xm* proportions is thus demonstrated spatially in the rectangle of the whirling square. We are not surprised to be told that phyllotaxis—the law that governs the growth of leaves on a plant—progresses in this proportion.

The *xm* rectangle possesses the fault of all extreme–mean ratios of growing or diminishing too fast. And, rather than follow the example set years later by Alice in Wonderland of drinking or eating an antidote, the ingenious classical designers discovered another set of rectangles that were more suited to their needs (Figure 5.5).

They began with the root 5 rectangle and made a series of root rectangles, in each of which the relation between the short side to the long side is as one is to the square root of the number that gives the rectangle its name. Only in occasional cases such as the root 4 rectangle is this ratio a numerical one. In the root rectangles the members of the series are not interlocked by an identical ratio but by geometrically related factors. Each successive rectangle is related to the one of a lower root number through the identity of the diagonal of the smaller rectangle with the longer side of the larger rectangle. Since all of the root rectangles evolve from a basic square, a very effective growth propulsion is felt due to the interrelations.

In Figure 5.6 it can be seen how a handy designer's tool can be made from the root rectangles.[4] The illustration shows such a tool, called a proportional triangle, made from the root rectangles. Here the triangle is made from the diagonal *AF* of a root 5 rectangle *AEFJ*. The triangle is *AFJ*. The diagonals of

---

[4]In a similar way a triangle could be made from an *xm* rectangle that would divide a line into *xm* ratios. A study of mathematics will reveal a number of such applied devices that help the student get ordered relations into a design.

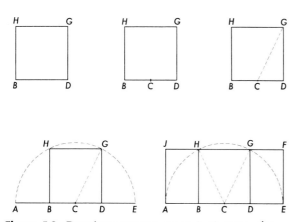

Figure 5.3. Drawing extreme-mean (*xm*) rectangles from a square.

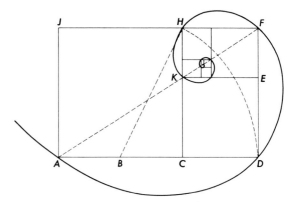

Figure 5.4. Drawing a spiral from the extreme-mean rectangle.

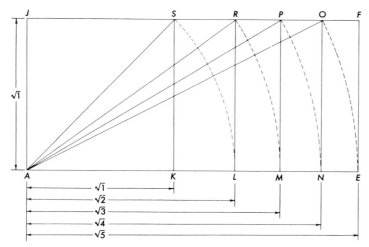

Figure 5.5. Drawing root rectangles from a square. The progression can also be drawn in the opposite direction, beginning with the root 5 rectangle and working down to the square.

Figure 5.6. A designer's tool: the proportional triangle.

Figure 5.7. Mathematical proportions can be used by the artist as training for sensitivity. (A) A root 3 rectangular picture in relation to a root 2 rectangle fireplace creates a pleasing variation in proportion. The wall is a root 3 shape. (B) Lamps frequently use the root 2 rectangle as the basis for their structural shape. (C) An entire wall with root 3 proportions is broken at the root 1 position, forming a square. Within the square, the upper part of the drapery is a root 2. The bands are designed to progress upward from a base square at the root 2, 3, and 4 division lines. (D) A wall with root 3 proportions has a fireplace or wall cabinet in a root 7. The break in this creates a root 3 horizontal and a root 2 vertical. The plant base is a root 3 horizontal and the entire plant occupies a root 7 vertical. The ends of the long, narrow picture come at the root 1 and the root 4 diagonals of the fireplace rectangle.

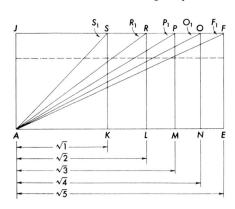

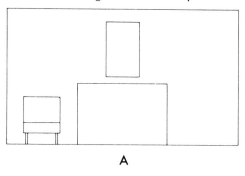

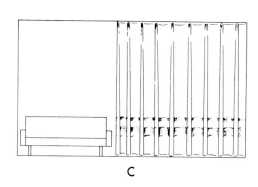

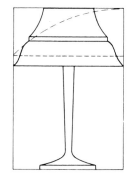
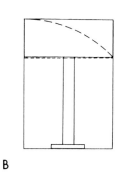

A

B

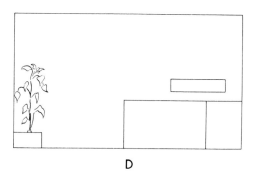

C

D

the corresponding root 4, 3, 2, and 1 rectangles mark off root proportions on the line *JF*. If it is desired that any other line should be divided into these proportions, it is only necessary to insert the line to be divided into the triangle so that it lies parallel to *JF* and is cut by the diagonals.

In these several pages we have considered a few of the fascinating relations that order shapes and their behavior in space. These thoughts provide an initial glimpse of the truth that there is no beauty without some kind of order and underline Edna St. Vincent Millay's assertion that "Euclid alone has looked on beauty bare." Mathematics is capable of demonstrating this order because it is a method of reasoning from cause to effect about those things that can be measured, counted, and related (Figure 5.7).

Most compound sensations and their resulting affections are at present beyond measure. Mathematical proportions can and possibly should be used by the artist as initial training for sensitivity to such complexity.

Artistic Shapes

Shapes become aesthetically enjoyable when their parts bear pleasing interrelations. One way of stating these relations is to suggest that the parts bear quantitative relations that are called rhythmic (see Chapter 4). Rhythm in the spatial arts is a term borrowed from the temporal arts. It signifies a repetitive or orderly varied quantitative relation. Thus a line is said to be rhythmic when it changes its width or direction according to an ordered proportion. It might be called graceful when the order of change is continuous and not abrupt. In two-dimensional areas the relation of length to breadth should possess a pleasing ratio. When an object is seen in three dimensions, the problem of design becomes more involved. Sometimes in considering a three-dimensional object it is helpful to run one's hands over the surface trying to feel the rhythmic relations of mass to mass. This act helps us appreciate the great artistry that exists in the apparently most simple forms. Interesting simplicity can be great art.

Shapes bounded by curved lines may be described as geometric (mathematical, regular) or organic (freeform, irregular). Geometric curves are arcs of simple mathematical shapes such as circles, ellipses, hyperbolas, and parabolas. These curves, changing their direction in a consistent manner, cause effects that are similar to those of a straight line.

Organic and freeform curves are less regularly ordered. They are the artist's creation. In addition to having a good irregular curved outline, a freeform area or volume should be designed so that there is variety as well as repetition in its opposing sides. Its longitudinal and transverse axes should not be at right angles to each other. Thus opposite contours do not run parallel for any extensive distance (Figures 5.8, 5.9, and 5.10). They should be similar to the curves of a vertebrate in action where the stretched muscles of the forward members bear a relation to but do not parallel the untensed muscles. To give a homely example, when a snake moves, the edges of its body are parallel. When a tiger moves, there is an interesting variation of the masses from haunches to thorax to head. Organic curves hold the interest for a comparatively long time. They can be used as relief for the precise character of straight lines and regular curves. It is a very interesting fact that much contemporary design seen in all kinds of objects from pictures to buildings makes use of easily seen geometric ratios. Can it mean that as a culture we are not aesthetically subtle?

Having chosen a well-designed basic or structural shape, we then must consider standards for its embellishment. Decoration may be desirable. It may make an object personal, unique, or more interesting. It may soften the structural contours. It can be beautiful in itself. Occasionally we discover an object of such ornamental character that it can act like costume jewelry to adorn a plain background. The decorative character of such an object should be of a very high order of artistic excellence if it is permitted center stage.

The modern designer accepts certain disciplines in regard to decorative design. The structural design is of prime importance and it must be good. Decorative design should not detract from structural design but should strengthen it in every way. Good decoration, like good structure, should evolve from the medium and the function. In short, it should not be easy to differentiate between basic structure and added decoration. The two should be a unit in purpose, expression, and design.

An analysis of chair shapes might clarify the standards that have been discussed. Consider the chairs illustrated in Figures 5.11 and 5.12 (traditional ones could be substituted) in the light of the following questions.

Functions

What are the overt functions of a chair?

What are some types of chair that might modify some of these functions (e.g., typist's chair, church pew, lounging chair)?

Analyze the functions of a particular type of chair.

Structure

What new structural principles are used in some of these chairs?

Does the visual form seem in harmony with the chair's structure?

Are you aware of an empathetic response to the chair's shape (an empathetic response is the feeling that the chair shape clearly illustrates its supportive function)?

Figure 5.8. Organic forms: I. Chinese pottery: horse, Northern Wei Dynasty; bull, T'ang Dynasty or earlier.
The Cleveland Museum of Art, horse, Purchase, Charles W. Harkness Endowment Fund; bull, Purchase from the J. H. Wade Fund
Photograph: Courtesy of The Cleveland Museum of Art
Artists of every age have understood the rhythms of organic forms, especially those of the vertebrates in action.

Figure 5.9. Organic forms: II. Carpet, "Smoke and Flame," 1959.
Artist: Stanislav V'Soske
Photograph: Rooks Photo, courtesy of the artist

Figure 5.10. Organic forms: III. Water pitcher, Steuben Glass.
Photograph: Courtesy of Steuben Glass.

Figure 5.11. Chair shapes: I.
Designer: Harley Edward Luyk
Photograph: Courtesy of Mueller Furniture Corporation, P.O. Box 2624, Grand Rapids, MI 49501
In Figures 5.11 and 5.12 we see quite differently designed chairs of recent production of a highly regarded furniture company. Why are their shapes so different? In what ways might each function in an office suite?

Figure 5.12. Chair shapes: II.
Photograph: Courtesy Mueller Furniture Corporation, P.O. Box 2624, Grand Rapids, MI 49501

Has the new type of structure been well or poorly handled with respect to function (e.g., balance when holding a seated person)?

Expression

What expressive form do you find in the various chairs?
Do the chair shapes seem compatible with the twentieth century?
Do the shapes appear to change as you view them (e.g., swell, contract, rise, fall)?
To what do you attribute these forces?
Are such forces desirable in this particular piece of furniture?

Organization of Parts

Does the chair stand up as a visual unity?
Was the designer motivated wisely in creating any disunity (e.g., functional considerations)?
Does the chair possess any interplay of mass and void?
Is this interesting? Is it functionally desirable?

Organization of Shapes

A shape has an individual character because it is an entity. Shapes, like colors and textures, do not stand alone. They have a placement or position relative to other shapes. Some writers even make of position another component, but it is simpler to think of position as a relation between shapes.

Placed in location, shapes immediately begin to organize the surrounding space. Chapter 4 has a summary in the abstract of the principles that relate to what can happen. Shapes can change; their qualities can become less obtrusive or more so; their visual force or power to attract can be minimized or magnified; and all that we have spoken about with respect to good and poor design organization can be affected thereby. On the basic level good spatial design is dependent on planned use of repetition, variation, and contrast. Throughout the rest of this text comment is made with respect to many illustrations of space organization—a subject that becomes abstruse and mind-boggling unless it is understood in terms of concrete examples. Good space organization is the first requirement of any significant spatial form such as an interior design. If the original architectural form is regarded in the space organization of the interior, we have what is known today as architectonic design (see Color Plate 8). Wherever it is possible to organize space in an architectonic way through shape qualities and their positioning, it is highly desirable to do so.

Illusion

When perceptual changes are phenomenal, we speak of them as illusions. Every designer must at times be their master. Optical illusions are caused by visual laws in accordance with which effects differ from those expected from the stimulus. Shape interrelations are especially able to create illusions through spatial proportions.

The following suggestions indicate a procedure to follow in seeking any illusion in interior design. First state the problem positively. If a room is 13 feet wide and 27 feet long, it is poorly proportioned. The problem is to shorten the long wall. The secondary problem of elongating the short wall need only be considered if it seems impossible to solve the first problem.

Then suggest a physical answer such as, in this hypothetical case, erecting a cross wall (see Color Plate 4) or eradicating the long opaque wall by opening it with windows. If these solutions are undesirable or impractical, try the next line of attack. Marshal visual forces in such a way that the eye is kept from traveling the length of the room. Force eye movement toward the ceiling or toward the center of the long wall. The shapes placed on or against this wall may be given vertical emphasis. Or the commanding shape forces can be concentrated near the center. This may be done in one of several ways. Place a large shape or a grouping of small shapes there. Or the shape rhythms can be arranged so that the eye is carried to this central axis. For instance, a vertical picture may be placed over a central mantel. Two low pieces of furniture and two well-placed objects can flank the mantel. This entire grouping would make a triangular rhythmic closure to attract the attention from the corners of the room. A contrasting shape placed over the mantel could also accentuate this effect.

When the possibilities of shortening the long wall are exhausted, one can then turn to the equally challenging likelihood of lengthening the 13-foot wall. Furniture placed parallel to this but nearer the center of the 27-foot wall would serve the double purpose of extending the direction of the first and breaking up the second.

Handling Space as Spaciousness

The most prevalent shibboleth of the architectural and design vocabulary today is the word *space*. By space, as the word is currently used, we mean the sense of spaciousness,

which, because it is in such scarce supply, is given special importance. But to function well in our lives space must be qualified (Figure 5.13). Therefore a few philistine remarks follow.

In your designing, don't let inhabited space fly counter to gravity (weightlessness fights with our present state as earthlings). At least balance its soaring by some earthbound weight. Vast window areas in tall buildings may look with pleasure at the sky provided some large shapes, some charcoal colors (if lighting standards permit), or some deep textures preserve an opposing balance.

Very large (always a relative matter) interior spaces (unless they are planned for the occupancy of many people, large parties, or much traffic flow) may provoke an impish desire to introduce a human-scaled wigwagging system for communication through their extent. Those two masters of space, Mies van der Rohe and Frank Lloyd Wright, knew this. Mies placed discrete internal groupings and decorative elements separate from the walled enclosure, thereby creating internal interest factors that belied the tendency of space to become centrifugal. Wright was not sparse with his furnishings. He placed objects, however, so that they aided our comprehension of the basic spatial rhythm.

Create some interesting vacant spaces (Figure 5.14). They are important and, if brought into rhythmic relation with accent shapes, can induce movement from one detail to another and thus lead to an enlarged sense of space. This kind of empty space can be at once stimulating and restful.

How much pattern? A blanket statement that absence of pattern creates the greatest illusion of space is simply not true. Actually, much depends on the particular quality of the pattern, and that must be considered in relation to its placement. Pattern of poor quality is of course always taboo (see Chapter 12, on wall treatments). It would be hard to deny fine art and its pattern in any location. Pattern, then, we first assume to be of good quality. Some repetitive pattern can serve as textural relief. But it must be allowed to serve as background. Pattern organized in rhythmic sequences that incorporate the requisite amount of rest can accentuate spaciousness (Figure 5.15). However, handle with caution until mastery is acquired. And be able to criti-

Figure 5.13. Design with an unusual sense of spaciousness. Private residence, Philadelphia, Pennsylvania.
Architect: Hugh Newell Jacobsen
Photograph: Maris/Semel, Reprinted from House Beautiful, *Copyright 1974,*
The Hearst Corporation, All rights reserved.
The sense of space in this country place is augmented by skillful designing.
The high ceiling follows the pitched roof. The walls are all white. The floor is
black slate. The furnishings are understated and are in a monochromatic brown
and white color scheme.

Figure 5.14. Significant use of vacant space. Residence of Mr. and Mrs. R. D. McGranahan, Fox Chapel, Pittsburgh, Pennsylvania.
Architect: John Pekruhn
Photograph: Joseph Molitor Photo
The fireplace wall in the family room of this interesting home creates an excellent example of meaningful space division and the relation between occupied and vacant space. Space so well arranged is always challenging—far more so than if it were broken into several poorly designed divisions.

Figure 5.15. Pattern accentuates spaciousness. Wallpaper: "Blooms."
Photograph: Courtesy of Albert Van Luit & Company
When spaces are very small and walls irregular, a rhythmic small pattern actually may appear to increase the size of the space.

cize the inept handling of patterns in interiors. Better still, be able to foresee and prevent.

Furniture Arrangements as Visual Space Problems

In Chapter 3 we deal with a house plan but suggest that the principles learned in its designing are applicable to many different types of structures. Here we apply the same logic to furniture arrangements.

Furniture arrangements, after they satisfy functional considerations, must be appraised as visual shape designs. The work now will be a process of plan and replan, check and recheck. Have some lightweight tracing paper handy. Paper is cheaper than the actual furnishings.

First estimate the architecture. What is the room rhythm? A space with a 4-foot window module will have a quieter, more stately movement than one with 3-foot modules or one with windows broken into small panes. A room with large windows is liable to show flatter planes. What is the room symmetry? Are its points of interest formally or informally disposed? Are the space axes at right angles to each other? What are the architectural climaxes and center of interest? Our furniture placement should strengthen the architectural design if it is good.

In furnishing any space, give consideration to the question of whether everything is to be purchased at one time or bought over a number of years. In either case it is good policy to keep the design of the nucleus simple and thus keep the emphasis on space (Figure 5.16).

We may have decided on certain shape

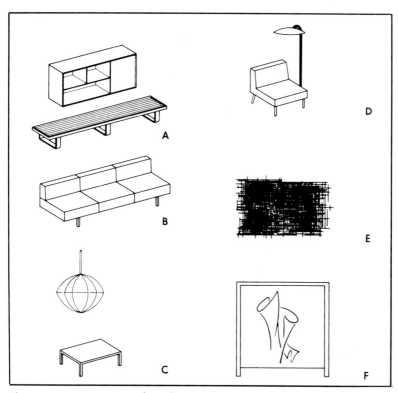

Figure 5.16. Suggestions for a living room starter set: keep it simple—keep it functional—keep it spatial. (A) A platform bench to use as a seat with cushions, or as a base for shelves and drawer units. (B) A daybed with bolsters, that can serve as a sofa or a bed. (C) A low, square table functional for corner groupings, between chairs, or as an individual piece of furniture. The hanging light provides good illumination in sofa and table groupings. (D) Two straight-line chairs with backs of comfortable height. An inconspicuous reading lamp. (E) A plain, woven rug that can be used later elsewhere. (F) A screen, a wall hanging, an interesting piece of sculpture, or a piece of driftwood that may relate to the personality of the owner.

traits that we wish to make dominant to establish the effects desired. We should also decide whether we wish to intensify these traits largely by use of repetitive, similar, or contrasting shape traits. The first will create the most easily perceived harmony, the last the most dramatic. In our projected purchases the dominant and subdominant themes are assigned their proportional emphasis.

Now draw elevations of the four walls of the area showing the furniture in place. These walls may be raised to surround the floor plan to make a more realistic depiction. Perspectives, of course, may be substituted.

At this stage, check the furniture groupings critically. Is there too much of one kind of size, direction, or line quality in some part of the room? Do the individual groups hold together as three-dimensional designs? If not, draw in a proposed remedy. It might consist of a few branches in a vase, a picture on a wall, an area rug, or a screen. Its embodiment should perform the essential visual task and it should not destroy the functional operation of the grouping.

When the internal furniture organization seems satisfactory, the next problem is to secure the necessary design integration between groups. This is done by introducing some rhythmic relations. Perhaps a picture may be chosen, the shape and placement of which helps group unity but the internal lines of which carry the eye to the next group. A repetitive or progressive rhythm of wall shapes from one group to the next may be the solution. The placement of an object in relation to the blank space beyond may direct the eye onward.

At this point (actually all of these considerations are probably occurring at once), note whether your predetermined centers of interest have been established. Has the eye been carried to them in the order desired?

For additional interest, some details might lead to several visual bypaths. The possibility is increased as color and texture are added.

Finally comes the appraisal of room balance. There should be a balance both of shape qualities and of shape forces on either side of the room (or visual area) axes. The nature of the room balance—bisymmetrical or asymmetrical—usually should correspond to the room design. Within the prevailing balance some minor diversions of the opposite type may prove welcome. With large window areas the outdoors can be a balancing factor.

6

LIGHT AS AN AESTHETIC FACTOR IN INTERIOR DESIGN

And God said, Let there be light: and there was light.

And God saw the light, that it was good: and God divided the light from the darkness.

And God called the light Day, and the darkness he called Night. And the evening and the morning were the first day.

Genesis, 1:3–5

With our present methods of producing tremendous brightnesses within very small areas and controlling them almost completely both as to intensity and as to spatial position, man's triumph over night has been rendered practically complete. . . . Leading illumination engineers are now willing to recognize that their science can no longer be considered as simply a branch of physics. It is realized now that a study of the effects of light on the human organism is equally important, so important in fact as to constitute a separate branch of illumination engineering.

David Katz, *The World of Color*[1]

The Importance of Light

Before the coming of light—nothing. Give first thought to light and lighting in interior design. Make no mistake: light can form, change, or devastate a space and all that it contains. Color itself, with which the designer has a longtime liaison, is nothing more or less than the effects of light bouncing off or passing through various objects. The light in a building often unfortunately seems beyond the designer's control—all the more reason to possess good firm knowledge of the

[1]London: Routledge & Kegan Paul Ltd., 1935.

90

subject so that one can modify the light if called in after the planning stage.

What Is Light?

As the elephant appeared in several aspects to the three blind men from Hindustan depending on their diverse approaches, so light is various things to different investigators. The person who intends to realize the design potential of light must begin understanding at the basic level.

To the physicist—master of twentieth-century encounters with space—light is a species of a particular form of energy known as electromagnetic energy. To humans, light is a sensation or a perception. To the psychophysicist it is a concept expressed through a measurement taken by comparing an unknown light with one that is known by having been physically measured.

Physicists know what energy can do and harness it to their will—a quantitative achievement. It is rather an encouraging thought that energy—the capacity to do work—is the basic entity of the universe.

Radiant (electromagnetic) energy is usually spoken of as having a wavelike motion. According to this concept, light is a narrow sector of a vast continuum of electromagnetic rays that can be measured in relation to their wavelengths from crest to crest. Its ordinary unit of measure, the nanometer (nm), is one billionth of a meter.

Electromagnetic waves travel through space at a uniform velocity. These waves differ a great deal from one another in wavelength (the distance between neighboring wave crests), and they also differ in corresponding frequency (the number of waves that pass a given location in a span of time). It can be seen that wavelength (λ) varies inversely with frequency (f). Therefore, either one of these qualities may be used to describe a particular kind of wave. When we speak of light, reference is usually made to its wavelength.

Radiant waves may also differ one from another in the amount of energy (capacity for work) that they contain. The power of radiant waves (their rate of doing work) is related to their amplitude. The amplitude of a wave is its height or depth as measured from its point of equilibrium. Like the waves of the sea, those that rise to the highest peaks and have

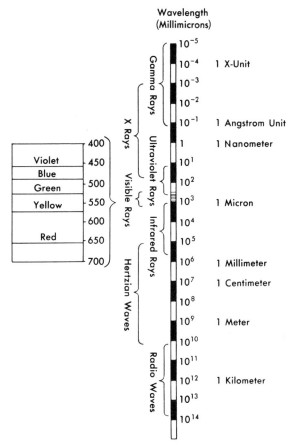

Figure 6.1. Light: a part of the electromagnetic band.

the deepest troughs possess more vigor than shallow little ripples do.

The Designer's Concern with Light

The interior designer must know how to use two kinds of light—light from natural sources (primarily the sun) and light from artificial sources (primarily electrical). Although a lighting designer may not be called upon to make the detailed calculations involved in gaining light of desired quantity and quality, he or she should understand the underlying concepts involved. One must consider the light source, the distance this light must travel, how it is modified enroute, and its nature at its destination. In all aspects of designing, the choice of lighting equipment and the surfaces and colors chosen for a space affect the resulting environmental pattern.

Designing well with light requires a knowledge of the meaning of its fundamental terms. Lighting technology is now in the process of change from a system dependent on the foot as the unit of linear measure to the metric system, which is, of course, related to the meter. Because this conversion is currently taking place, terms are given here in the metric system, although frequently they are correlated with the older vocabulary.

When lighting engineers measure light, they are interested in evaluating its capacity to produce visual sensation. The basic instrument for such psychophysical measurement is the photometer, an electrical device carefully designed to have a response resembling that of the human eye. (The photographer's light meter is a similar device arranged to match the responses of photographic film.) The earlier photometers required the operator to equate a light of unknown intensity with one whose intensity was known, but today's easy-to-use instruments give readings directly.

Most of the words used in light calculations are derived from a hypothetical power source—originally a specifically constructed "standard candle." This is imagined as being in the center of a hollow sphere with its flame—the point source—emitting light evenly in all directions. According to the older definition, the sphere surrounding the candle has a 1-foot radius, and the amount of illuminance that reaches any 1 square foot of its surface is 1 *footcandle*. Nowadays the materials of the light source and the sphere are ac-curately specified and the measurements are metric, so that the sphere's radius is 1 meter and the amount of illuminance that reaches any 1 square meter of its surface is called the *lux* (Figure 6.2). If a recipe for illuminance is stated in footcandles, multiple the number roughly by 10 (more exactly, by 10.76) to obtain the equivalent number in units of *lux*. The *lumen* is a unit of luminous flow equal to the light emitted from the standard point source within a solid angle of one steradian.

The rate at which energy is fed to a light source is expressed in watts, whereas the rate of light production by this source is given in lumens. The ratio (lumens produced/watts expended) is the normal way in which the luminous efficiency of a source is specified.

To describe the light in a complex situation further, the lighting scientist needs a term for the light that leaves a surface. This is luminance, again a psychophysical quantity. It is expressed in *footlamberts*, defined as the amount of light equal to the light coming from a surface at the rate of 1 lumen per square foot. There is yet no universally recognized term for footlamberts in the metric system.

Last, we arrive at a consideration of light as a sensation. The term *brightness* is here applied. Brightness may be defined as the attribute of sensation whereby an observer is made aware of differences in luminance—in

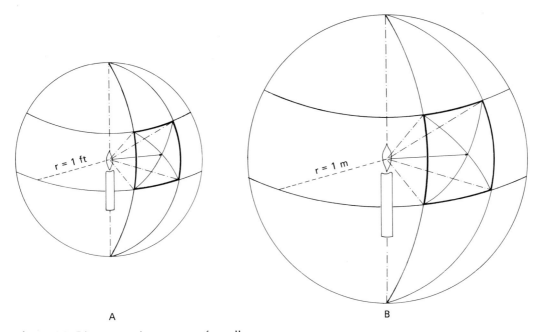

A   B

Figure 6.2. Diagrammatic concept of candle power.

other words, a subjective evaluation of luminance. It cannot easily be measured objectively inasmuch as there are many factors that influence the estimate of brightness such as illuminance, the character of the surface, the angle of vision, the surround, the duration of observation, and even the characteristics of the eye.

The eye alone, however, can make very useful comparisons of the brightnesses of two surfaces. This can be done by punching two small holes in a card and holding it about two feet from one eye with the other closed and then equating a known brightness through one hole with an unknown through the other. Such a comparison reading is often taken by the artist/designer when estimating the brightness relations of surfaces. A brightness meter operating on a similar principle can also be used.

It is within the power of the designer to change apparent brightnesses in a space. It is all a matter of relationships, and if well understood it provides some of the character of wizardry.

Modification of Light by Matter

Material in the path of light can affect it in three ways (Figure 6.3). Some of the light may be bounced off in the way that sunlight ricochets off the moon and illuminates our night. This is reflected light. Light energy can also be absorbed by an object. Absorbed light is then invisible. Some of the light may seep through. This is transmitted light. The total amount of light that strikes a surface must be accounted for in these three ways: reflection, absorption, and transmission (often called the R–A–T formula).

Several laws relative to this behavior of light have been known to us from our earliest contacts with mathematics. One is that when light is reflected from the surface of an object, the angle of incidence is always equal to the angle of reflection. Every billiard player learns this. Another commonplace is that when light enters most objects it can be bent or refracted, and it leaves the object in another location from the one it entered. This we see when we look at an oar partially submerged in water. It seems to be displaced, although we know through touch that this is not true. A third characteristic of light is of great consequence to our understanding of

chromatic color—in many cases when light enters an object it is selectively reflected from or transmitted through that object. This means that part of it may be influenced by the molecules within the object and may be cast forth in an altered form. We refer to this phenomenon in greater detail later in this chapter.

When light strikes a smooth surface, its boundary reflection is said to be directional light, or light reflected in a definite direction or pattern. This is also known as mirror or specular reflection. It accounts for the glossiness of a surface. Transparency of a material results when transmitted light leaves a substance in a regular directional manner.

Nondirectional light is called diffuse light. It may be a result of nondirectional reflection from a relatively rough surface or from internal refraction, reflection, and transmission of light from inner particles that are

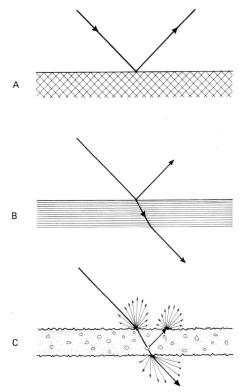

Figure 6.3. Light energy from indirect or non-self-luminous objects. (A) A smooth surface gives directional or specular reflection. (B) The total light that impinges on a surface is accounted for in one of three ways—reflection, absorption, or transmission. (C) Diffusion of light may result from nondirectional reflection from a relatively rough surface, from internal reflection and refraction, and from resulting transmission.

relatively large. Diffuse light produces the appearance of a matte surface in an opaque material and a translucent light from a transmitting material. Many surfaces reflect and transmit some directional and some diffuse light. Each has its use in interior design.

Reflection of light occurs at the boundary between any two substances when the differences between their indices of refraction is high. Light enters a material when this difference is less. Light passes through when the difference approaches zero. The index of refraction of a substance corresponds to the rate at which the velocity of light is slowed by the substance relative to its velocity in outer space.

Because surfaces in the path of light can affect its quantity and its quality, it behooves the designer to choose them carefully. Dark, shiny surfaces in a work space must be shunned at all cost if maximum use of available light is important. All designing is a matter of problem solving, but coming up with the wrong answer when planning for lighting can wreak physical handicap.

Requirements of Adequate Lighting

There are three sets of interdependent requirements for adequate lighting. First there is the functional requirement exacted in the interest of securing adequate light for the physical task of seeing. Then there is the psychological requirement that lighting contribute its share toward the establishment of the atmosphere of a space. This is the phase whereby lighting communicates its message to an interior. Lighting that focuses on such communication is sometimes known as mood lighting. Last there is the design requirement for good lighting. In fulfillment of this requirement the light must enhance the visual design of the interior directly. It is easy to see that the planning of lighting is a multi-purpose task and that no easy solution is forthcoming. However, all aspects must be considered one at a time and then an attempt made to synchronize them.

PHYSICAL FUNCTIONAL REQUIREMENTS

The first functional specification for light is quantitative: enough light to perform a task. Where critical eyework is performed for long periods at a time, for instance, when a typist needs light for 8 hours a day, the securing of the proper amount of light for this

task becomes of prime concern. Even here, however, illuminating engineers are discovering that qualitative standards should not be disregarded and a range of quantitative ones that depend on the nature of the task, the condition of the eyes, and the character of the surround should also enter the picture.

There are so many variables that affect a recommended level of illuminance that it is best to consult a source book (such as the *I.E.S. Handbook* listed in the Bibliography)[2] for specific information. For instance, entrance halls in private homes can vary in general lighting levels from 50 to 100 lux. Study at a desk might require 200 to 500, whereas difficult tasks performed over long periods could easily require ten times this amount.

If a calibrated photometer is available, take some readings following the directions for handling the instrument with regard to the angle it should make with and the distance it should be held from the plane to be examined. It may surprise you to see how inadequate the lighting is in some essential locations.

It is obvious that certain quantitative lighting requirements are imposed by whatever task is being done. It is also necessary to note that these may change in relation to the eyes of the viewer. Sight varies from person to person and with the years in the same individual.

The surround of a lighted task is of importance to ease of seeing. Light must be of the right quality for comfort so that one may work with a minimum of nervous fatigue and thus with the least physical exhaustion. Comfortable light is light without glare. Glare may be defined as any brightness within the field of view sufficient to cause annoyance, discomfort, or interference with vision. Glare can result from light coming directly from a source, for instance, when the light from a luminaire[3] shines directly into the eyes, or it may come from reflected light (often called a veiling reflectance), for instance, off shiny paper that is within the

---

[2]The IES publishes many pamphlets on specific lighting applications. Their address is: IES Publications Office, 345 East 47th Street, New York, NY 10017.

[3]A luminaire is a complete lighting unit, usually including base, bulb, diffuser, shade, and switch. Some confusion can result from the fact that luminaires are commonly called lamps (e.g., floor lamp), whereas the lighting industry uses the word lamp to refer to the replaceable light-generating part that we usually call a bulb. The context will usually prevent misunderstanding.

field of the visual task. (This lessens the contrast between the printing and the paper on which it is printed).

The visual field within range of one performing a task that requires visual acuity can be divided into three zones: the first zone comprises the task itself, the second is the area immediately surrounding the task, and the third is the general surroundings. The illuminance at zone 2 should be one third that of the task, and zone 3 should not be more than five times the task illuminance or less than one fifth of it.

EXPRESSIVE REQUIREMENTS

Lighting can be an agent in creating the kind of atmosphere that is conducive to carrying out the purposes of a building. There is a very close relation between light and mood. Extremes of light and sound are disconcerting. We shrink from excessive brightness as we do from a blast of noise. A pleasurably high level of light is like a paean of music that can stimulate and arouse, whereas twilight is the softness of the kitten's purr that ministers to relaxation. Entirely diffused light that casts no shadows is apt to be monotonous and undramatic. At times it is even unsafe light because some shadows are necessary to disclose the shapes of things. Directional light casts highlights and shadows on the various surfaces of a room. These move with the observer and help produce visual mobility and excitement.

Buildings are for shelter. Light and darkness can only provide visual shelter, privacy, and protection. This can be augmented by the psychological feeling of security that derives from various levels of illumination. There should be areas of sunlight and areas of shadow, large windows and shaded porches, gardens with sunny flowers and cool trees. Inside it is good to have high and low levels of artificial lighting.

Many special kinds of activities invite mood lighting. One of the most important of these is conversation, that social attainment that some say we are losing in the easy alternatives of television, loud music, and electronic games. Lighting for conversation should go beyond the negative aspect of not being annoying: it should create the mood, the psychological set for discourse (Figure 6.4). For this, lighting of a medium level should be specified, neither too high nor too low. Thus it will steer between the Scylla and Charybdis of being too stimulating or too depressing. Good conversation is aided by a cloistered feeling, by that atmosphere that is sometimes described as being cozy, by those surroundings that accentuate the feeling of shelter and privacy. This can be accomplished by reducing the general room background to as low a brightness as is compatible with the five-to-one functional brightness level. Low-placed lighting fixtures aid the feeling of intimacy requisite to a conversation area. Particular care should be taken to see that the lighting is warm in tone (see Chapter 7).

There are occasions when a space is the setting for a festive grouping, when a reception, a cocktail party, an after-theater gathering, or just the preliminaries of a lively dinner are going on. Gaiety and heightened spirits are the order of the day. Pleasantries and chatter fill the air. Greetings are exchanged and a few words spoken without any intent of entering into the give and take of more serious conversation. What of the lighting requirements for such activities— certainly neither the full brightness of noonday nor darkened concentrated lighting would answer. Lighting of a somewhat higher level than that provided for general conversation should fill the room, but it must do so in a dramatic, exciting way (Figure 6.5). Glareless lighting is certainly required, but a pleasurable exchange of light and shadow from directional sources should play its part, too, in this sort of decoration.

Light for dining also should be suited to its program. Dining is eating with ceremony for the purpose of furthering pleasant, friendly intercourse. The room lighting should be a combination of lighting for conversation and the more dramatic lighting with focus on table ceremonials. The general lighting should not be too high and it should be diffused. But there may be a higher level of light directed onto the table. Such lighting will make the table appointments gleam and will be flattering to the guests. One should be careful to see that no light shines in the eyes of any person seated at the table or obstructs the view of anyone so seated. This precaution is particularly important when the table is lighted by candles. Candles as they burn down are apt to come to eye level. Aside from this, candlelight is soft, warm-toned, dramatic light for dining. Marginal

Figure 6.4. Light and color. Apartment of Thomas and Zehra Boccia, Manhattan, New York.
Designers of interior and furniture: Thomas and Zehra Boccia
Photograph: © Jaime Ardiles-Arce
This apartment that belongs to a husband-and-wife team of designers illustrates well the changes that are occurring in the contemporary design field. Emphasis is placed on beautiful works of art, such as the antique Japanese silk embroidery on the paneled screen. Textiles are also rich, sensuous, and frequently old. The richness of effect is accentuated by the colors chosen—here lacquer-stained black floors and plum tones in the fabrics and related walls, which are lighted with fixtures tempered with colored filters. Spot lighting is focused on the important centers of interest. In the overall lighting scheme, however, the conversational grouping is emphasized. Although the window surrounds are canted to provide an added feeling of openness, the windows themselves are covered with pleated plain solar screen fabric that serves, especially at night, to enhance an effect of inwardness.

Figure 6.5. Light for sparkle. The Versailles Ballroom at the Helmsley Palace Hotel, New York.
Architects: Emery Roth & Sons, Principal architect in change: Richard Roth, Jr.
Interior designer: Tom Lee Ltd. Principal designer in charge: Sarah Tamerlin Lee; senior designer: Warren McCurtain.
Architect for preservation: William C. Shopsin
Project architect for renovation: James W. Rhodes
Lighting designer: Howard Brandston

Photograph: © Jaime Ardiles-Arce
This luxury hotel in Manhattan is a rebirth: a new high-rise hotel that incorporates the famous Villard houses on Fifth Avenue designed by the firm of McKim, Mead & White. With a frank attempt at romanticism but with consideration for the preservation of historical details, this ballroom tastefully conveys an impression of the eighteenth century. Much of this atmosphere is due to the sparkling illumination from the large crystal chandelier.

room light should be provided to further ensure comfort.

Listening to and playing music are pleasurable activities that are benefited by proper lighting. The performance of music, like reading or studying, inaugurates its own set of visual requirements. The listener appreciates the kind of lighting provided at the concert hall: of a general level that is not very high, and nondirectional, without brightness contrasts. The desired atmosphere is that of the twilight of a dream world.

Much the same advice can be repeated for television viewing. The prescription is for a general light of moderately high level, well distributed throughout the room, and having no spottiness or source of glare. The television receiver is a light source in itself and should be balanced with other illumination. The surface of the receiver is glass that acts like any other reflecting surface. No room light should rebound to the eyes of the viewer. The use of an even and low level of illumination is also desirable wherever film projection is intended.

The area of a building that is set aside as a reception area or as a traffic artery has unique functional and psychological illuminance requirements. These are similar for any traffic area, although when dealing with a large public traffic situation the level of light necessarily must be higher. In public traffic areas functional safety requirements are of paramount importance. Here the designer will often need to draw that close line between drama and pragmatism. The hall area is the main flume of a building and echoes the tone of all subsequent spaces, although it may do so in a more exciting way. Because a hall in a house may be the outsider's only contact with the interior and because it is the guest's introduction to it, the lighting of a hall should be particularly cheerful. Few spots are as dejected looking as a dismally lighted hallway.

The private apartments of a house should have thought given to their lighting. When sections of those areas duplicate the functions of the general living room, the type of illumination should also correspond. Sections of these areas serve overtly functional needs. Then the type of illumination should be planned to such purpose. For instance, it is essential that adequate diffused light should fall on the person who is dressing.

The sleeping compartment of a bedroom exerts definite lighting demands. The quality of comfort, essential to all good lighting, is of prime importance, especially during illness. There must not be glare within the angle of vision of the person in bed. It is important that light should be cheerful, warm in tone, and of sufficient brightness not to be depressing. However, it must also be restful. Therefore, a very high level is not desirable. It is also necessary to be able to darken the room for sleeping.

Many, many are the different uses for which light must be planned in interiors. The only way to solve the problems involved is to arm yourself with the basic principles, understand the variety of the machinery now on the market, study the pamphlets or books of the best light companies and of the IES, and then go ahead and plan. A word might be said, however, as general advice for several common situations.

It is wise to think about the lighting requirements for specialized building types (Figure 6.6). For instance, consider restaurant lighting. Basic illumination should be from glarefree down lights spaced uniformly so that table placement is not necessarily fixed. These lights may be accompanied by dimmers to change the specific mood. Strategically placed indirect (diffused) lighting should supplement the down lighting to reduce the shadows that might be unflattering to patrons. Special lighting may be placed in restaurants of specific types, say sparkling chandeliers in one that has delicate, feminine decor or large iron housings in one that features masculine clubroom decoration. Particular provisions should be made for the illumination of art objects (see the following section).

DESIGN THROUGH LIGHT

Light, although it is not usually called a design component, is a most potent design factor. Light can be secured in forms that range from sharp pinpoints to amorphous shapes. Often one fixture can produce several of these results. It is the designer's privilege to use these sources as agents through which to work.

There are five different classes of results that a designer should know how to achieve. First one should be able to illuminate and

Figure 6.6. Specialized lighting. Entrance foyer to the Grasselli Library, John Carroll University, Cleveland, Ohio.
Architect: Ernst Payer
Photographer: C. W. Ackerman
Buildings not only require specialized lighting for various needs, they frequently require unique fixtures for special locations. This large multi-storied foyer is dramatized by the fixture illustrated. It was designed by the architect to become a focal spot in an area that is otherwise largely illuminated with well-placed ceiling fixtures.

Figure 6.7. Light as a design factor. Corporate offices for a large company.
Architects: Schmidt, Garden & Erickson
Interior Designer: Beverly Jablonski
Photographer: James R. Norris
A repetitive pattern of oval-shaped light leads the eye to the hanging tapestry.

direct attention to objects of interest. This job is comparatively easy. In a more imaginative vein a lighting system can be designed so that the shapes of the light will be capable of setting up patterns and rhythms that are of interest in themselves (Figure 6.7). We speak of bands, circles, or pools of light—all testimony to the fact that light presence is a design factor.

Third, diffused light may show pattern. On occasion this is due to the shape of the luminaire from which it comes. The Japanese *akari*, which resembles a large paper lantern, gives pattern to diffused light (Figure 6.8). The pattern is actually that of the glowing receptacle. Large diffusing panels are similar. They can define areas, connect subdivisions, and of themselves create rhythms.

Fourth is formless light, which can flood a room and make it appear more spacious and sometimes limitless. Last, attention should be given to the potential of shadows that have shapes (Figure 6.9). The considerations here are similar to those affecting light. However, a thorough knowledge of how to harness shadows requires that understanding that comes from the graphic study of how to draw them. This is one of the values

of training in draftsmanship. Even some shadows thrown on a screen by hidden light sources can have merit. If the light is from a natural exterior source, the mobility of light and shadow is in itself a source of delight (Figures 6.10, 6.11, and 6.12).

In designing with light, a great deal of attention must be given to its color. This is not only important for itself, but because of its direct influence on all object colors. Color is so important that it necessitates a separate chapter in this book (Chapter 7). A hue must be in an emitting light if it is to enhance a surface that would normally contain that hue. That is to say that a light must contain a yellow wave band if it is to reflect yellow from a surface.

Light alone does not have texture, yet sharp pinpoints of light seem brittle and large pools of light seem soft at their edges. This projection of texture into the light itself probably results from the fact that the character of the visual texture of materials is dependent on the character of lighting. Visual texture results from visual nonuniformities in the reflectance of a surface. When light is directional and it creates much brightness contrast, it enables a textural nonuniformity

Figure 6.8. An akari lighting fixture. Residence of Mr. and Mrs. Bruce M. Walker, Spokane, Washington.
Architect: Bruce Walker, Spokane, Washington.
Photograph: © by Morley Baer
The *akari*, which is the word for *light* in Japanese, is a paper and wire structure that is the direct descendant of the Japanese lantern. Such lamps are simple solutions to low-cost, low-brightness lighting and can add drama and fantasy to an interior.

Figure 6.9. Shadows. Medusa Portland Cement Company, Cleveland, Ohio.
Architect: Ernst Payer
Sculptor: William M. McVey
Photograph: Hube Henry, Hedrich-Blessing
Directional light from the sun casts shadows on the building and creates highlights on the contours of the sculptured head of Medusa.

Figure 6.10. Contemporary and traditional blend. Residence of Mr. and Mrs. Richard Dickson, New Vernon, New Jersey.
Architects: Crissman & Solomon
Photograph: © Steve Rosenthal
This home, interiors of which are shown in Figures 6.11 and 6.16, exemplifies the eternal beauty of a rational basis for design used in the spirit of the traditional idiom.

to throw the deepest shadows and a smooth texture to give the most brilliant reflections. By comparison, diffused light tends to minimize textural differences and thus may soften all textural aspects of a room. It is good to develop a relationship between the textural quality of the light in a room and the rest of its decoration.

The Lighting of Art Objects

Lighting can be planned to display art objects to best advantage. The ideal light source for illuminating paintings should be similar in all respects to that under which the painting was made. Care should be taken to see that no reflection of the light source rebounds from the painting to the eye of the observer. A good position for the light is a high one

whence relatively diffused light falls on the painting at an angle of 45 degrees.

The surface surrounding a painting should be between 50 to 100 percent as bright as the average brightness of the picture. This will facilitate visual adjustment to the latter. The background should be somewhat neutral in tone so that little saturated chromatic light will be reflected to interfere with the colors of the painting. A surround that echoes the dominant painting tone at a lower saturation and value level (see Chapter 7) is excellent because it inaugurates a color rhythm that has its climax in the painting itself.

It is best to place sculpture that was designed to be seen from all sides so that it may be viewed in this manner. Light directed on sculpture should create shadows that will display its three-dimensional shape to good

Figure 6.11. Movement of light: I. Residence of Mr. and Mrs. Richard Dickson, New Vernon, New Jersey.
Architects: Crissman & Solomon
Photograph: © Steve Rosenthal
Using pitched roofs and white clapboarding, the architects have created a delightful contemporary house that seems to fit in with the surrounding architecture. One of the chief charms of the house derives from the play of sunlight that slants into many inside corners.

advantage. A satisfactory light source is a unit of low brightness directing light from an overhead angle of about 45 degrees.

A sculpture should be placed so that reflected light will impinge from two or three sides and from below. Thus the environment should be light enough to be an efficient re-

flector but should not be brighter than the sculpture surface.

A transparent or translucent object is best displayed by introducing light through one or more of its edges if it is flat or by illuminating it through opal glass from below if it is three dimensional (see Figure 11.9b). A dark

Figure 6.12. Movement of light: II. Church of Maria Königin, Cologne. *Photograph: From The New Churches of Europe by Kidder Smith.* The light from the stained glass of these tall windows as it moves around the small sanctuary is a constant source of joy and inspiration, strongly suggestive of the aesthetic force found in the great stained glass windows of Gothic cathedrals.

surround is advised to minimize distracting reflections and to make the sparkle of the transparency more evident.

It is interesting to note here that certain changes in the guidelines for the illumination of art objects have occurred in some recent installations, notably those in the new André Meyer Galleries at the Metropolitan Museum of Art (Figure 6.13). Here the collaborative thought of museum personnel and architects decided against the usual closely regimented gallery lighting in favor of what, on casual view, appears to be a return to that of an earlier date. This misconception is due to the fact that the subtlety of the Metropolitan lighting installation is not immediately apparent and would not have been possible in early gallery lighting because it involves sources not then in existence. The light for the Meyer Galleries appears to come from ceiling skylights that allow natural light with all its vagaries of sun and shadow. Actually the first control is at upper skylight level, where the ultraviolet rays that are harmful to art objects are screened. Six feet below are light-diffusing panels. Here artificial light must supplement the unpredictable sunlight. Between skylights and panels a stainless steel baffle has been placed that reduces shadows and reflections. Light from quartz lamps and from outdoors is directed to wash the vertical surfaces of gallery walls. Although this lighting may not be the ultimate solution, it points the way to answer the question posed in Chapter 1: how to work with all the available means to improve on the rigid rule book that has somehow grown out of the mechanized prescriptions of this age.[4]

Ways of Securing Light in Interiors

NATURAL LIGHT

Natural light should furnish as much as possible of the illumination for an interior (Figures 6.14 and 6.15). Contemporary buildings are planned to make the best use of the sun. In the northern hemisphere, large glass areas are oriented to the south or the southeast. These windows should contribute to the temperature conditioning as well as to the light (see Chapter 2).

Expansive windows provide comparatively glareless illumination. Light from an exten-

[4]The museum is represented in this solution by Sir John Pope-Hennessy, Chairman of the Department of European Painting; the architects were the firm of Kevin Roche, John Dinkaloo and Associates working with Arthur Rosenblatt, the Museum's Vice President for Architecture and Planning. This account is taken from an article by Ada Louise Huxtable in the *New York Times*, March 25, 1980.

sive source falling on a matte surface is diffused. It creates less brightness contrast with surroundings than a concentrated beam from a small source. More reflective space is used when light enters an interior from a high origin rather than from a low one. Consequently, large window areas reaching to the ceiling are ideal for capturing southern light.

Auxiliary light should be planned in other places for balance. Clerestory lighting, which, as the term is currently used, means lighting from small windows placed high in a wall, is frequently designed to open the other facades. Skylighting that employs a diffusing material is another way to light inner areas. Ribbed glass can direct the light that enters. Glass partitions between functional spaces increase the availability of the light supply.

Even benefits sometimes require control. Control of window light becomes a liability only when it is unduly expensive or when decorative considerations negate the functional. (The decorative consideration of windows is discussed in Chapter 12.)

At times natural light, possibly not well planned, requires functional regulation. If the light must be redirected, this can be accomplished by vertical or horizontal reflec-

Figure 6.13. New lighting in the Andre Meyer Galleries of Nineteenth-Century European Painting, the Metropolitan Museum of Art, New York.
Photograph: The Metropolitan Museum of Art

Figure 6.14. Natural light: I. Centre Street Addition, the Walters Art Gallery, Baltimore, Maryland.
Architects: Shepley Bulfinch Richardson & Abbott
Photograph: Courtesy of the Walters Art Gallery, Baltimore
The addition of the new section to the Walters Art Gallery presented many problems: those dictated by the site, the requirement for maximum space, and the necessity of designing a building that would harmonize in scale and character with the old gallery that had been built in 1905. The exterior walls were designed in glass to reduce to a minimum the necessity for artificial lighting. These glass walls are shielded by concrete screens, which diffuse glare, enable outer gallery walls to be used for exhibition space, shut out the distraction of street views, and above all provide natural lighting for the inner spaces.

Figure 6.15. Natural light: II. Interior, Centre Street Addition, the Walters Art Gallery, Baltimore, Maryland
Architects: Shepley Bulfinch Richardson & Abbott
Photograph: Courtesy of the Walters Art Gallery, Baltimore
A section of the gallery as illuminated with natural light.

tors such as Venetian blinds or screens with tilted meshes. This sort of control may be necessary when a finely finished piece of furniture stands near a southern window.

Light can be diffused when it enters. The translucent or "glass" curtain is the usual medium for accomplishing this. Many draw curtains are not lined and are made of a translucent fabric. Shades made from narrow strips of bamboo can modify the entering light. Translucent glass is excellent when it is not necessary to look through a window. Translucent shades will also diffuse light.

Often, particularly in commercial installations it is desirable to shut off a window. Privacy or a variable degree of openness is necessary. Here we need the functional control given by shutters, Venetian blinds, opaque draperies, or some of the new opaque and fireproof substitutes that are on the market. Many give a convincing appearance of architectural barricades.

ARTIFICIAL LIGHT

Artificial light is certainly mandatory in all buildings today. In general it is electrically powered. For installations, a registered electrician must verify legal compliance to wiring codes, and for complex work, the advice of an electrical engineer must be sought. Ideas and planning, however, should be within the competence of a well-trained interior designer to supply.

Having considered where the light should fall and of what quality and quantity it should be, the designer then decides about the placement and types of sources. When possible it is wise to incorporate these with the architecture. The first location is in the plenum, the cavity between the structural ceiling and the finished ceiling. Inasmuch as this is usually large enough to accommodate the plumbing ducts, it is also of sufficient size for the electrical. Next, the electrical panels may be placed in the finished ceiling or may hang from it. In the same manner a ceiling track can be designed for the use of several varieties of fixtures (Figure 6.16).

From the walls we have cornice, cove, valance, soffit, and panel lighting, all fairly easy to install and often incorporated in house lighting where the fundamental structure, as in a rental property, cannot be tampered with (Figures 6.17, 6.18, 6.19, 6.20, and 6.21). Then, of course, there is the portable luminaire or lamp that does indeed have func-

tional and aesthetic validity but may well be supplemented by architectural light.

After placement, one must consider the available types of bulbs or lamps (in the meaning of the generator of the light and its immediate housing). Inasmuch as the ultimate power is electricity, the lamp must provide a means of turning this into light. First, the incandescent bulb. This is a filament wire, usually tungsten, sealed into a glass tube, with a metal base for connection to a power source. Electric current passing through the filament must overcome its resistance, and the energy consumed heats the filament to incandescence.

Principles rarely go out of date. Fixtures do. The electrical engineers are forever improving on their product, from the viewpoint of creating light of better quality, of conserving energy (giving more lumens per watt) or of prolonging effective life and thus saving money. Lighting is a field in which the designer must continually investigate new sources and consider manufacturers' recommendations.

Fluorescent sources are the second kind of planned lighting to be examined. Fluorescence is the property of a material to become self-luminous when acted on by radiant energy. Evidence of this phenomenon can be seen in the glowing of phosphorescent and fluorescent materials in decaying bogs. In fluorescent lamps, mercury vapor is charged with an electric current. It then emits ultraviolet light that activates the fluorescent powders lining the tube to emit light in the visible spectrum.

Recent innovations in fluorescent lamps are planned to improve energy efficiency, prolong efficiency, prolong lamp life, and enrich color quality.

Bulbs that owe their light to fluorescence must be operated with a ballast, a device used to obtain the necessary electric circuit conditions. Certain fluorescent lamps of lower wattage (e.g., General Electric's *Circlite*) do not need this additional fixture.

Another type of bulb that must be operated with a ballast is the high-intensity discharge lamp. Here the light is produced when vaporized substances (e.g., mercury, sodium) in the lamp are activated by an arc struck between the anode and the cathode of these tubes. Low-wattage mercury lamps are used efficiently in residential exterior lighting, but the primary purpose of the high-wattage

Figure 6.16. Illumination: ceiling track. Residence of Mr. and Mrs. Richard Dickson, New Vernon, New Jersey.
Architects: Crissman & Solomon
Photograph: © Steve Rosenthal
In this view of the living room interior of the Dickson home, a ceiling track for down lighting is seen. The interior illustrates the enlargement of visual space by the use of partial walls and the selection and good placement of decorative accessories.

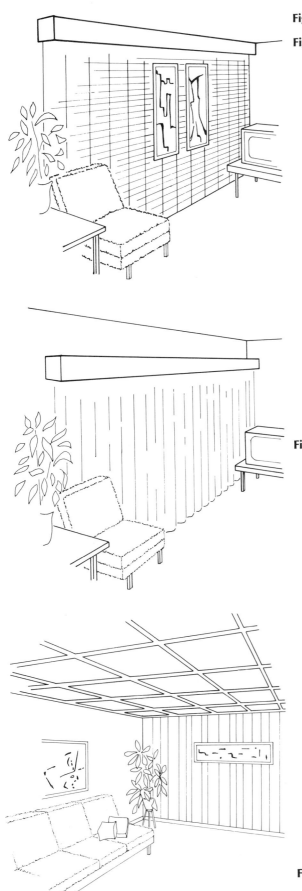

Figure 6.17. Cornice lighting.

Figure 6.18. Cove lighting.

Figure 6.19. Valance lighting.

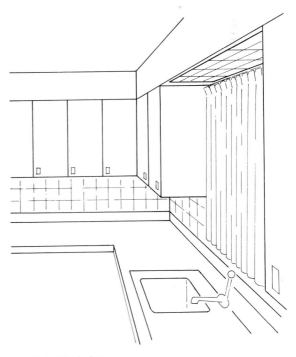

Figure 6.20. Soffit lighting.

Figure 6.21. Panel lighting.

bulbs is to illuminate such large areas as sports fields, outside grounds, lobbies, and so forth. The high-intensity discharge lamps offer very intense sources of light and have a very high lumen output per watt.

Thought also must be given to the shape (or, conversely, the amorphism) of the desired light. Diffused light is to a certain degree incorporated in most lamps by means of a powdered or enameled coating on the inside surface. Diffusion can also be obtained by using some secondary reflective source that provides a wide light spread and consequently a "soft" light. This may be the translucent shade of a luminaire or the indirect light sent back from an illuminated large area of ceiling, wall, or even floor.

We are most apt to wish for light with a precise shape and a definite direction. The shape we are talking about may have a hard or a soft edge, and may cover a small or a large area. The beam may have parallel sides or be converging or diverging. Obviously some careful study of existing sources is necessary to learn which one is most suitable for a particular use.

The principles used in beam direction are those illustrated by reflection, refraction by a lens, transmisson, and, on occasion, absorption of light. Several of these means frequently are operative in a single fixture type. For directional light, fluorescent lamps need to have some sort of directional apparatus supplied by the lamp housing as, for instance, when they are installed in a ceiling panel the glass downface of which is supplied with a lens. Incandescent lamps can use the shape of the lamp itself to control the beam (a concentrated beam is a *spot*, a broader beam is a *flood*), although additional control is often found external to the lamp in shaped reflectors. Thus a pinpoint of light can be secured from an elliptically shaped reflector (called an ER lamp), where the concentrated light source is placed at one focus of the ellipse and the convergent rays focus on the other. The parabolic reflector is probably the most widely used shape. When the light source is placed at the focal point of a parabolic reflector (P lamp—often known as the PAR lamp when coated with aluminum), the reflected rays of light will be essentially parallel. This reflector shape is used in spotlights and, in combination with a lens, in automotive headlights.

The principle of absorption is seldom used in planning light sources because light is costly, and its absorption is not desired from an economic standpoint. However, black is often used as a coating when some shielding is necessary.

Anyone who is knowledgeable in the subject of lighting for such tasks as reading is often appalled at how poorly designed for this purpose many portable luminaries are and at the errors so often shown in their placement. A luminaire is first and foremost a functional housing for light, and its choice and placement should put that consideration first. The rules are simply demonstrated. Light the luminaire in a dark room in the position that it is supposed to function. Notice where the cutoff of its light falls, or find it by taking footcandle readings. Do the tasks that are to be lit by this source fall easily within this cutoff line? The height of the bulb within its shade, the dimensions of the shade, the positioning of the luminaire, and the reflective register of the shade itself will all enter into solving the problem of proper placement (Figures 6.22 and 6.23).

Ambient Lighting

Ambient lighting, of course, is not a new idea (Figure 6.24). What are our household lamps or ceiling tracks but ambient lighting? However, the combination of lighting with a furniture grouping (now called ambient lighting systems) does offer something new. It is a conception that seems to have possibilities, particularly when flexibility and movability must be worked into many living and business situations. In this system the purpose is to incorporate lighting for task visibility in the furniture, with reduced light levels elsewhere. It has been developed most extensively in relation to office systems, although to a certain extent it is found in light sources incorporated in bedroom and library furniture.

Although the complete designing of ambient lighting systems is in its infancy, if properly developed by the lighting engineer working with the furniture designer and manufacturer, it holds some promises. Not the least of these is the breakup of uniform ceiling luminance (now found in many offices) that is acknowledged to be psychologically unsatisfactory and highly impractical.

Figure 6.22. A good luminaire: I. Lamp: Paul Hanson Company, Inc.
Photograph: Courtesy of Paul Hanson Company, Inc.
This porcelain lamp in Chinese red with brass fittings is well designed for adequate light for reading. The height of the lamp and the width and depth of the translucent shade provide suitable light and enhance the surroundings of the room.

Figure 6.24. Ambient or task lighting. A grouping of Herman Miller Action Office™ units.
Photograph: Herman Miller, Zeeland, Michigan
The concept of task-oriented lighting is illustrated in this flexible office system incorporating four work centers. Here the light sources are both those that are furniture-integrated and those that are incorporated

Figure 6.23. A good luminaire: II. Lamp: Nessen Lamps, Inc.
Photograph: Courtesy of Nessen Lamps, Inc.
This floor lamp not only is well and simply designed from a visual point of view, it also serves well as a luminaire for reading because of the height, proportions, and translucency of its shade. Doing double duty as a small side table, it would be a welcome addition to any room.

with movable partitions. The system is designed to put lighting of requisite quantity on the task and to supplement this with appropriate ambient lighting. The light matte-finished surfaces aid both the quantity and the quality of the reflections.

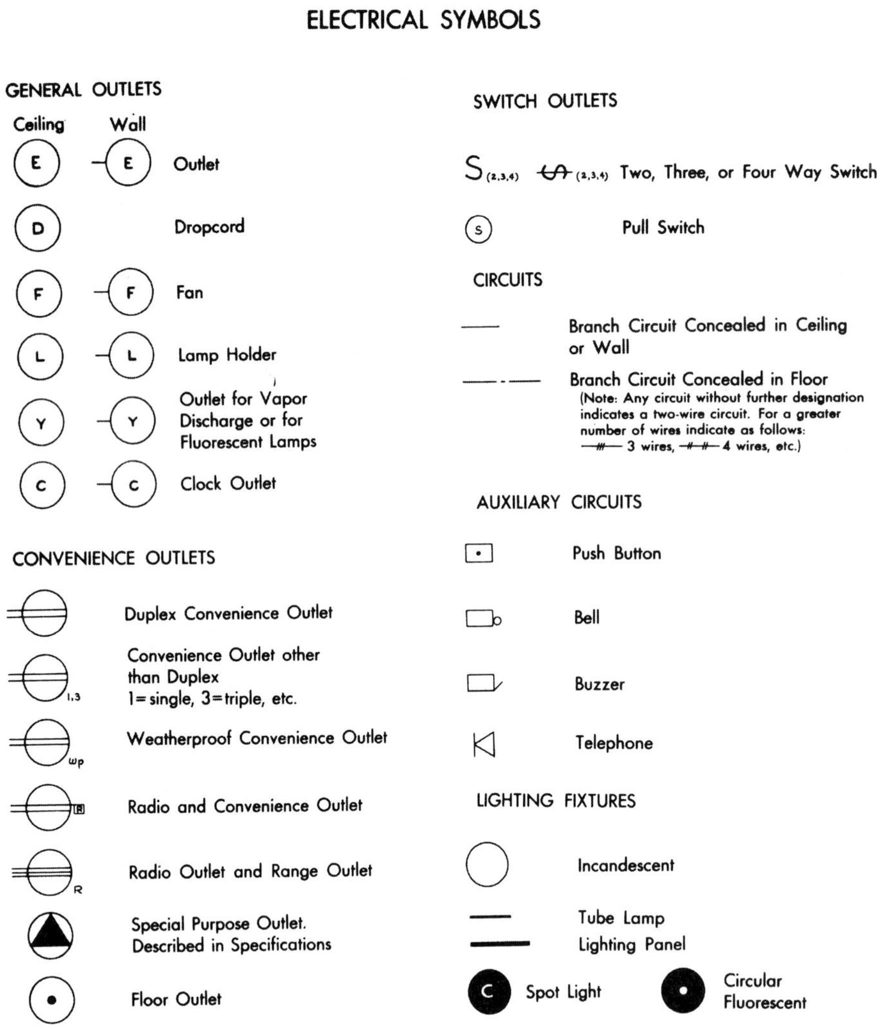

ELECTRICAL SYMBOLS

GENERAL OUTLETS

Ceiling   Wall

(E) —(E)   Outlet

(D)   Dropcord

(F) —(F)   Fan

(L) —(L)   Lamp Holder

(Y) —(Y)   Outlet for Vapor Discharge or for Fluorescent Lamps

(C) —(C)   Clock Outlet

CONVENIENCE OUTLETS

Duplex Convenience Outlet

Convenience Outlet other than Duplex 1=single, 3=triple, etc.

Weatherproof Convenience Outlet

Radio and Convenience Outlet

Radio Outlet and Range Outlet

Special Purpose Outlet. Described in Specifications

Floor Outlet

SWITCH OUTLETS

S (2,3,4)   (2,3,4) Two, Three, or Four Way Switch

(s)   Pull Switch

CIRCUITS

———   Branch Circuit Concealed in Ceiling or Wall

—— · ——   Branch Circuit Concealed in Floor
(Note: Any circuit without further designation indicates a two-wire circuit. For a greater number of wires indicate as follows: —#— 3 wires, —#—#— 4 wires, etc.)

AUXILIARY CIRCUITS

Push Button

Bell

Buzzer

Telephone

LIGHTING FIXTURES

○   Incandescent

——   Tube Lamp
Lighting Panel

(C) Spot Light   Circular Fluorescent

Figure 6.25. Electrical symbols.

Planning for Room Lighting

It is now time to take the problem that we began in earlier chapters and carry it a step further to ensure good lighting (Figure 6.25). We already have a plan for this space and the furniture in position. It is now feasible to design for movable lighting in the form of lamps and/or installed architectural lighting.

The lighting plan starts with provision for local lighting at the major furniture groupings. Much of this may be supplied by recessed down lights of the reflector spot type. If these are not placed above the ceiling they can be run on a track below it. They provide high wattage and controlled distribution. Pinpoint refractive spots or flood lights may be used to dramatize and wall-wash limited areas that are intended for decorative purposes. When architectural lighting is not feasible, an average size living room will require from four to six portable lamps carrying about 900 watts for local lighting.

Thought also must be given to the general lighting of a room. Many structural devices supply large sources of indirect or diffused light. If portable lamps must be relied on for this general illumination, certainly some of them should have diffusing rather than opaque shades, with the walls, floors, and ceilings used as reflective sources.

The task of supplying adequate light for all of the areas of an interior can be analyzed in the manner just outlined. A careful examination of the current market will show that lighting engineers are constantly improving the means for securing desired results, and today they are also designing with energy conservation in mind.

CHAPTER
7
UNDERSTANDING COLOR

In ink-sketches the brush is captain and the ink is lieutenant,
but in coloured painting colours are the master and the brush
is the servant.

Sei-Ichi Taki, in Laurence Binyon, *The Flight of the Dragon*[1]

The Importance of Color and Its Study

Color is one of the three visual components—shape, color, and texture. It is difficult to describe color except by saying that it is one aspect of everything we see. It is red and orange and yellow and all the hues of the rainbow. It is also black and white and grey that we seldom see in nature. Even the white paint on a house or the new white of the snow borrow a green from the trees or a yellow or blue from the sky.

If we half close our eyes and if we possess good long eyelashes, we suddenly find that we have left the rainbow world and have entered the black, white, and grey one. This is a world peopled with shapes because it is the position of light and dark on a shape that helps us locate and identify it. We glean much of our visual understanding of the real world from our black and white knowledge of it—all that we need to travel safely. Chromatic color is an extra gift of the gods. When we use it well we are playing on an instrument that can turn prosaic lives into poetry.

Many color wizards are untutored in its use. Color is such a complex subject that a scientific comprehension of it cannot be a substitute for an emotional sensitivity. It

should be an aid to such sensitivity. Indeed, in this age of artificial lighting, of standardization and duplication of colorants, of physiological color interactions, the science of color should not be *terra incognita* to the interior designer.

Knowledge of color helps provide certainty of results. Variations in the color stimulus, in the eyes and nervous system, in the physical and mental state of the observer, and in the total color design will affect the colors seen. Only with knowledge of all the attendant factors can artists control their products. In an interior there is no escape from the pervading colors. Emotional responses even to small areas of color can be explosive. Color mistakes that would be magnified, costly, and dangerous must be avoided.

Color knowledge comes from many sources. The physicist tells us that color is light as a form of energy. The psychologist is interested in the entire process of color perception and is helped by the physiologist who studies the eye and the brain. The aesthetician is concerned with our color preferences. The chemist tells us how to control color through pigments and dyes, the lighting engineer through light. As artists, we wish to use color as an aid toward creating a good interior design. We must not lose sight of our purpose as we study each branch of color science.

[1] London: John Murray (Publishers) Ltd.

113

A story, oft repeated, is told about Whistler painting the famous picture of his mother. As twilight and eventually darkness fell upon the room, the artist saw all the trivial aspects of the sitter disappear until only the significant qualities remained. So it is with color. One should learn to progress from the many facts that surround the subject to an understanding of the relevance of fact and fancy to creation.

The Psychological Aspects of Color

It is difficult to think about color without using some color names. Color concepts, like those of light, have been given many designations, each set related to a particular type of use. The terms most essential to the artist are those that specify basic color responses. These are called the psychological color attributes. The first is *hue*. If we see several samples of colored cloth, we first notice whether they resemble one another in hue. Hue is that attribute of colors that enables us to distinguish them from black, white, and grey. The latter are the *achromatic colors*, those that do not have hues. Colors (such as red, orange, or yellow) that exhibit hue are known as *chromatic colors*.

If we observe further, we notice that some colors are light and some dark. We recognize this more quickly among the achromatic tones. In naming this lightness–darkness aspect it is proper to adopt the shorter term and speak of the *lightness* of the color. Lightness is defined as that attribute by reference to which a color is classed as equivalent to a member of the achromatic series from black to white. (Again half close your eyes and try to determine relative lightness among your samples.) Thus we describe a color as being about as dark as a certain grey or as light as white. A lightness–darkness sense is extremely important both to artist and to designer.

If we study our samples once more, we may notice that there is a third kind of difference between them. We might say that one is more "colorful" than another. To this kind of difference the name *saturation* is given.[2] Satura-

tion is the attribute of any color that determines its degree of difference from a grey of the same lightness. Thus we discriminate between two red samples that are equally light by saying that one of them is more nearly grey or is less saturated than the other. Saturation refers to the strength of a color.

Chromatic Light

Although all color is light, we perceive it in different phenomenal ways known as the modes of color appearance.[3] One of these is the illuminant mode in which the color stimulus is perceived as light. Color viewed as light can be chromatic. Chromatic color is the sensation we experience when we look at a fractionally narrow band of the total span of light. For instance, a band of wavelengths measuring from 380 nm to 450 nm will be seen as violet light, from 450 nm to 490 nm as blue, from 490 nm to 560 nm as green, from 560 nm to 590 nm as yellow, from 590 nm to 630 nm as orange, and from 630 nm to 760 nm as red.

How is light broken up into these smaller bands (Figure 7.1)? We already know that light traveling through space has a constant speed or velocity. When this light strikes an obstacle in its path, it may be slightly retarded. The shortest wavelengths are slowed down most and the longest wavelengths least. As a waveband of light is delayed it is bent proportionately off its straight course. Thus the shortest or violet-hued lights emerge from such an obstacle in a most oblique direction. The long or red-hued lights emerge with the least deviation from the normal, and the other bands are relatively situated between these extremes.

The name given to the bending of light rays when they travel through a medium of greater density than a vacuum is refraction. It is commonly demonstrated by means of a glass prism, which is a piece of clear glass having triangular ends and nonparallel sides. Inasmuch as glass is denser than air and is transparent, the white light will be refracted and will emerge in narrow bands each having a different hue. This we see in the rainbow, where the drops of moisture in the air have acted as myriad prisms to refract the sun's

---

[2]The color terms used throughout this chapter are taken from *The ISCC Comparative List of Color Terms*, compiled by Sidney Newhall and Josephine G. Brennan, Washington, DC: Inter-Society Color Council, 1949. This publication is now in the process of revision by a committee of the Inter-Society Color Council (ISCC) under the chairmanship of Dr. C. J. Bartleson, Eastman Kodak Company Research Laboratories.

[3]Robert W. Burnham, Randall M. Hanes, and C. James Bartleson, *Color: A Guide to Basic Facts and Concepts*, New York: Wiley, 1963.

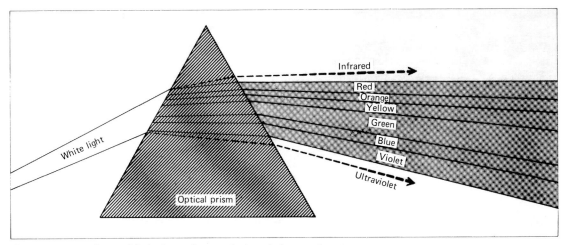

Figure 7.1. Breakup of light into chromatic bands by a prism.

rays. The process of breaking up a total band of light into its component rays is known as dispersion. The band of colored light that results from dispersion is called the visible spectrum. The hues seen in the spectrum are the spectral hues. (Diffraction, interference films, and polarization are other means that can be used to isolate portions of the spectrum. These may be studied in any text dealing with the physics of light.)

Every hue in a continuous spectrum merges imperceptibly into its neighboring hue. The average eye can differentiate about 125 different spectral hues. However, for the sake of convenience, the spectrum is frequently and arbitrarily divided into the six broad visual regions previously mentioned.

Additive Color Mixture: Light

Not only is it possible to break chromatic light into chromatic bands, but these bands can be recombined into achromatic light. This process of adding lights together and obtaining a light that is an integration of all their characteristics is frequently called additive color mixture (Figure 7.2).

The results of additive color mixture are readily predictable. In the first place, the amounts of the component lights add up as simply as a sum in arithmetic. Thus if we add together several dim lights we obtain a much brighter light. Note again that when we talk about light as so much illumination, we speak of its brightness rather than of its lightness. The two words refer to different visual aspects of the same thing—namely, the amount of light.

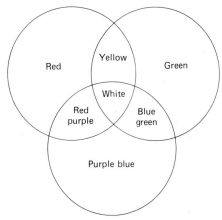

Figure 7.2. Additive light mixture.

The combination of the hue and saturation of a light is known as its *chromaticness*.[4] If several lights are added together, the chromaticness of the resulting light is predictable. Now, however, the process is not exactly like adding together two things that have the same sensation quality. That is, two brightnesses. We are combining two lights that may have different qualities of chromaticness. Perhaps one light is a strong blue light and the other is a weak yellow light. Blue and yellow seem to be different in quality, although their saturations may be visualized as magnitudes or quantities.

The process at this point more nearly resembles a combination of tones of several instruments in an orchestra. The *amount of*

[4]*Chromaticness* indicates hue and saturation, without the aspect of brightness. The term *chromaticity* is more generally encountered. This rightly refers to the physical synthesis of two or more lights integrated in all of their aspects. See R. W. Burnham, R. M. Hanes, and C. J. Bartleson, *Color: A Guide to Basic Facts and Concepts*, New York: Wiley, 1963.

sound that the instruments make in unison is equal to the sum of what the individual instruments make solo, but the *kind* of sound made in unison is a new kind that is a composite of the pitch and timbre of the individual instruments.

In general, we can say that any two lights added together will have the hue of a light that is halfway between them on the spectrum. A red and a yellow light will make an orange light. Thus two chromatic lights could be found, each of which would be a combination of the lights of one half of the spectrum. These two lights then would combine to make the entire spectrum, or achromatic light. Two such paired lights which, when added together make achromatic light, are called *complementary lights*. It has been found that for every monochromatic light (one-hue light), with the exception of the green band, there is a complementary light. Monochromatic light (light energy of a single wavelength) is more accurately called homogeneous light as opposed to that composed of several or all visible wavelengths, which is heterogeneous light.

We may wish to predict the saturation that will result when several lights are combined. The more homogeneous a light, the more saturated it will appear. The more heterogeneous, the more achromatic it will appear. In a familiar color diagram the spectrum band is represented as a circle. This is the way that Sir Isaac Newton (1642–1727) illustrated it. It was he who first demonstrated that white light was composed of chromatic light. The circle diagram is useful in helping us determine the quality of a combination of lights.

If we take the spectrum band and join its short-wavelength, or violet, end to its long-wavelength, or red, end, it becomes apparent that the spectrum does not contain colored lights of the hue that we call purple. This hue, however, can be formed by the addition of red and violet light. When this synthesized purple light is added to green light, white light results. Here is the missing complementary range for the green light band.

If a purple band is included between the red and the violet bands, our circle diagram of chromatic light is complete. The circle should be arranged so that complementary lights are opposite each other and thus lie on a straight line extending through the center, where will be found the achromatic light that results from a mixture of the complementary lights. Such a circle diagram is known as a chromatic light circle because it illustrates the interactions between chromatic lights in relation to their appearance of chromaticness.

On this chromatic light circle the hue resulting from the addition of equal amounts of two lights can be visualized by connecting the two with a straight line. At the midpoint of this connecting line place a point. Project a radius of the circle through this point. The new hue is located where this radius meets the circumference. Where two complementary lights are mixed in equal amounts the point falls on the center and an achromatic light results. If two lights are not complementary, it will be seen that their summation light will be pulled toward the center (achromatic light) by an amount commensurate with their distance apart on the circle. If two lights are combined in unequal amounts, the resultant light will be of a chromaticness that is proportionate to their relative amounts but is dictated by the general principles outlined above.

The procedure just outlined will also indicate the saturation of two combined lights of less than spectrum saturation. The new saturation will fall on the line connecting the diagram positions of the lights. For prediction on several lights, work from the extremes to their adjacent lights and proceed until the number has been reduced to two.

Since lights always combine qualitatively to form an intermediate light, it is possible to match the chromaticness of any light by the proper selection of several carefully chosen chromatic lights. Three chromatic lights have been found to be the smallest number that would accomplish this satisfactorily. These are spaced so that if combined in equal amounts they will form achromatic light. In other words, they are about equidistant from one another on the spectrum. The three lights usually chosen for this purpose are of red, green, and violet blue hues. They are conveniently located at the extremes and in the center of the visible spectrum. They are sometimes called the *primary lights*. Here the word primary means coming first in a process. They are the basic lights that are used in larger or smaller amounts to match any other light in color.

Object Color: Colorants

The ratio of incident light to reflected, transmitted, and absorbed light with respect to any object is constant. This causes us to think of the color of an object as unchangeable, inherent, and in the *object mode*. The object mode is often called the *surface mode* or *volume mode* when we appraise colors as belonging to a surface or to a volume, respectively. Here again we are seeing color in a phenomenal way, for no color really belongs to an object—color is always light, and light fluctuates.

We speak of both *genuine color* and *apparent color*. The first is the color seen under white light or sunlight; the second is the color seen under any other light. Sunlight is a warm yellowish hue. Skylight is the bluish light from the sun when it is near its zenith. Its color is derived from the *scattering* of light by small particles of matter in the air, the short rays being affected most readily.

Any object that can modify the color of the original impinging light is technically known as a *colorant*. Thus a colorant is any substance used to produce the color of an object. The chief colorants are the pigments and dyes—pigments are insoluble in their liquid media whereas dyes are soluble. Toners are concentrated dye salts. When mixed with a carrier, colorants become the paints, lacquers, varnishes, dyes, and lakes of commerce. But we must not forget that the green of grass, the grey of slate, or the brown of earth owe their colors to natural substances that they contain. Colorants extracted from natural sources were the only ones available until the eighteenth century.

In large-quantity commercial work, powdered colorants mixed with an appropriate extender vehicle provide the most economical source for desired colors. Since the formulas for pigmented coatings are frequently merchandising secrets, it is advised that the individual seeking sureness of colorant knowledge begin by studying the fundamental artists' colorants. The paint manufacturer uses these while considering many functional facts about them such as their tint tone (in combination with white), tinting strength, relative permanency, covering power, their resistance to chemicals, their bleeding into diluents, and their combining character.

Colorants are divided into two large classes, the inorganic and the organic. These are distinguished primarily by the absence or presence of carbon in the molecular structure. The inorganic compounds in general are salts of the minerals to which they owe their color.

A second major colorant division is that by which the synthetics are distinguished from the natural pigments. The synthetics are made largely from basic raw materials (e.g., carbon, oxygen, hydrogen, and nitrogen) obtained from intermediate crude products (e.g., benzene, naphthalene, anthracene, toluene, and xylene) of the coal tar industry, and built into structures for color. The visual and practical qualities of the synthetics have given them precedence in the commercial field. Only a few are obtainable as artists' pigments.

Many important colorants are given in the following reference list.

Inorganic

1. Native earths (ochre, sienna, umber—raw or burnt): permanent—ochre is opaque, the other native earths are somewhat less so—tinting strength not great—frequently used to dull other colorants while supplying a warm tone—useful for antique glazing.[5]
2. Minerals (aluminum, copper, gold, zinc): difficult to keep in solution—uses are specialized.
3. Mineral compounds.
   a. Alumina hydrate (or aluminum hydroxide): an inert base for lakes.
   b. Cadmium compounds (usually as a sulphur salt): hues are red to yellow—permanent—opaque—great saturation and tinting strength—largely used in artists' pigments.
   c. Chromium compounds (lead chromate): hues similar to cadmium compounds but less saturated—not sufficiently permanent for artists' use—economically used for exterior and interior house paints.
   Chrome orange: used as a metal primer.
   Chrome oxide green: relatively permanent—opaque.
   Chrome green: Prussian blue plus chrome yellow—not permanent.

---

[5]A good glazing medium is as follows (it may be used as the vehicle for incorporating thin glazes of transparent colorants over an opaque coating): Mix 1½ oz damar varnish, 1 oz stand oil, 5 oz turpentine, and ¼ t cobalt linoleate (drier).

Hydrated chromium oxide (better known as viridian): saturated green—permanent—transparent.

d. Cobalt compounds (cobalt aluminate): blue hue with slightly greenish undertone—relatively permanent—nearly transparent—cobalt greens and violets are available, some of the latter being poisonous and must be used with care.

e. Iron compounds (iron oxide): hue of dull red—in natural state known as Indian or Venetian red—synthetics known as Mars colors—permanent—opaque.

Prussian blue (or ferric ferrocyanide): not absolutely permanent—transparent—high tinting strength.

f. Lead compounds:

Red lead: various lead salts—not permanent—opaque—used industrially as a priming coat for steel and as a drying agent.

Flake white: basic lead carbonate (organic)—high quality corroded, so-called Dutch process lead—poisonous if taken internally, even after it is dry.

g. Lithopone composed of zinc sulphide and barium sulphate (blanc fixe): extensive use for white interior house paint because of good performance and low cost.

h. Titanium dioxide: a permanent white of great opacity.

i. Ultramarine: originally ground lapis lazuli—now a form of colloidal sulphur blue—best are permanent—semitransparent.

j. Vermilion (or mercuric sulphide): red—replaced largely by the cadmium colors.

k. Zinc oxide (Chinese white): a permanent opaque white.

Organic

1. Vegetable (indigo, madder): seldom used except in craft work.

2. Animal (cochineal, lac, Tyrian purple): seldom used.

3. Carbon black: often used as a generic name for all blacks made from carbon—specifically made from natural gas—mixes well with water—permanent—opaque.

Lamp black: pure carbon—permanent—slightly bluish in color.

Ivory black: impure carbon—generally a high grade bone black—brownish undertones—mixes well with water.

4. Synthetics: the principal synthetic lakes available as artists' colorants are:

a. Alizarin: produced from anthracene—blue red hue—permanent—transparent.

b. Phthalocyanine green and blue: saturated tones—high tinting strength—deep copper mass tone overcome by preparation with a percentage of inerts—permanent—transparent.

Paints and Protective Coatings

Manufactured colorants such as those listed above provide the coloring matter for all objects that are artificially colored. When such coloring is placed on the surface of an object (as opposed to being integrally incorporated, as with a dye) it must be manufactured further into a paint or similar product.

These commodities are produced by a vast industry dealing in protective and decorative coatings. A protective coating may be very specialized in its purpose. Those the designer uses protect a surface from harmful atmospheric, bacteriological, and chemical action. They also are intended to improve its appearance and modify its light reflection.

Early developments in the use of decorative wall finishes were slowly attained through the empirical methods of the artist. Crayons made from natural earths and used in early cave paintings have been found. Other media, variously known as tempera or gouache, add a binder of casein, egg, glue, or gum to opaque earth colors, with water as a diluent. There is little excess binder in these coatings and the film dries by coagulation to a matte, porous finish. Therefore these paints have little protective value and their color can be washed away.

This fault is remedied in two forms of mural painting being revived today. The first of these is fresco painting, in which pigments ground only in water and inert to lime are placed on a newly laid plaster wall. The pigments set with the plaster and so are as permanent as it is.

Encaustic painting is also an early decorative technique. It is pigmentation applied in hot wax and sets as a hard film when cool. Waxes possess great protective value because they are practically impermeable to atmospheric moisture. Therefore, thin coatings of wax alone are frequently used for finishes. Their disadvantage is that they are not impervious to dirt.

The film-forming property of a coating is very important. Such a film must be hard enough to be protective and have other desirable physical qualities such as adherence, durability, ease of application, and quick setting. It is counted on to provide the appearance quality (i.e., surface mode of appearance) of gloss. Various film-forming ingredients excel in various ways; therefore, combinations are often used.

When drying oils and resins were added to paint composition, the protective function of paints began. These substances are second to the waxes in resisting atmospheric changes. The oils belong chemically to the same category as the animal waxes, for instance, beeswax. The drying oils are a number of vegetable oils such as linseed and tung (Chinese nut) that dry by oxidation to a hard solid film. In oil paints the pigments are not only ground in oil as a binder, but additional oil also serves as the film-forming material. A dried oil film permanently encases the pigment particles in its glossy surface.

Resins are substances that can be dissolved in suitable solvents and will harden to a glossy film either by oxidation or by evaporation of the solvent. Natural resins are usually formed in plant secretions. Synthetic resins have practically revolutionized the protective coating industry within the last fifty years. They have made possible durable films that dry quickly and adhere to all kinds of surfaces.

Some resins are soluble in drying oils. A homogeneous solution containing such resins and oils is the traditional recipe for a varnish. The word *varnish* sometimes is used loosely as a generic name for all clear resinous finishes. Many of today's oil paints and varnishes contain synthetic resins that impart desired qualities of gloss, hardness, and quick drying. The paint or varnish vehicle must then contain suitable solvents for these resins. Such paints are frequently known as *enamels*.

Spirit varnishes contain resins that are dissolved in mineral spirits such as alcohol. Film hardening is the result of the evaporation of the solvent. *Shellac* is a spirit varnish made from a natural resin. Its solvent is alcohol. *Lacquer* is made from a synthetic nitrocellulose resin dissolved in a suitable solvent.

Instead of being dissolved in a solvent, some synthetic resins of high molecular structure can be dispersed in a medium in the same manner that pigment particles are. This produces a coating that has many advantages of application. A recent development in a dispersed resin paint is *latex paint*. A latex is a colloidal dispersion of a high molecular resin in water. It can be combined with pigment and oil to make a paint. This paint unites the advantage of drying to an oil-and-resin film with the ease of application of a water-base paint.

In addition to pigment and added film-forming ingredients with binders and solvents (known collectively as the vehicle), paints may contain diluents, fillers, driers, and other constituents to provide practical qualities. Turpentine is a diluent for oil-base paints, alcohol for shellac, special diluents for lacquers, and water for latex and all water-base paints.

Coatings are classified according to their functional uses, and paint companies have produced products that are balanced carefully to perform their specific purpose well.

1. *Primer and sealer:* designed to prepare and seal a porous surface such as plaster so that it will retain finish coats. Some sealers are especially designed to seal against bleeding by stains.
2. *Surfacer* (which may also be a primer and sealer): designed to provide a smooth surface for finish coats.
3. *Enamel undercoater:* for use with one-coat enamels in place of primers and surfacers.
4. *Finish coat:*
   a. Flat and egg shell: no gloss.
   b. Gloss paints: paints that come in a variety of sheens and are called by a variety of names.
5. *Floor paint:* designed for hard use and to counteract the harmful effect of moisture on some resins.
6. *Spar varnish:* designed for use on surfaces exposed to moisture.
7. *Paint for metal surfaces.*
8. *Stain:*
   a. Wiping stain: pigmented linseed oil in diluent—designed for use on nonporous wood or to create special effects on porous wood. The pigment percentage is low compared to that used in paint. A preservative such as creosote is usually a component of shingle stain.

b. Water or penetrating stain: dyes immersed in water—designed for use on porous wood—should be followed by a coat of diluted shellac or lacquer—the surface when dry should be sandpapered to reduce any raised grain.

c. Nongrain-raising (N.G.R.) stain: dyes dissolved in alcohol.

9. *Wood filler:* designed to fill pores in open-grain wood.

10. *Plastic wood:* designed to fill larger holes in wood.

Luminescent paints are composed of pigments plus radioactive substances (those that emit ultraviolet rays). These rays convert some of the light energy normally absorbed by the pigment to the wavelengths normally reflected by it. Thus these pigments reflect more energy of a specific wavelength than is present in the impinging light. Colorants can be made to fluoresce in the dark by being activated similarly by a special ultraviolet or so-called black light.

Subtractive Color Mixtures: Colorants

Colorant mixtures are not as predictable as light mixtures. Many factors, not always recognized by the artist, enter into the problem. In the first place, the exact physical composition of the reflected light is a factor. Likewise such characteristics as the relative size of the particles in the coloring media, their relative opacity, and their chemical activity and permanence are important. General rules, therefore, can serve only as a guide.

What may be expected to happen in a colorant mixture (Figure 7.3)? It is important to notice that the resultant color will be duller than that of any of the separate colorants present. This is due to two causes. The first is the fact that no colorant can be manufactured so that it is completely physically unadulterated. In multiplying the colorants we multiply the impurities that usually are achromatic. Second, no colorant is spectrally pure. A yellow colorant may reflect some green and red rays. A red colorant may reflect red rays plus a small amount of yellow and blue. A mixture of the yellow and red colorants reflects red, yellow, and small amounts of green and blue rays. The green rays tend to dull the red, and the blue to dull the yel-

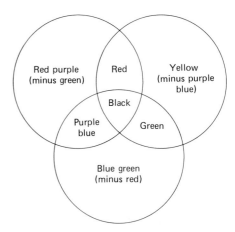

Figure 7.3. Subtractive colorant mixture.

low, resulting in an orange that is duller than either the red or the yellow. Thus painters wishing very saturated colors should use them as free from admixture as possible. Colorant mixture is always subtractive mixture.

With this proviso, the first thing the painter should do in mixing colorants is to try to obtain the desired hue. When the colorants are arranged in the well-known rainbow sequence, this should not be difficult to do, because the mixture of any two colorants usually results in the intermediate color. Blue and yellow, for instance, should make green. Here we obtain our definition for *colorant primaries*. A colorant primary is primary because it cannot be obtained readily from the admixture of any other two colorants. From three primaries any other hue can be made. At least these colorants will give the painter the maximum range of colors on mixture. The usual colorant primaries are yellow, blue, and red. When the colorant primaries are defined as those colorants that will absorb the primary lights, the primary yellow is a pure lemon yellow, the blue is really a bluish green, and the red is close to the color we know as magenta.

In mixing pigments, the painter finds that the yellow and blue combinations will make the greens, the yellow and red combinations will make the oranges, and the red and blue combinations will make the violets. If red is then mixed with the combination of the yellow and blue (the green), a darkish grey is secured. Theoretically this color should be a black, but impurities in the pigments make the obtaining of a good black unlikely. In other words, a combination of all three of the primary colorants is capable of absorbing all of the light rays. Every colorant added to another colorant subtracts more of the total rays, and when these colorants are capable of supplementing one another to subtract all the rays of visible light, the sensation of black results. Black as a color exists whenever the amount of light reflection is exceedingly small compared to that of the surroundings.

One can understand why the mixture of colorants is known as subtractive color mixture. It is because colorants selectively subtract (or absorb) light. This is the negative side to their positive reflection of light. Any two colorants that when mixed in the proper amounts subtract all of the visible light rays are said to be *complementary colorants*. Inasmuch as a saturated colorant absorbs the light ray that is complementary to the one it reflects, it will be noted that the three primary pigments absorb the three primary lights. This fact is used in color photography, where the filters that screen out colored light are the three primary colorant hues.

Any arrangement of colors in a circle is purely arbitrary and therefore should be dictated by some type of use. A color circle arranged so that complementary colorants can be visualized quickly because they are opposite one another is called a painter's color wheel. Such an arrangement is made to facilitate the work of the painter in mixing colors.

Once we understand the principle of subtractive color mixture we know how to lower the saturation of a color to any desired degree. This is done by proportional mixture with its complementary colorant. Or a color may be mixed with proportional parts of black and white or of their admixture—a neutral grey—to lessen its saturation.

As paints dry they often seem to change in saturation. This is due to changes that take place in the indices of refraction of the vehicle during the drying process. In general, watercolor paints become less saturated and oil paints more so during the drying process.

After the desired hue and saturation are obtained in a colorant mixture, the last problem is to create an acceptable lightness. For opaque paints this requires the addition of an achromatic extender of the proper degree of reflectance. Transparent colorants can be diluted but will only be lightened if the material that supports them is light in color.

Extension of colorant mixtures in this manner presents special difficulties. When white pigment is added or when concentrations are changed, the hue is frequently altered too. The reds are apt to slide counterclockwise in the colorant circle toward violet, and the greens clockwise to blue. Moreover, when light colors ground in oil are used for tinting, they frequently contribute the yellowish cast of the oil. A black colorant may be a dark tone of a chromatic hue. When extended or diluted this basic color becomes apparent. Lightening or darkening colorants is known as tinting and shading, respectively. In this process a reduction of saturation will occur because of subtractive mixture and lessened concentration. Compensation must be made by the painter for all of these changes.

The painter should also realize that achromatic boundary reflection will weaken the apparent saturation and lighten the tone of chromatic color by adding white light. The extent of such boundary reflection also allows less internal selective reflection. This dulling is particularly noticeable when a gloss paint is illuminated by a large source of diffuse light.

Color Blindness and Tests for Color Vision

The first requirement for color perception is normal eyesight. Many persons are color-blind and are not aware of the fact. For this reason we tabulate the color defects of the eye. Such defects are possibly due to some malfunction of the cones (the chromatic receptors) that line the retina.

There are several tests for color vision, and one of the first duties a prospective interior designer should perform is to make certain that he or she is able to see chromatic color in the normal way. Nevertheless, designers who are color-blind have been known to perform well with color, although in a somewhat limited fashion.

The chief types of color blindness are:

A. Monochromatism or achromatopsia: complete inability to experience chromatic sensation.
B. Dichromatism: chromatic sensations consisting of only two hues.

1. Common forms:
   a. Protanopia: red and bluish green seen as grey—no light seen at extreme long wavelength end of spectrum.
   b. Deuteranopia: bluish red and green seen as grey.
2. Rare forms:
   a. Tritanopia: purplish blue and greenish yellow seen as grey—there is a possible weakness in seeing light at extreme short wavelength end of spectrum.
   b. Tetartanopia: the spectrum appears red at the long and at the short wavelength end but green in the middle.
C. Anomalous trichromatism: all hues are frequently recognizable but occasionally there is confusion among them.

Normal color vision requires three primary chromatic lights to make a match for any color; dichromatism requires two and monochromatism one. Monochromatism generally occurs when there is complete destruction of the fovea with attendant loss of cone function.

Following is a list of the most noteworthy tests for color vision:

The American Optical Corporation's Pseudo-Isochromatic Color Test (A O Test) for color perception, available through the Optical Products Division, American Optical Corporation. This test consists of a series of charts composed of figure and background that can be distinguished by a person with normal color vision but which are confused by a person with abnormal color vision.

The Farnsworth-Munsell 100-Hue Test, available through the Munsell Color Company. This test has been designed for the dual purpose of determining color blindness as well as color aptitude.

The Inter-Society Color Council Color-Matching Aptitude Test. This test is designed to teach color aptitude, which is the ability to make nice distinctions in color whether acquired as a result of color training or inherent because of good color vision.

Apparent Changes in Object Color

CHANGES DUE TO ILLUMINATION

With color, as with shapes, changes amounting to illusions can occur and can be maneuvered to the designer's advantage. Most al-

terations, however, happen so naturally with light fluctuations that they are scarcely noticeable and are only of importance as they help the painter visualize more interesting color schemes.

Groups of colors seem constant when all conditions of illumination change in a uniform way over the entire field. When a sight range is split, for instance, when one section is illuminated by a warm incandescent light and another with a colder fluorescent, the colors within the view become obviously altered and the result may be visually irritating.

Shadows and shades—those cut-offs of light that are found on adjoining and conjoined surfaces, respectively—are chromatic phenomena understood by painters but seldom noticed by the layman. Shadows and shades in nature are both pushed in all three of their color attributes toward the bluer, darker, and greyer. So, too, highlights become yellower, lighter, and in some instances more saturated. Often, if the light on a reflective surface is intense, the color as well as the texture of the underlying shape is obliterated and is replaced by a dazzle of white light.

If the light on an object is relatively homogeneous and strong, for instance, an intense yellowish light, the shadow partakes of the complementary color. All of this, however, the layman can leave unnoticed and know only that it serves to enliven our daily scene.

The description of one illumination phenomenon states that with greater intensity of illumination, colors differ in their ability to evoke the brightness attribute. If illumination goes from phototopic (daylight) levels to scotopic (very low), the short wavelengths gain over the long ones in their ability to evoke brightness. Red, for instance, fades quickly in twilight. If a room color scheme is to look bright under lowering illumination, green yellows or light blues rather than yellow should predominate. Yellows and their close partners owe their very life to adequate illumination.

CHANGES DUE TO THE PHYSIOLOGY OF THE EYE

Certain well-established physiological facts serve to explain our next consideration—apparent changes in object colors due to juxtaposition. The first of these effects is an example of additive color mixture. When the space or time difference separating two colors is small, they add up in the eye to an intermediate light, strengthening each other in hue if they are proximate on the color circle and neutralizing each other if their hues are far apart.

Another well-known physiological fact is that when the color nerves of the eye become fatigued, they take matters into their own hands and project a color on the retina that is the exact opposite in all respects from the tiring culprit. This projected color is known as the *after-image*. It is easily demonstrated by holding a saturated red spot close to one eye with the other eye shut and then, after an interval, looking at a blank piece of white paper, on which a bright green spot will appear—the after-image.

CHANGES CAUSED BY JUXTAPOSITION

The following phenomena should be observed carefully by the designer, who is constantly placing colors adjacent to one another and must be aware of their interactions. The illusions that occur are in strict accord with the optical laws that we have just discussed. The following, therefore, are simply exam-

ples of what to expect and to be on guard about.

Colors in juxtaposition can have their differences accentuated or minimized (Figure 7.4). This is a piece of self-evident wisdom but is an important statement nevertheless. To help in the understanding of this we introduce a diagram to which the nineteenth-century colorist Ogden Rood contributed his name (Figure 7.5). Note that one phenomenal effect takes place when we work with fairly large areas in relatively close juxtaposition. It is most strikingly seen when two colors are alike in two of their color attributes and different in the third. It is an example of after-image effects presumably due to eye fatigue. It is frequently called the *color contrast effect*.

Imagine two color circles of equal size and corresponding hue placements, the one circle of dotted outline falling slightly to the right of the other. On the circles here illustrated we observe first the effect of red on orange. On the solid circle at the left locate the two colors. Then glance at the position of the orange on the dotted circle at the right. The center of the first circle illustrates neutrality

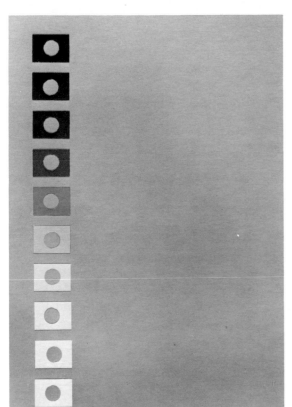

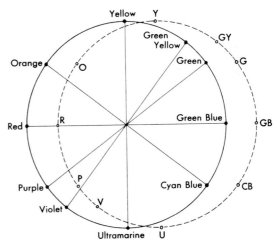

Figure 7.5. Rood's diagram: the contrast effect of one color on another.

Figure 7.4. *(left)* Color contrast effect.
Standardized papers courtesy of Munsell Color, 2441 North Calvert Street, Baltimore, Maryland 21218
In this illustration the background is kept at a constant lightness–darkness level (Munsell Value 5). The graded rectangles with the circular openings advance by ten equal visual steps (approximately Munsell Values 1 to 10) from dark to light. Notice how the background grey seems to change in tone due to the effect of contrast in values.

and as a color moves nearer to this center it becomes less saturated. Notice that the position of the orange of the dotted circle has moved nearer to the yellow of the first circle and that it has also moved nearer to the center. This illustrates the fact that when red and orange are seen together, the orange becomes more yellow and less saturated. The red would also be affected by an orange and would become more blue and less saturated. Here, for the purpose of controlled experimentation, we are keeping the red constant. This effect of contrast can be stated as a general law: *When two colors lie in the same hemisphere of a color circle (i.e., are similar in hue), they will push each other farther apart in hue and will weaken each other in saturation.*

Now observe the effect of a red on a green yellow by observing the position of the green yellow on the dotted wheel. The green yellow has moved toward green. Thus the first portion of the general law holds true and the two hues (red and green yellow) are seen to be pushed farther apart on the color wheel. The green yellow, however, is seen to be farther away from the center of the original wheel. This signifies that it appears to be more saturated when it is placed next to a red. The second part of the general law reads: *When two colors lie in different hemispheres (i.e., are very different in hue), they will push each other farther apart in hue and strengthen each other in saturation.*

Notice again that the color that red cannot displace from its hue position on the circle is its visual complement or, in other words, blue green, the color that is projected as an after-image when one focuses on red. The only way that red can alter this opposite color is to strengthen its apparent saturation. Thus the third part of the general law reads: *When two colors are visual opposites, they will not change each other in hue and will strengthen each other in saturation.*

The reason and the logic behind this phenomenon and Rood's diagram are not difficult to find if we return to the fact of after-images. Look again at the Rood chart. The after-image of red would be a blue green. This blue green projected onto orange would dull it slightly and would make it slightly more yellow. We see that the law of color contrasts is an example of the occurrence of after-images except that the after-image falls on another chromatic color and thus affects it.

When areas are sufficiently small and the eye has little time interval for adjustment, the optical laws governing additive light mixture operate rather than those for color contrast. The end product of additive mixture will be an intermediate hue and lightness with a saturation lowered to the degree represented by the separation on the color circle. Light mixture between colors with related attribute traits can produce a lively result if carefully handled.

One effect that has puzzled colorists and for which they offer no certain cause is the so-called spreading effect (assimilation effect). A fine black or white line surrounding a chromatic area seems to spill over and alter the tone of the area. This, like several other uncommon phenomena, is more of interest to a designer of flat patterns such as textiles or wallpaper.

The Organization of Colors

NATURE AND IMPORTANCE OF A COLOR SYSTEM

Most of us enjoy listening to good musical improvisation. At the same time there are few who would be willing to give up the great written symphonies or operas for transient unrecorded music. Registered music is made possible because of the standardized arrangement of instrumental tones and of musical notation.

Colors too have been placed in systematic order within this century. This makes color work easier because color interrelations are seen. If this order is carried out in any comprehensive way, it amounts to a color system.

A *color system* is an ordered but arbitrary and limited sampling of color. All colors, like all sounds, would merge into one another in a natural kind of arrangement if all the intervals were represented. When it becomes expedient to limit the color selection, the basis for choice must necessarily be an arbitrary one. That does not mean that the basis for selection should be a capricious or a useless one. Every good color system should be designed to serve some particular kind of function.

TESTS OF A GOOD COLOR SYSTEM

What are the tests of a good color system? First the color order should be dictated by a particular kind of use. Then there should be sufficient color samples chosen to make the system really serviceable. These samples must be standardized and permanent. It is helpful if their measurements can be transferred to other kinds of systems. Finally, it is most important that the system should be demonstrable in some manner that will make it convenient to employ for color work.

It should be clear at the very beginning that a color system is no more a recipe for color harmony (good color relationships) than an ordered piano keyboard is a recipe for musical composition. A good musical composition is a selection from the symmetry of the keyboard. But it is a varied and interesting selection. Given the keyboard and an understanding of its relations, the musician is helped in creating harmony. So much and no more can be claimed for color systems in relation to color harmony.

COLOR MIXTURE SYSTEMS

A color mixture system is dictated by mixtures of colored lights. Additive mixtures of colored lights are used in lighting, in halftone screen printing, and in all color processes that obtain color effects by juxtaposing small areas of color. An easy way to visualize the effects of color mixture (as additive light) is by rotating sector disks. A disk is constructed so that its sectors can be adjusted in size. When the disk is spun rapidly, the light reflected from the various sectors merges so that a single color sensation results. The percentages of the colored disk areas then become an automatic measure of the light and indicate its place in the color order system. The color obtained by disk mixture can be duplicated in colored material standards for convenient reference use.

Certainly one of the best examples of a color mixture system is the Ostwald color system. The German physical chemist and psychologist Wilhelm Ostwald (1853–1932) worked on the problem of systematizing colors during and following World War I, when an enforced absence from his daily routine gave him more free time to devote to a study that had long held his interest. His concern in perfecting a color system was associated with his thought for demonstrating color harmony. However, both the Ostwald color system and Ostwald's theories on color harmony have independent merit.

In a color mixture system, the colors of the primary lights or primary colored disks are important because they determine the range of colors. Ostwald used a near black and a near white for two of his disk sectors. The third sector was a hue that was as near as possible to a chromatic light of 100 percent purity. Any color can be matched by a suitable mixture of monochromatic light plus white light in the same manner that it can be matched by three primary lights. Therefore, the Ostwald disk sectors provided a complete color gamut. (For many years an excellent range of material standards for the Ostwald Color System was supplied by the Container Corporation of America in its Color Harmony Manual. Although this is no longer commercially available, it can still be found in libraries and established departments of design.)

COLORANT MIXTURE SYSTEMS

The second type of color system is one in which the sampling of color space is made by adjusting ratios of colorants in a prescribed manner. Although a basic knowledge of the laws of colorant mixture is indispensable to anyone who would make minor adjustments in colorant tones, it is more economical in large-quantity work to refer to a colorant mixture system to visualize the results of the major mixtures. Most of the large paint companies have compiled recipes for the admixture of their paints and have charts to illustrate the results. When these recipes provide a wide selection of colors and when they are systematically developed, they make what amounts to a colorant mixture system.

VISUAL COLOR ORDER SYSTEMS

The third and last type of color system is that in which the sampling is based on uniform visual steps. The step between any color and its neighbor should appear to be the same as the step between the next two colors extending in the same direction on that system. A color system that is arranged on the basis of visual order is basic for the artist, and the Munsell color system is, in the opinion of many colorists, the most adequate system yet devised for describing color as it is actually seen.

The Munsell color system[6] was the work of the Boston art teacher and artist, Albert

---

[6]Many informative books and pamphlets are published by Munsell Color, 2441 N. Calvert Street, Baltimore, MD 21218.

Munsell. During the years 1900 to 1912 he became impressed with the need for some systematic arrangement of color to help him in his teaching, and he devoted the major part of his time and attention to the task of perfecting such a system. Since his death, his work has been continued by the Munsell Color Company.

The Munsell system is illustrated on a three-dimensional solid in which lightness–darkness (Munsell *value*) is the vertical axis, saturation (Munsell *chroma*) is the horizontal axis, and the hues progress clockwise around the central pole (Figure 7.6; see also Color Plate 1a). Thus the directions on the Munsell solid illustrate the psychological attributes of color.

The neutral central pole of the Munsell solid is divided into nine (theoretically ten) steps of value numbered from 1 (near black) to 9 (near white). The purpose that dictated

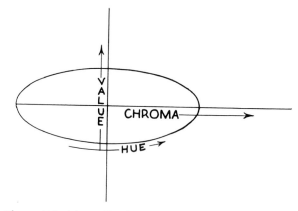

Figure 7.6. Munsell color space.
Diagram: Courtesy of Munsell Color, 2441 North Calvert Street, Baltimore, Maryland 21218

Figure 7.7. (*below*) Munsell hue, value, and chroma scales in color space.
Illustration courtesy of Munsell Color, 2441 North Calvert Street, Baltimore, Maryland 21218

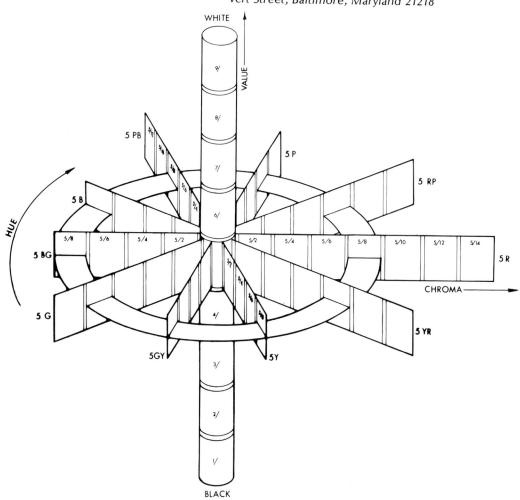

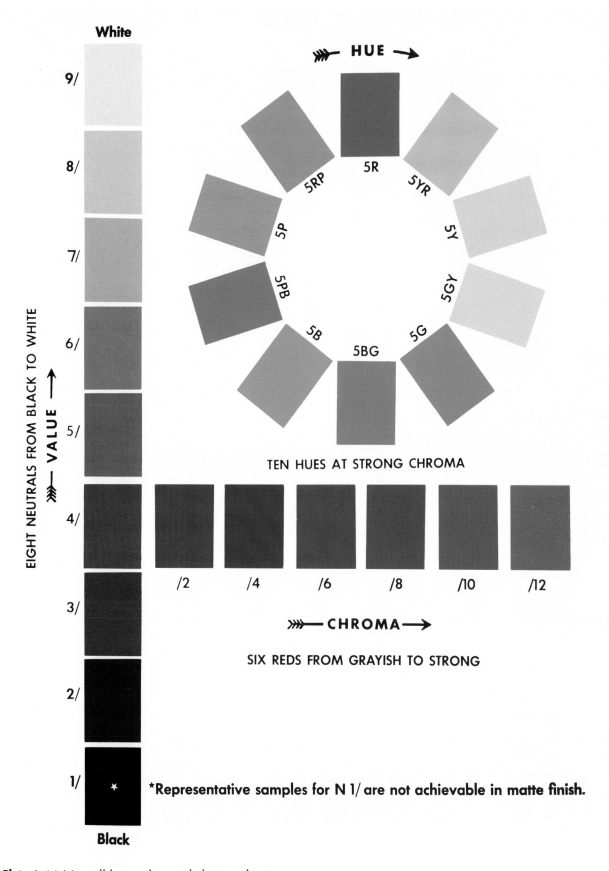

Plate 1. (a) Munsell hue, value, and chroma chart.

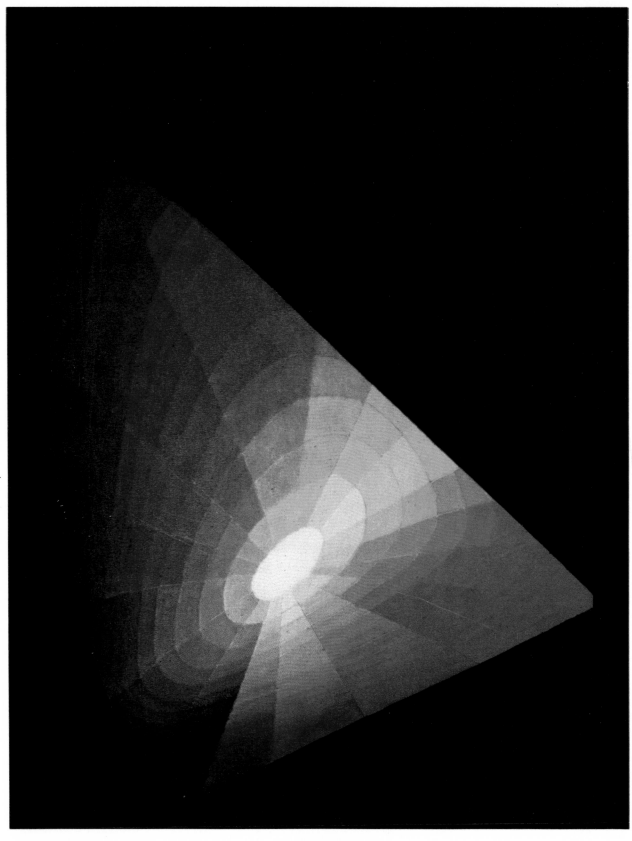

Plate 1. (*b*) The C.I.E. chromaticity diagram with colors superimposed.
*Photographs: (a) courtesy of Munsell Color, 2441 N. Calvert Street, Baltimore,
Maryland 21218. (b) from an oil painting by L. Condax, reproduced by per-
mission of the Eastman Kodak Company.*

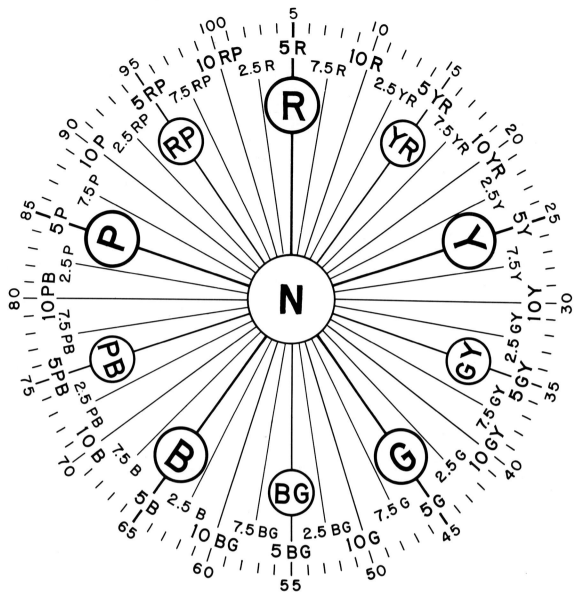

Figure 7.8. Munsell hue symbols and their relation to one another.
*Illustration courtesy of Munsell Color, 2441 North Calvert Street, Baltimore,
Maryland 21218*

their spacing was that they should appear visually equidistant.

The five principal Munsell hues are called red, yellow, green, blue, and purple. To these were added five intermediate hues that combined the names of the original hues in counterclockwise order and were called green-yellow, blue-green, purple-blue, red-purple, and yellow-red (Figure 7.7). For further discrimination, numerals are now used before the hue name (Figure 7.8). Each of these ten principal and intermediate hues is designated by the number 5. This number is understood even when it is not expressed. The numerals 1 to 4 refer to gradations that become pro-

gressively more like the designated hue and the numerals from 6 to 10 refer to variations more like the hue found clockwise. Thus 100 hue steps of the Munsell hue circuit are arranged with the purpose of having them visually equidistant. Opposite hues are those that the eye projects as visual complements.

The Munsell chroma scale (Figure 7.9; see also Color Plate 1a) extends from zero at the neutral pole out to fourteen or more steps for some of the most vivid color chips. Hues come to their fullest visual saturation at different lightness (Munsell value) levels. This is seen in the spectrum where yellow is lighter than blue. The normal lightness level of a hue as seen in the spectrum is called its spectral level. The Munsell color solid places each hue in its most saturated chroma at its spectral value level. Thus the chroma steps of yellow extend farthest from the neutral pole at value 8, whereas red extends farthest from the neutral pole at value 4.

Munsell chroma steps project varying distances from the neutral pole for different hues. In depicting saturation, Munsell first began with a physical circumstance.[7] He too began with disk mixture. Complementary

hues in the strongest colorant saturation were revolved in equal sector amounts. He found that the resulting sensation was not a neutral grey but a very warm or reddish grey. This meant that the strongest colorants of the warm hues were visually more forceful than those of the cool hues. Working with

[7]It was Munsell's original belief that one system would be found to illustrate all types of color relationships. This idea had to be abandoned, and the present Munsell system has been developed along the lines of visual order for which it was uniquiely suited.

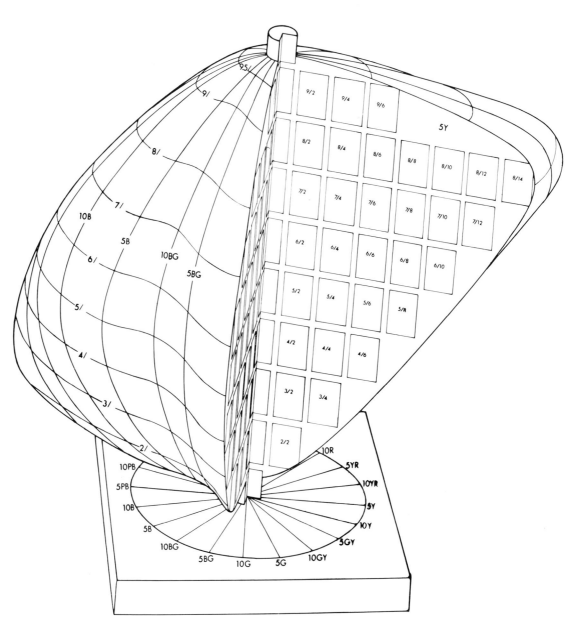

Figure 7.9. Munsell color solid cutaway to show constant hue 5Y.
Illustration courtesy of Munsell Color, 2441 North Calvert Street, Baltimore, Maryland 21218

red, he reduced it in saturation until the red sector would neutralize blue-green. This saturation was assumed as chroma 5 or five steps of chroma from the neutral axis. Visual chroma steps were then adjusted with reference to this. Therefore, the number of chroma steps assigned to each hue is dependent on the strength of the available standardized pigments in that hue. As colorants exhibiting stronger visual saturations are developed, the chroma steps can be projected farther without disturbing the internal arrangement.

A Munsell designation of a color is given as number and hue name, followed by value and chroma designation, for instance, 5R 4/14, which designates a very strong red.

OTHER SYSTEMATIC COLOR ARRANGEMENTS

Systematic color arrangements constructed for specific purposes abound. Some are more copious in their samplings than others. Although it is not practical to mention them all here, the designer should be aware of their existence and their use and should be able to see how they correlate with other systems.

Several color dictionaries are available that present an array of colors made with colored inks. Others present textiles in ordered color relations. Some of the latter give the current fashion names for colors. Popular color names are important to merchandising. Think of the verbal suggestions in "jungle green" and "misty dawn."

One color name system is that of the Inter-Society of Color Council and the National Bureau of Standards. This group publishes *The ISCC-NBS Method of Designating Colors and a Dictionary of Color Names*. The charts in this book block off areas of color that have been defined in terms of Munsell notation and to which names have been assigned that are most used by colorists and laymen. The arrangement of colors combines features of the Ostwald and the Munsell systems.

The Measurement and Specification of Color

THE NEED FOR MEASUREMENT AND STANDARDIZATION

The uses of color and the various industries connected with these are so numerous that some measurement for the purpose of intercommunication and standardization is requisite. Color measurement is known as colorimetry, and it is a large professional field that has many ramifications. The colorist encounters technical terms and meets problems of color exactness frequently, and one is better equipped to talk color language and to obtain specific results if one tries to understand the science of color calculation.

The methods employed for color measurement correspond closely to those used in the computation of light. But color measurement may go a step further and measure the light coming from colorants in terms of separate wave bands.

GRAPHS

Quantitative ideas must be conveyed in as unambiguous, precise, and concise a manner as possible. That is the reason for using exact definition, symbols, and equations. Graphs—or diagrammatic pictures explaining interrelations—are helpful. A rectangular graph showing the spectral distribution of light reflected from a green paint is illustrated in Figure 7.10.

On the horizontal axis (called the abscissa) are located numbers that designate the component wavelengths of light. On the vertical axis (the ordinate) is a scale showing the relative amount of radiant energy reflected. The curve traces a path derived from many points of separate measurement that tell what reflection factor is found at a particular wavelength.

PSYCHOPHYSICAL MEASUREMENT

The psychophysical measure of a light source is taken on an instrument known as a spectrophotometer. This measures the amount of energy given off by a light at various wavelengths compared to that from a standard light measured on a radiometer.

We now wish to ascertain the light reflected or transmitted (given off) by a colorant. Therefore, a new comparison factor must be considered, namely the reflectance, wavelength by wavelength, of the colorant compared to an ideal reflector such as magnesium oxide or a transmitter such as distilled water.

The spectrophotometers used to determine these measures of colorants are very complex instruments (Figure 7.11). The sepa-

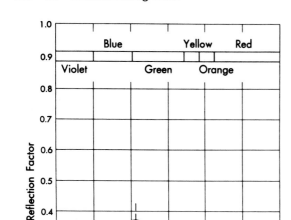

Figure 7.10. Graph of light energy reflected from a typical green paint under a standard light source. Graph adapted from A. C. Hardy, *Handbook of Colorimetry*, Cambridge: The MIT Press, 1936.

rate rays of a standard light are directed to the standard reflecting or transmitting substance and to the trial substance. A photoelectric cell registers the relative energies reflected or transmitted by each. The result appears automatically on a graph known as the spectral reflectance or transmittance graph for that colorant.

Strangely enough, after you have seen numerous such graphs you may begin to imagine that you visualize the color. Of course this is not so, for a graph is a graph, simply a black and white chart. It bears no visual correspondence to the sensation of color as experienced.

THE EYE AS A FACTOR

One of the puzzling color phenomena is the fact that two samples may look alike under certain viewing conditions and yet have very different spectral reflectance or transmittance curves. These color samples might appear dissimilar under other viewing conditions. Colors that are visual rather than physical spectral matches are known as *metamers*. The existence of metamers is a clear indication that there is more to the appraisal

of color than a spectrophotometric reading. The reason for the matching of metamers, inasmuch as it is not to be found in the physical composition of the colored lights that are the source of the stimulus color, must reside in the visual process. For source (light) plus receiving instrument (visual process or organism) always equals response (sensation of color). Therefore, a measure of visual efficiency must be added to the physical measurement to give the correct picture of a color. In other words, the photographer needs to know the camera as well as the subject to get a good likeness.

The process through which a visual evaluation of color is made is described as *the eye of the normal or standard observer*. This merely means that the characteristics of a number of normal eyes with respect to their reaction to color have been averaged, and this has been taken as the standard way in which normal eyes work.

The eye registers brightness differently for different wavelengths. It responds from zero just below 400 nm to a maximum at 555 nm and retrogresses to another zero just beyond 700 nm. This ability of the eye to evoke the sensation of light is diagrammed on a curve known as the relative luminosity curve or graph of the eye (Figure 7.12).

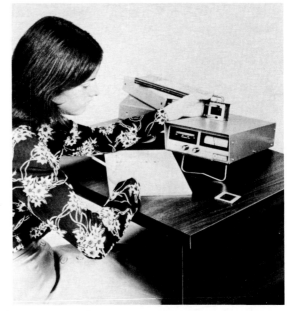

Figure 7.11. Student spectrophotometer. *Photograph: Courtesy of Munsell Color, 2441 North Calvert Street, Baltimore, Maryland 21218* Macbeth's Student Spectrophotometer is a quality educational instrument available at low cost.

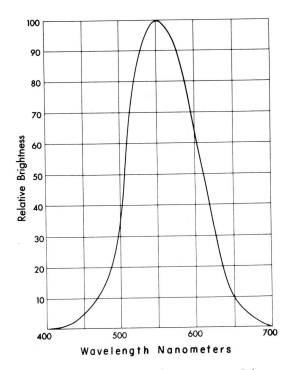

Figure 7.12. The relative luminosity curve of the eye.

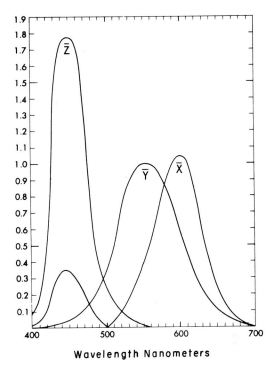

Figure 7.13. The standard C. I. E. color mixture curves of the eye, or the tristimulus values of the spectrum colors. Graph adapted from A. C. Hardy, *Handbook of Colorimetry*, Cambridge: The MIT Press, 1936.

If the eye luminosity curve is integrated with the spectral reflectance curve (SRC) or spectral transmittance curve (STC) that defines a colorant, the resulting measure will be a physical estimate of the amount of light evoked by that color by the normal eye. The word *integrate* here simply means to employ the mathematical process of uniting two graphs into a single one, and we shall see that integration is constantly an important factor in the science of colorimetry. It can be performed mathematically even in the classroom. However, it is a tedious and lengthy task. The process can be automatically calculated today as a function of an integrating spectrophotometer.

The eye also reacts differently to different wavelengths with respect to the ability to produce chromatic sensation. The measures for this reaction are taken on a colorimeter, an instrument that uses varying amounts of the three primary lights to make a visual match for any color. These amounts are known as the *tristimulus measures* of a color. If the tristimulus values are taken for a hypothetical spectrum composed of light of equal energy at each wavelength (known as the

equal-energy spectrum), they will describe the sensitivity of the eye to an interpretation of color at each waveband. The luminosity curve measures can be omitted when the tristimulus measures are used, since the latter incorporate the former (more integrating!). This chromatic sensitivity of the eye has been diagrammed on graphs known as the tristimulus specification of the equal-energy spectrum or, more simply, as the *color curves of the eye* (Figure 7.13).

If the color curves of the eye are integrated with the spectral reflectance or transmittance measure of a color, the resulting measure will be a physical estimate of the amount of the three primary lights needed to match that color. If the dials of the visual colorimeter are turned to the required amounts, the appearance of the color can then be seen.

Disk colorimetry can be used to demonstrate the principles of modern colorimetry (Figure 7.14). It requires a few carefully measured disks, a disk spinning motor, and standard lights focused on the spinning disks. One of the color systems companies can advise a laboratory about the ideal equipment to obtain for this purpose.

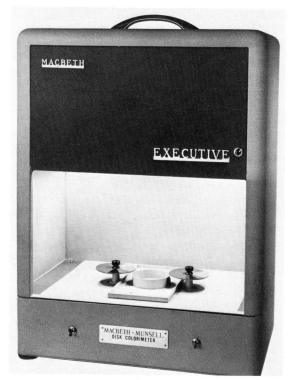

Figure 7.14. Disk colorimeter.
Photograph: Courtesy of Munsell Color, 2441 North Calvert Street, Baltimore, Maryland 21218

THE C. I. E. SYSTEM OF COLOR NOTATION AND MEASURE

The psychophysical measurement of an unknown sample of color can vary, as we have noted, with viewing conditions and with the characteristics of the eye of the viewer. Therefore, as many different correct measurements can be obtained as there are changes in these two factors. To standardize at least one procedure, the International Commission on Illumination met in England in 1931 and decided to adopt certain viewing conditions and one set of reaction characteristics for the normal eye. This recommended procedure is now called the C. I. E. Standard Observer and Coordinate System of Colorimetry (the initials abbreviate the French name of the Commission).

The C. I. E. specifications involve standard viewing conditions that are prescribed for the purpose of eliminating all distracting effects such as gloss or flicker. They specify three standard light sources under one of which a color sample could be viewed. The particular source used must be stipulated

in giving the measurement. These light sources are typical of the light under which color is usually seen. Thus light A is spectrally similar to the light from a common tungsten filament light, B is similar to noon sunlight, and C corresponds to average daylight illumination.

The C. I. E. specified the three primary chromatic lights that they used in the original colorimeter determinations. These are light of 700.0 nm (the red light), 546.1 nm (the green light), and 435.8 nm (the blue light). These primary chromatic lights were used only on the original experiments. Again, standard lights were hypothesized to straighten out certain difficulties that arose in subsequent calculating. This kind of alteration is not difficult to understand. It is a simple case of shifting boundaries on a graph so that the initial inner relations are not altered. In a sense it is the old story of robbing Peter to pay Paul. One area or quantity substitutes for another for the purpose of expediting calculations. The final color mixture curves evolved in this manner become the *Standard C. I. E. Color Mixture Curves of the Eye* (see Figure 7.13).

The C. I. E. uses the symbols X, Y, Z to represent the amounts of the three primary lights—red, green, and blue respectively—needed to make a metameric match for any heterogeneous color. The C. I. E. system uses the lowercase letters with a bar over each—$\bar{x}$, $\bar{y}$, $\bar{z}$—as symbols for the amounts of the primary lights needed to make a match for any spectrum light of one wavelength. Another way of using these symbols consists in finding the ratio of each of the integers X, Y, Z to their sum. The coefficients x, y, z are thus obtained, which represent the fractional part of the total light supplied by that particular primary light. It must be remembered in using all of these symbols that luminosity is expressed by the Y (or $\bar{y}$) evaluation. Thus the luminosity of X, Y, Z (or $\bar{x}$, $\bar{y}$, $\bar{z}$) is 0—1—0 respectively. In referring to the tristimulus coefficients x, y, z, the total luminosity Y is usually expressed separately.

The psychophysicist uses a graph on which to arrange all colors with respect to their tristimulus values. The C. I. E. Chromaticity Diagram is one such graph most frequently used.

Since there are three tristimulus values,

one would expect them to be located on a triangular graph. Such a graph was originally used by the famous physicist James Clerk Maxwell (1831–1879), who located a color on a triangle by charting the relative amounts of three primaries used to match it. The C. I. E. tristimulus evaluation of a color is charted, however, on a rectangular diagram (Figure 7.15; see also Color Plate 1b). On this diagram obviously there can be only two coordinates of a point. But if x plus y plus z equals unity, then z can always be found when x and y are known.

The point at the left-hand corner of the C. I. E. diagram represents zero percent of both red and green light. Therefore it represents 100 percent blue light. From this as a reference point the abscissa indicates the fractional amount of the red light used in making the color match, and the ordinate represents the fractional amount of the green light. The value of Y given independently indicates the luminosity. The point representing the total red light is located at the lower right-hand corner of the graph

and the total green light at the upper left-hand corner.

Perpendiculars erected at the appropriate spot on the abscissa and horizontals placed on the ordinate representing the x and y values, respectively, would locate a position for the color to which these linear coordinates (two lines that locate a point) refer. When the tristimulus coefficients of the spectrum colors are used to locate the spectrum on this graph, they take the position illustrated by the triangular-shaped locus on the C. I. E. diagram. The purples are located on the straight base line connecting the reds and the blues. The fact that even the spectrum colors are within the rectangular graph indicates clearly that the colorants we are measuring are never as pure as the standard lights.

The C. I. E. diagram of a color can give some information to the physicist even though no spectrophotometric measurements of the specific colorants are available. The standard illuminant that was used for computation is always given and can be located on the chart. Inasmuch as it approaches white light, it will

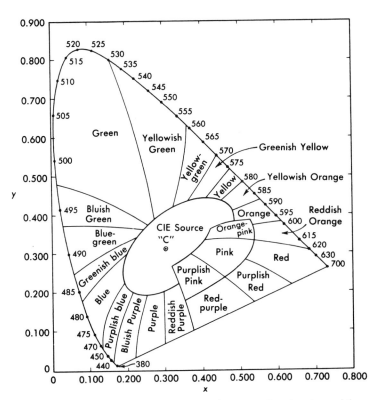

Figure 7.15. The C. I. E. chromaticity diagram. Graph adapted from D. B. Judd, *Color in Business, Science, and Industry*, New York: Wiley, 1952, p. 147.

be located near the center of the diagram, because white light is composed of equal amounts of the primary lights. A straight line drawn from the illuminant point A (or B or C, depending on which standard illuminant was used) through P (the point for the color under discussion) will intersect the spectrum locus at a point S that locates the dominant wavelength (λd) of the color. All points on this line have the same dominant wavelength. By taking the ratio of the distances CP to CS a percentage is found, which is the measure of the purity (excitation purity, P) of the sample color. Dominant wavelength is the psychophysical term that is roughly the counterpart of the psychological attribute hue, and purity is approximately the counterpart of saturation. These two psychophysical concepts denote chromaticity. Luminance is the psychophysical correlate of brightness and this can be found from the Y value.

If the line of the C. I. E. diagram connecting the dominant wavelength to the illuminant source is projected to the opposite side of the locus, it will cross the locus at a point indicating the complementary wavelength. For the greens there are no complementary wavelengths in the spectrum, although they are the complementary wavelengths of the purples.

This color diagram will also tell us something about the effects of color mixtures. If two colors are located on the diagram, their mixture will lie on the straight line connecting the two colors. The exact location on the line will be relative to the percentages of the two mixture colors. Thus it will be seen that mixtures in the yellow red range will be as pure as spectrum colors because the spectrum locus in that region is a straight line. Mixtures of greens, however, will not be as pure as spectrum colors because the locus in this range is a convex curve. The line connecting the red and violet ends of the spectrum locus is drawn straight because the purples must be made by a combination of red and blue, there being no purples in the spectrum.

It should be made clear that, although an experienced worker may be able to visualize a color through its position on the C. I. E. diagram, there is no color that is inherent in the diagram. Only through translating the diagram data to some sort of visual standard will its colors really be seen. Frequently a C. I. E. diagram is shown with the various

colors charted on it. This is an aid to the colorist but is, of course, an addition to, rather than an integral part of, the diagram (see Color Plate 1b).

Laboratory Exercises in Color

These exercises are merely suggestions to be carried out insofar as there is opportunity and equipment for this sort of procedure.

Exercise 1
Purpose: To learn to differentiate between colors with respect to their attributes. The exercise trains the eye.
Materials: A large sampling of colors in any medium.
Procedure:
  Separate the samples with respect to hue.
  Separate the samples with respect to lightness.
  Separate the samples with respect to saturation.

Exercise 2
Purpose: To recognize a gamut of hues with respect to the usual spectral values and saturations.
Materials:
  White drawing paper.
  Compass and pencil.
  A range of tempera pigments sufficient to cover the primary colorants as approximated in commercial colorants.
Procedure:
  Draw a 6-inch circle and place these hues equidistant so that complementary colorants are opposite one another.
  Letter and connect with diameters through the center.
  This exercise may be carried further, and a lightness scale can be included.

Exercise 3
Purpose: To gain skill in color matching.
Materials:
  Tubes of oil pigments (oil paints are most commonly used for interior work); a suggested assortment that would provide a good gamut would be:
    yellow—chromium or cadmium yellow
    green—viridian or chrome oxide green
    blue—cobalt blue
    purple blue—ultramarine blue
    red—cadmium red
    orange—chrome or cadmium orange
    white—zinc oxide (Chinese white)
    black—ivory black

A diluent and film-former (the vehicle), for instance, 2 parts turpentine and 1 part linseed oil mixed together.

Several oil brushes of appropriate size.

A small cup to hold oil and turpentine.

A small mixing spatula.

A board covered with foil to act as a palette.

Canvas or canvasboard.

Procedure:

Mix the pigments that should provide the desired hue (you can test on your wrist).

If necessary, dull with complementary color. Black and white can be used for this purpose. It is interesting to note the different results obtained by these two methods.

Lighten with white or darken with black as necessary.

You will note that matches are not easily obtained. Often compensations have to be made all along the way.

Commercial paint may well be the most economical starting point for securing a desired color in interior work. This exercise should teach something about the direction in which to go for modification.

If the sample prepared in this exercise is done on wallboard, it may be used as the wall color for the color plan that will be carried through for the initial project suggested in Chapter 3.

Exercise 4

This project is certainly not one that can be considered necessary or even possible in most class situations.

Purpose: To demonstrate how a color can be reproduced commercially within an allowable range—indeed, how the entire commercial enterprise of paints and protective coatings can become a large industry producing guaranteed quality.

Materials:

An analyzing spectrophotometer. (This instrument is sometimes available in the chemistry departments of universities. However, it is not recommended that it be used unless an automatic integrating tristimulus calculator is attached. The tristimulus values can be figured mathematically from the spectrophotometric measure, but such calculation is too extensive an operation to be valuable in a laboratory designed for the training of interior designers. Large paint companies often have spectrophotometers with attached integrating tristimulus calculators, and in the past they have been most cooperative in helping with this kind of class problem.)

A small sample of the desired color, as made in Exercise 3. This should be on thin canvas and should be no more than 4 inches in diameter so that it will fit into the eye of the spectrophotometer.

A Munsell reading for the sample is desirable because the C. I. E. tristimulus readings for all of the Munsell colors are available. (If the exact values are not available, the Munsell Company can provide conversion diagrams illustrating the positions of their colors on the C. I. E. Chromaticity Diagram, at the various value levels.)

Procedure:

Locate the original Munsell color on the C. I. E. Chromaticity Diagram.

Using the tristimulus values as given by the spectrophotometric reading, locate the position of the sample on the C. I. E. Chromaticity Diagram.

Note the correspondence or the degree of difference between the standard color and the sample. Would this be allowable in commercial productions? (The answer to this question must, of course, be a conjecture, but in much commercial work, parameters are definitely stated.)

8

USING COLOR
IN INTERIORS

There was a child went forth everyday,
And the first object he look'd upon, that object he became,

. . . .

The early lilacs became part of this child,
And grass and white and red morning-glories,
*   and white and red clover,*
*   and the song of the phoebe bird.*

Walt Whitman, *Leaves of Grass*

But she may well fail to find again her childish subtlety and
the keenness of her senses, that can taste a scent, feel a
colour and see "thin as a hair, thin as a blade of grass"—the
cadence of an imaginary song.

Collette, *My Mother's House*[1]

There is a close analogy between what takes place in the mind
of a military commander when planning an action, and
what happens to the artist at the moment of conception. The
former does not renounce the use of his intelligence. He draws
from it lessons, methods and knowledge. But his power of
creation can operate only if he possesses, in addition, a certain
instinctive faculty which we call inspiration. . . .

Charles de Gaulle, *Le Fil de l'Epée*[2]

The Importance of Color Facts for Use

Color facts should help us obtain color effects. Otherwise they are meaningless for us. A constant association with ordered color is almost certain to suggest color images made from that order, and a knowledge of the methods of color measurement and standardization should help us secure them. Such a background will make our work easier, since

[1]Reprinted by permission of Farrar, Straus and Giroux, Inc. Selection from *My Mother's House* and *Sido* by Colette. Copyright 1953 by Farrar, Straus and Young (now Farrar, Straus and Giroux, Inc.).

[2]Reprinted from *The Edge of the Sword* by Charles de Gaulle, New York: Harper & Row, 1960.

many of our technical difficulties will be solved.

All this is helpful but not enough. Living colors, feeling colors, imagining a world of colors, having a love for colors—this is the only talisman that will inspire and guide us step by step to success.

Master color facts so well that you apply them almost subconsciously. Study the suggestions in this chapter that may help in harnessing colors to your purpose. But never lose that passion for the most emotional of components that will only be satisfied when you create anew what you feel and see.

Choice of Color Traits

Our object is to create well-designed color groupings that will be functional and significant for an interior. For this, one must first choose color qualities that seem to assure the desired results. Let us think first of hues,

realizing that hue messages are modified by lightness–darkness and by saturation. Table 8.1 is a chart of some hue effects. It is not meant to be exhaustive but merely suggestive. Notice how the communications in color, just like those in shape, progress from those interpreted as physical, about which most of us seem to agree, through the emotional effects, about which there is some difference of opinion, to those responses that are more intellectual and that project a characterization and hence an evaluation on the color. About these last messages there is even less unanimity of judgment.

The saturation of a color will modify the impressions caused by the other color attributes. In the first place, the physical and emotional tone of a hue will be emphasized through greater saturation. Greyed colors are emotionally balanced in tenor. Black and white, being extremes of the lightness–darkness scale, confer qualities that extreme light-

TABLE 8.1
Effect of Hue

Feeling in Terms of	Red	toward	Green	toward	Blue or Purple
Physical response (effects interpreted as affecting us bodily)	Advancing Hot Loud Glowing				Retreating Cool Quiet
Simple emotional response (effects interpreted as affecting us emotionally)	Exciting Stimulating		Restful Cheerful (especially yellow)		Depressing Subduing
Complex intellectual response (projection of character-meaning)	Garish Primitive Vivid		Youthful		Regal Conventional Drab

The Lightness–Darkness Effects Will Modify Those of Hue

	Light	Medium	Dark
Physical effect	Light		Heavy Stable
Emotional effect	Cheerful Gay	Restful	Depressing
Intellectual response	Frivolous Feminine	Mysterious	Dignified Masculine Impressive Somber

ness or extreme darkness would give. In addition, they are such pure sensations that they provide an impact similar to that given by a saturated color—a sort of visual electric shock. In this they are dissimilar to a greyed color.

Colors as Visual Forces

The visual force of a color is its ability to attract our attention and thus to influence us. The visual force of colors must be appreciated from the start. Color pervades everything. If it comes forward it likewise brings objects into focus. If it recedes it creates space.

The intrinsic force of a color is a composite of its hue, lightness–darkness, and saturation. The hues on the warm side of the color circuit are advancing. The strong saturations are more forceful than the weak ones. Relative loss of saturation is one of nature's ways of making distances recede. Thus greyed colors will also seem more distant than saturated ones.

Lightness is a more powerful magnet than darkness. Distant colors in nature approach a medium lightness–darkness range. Dark trees seem very dark and white snow very white when close at hand and almost the same tone when far off. Therefore, middle tones are less forceful than either extreme.

Color Effects Due to Interrelations

As with other visual forces, color can be manipulated in a design by means of the other colors with which it is associated. The extent of a color force can be enlarged (1) by repetition, (2) by placement in a rhythmic sequence, or (3) by being opposed by severe contrast. These ways of modifying a color force may often make a less important color take precedence over a more forceful one. Because color is related to shapes, it is obvious that the magnitude of a color force bears a direct relation to the size of the area on which it is seen.

In working with color we encounter the problem of creating what is frequently called a color harmony. We use the phrase to mean a grouping of colors that will seem pleasant in ensemble. It is too much to expect that everyone will like all color groupings even though we think they are well ordered. Color preferences for individual colors are difficult

to anticipate. For grouped colors they are even more unpredictable. The emotional and consequent evaluative responses to color are so strong and closely related that some people are prone to condemn a color scheme as poor simply because they do not like it.

Frequently distaste for certain color combinations can be analyzed. Often it is due to the fact that a particular kind of color order, a particular grouping of colors, is unusual. If such a novel combination is well planned, we may expect that a general liking for it will grow. It is hard to realize that when the van Gogh color scheme of yellow and orange first became apparent, it was disliked by many who now enjoy it because they have seen it more often. Mexican color schemes combining red purples with yellow reds are still too novel for many people to give them wholehearted approval.

If we are sensitive to color relationships and have achieved a grouping of colors that is pleasing to ourselves, we can be reasonably certain that it will eventually be appreciated by others. In every phase of design, observers enjoy well-considered groupings despite their personal preferences for other particular kinds.

A harmonious color grouping will be made of colors that are related, that have something in common (see Color Plate 3). What are the various ways in which we can relate a group of colors?

By the repetition of a color attribute trait, that is, the repetition of the exact hue, or lightness, or saturation.

By an orderly arrangement of color intervals, that is, the repetition or ordered variation of the spacing between colors as visualized on a color order system.

By the positioning of colors in a design to use optical laws that will create illusions of the above.

REPETITION OF COLOR TRAITS

The first idea is expressed most definitely in the work of Wilhelm Ostwald. He said that object colors were harmonious if they contained equal amounts of pure color, white, or its absence, black. Such colors can be located on the system of Ostwald color standards.

In the language of color in psychology, a group of colors could be related by repeating the same hue, lightness, or saturation throughout. Such combinations may be located on a visual order system.

ORDERLY ARRANGEMENT OF COLOR INTERVALS

Repetition, as we know, may create monotony. The complete and undeviating repetition of an original color throughout a room would not result in the emphasis of this color in an interesting way. Therefore some change from the original color must be considered. This may be in hue, in lightness–darkness, or in saturation. Indeed, unless all attribute traits are duplicated in a color grouping, some must automatically be varied. Alteration may occur in all three attributes. In change (variation), what the mind records is the measure of the change, the interval. This is evident in the analysis of proportional relation through shapes. It is equally true in interval relations in color.

Paths through the Color Solid. All color systems are based on the idea that, in relation to some point of reference, the intervals between adjacent colors are even. Thus on any good color system we can trace paths or scales the steps of which are equidistant with respect to an ordering factor (Figure 8.1). It is excellent color training to trace paths through a color solid or to arrange colors so that their intervals of change are repetitious.

There are seven principal routes or progressions through a color solid. The first three of these can be found on any slice of a color sphere where the hue or dominant wavelength is kept constant. On the Munsell solid we could travel vertically on a path of changing value (progression 1), horizontally on a path of changing chroma (progression 2), or diagonally on a path where both value and chroma change (progression 3).

In the next four routes the hues are varied in orderly fashion. Progression 4 is a duplication of progression 1, where saturation is constant and lightness changes in an orderly fashion with the hues. A counterpart of progression 2, where lightness is constant and saturations change in an orderly fashion with the hues, makes progression 5. A duplication of progression 3, where both lightness and saturation change in orderly fashion with the hues, makes progression 6. In progression 7 hues change in an orderly fashion, but both lightness and saturation are repetitive. Similar kinds of progressions could be located on other color systems, although their repetitive and variant factors would be related to the ordering of the system.

Progression 1, where colors change from dark to light without altering their hue or saturation, is found in nature on overcast days. It is a good relationship to use when large surfaces are planned to be united as background. This might be in a carpet and wall harmony where the floor would be of darker value and the same hue and chroma

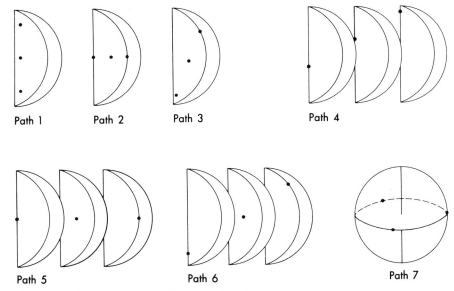

Path 1   Path 2   Path 3   Path 4

Path 5   Path 6   Path 7

Figure 8.1. Seven regular paths through color space.

(Munsell) as the walls. An example would be the use of a dark, greyed green carpet and lighter, greyed green walls.

Progression 2 is reserved for using the same hue on two different planes of attention. A wall might be a greyed yellow and a saturated yellow could appear in a picture used as foreground area.

Progression 3 is a force in directing the eye toward a lighter color. This could be used where a window was focal and its curtain was a lighter and more saturated example of the wall hue.

Progression 4 is frequently seen in nature, where hues are generally varied. This may be used in the same manner as progression 1. It introduces a little more variety and in-

terest. A darker blue green carpet could be combined with a slightly more yellow and lighter wall. In this kind of order saturations are not changed (Figures 8.2 and 8.3).

Progression 5 functions in a manner similar to path 2 but introduces greater change. It is sometimes interesting to use in a minor portion of a design, for instance, when a more saturated green is used in an enamel placed near a duller blue chair of the same lightness.

Progression 6 goes from the dark and dull of one hue to the light and saturated of a neighboring hue. It is one of the most exciting progressions found in nature. It invariably suggests bright sunlight and it swiftly moves the eye toward the parts of the design

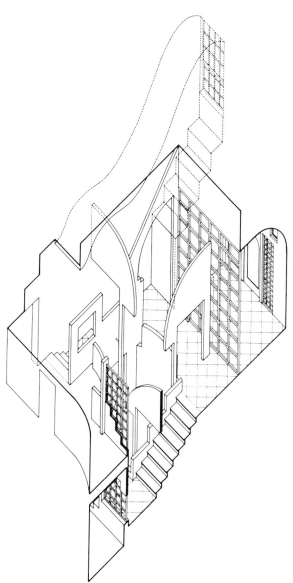

Figure 8.2. (*opposite*) Stair hall at the School House, Boston, Massachusetts.
Architects: Graham Gund Associates, Inc.
Photograph: © Steve Rosenthal
In the stair hall of this renovated Boston school house turned condominium, the architects have allowed themselves a little whimsy. Note how the area pictured here is handled skillfully so that it does not clash with the generally rational character of the apartments and the building exterior. The three arcs are painted fancifully in greyed tones of green against a background that has the same low chroma in a warm tan. There is a slight difference in the lightness–darkness (i.e., the value) of the two colors, and this appears in the black-and-white photograph, whereas the hue difference is pronounced in the actual interior. The artist conceived of the hall design as a "metaphorical garden." In reality, however, it is consistently geometric and abstracted from nature. This makes a very pleasant and interesting introduction to the living suites. (For other views of the School House, see Figures 1.4, 1.5, 1.6, and 1.7.)

Figure 8.3. Isometric view of stair hall at the School House, Boston, Massachusetts.
Architects: Graham Gund Associates, Inc.
Drawing: Courtesy of Graham Gund Associates, Inc.

that are most brilliant. In a room scheme this kind of order is very forceful in directing the eye to the chief centers of interest.

The seventh path (progression 7) through color space can be visualized on a Munsell solid by sampling all the hues at some arbitrary value and chroma level, say 4/6. The colors then become so very much alike that they can be mixed at will in one attention plane of a design. A rainbow of hues can be used as one pattern in the back-, middle-, or foreground if the intervals between are interesting and if their saturations and lightness—darkness are constant.

Progressions 1, 4, and 7 are especially useful in coordinating eye movement on one plane of attention. In progressions 2, 3, 5,

and 6, transitions between planes of attention can be made more readily. It is wise to seek some color bridge, in the form of hue, value, or chroma, that will coordinate the various levels of attention. It is also good not to attempt too much in one scheme.

The Natural Order of Colors. If for a moment we reconsider progressions 4, 5, and 6, we note that they are characterized by a change of hue accompanied by a change in either one or both of the other color attributes. In the natural phenomenon of the rainbow spectrum, the hues become lighter as they approach yellow and darker as they approach the purples and blues. This has been called the natural order of colors.

In using the natural order in a decorative scheme, first note the respective positions of the hues on a circle, with blue placed opposite yellow. Then use the color that is nearest to the blue as the darkest and probably dullest color. The others are regulated in saturation and lightness–darkness according to their respective positions between blue and yellow. This applies as a somewhat reliable guide when close progressions between hues are used. Thus a green wallpaper would be lighter than a blue carpet. When many hues are involved, problems of planes of attention and of major and minor emphases are apt to introduce considerations that would invalidate such oversimplification of precept.

As safe and usable as the natural order of colors has proved to be, a slavish following of this order at all times is not essential. Even nature shows us a blue in the sky that is lighter than the green of the grass or the brown of the earth. It may suit our purpose for sparkle or for dramatic effect to use a topsy-turvy order in our hue–lightness–saturation relations. How about a saturated vermilion (slightly yellowish red) and a crimson pink (blue and lighter red)? The Indian maharajahs often caparison their elephants and entourage in these colors. Observe the dark yellow reds or oranges used with light lavenders on many Persian miniatures.

The Kinds of Intervals. The kinds of intervals chosen in color work are very important to the securing of an effect and should go hand-in-hand with any discussion about the choice of color traits. Small intervals result in greater uniformity and quietness of effect. Wider intervals create more drama. Intervals can be measured on any color progression. Even intervals would be 1—2—3—4—5 or 1—3—5—7. Variant intervals would be 1—5—7. For contrast, intervals 1—8 might be considered.

Many texts in the past have given names to different kinds of intervals with respect to hue schemes. These names, however arbitrarily assigned, are frequently useful in color work. They afford a firm handle by which to grasp color combinations. In one frequently used group of nomenclatures we find such labels as monochromatic, analogous, triadic, and complementary color schemes. These represent a progression of color groupings, the hues of which range from small to large interval spacing. Inasmuch as it is natural to think of color first in terms of hue, we might consider these different types of hue schemes at much greater length.

Monochromatic or *one-hue harmony* indicates a group of colors all of which possess the same hue, with changes introduced through lightness–darkness and saturation. An *analogous* or *closely related hue harmony* uses a group of colors with closely related hues. A group of colors such as the purples that have varying amounts of both red and blue in their composition are very closely related. Two colors such as yellow red and red purple that have only red in common are less closely bound. Using any of these closely related hue schemes is apt to be overpowering in its one-sided emotional effect and may fatigue the eye unless precautions are taken to introduce contrast in some subtle way.

A *triadic hue harmony* is a scheme that uses three hues about equally spaced around the color circle. A *complementary hue harmony* consists of hues that are approximately opposite each other on the hue circuit. Or we could use four hues equally spaced on the hue circle, which achieves a *quadratic harmony*. The schemes that use all of the various hue sensations are often most satisfactory in a space that is much occupied. At the same time they can be more restless than more closely related hue harmonies.

The major notes on any of these hue harmonies will be regulated by some clearly expressed order found on one of the color progressions. They are like musical chords with definite relations between tones. Minor developments must also be ordered, but they need not follow the major progressions.

Relation between Color and Spatial Design

The selection of colors and their placement is governed not only by the intent to create a pleasant color grouping but also to create one that will promote all of the spatial design purposes. The artist selects and arranges so that the colors will fit into the room plan: (1) some colors will group with others on the same level of attention, (2) some progressions will direct eye movement, and (3) some repetitions will aid stability.

There are innumerable ways of doing all this, each of which will seem particularly right to the designer for a particular set of conditions. An example follows.

A decision is made to organize the background of a room by means of path 1, holding all of the colors together by use of the same hue and saturation. Assuming the carpet to be a dark yellow red (brown), the upholstery of the largest pieces could tie in with this background by picking up the same saturation of the hue in a lighter tone (tan). From there the rest of the furniture could move by progression 2 to a more saturated color (orange) for smaller pieces. Accents could begin with this strong note and pick up a triad of hues in progression 7. This would give the eye many chances for movement in color, along the background tones, in the linkages from background to middleground, along the middleground, in the linkages from middleground to foreground, and along the foreground path. If in all of these there was some additional linkage of lightness–darkness, the eye would pick up this route. If the possibilities of choice in visual channels of shapes were added, it is easy to see that the design would become vitally complex.

Spatial Illusions through Color Interrelations

The adjustment of visual forces creates effects that may be illusionary. The following are a few of the spatial illusions that may be accomplished through color.

1. To create space through color.
   Use cool hues.
   Use light tones.
   Use dull saturations.
   Keep contrasts to the minimum dictated by the necessity of relieving monotony.
   Use color rhythms to direct the eye to more expansive space.
2. To contract space.
   Use the reverse of the suggestions in 1.
3. To lower a ceiling.
   Use warm hues.
   Use dark tones.
   Use strong saturations.
4. To heighten a room.
   Use the reverse of the suggestions in 3.
5. To shorten a room.

Use any of the suggestions under 2 on the narrow wall of the room.
6. To lengthen a room.
   Use any of the suggestions under 1 on the narrow wall of the room.
7. To take away from the squareness of a room.
   Use different hues, lightness, or saturations on one or several walls.
8. To obliterate an undesirable feature.
   Use colors for the surroundings that present little color contrast with the object.
   Break up the object by color areas so that it can no longer be seen as a complete object.
   Extend the object through the use of color to make it part of a more desirable object.

Color Planning Procedure

When one has mastered the ABCs of color order, it is time to go to work, analyzing and trusting what one does, trying many ways of solving color problems, and learning from each new attempt.

You might think of your progress in this order:

1. Choose the emotional effect that in your opinion should dominate the space.
2. Consider the practical aspects of the problem. They will incorporate cost, durability, cleanability, availability—factors necessarily interrelated. For instance, unusual colors, dark ones, and colors incorporated with practical finishes cost more but may be worth the price.
3. What about the personal expressions of the buyer? In spaces intended for group occupancy this can be least indulged, and attention to average desires must take preference. In private quarters, personal preferences should certainly be considered and be modified only to the extent necessitated by the general problem. It is frequently good to allow children to choose the dominant color for their surroundings. Such opportunity makes them color conscious. It is an equally sound idea to show children how their choices must fit into the wishes and economics of the group.
4. Consider the space as a factor. Thought should be given to the unity of color schemes throughout a building, the colors of an entire plan being something like a symphony. The principal room is possibly the first movement with its statement and elaboration of the first themes. The other spaces may use these ini-

tial harmonies as points of departure, always bearing some relation to them. At times the secondary rooms may restate the first color idea in another way, perhaps adding something to its development, but rarely should they start off on new channels. The entire suite should present a unified color experience but not a monotonous one.

In dealing with various kinds of interior spaces, consider the surroundings and structure of the building, the size and integral coloring of permanent fixtures within the building, and last, whether it seems to be in accord with these defining elements or to oppose them.

5. Decide on a dominant hue. Here we must explain what this term means. It might be easier to explain what a dominant hue is not. It is not necessarily the color most in evidence. Nor need it be the most saturated color. It is the color from which all others take their point of departure. It is the color by which the relationship of all other colors is gauged. It is the starting point of a color scheme, much in the same way that a keynote establishes the tonal relations in music. The effect of this color is to be enhanced through the design. Keep it at hand for ready reference. Since we are about to embark on a chromatic journey, we must at all times be aware of our starting point because from this we take our moorings. Without it we are adrift.

6. Look at the plan or perspective of the space. Decide which elements are to be background, middleground, and foreground. Today one is liable to plan just for background and foreground or perhaps to envisage colors only as an understructure for the activities the space must serve.

7. The next decision should be concerned with the hue harmony. Do we wish to effect a close or a divergent one? A flip of the hand on a color wheel will disclose what other hues might accompany the dominant.

8. Scarcely to be divorced from hues are the problems of what lightness–darkness and saturations to choose.

9. Having arrived at some tentative answers to these questions, we are ready to progress to particulars. Here, of course, pages could be written because in all color work, indeed in all interior design, myriads of solutions suggest themselves. Select one and follow it consistently.

10. Consider the floor treatment first. Flooring is one of the most expensive items in furnishing. It has the hardest wear. It is the most difficult to change. It is more pervading in its color potential than any other feature.

We can assume the most common plan of placing the darkest shade on the floor. This gives the greatest sense of stability. If any hard material like slate, tile, or wood is to be used, keep it dark and neutral. Place on top of the foundation floor a dark carpet in the range of Munsell 1 to 5, chroma 1 to 6. The hues would be the bluest of those chosen.

However, don't by any means consider this the only solution. Possibly a light ivory rug would offset darker values elsewhere. Figure what you want that floor to do in your color planning and act accordingly.

11. Choose the wall color or colors. The hue may be the same as the carpet or it may be any other of those selected. The usual thinking will place it in the middle-to-light range, Munsell value 5 to 8. The saturation would be the same as the carpet. Wall arrangements sometimes use several hues and values within one space. This might be considered under certain conditions in order to divide space.

12. The wood trim may be in the same tone as the walls. In many cases the designer must decide whether to use a natural wood or metal structural trim as it stands or modify it. Just a few things to think about. Don't change any beautiful woodwork. Rather, if it was originally part of the room schema, give it prominence. If necessary, change only its tone, preserving its grain by means of the appropriate use of stain. If white trim is proposed, do not forget that it immediately becomes a very saturated note or theme and be certain that it is not destroying other values.

13. The ceiling demands some attention. If the space is under 8 feet in height, it will probably be most satisfactory to paint the ceiling off-white. With low ceilings, either a saturated hue or a very dark tone will cause uneasy eye movement. If such solutions are selected, they can be balanced and hence become less insistent through eye-attracting floor treatment. On occasion, midnight blue in a ceiling can become like the night firmament—receding.

14. What about the window treatment? If a quiet effect is desired, duplicate the hue of the carpet, walls, or trim for the background of the

draperies. The choice of the same hue as the walls will give the most restful effect, and a repetition of the tone of the walls will combine the two elements visually. Remember: repetition and variation align; contrast separates.

15. Now, the main furnishings. Older schemes planned the hues to correspond to floors and walls, possibly adding a third that would be dictated by the hue plan. Today furnishings more frequently use one hue, possibly in the unsaturated range. This could be an ivory, a light blue or a green. In some instances a very dark example of these is dramatic.

16. Plan the foreground colors, those to be found in small chairs, pictures, drapery patterns, and accessories. The hues will be a repetition of those used or they will be an orderly variation from these. The tones will be those that fit neatly into the well-established tonal patterns. The saturations can be strong.

17. Place swatches of the colors on the preliminary room sketch. Observe how they rate in integrating the room design. Do this before purchasing, because at this stage it is possible to make changes without cost.

18. If some fortuitous advantage of the marketplace indicates the need for a shift in colors, shift all of the colors to the same degree. For instance, you may have placed your dominant hue on the walls and then find that the available paints are slightly more red-purple than you had wished. Feed that into the computer and search for a whole new gamut of related colors by shifting, in this case, the hue circuit.

Color Design Examples

A Restful Living Area

Space	Hue	Value (lightness–darkness)	Chroma (saturation)
Upholstery	PB—purple-blue	5—Medium	6—Moderate
Wood	YR—yellow-red	4—Medium	2—Weak
Carpet and wall	Y—yellow	8—Light	4—Moderate
Accent 1	YR—yellow-red	7—Light	8—Strong
Accent 2	GY—green-yellow	Various	Various

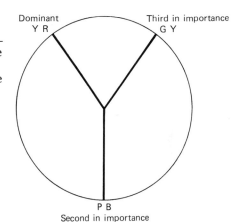

Dominant
Y R

Third in importance
G Y

P B
Second in importance

Medium to light values
Weak to strong saturations

The emotional effect desired here is one of dignified and reserved friendliness. Perhaps this is the home of a mature couple, a retired banker and his wife. The latter is very fond of blue and so wants to use it for the dominant hue. Moreover, old Dutch blue tiles line the fireplace, each tile depicting an indigenous herb, of which plants she is a notable cultivator. She selects a soft blue quilted chintz of a medium lightness for the upholstering of a davenport and two major chairs. The chair for the husband is in a light-toned tweed that combines the blue with a predominance of warmer hues. (We note that Mr. B wears brown and rust shades.)

The house, although contemporary in its outspoken emphasis on wooden-beam structure, does not have large windows. They are, however, sufficiently sizable to create a sunny aura, and they possess a beautiful dark wood surround. In those that are casement, the panes are fastened with leaded strips, an unusual but texturally lovely indulgence. No curtains have been used, thus the window frames are displayed to advantage.

The base floor is dark stained quartersawed oak. An ivory colored rug echoed in the wall color lightens the entire ensemble.

Accent hues are found in the subtle patterns of chintz and threads of tweed. These are in apricot, rust, and tones of green.

This is basically a complementary hue color scheme, with relief from the adjacent hues. A glance at the chart shows how values and chromas fit into the pattern in its entirety, interlocking various paths.

A Dramatic Lounge in a Country Club

Space	Hue	Value (lightness–darkness)	Chroma (saturation)
Wall and carpet	2.5 G—green with some yellow	Darkish	Strong
Wood and background of draperies	White	Light	Strong
Pattern 1	10 RP—red with some purple	Medium	Strong
Pattern 2	2.5 G—green with some yellow	Dark	Strong
Pattern 3	10 Y—yellow with some green	Light	Strong

Our second color scheme is more stimulating. It uses strong contrasts in hues and eye-arresting color traits. We can imagine a small room in a country club that is planned for sparkling occasions. The woodwork, fireplace, and furniture are painted white. White always gives the emotional effect of a strong saturation. Draperies are chosen with a white background on which bouquets of saturated cherry red, green, and yellow flowers are splashed. The textile artist will have enlivened these with darker greens and some variant hues. The principal chairs have green or red seat coverings. The chart of the room, a complementary hue harmony, indicates contrasts in values and strength in chroma.

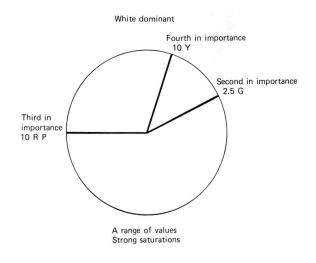

A House of Steel and Glass

Space	Hue	Value (lightness–darkness)	Chroma (saturation)
Walls and curtains	2.5 YR—red with some yellow	Light	Weak
Floor	2.5 YR	Dark	Weak
Upholstery	YR—orange	Medium	Moderate
Traverse screen	2.5 RP—purple with some red	Dark	Moderate
Glass	7.5 PB—blue with some purple	Medium	

This is a plan in which the lightness–darkness of the colors is the most important consideration. The walls must be just off-white and could be slightly warm in hue. The color must be very much greyed and not just an admixture of white paint with yellow-red. The curtains are the same. They will be pulled back generally and only traversed for privacy. The flooring is the same hue but almost black, and the leather upholstery on the steel chairs can be similar and lighter in value. The only accents are dark. One is a ceiling track that houses a drapery that would shut off the dining area. When not in use, it folds back along a corner of the dining space. This has blue and red threads interspersed, which add to the mingling of the secondary hues. Between two of the windows onto the court is a nar-

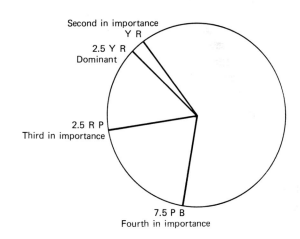

row clear glass panel in the purple-blue tone. In front of this might be placed an off-white piece of sculpture. One large painting diagonally opposite the ceiling drapery could pick up colors similar to it. These accents, the only ones, are spaced to direct the eye toward the rich greenery of the patio.

One interesting thing about a suite of this sort is that it could be altered easily without doing damage to the plan. For instance, the floor and/or the upholstery might well be in an almost black tone of any of the hues. This would fall into the conceived contrasting value scheme.

A Contemporary Wood or Masonry Structure with Much Glass

Space	Hue	Value (lightness–darkness)	Chroma (saturation)
Floor and rug	Green	Medium to dark	Weak
Walls and curtains	Green	Medium to light	Weak
One wall	Purple blue	Very dark	Weak
Upholstery	Red or any other hue	Dark to medium	Weak
Accents	Red	Dark	Strong

This might be a house, a library, or an office executive suite. The hues are basically green and crimson. One wall is of charcoal purple blue; its dark value is repeated in the room. This wall might as easily be charcoal brown (yellow red) if a warmer room is desired. It must be deep, deep.

Draw curtains are used that are similar to walls. In public areas they could be wood or some type of vertical blind.

This entire interior should provide a quiet atmosphere similar to that of one type of oriental interior. The hues and even the value placements are not as important as the low saturation of all.

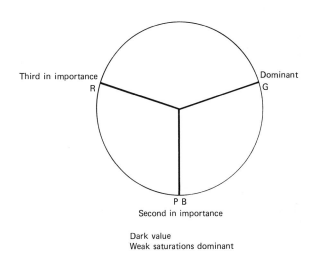

Third in importance R

Dominant G

P B
Second in importance

Dark value
Weak saturations dominant

Summary

It is hoped that several conclusions can be derived from the foregoing pages. One is that color enjoyment can be found in sensitive observation of muted groupings as well as in those that advance full force.

Second, it must be learned that in creating color designs for different purposes, interior designers cannot be limited to groupings that may particularly please themselves. This is the prerogative of the artist painting a canvas, but not of the one who must be oriented toward a world that is particularly demanding.

Third, it is true that after one settles on a dominant color the choice of which is the result of many factors, the resolution of completing the color design can wander in many directions. The colors added to the first may greatly increase its charm. However, they must preserve some order in relation to the dominant tone, and within the plan not many things can operate successfully at once.

Do not be afraid to use color. The opportunities are legion.

9

UNDERSTANDING TEXTURE

For texture has a unique dimension. The particular rhythm of light and dark that makes up visible texture is beyond our ability to distinguish in any form of visual organization in terms of modelling by shading. It has a fine grain of sensory impact which can be comprehended only in its structural correspondence to other sensory feelings. The surface texture of grass, concrete, metal, burlap, silk, newspaper, or fur, strongly suggestive of the qualities of touch, we experience visually in a kind of intersensory blend. We see, not light and dark, but qualities of softness, coldness, roughness, restfulness—sight and touch are fused into a single whole.

Gyorgy Kepes, *The Language of Vision*[1]

A white lace curtain on the window was for me as important as a great work of art. This gossamer quality, the reflection, the form, the movement. I learned more about art from them than I did at school.[2]

Louise Nevelson, *Dawns and Dusks*

The Meaning of Texture

The word *texture* comes from a Latin root meaning *to weave*. From this is also derived the word *textile*. Today we speak of texture in a broader sense. We refer to the texture of wood and say that oak is coarse whereas satinwood is fine. We refer to iron as being rough and silver smooth. What do we really mean by these phrases?

One aspect of texture refers to the structure of a material—the way in which it has been built from the microscopic particles to the mass. In wood, for instance, the structure is fibrous. A microscopic study can help the artist appreciate the potentialities of a material.

[1]Chicago: Paul Theobald & Company.
[2]New York: Scribner's, 1976.

Texture more frequently refers to the outer surface of material. Its qualities may be those that are the natural expression of the inner structure or a modification of these. Thus silver has a silvery grey metallic lustre that reveals its inner character. The silversmith may give it a highly polished surface or may hammer the surface and make it rough. The weaver may take advantage of the long silk filament with its natural lustre and produce a diapered cloth on which the textural reflections are tiny diamond shapes. Surface textures are most lovely when they are developments of inner structures.

The Intersensory Character of Texture

The tactile sense is used in an appreciation of textures. Touch is nature's most elemental sense. Through it the earliest living forms recognized danger and food and thus survived. We are told that the tactile sense is probably the last to depart. Nurses know that pleasant sensations from smooth sheets, soft blankets, and thin china are very satisfying to the invalid.

Impressions of texture are conveyed through the eyes as well as through the skin (Figure 9.1). We see light and shade and the

Figure 9.1. The intersensory character of texture.
Ceramic sculpture: "Loon," Thelma Frazier Winter
Textile: Dorothy Turobinski
Photographer: G. C. Ball
The aesthetic enjoyment provided by texture is particularly rich because several senses convey the message. In this example, the soft, rough feel of the textile contrasts with the hard, smooth ceramic; the similar yet different patterns of the light breakup make a counterpoint with each other. All this together creates a well-designed grouping that is in harmony with the proud bearing of the untamed loon.

indefinite pattern that characterizes a texture. It is through sight that textures acquire a lively quality. The surface of wood grain changes with the angle of view. Patterns of light and dark become moving rather than static.

Texture is also appreciated through kinesthesis. The weight of a material, its hardness—these are qualities determined through the use of our muscles.

Some textural qualities seem to require several senses for their comprehension. A coarse texture that has large particles in its structure gives a sensation of being heavy and rough. An open texture appears lighter in weight than a close-knit one. A highly reflective texture suggests smoothness to the touch.

Texture is the way a material feels, the way it looks as though it would feel, the way our minds interpret an inner structure from its appearance and feel.

Because the sense of texture represents an intersensory blend, a developed textural sense is very sophisticated. It is essential to the work of the interior designer.

Texture as the Basic Component

When we say that we see textures, the statement is different from that made in the previous chapter about the artist feeling colors. The first is a matter of fact; the second is phenomenal. There is a certain amount of poetic license, however, in the statement that texture is an intersensory blend. To the artist, texture in a very appreciable manner coils its tentacles around objects, dictating the manipulation of the medium, the scale of masses and voids, the colors and finishes. The sensitive artist works through textures from the beginning to the end of the finished product. It is doubtful whether this grip on the sensibilities would be so strong were not many senses engaged.

Moreover, the artist knows, again possibly through many messages, that texture can act as an interface between diverse expressions (remember the two lists in Chapter 4?). For instance, he or she may use fine, glazed cotton chintz with a large pattern on a heavy pine chair. The cotton is quilted to correspond visually to the felt weight of the furniture. In this way a world of refinement can be united with one of vigor.

Space and time are basic because we are creatures of action; color is basic because we have emotions; texture touches our many sensations and through them our mental conceptions.

The Quality of Material

Quality in a material is the result of its intrinsic textural nature and of the way in which this has been developed by both the craftsman and the visual artist.

What is good, better, and best in intrinsic textural quality? The standards for evaluation must be made in relation to some desired result. One result might be its suitability for a certain physical use. Thus mahogany has a texture that is good for carving. It is better than oak for this purpose because it is softer. Another measuring stick for a texture is its suitability in certain design relations. Thus leather has a texture that, because of its sheen, may align itself with metal furniture. And, again, we can evaluate a texture because of its expressive qualities, for instance in the way that softness suggests femininity.

Beyond all this, the phrase "good-quality material" implies that a substance has been developed in propitious surroundings. A fine-quality oak will grow tall and straight because its growth has been in an open expanse. Finesse of handling by artist and craftsman also contributes to the ultimate worth of goods. It may turn a rough diamond into the Kohinoor.

It is evident that a good-quality material will cost more than a poor one of the same type. The rarity of natural conditions favorable to growth, the skill and time required to duplicate these conditions, and the wages of labor involved in processing a material are all contributing factors to its worth. Moreover, these conditions make some kinds of materials cost more than others: silks are priced higher than cottons.

When artistic handling is given to quality materials, the product is invested with an aura of preciousness. The practical Cinderella of today realizes that she will have to wait for a fairy godmother before acquiring some such precious materials. In the meantime she is secure in the knowledge that there are ways with cottons and with plastics and with silks, and that each would lose if it were to deny its own potentialities. It is better to do well with pewter than to do poorly with silver. We are wise to remember Polonius's advice to Laertes to let his standard of worth be "rich not gaudy."

The Attributes of Texture

The successful aesthetic handling of any component depends on a sensitivity to its attributes. Because the component texture has so many facets, few comprehensive listings that systematize textural traits have been made. Some lists relate the physical qualities of a texture to its aesthetically apprehended qualities. Other lists classify in terms of qualities perceived through various senses.

It is difficult to describe a material with respect to its attributes unless one knows what weight of the material is intended. A steel beam and a steel wire have certain likenesses, but they also have certain differences. It is similarly difficult to find a basis for comparing different kinds of objects. What characteristics would be common to the texture of an oak table and a linen drapery?

The solution to the problem of thinking clearly about texture lies in dealing with one sensuous aspect of texture at a time. Table 9.1 consists of lists that attempt to classify textures and suggest their expressive qualities.

In describing materials, it is apparent that some of the words we use designate a combination of qualities. For instance, sheerness suggests lightness and openness; crispness suggests lightness and firmness. It is indeed difficult to describe some textures without resorting to words that defy analysis and that are compounded of several meanings.

Textural traits are especially capable of conveying complex mental characterizations. How easily a room can acquire a feeling of elegance, of honesty, of simplicity through texture. To this list may be added other character terms. Notice how our language has words for them—homespun naturalness, polished refinement, ingrained sensitivity, coarse-grained vulgarity, and rugged individualism. Such words suggest that through texture similar qualities may be expressed.

It is this powerful ability of texture to convey qualities of character that makes textural choices such an index to taste. Taste is really the ability to select good-character qualities and to make them explicit through good art.

Texture Design

The choice of a dominant texture for a room should be made after careful consideration of function, expression, and the existing design character. This decision is complicated by the fact that the expressive character of many delicate-appearing contemporary materials belies their practicality.

A room's dominant texture can be strengthened by a textural grouping the members of which have family traits. Even contrasting textures should possess some points of similarity. For instance, they may be harmonious in weight even though they differ greatly in light reflection.

Textures are part of the shapes to which they belong. Therefore, textural affiliations may begin with an attribute that can relate them to shapes. This could be size with its suggestion of weight.

A textural grouping to use with heavy oak furniture may serve as an example. Oak has relatively coarse fibers and large pores. Linen is the heaviest of fibers, so a coarse linen may be a good choice for a cloth to combine with oak.

As a substitute for the linen, fabrics could be chosen that appear heavy even though made of finer fibers. Cloths that are compact, or thick, or that have uneven yarns may answer. Sometimes a pattern applied to a fabric will give it a heavier appearance. Colorful, closely drawn designs give this illusion of weight.

Once a certain weight relationship is established, light reflection should be considered. If a hand-blocked linen were chosen for the draperies, its reflective character would be constant and luminous. It would be coarse, compact, stiff, and slightly rough. But now the woods and the textiles are too similar in texture. Like the old game of fine and superfine, what should the owner do to redeem them?

A couple of chairs may be upholstered in leather. Here is a heavy material that is as stiff and unbending as the linen. However, it reflects more light and, because of the natural unevenness of its pores, the light reflections from it are somewhat changeable.

Note that both the linen and the leather are relatively cold to the touch. What does the room now need? Certainly some fabric from which the light is deeply reflected. This is particularly true because oak itself, a rela-

TABLE 9.1

	Physical Expression	Expressive Character
Attributes Appreciated Primarily through Touch—The Feel of Material		
Surface contour		
Uneven	Roughness	Crudity
Even	Smoothness	Refinement
Surface friction		
Harsh		Brusqueness
Slippery		Slickness
Thermal character		
Hot		Friendliness
Cold		Austerity
Attributes Appreciated through Kinesthesis		
Compressibility (resistance to pressure)		
Hard	Rigidity	Masculinity
Soft	Plasticity	Feminity
Flexibility (resistance to bending)		
Stiff	Unbending	Severity
Pliable	Yielding	Grace
Weight (resistance to lifting)		
Heavy	Strength	Stolidity
Light	Delicacy	Imaginativeness
Attributes Sometimes Called the Hand of the Material— The Reaction to Handling		
Elasticity (reaction to stretching)		
Elastic		Uncertainty
Inelastic		Stability
Firmness (tendency to resist change of internal position)		
Firm		Substantiality
Sleazy		Fraudulency

tively open-pored wood, has deep light reflections.

Then there is need to introduce the characteristic of softness and perhaps a note of relative sheerness. A textured rayon or synthetic gauze at the window for glass curtaining may seem right. And so on, down the list of needed textiles one goes, never deviating too far from those characteristics that are basic to the texture-establishing woods but frequently using some variety and even some contrast for interest.

A textural grouping with mahogany (Figures 9.2 and 9.3) might be considered in the following manner (exact materials may be filled in after a study of textiles—similar harmonies for walnut, pine, and other commonly used woods are good textural exercises):

Wood: mahogany—medium heavy—fine grain—when given a rubbed-down varnish finish the light is highly reflected and is changeable due to figure in wood.

Carpet: wool pile of fine yarn and good quality—repetition of luster and lively character of light reflections due to resilient nature of fiber.

Upholstery: caning—repetition of lightness and finish of wood.

Cottons with firm weave, sometimes with glazed finish—repetition of fineness and luster.

Woven patterned materials—accentuation of changeable character of light reflection.

Fine-yarn pile fabric—repetition of depth reflection of carpet while keeping in family of weight and fineness.

TABLE 9.1 (*Continued*)

	Physical Expression	Expressive Character
Resiliency (tendency to return to position after deformation)		
Resilient	Liveliness	Youthfulness
Nonresilient	Lifelessness	Age

Attributes Appreciated through Sight

	Physical Expression	Expressive Character
Amount of reflection		
Shiny	Activity	Ornateness
Dull	Passivity	Simplicity
Continuity of specular reflection		
Changeable	Liveliness	Restlessness, flashiness
Constant	Lifelessness	Restfulness, constancy
Depth of reflection		
At the surface	Brittleness	Ostentation
Deep	Warmth	Luxury

Attributes Appreciated through Several Senses

	Physical Expression	Expressive Character
Size of structure		
Coarse	Heaviness, strength	Crudeness
Fine	Lightness, delicacy	Refinement
Density of structure		
Compact	Sturdy	Trustworthiness
Open	Airy	Ethereal

Nubby yarn—occasionally introduced in firm cloth to provide the contrast of softness.

Drapery: full-hanging gauze of raw silk yarn—addition of sheerness and crispness with irregular light reflections.

After securing a textural harmony (Figure 9.4), it should be arranged to aid the design. This means the ordering of textural forces. Intrinsic textural force may be found in extremes of rough and smooth textures (Figures 9.5 and 9.6). The first will attract because of the contrasts of surface and the second because of the amount of light reflection. Any texture will be made more forceful when it is incorporated in a rhythmic sequence or if it is contrasted with its textural surroundings.

Modern decoration places a great deal of emphasis on texture, but this emphasis frequently goes no further than an interest in conspicuous textures. The fact that textural harmonies can be highly developed in a room often is not recognized. Rhythms might be set up by gradually increasing the unevenness of surfaces or by gradually approaching a more highly reflective surface. A shiny texture on a small chair may give it the importance necessary to balance a large one with average reflection.

Textures can be used to create illusions. Forceful textures gain attention and thus increase the apparent size of objects. When there is reason to accomplish the reverse and increase the effect of space, you should steer a middle course between shiny, sleek textures

Figure 9.2. McGranahan house, Fox Chapel, Pittsburgh, Pennsylvania.
Architect: John Pekruhn
Photograph: Joseph Molitor Photo
The architectural details and finishes used in this building are not too coarse to blend with the use of fine-grained mahogany in the interior.

Figure 9.3. A textural grouping that works well with mahogany. Residence of Mr. and Mrs. R. D. McGranahan, Fox Chapel, Pittsburgh, Pennsylvania.
Architect: John Pekruhn
Photograph: Joseph Molitor Photo
It is frequently difficult to envisage fine eighteenth-century mahogany furniture in a contemporary architectural setting. Here the wall and ceiling finishes and the softness and depth of carpet and upholstery serve to overcome any harshness. The textiles are chosen carefully in relation to the size of the furniture and to the natural setting of the room. Reflections from ceramics, glass, brass, and fine leather echo the light from the wood.

154

Figure 9.4. A carefully designed textural harmony. Lobby of the Seagram Building, New York.
Architects: Mies van der Rohe and Philip C. Johnson
Photograph: Ezra Stoller © ESTO
This lobby illustrates some of the very best textural designing. To appreciate thoroughly the thoughtful planning, try to visualize the space if the walls were polished marble instead of the travertine used here which, although hard and fine grained, nevertheless possesses pores that give it just the right amount of change from the gleam of the polished steel surround. Even the floors have a lustrous rather than a highly reflective finish. Everything is hard and linear, but these qualities are given relief through subtle variations.

and rough, irregular or deep-pile varieties. Materials should be fine grained with a moderate amount of textural interest. Select furniture with a good bit of exposed wood. Choose upholstery fabrics with firm grain. A few highly reflective articles are appropriate.

One textural design problem—that of minimizing the apparent coarseness of architectural materials in a space where a fine textural harmony in furnishings is desired—may be solved with the use of a light-color stain applied to the woodwork. This again illustrates the fact that the senses overlap in any appreciation of designing with texture.

If one were to pinpoint a phase of contemporary interior designing that is most apt to be poorly done, it might be that of texture design. With the introduction of so many new materials, their textural compatibility seldom seems to be considered. Continued thought and training is strongly urged.

Texture and Pattern

When small shapes are regularly repeated, the parts merge and become to us not pattern but texture, that blend of tones that we sense as tactile rather than visual. This is particularly true when color values are close. As figures grow larger there is a point at which they become shapes—pattern.

The designer must learn to distinguish the fine line between texture and pattern. If this distinction is not made, one will have either poor texture or poor pattern. This subject is treated more fully in Chapter 12. The handling of the problem of visual texture versus pattern is of great importance today when designers use pattern to attract attention or combine a great number of different patterns in an interior. Although there is nothing wrong in attempting either, it requires skill to do them well.

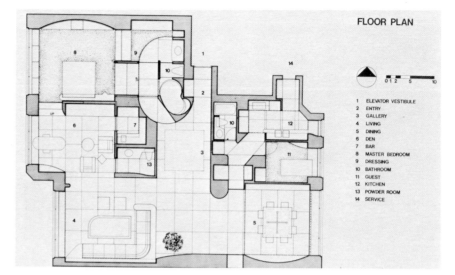

Figure 9.5. (*below*) Floor plan of a luxury apartment in New York City. *Architects: Charles Gwathmey and Robert Siegel*
Plan: Courtesy of Gwathmey/ Siegel and Associates, Inc.
This is the plan of the apartment pictured in Figure 9.6 and in Color Plates 4 and 5. Relate the pictured views to this plan and try to visualize the space relations.

Figure 9.6. A textural grouping showing high contrasts. Apartment in New York City.
Architects: Charles Gwathmey and Robert Siegel
Photograph: Courtesy of Gwathmey/Siegel & Associates, Inc.; © Norman McGrath, photographer.
Marble flooring and stainless steel are contrasted with warm-grained wood, pile carpeting, and a deep pile fox-fur bedcovering to make a dramatic study in textural contrasts.

10

THE MATERIALS OF INTERIOR DESIGN

Thus each material has its specific characteristics which we must understand if we want to use it.

Mies van der Rohe as quoted by Philip Johnson in *Mies van der Rohe.*[1]

Why should a designer have a fundamental knowledge of materials? The answer is threefold. First, a thorough acquaintance with material structure gives the designer increasing certainty about the use of materials. Second, one learns to separate the good from the spurious. And third, one begins to appraise any new and valuable substance that industry provides. Without this familiarity, some aesthetic failure is bound to occur. This knowledge is a requirement for anyone who practices the art of interior design.

Today's buildings are often constructed quite differently from the way they were in the past. The interior designer must estimate how these new modes of construction, along with the new materials such as steel and glass, have altered the effects of materials used in interiors.

And, as industry continually produces the new, so the interior designer must be able to evaluate not only with respect to use but also in relation to cost. One must have high standards within a range of legitimate prices for a particular assignment.

Wood

THE CHARACTER OF WOOD

Wood was one of the earliest materials used by man. It was used because it could do

so many wonderful things so easily. Moreover, it possesses such lovely sensuous qualities that it endears itself while it serves. It has changing color and pattern that pleases the eye, warmth and smoothness for the touch, and odor for the nostrils. A sensitive artist needs only to form wood into useful objects of artistic shape, and the wood itself will be its own enrichment. To say this is not to decry carving and inlay and finishing. It is to say that these embellishments are most lovely when they seem to enrich the natural beauty of the medium.

The knowledge of how a tree grows helps an understanding of this beauty (Figure 10.1). Wood is composed of both vertically and horizontally elongated cells. The vertical contain cellulose fibers interspersed with hollow pores through which the tree draws its sustenance. They resemble closely packed, open-ended tubes containing woody tissue. The transverse cells of similar but more compact composition are known as the rays. Their function is not clearly defined but they may act as food reservoirs or as binders for the vertical cells. A tree grows horizontally from year to year at the same time that it

[1]New York: The Museum of Modern Art, third edition, revised: copyright © 1978 by The Museum of Modern Art; second edition, revised: copyright 1953, first edition: copyright 1947, renewed 1975. All rights reserved.

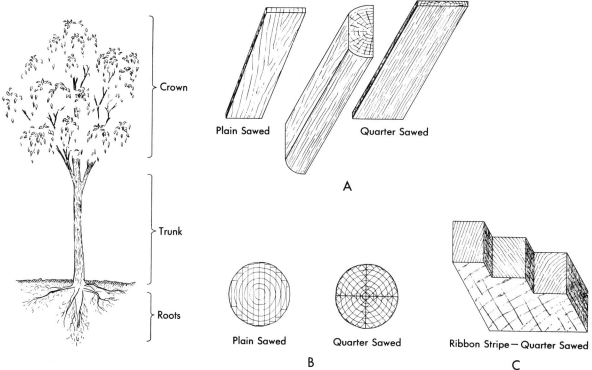

Figure 10.1. Wood grain.

grows vertically. This growth has been described as if the tree were like a huge cone on which a larger and taller cone was annually superimposed.

The outline of these cones is clearly indicated in trees that live in a climate where there are intermittent seasons of growth. A warm season will produce quick-growing large cells and a cool season will make slow-growing small ones. This difference in cell size is visible in many woods in which the more compact cells can be seen in cross section of the wood as annual rings. The age of a tree can be determined by counting these.

Figure or pattern in wood is of two main varieties. The first is that caused by light reflected from various kinds of cell arrangements and from various angles of the cells. This kind of pattern is one of the chief glories of wood, for it has infinite variety. No two pieces of wood, not even two adjacent and thin slices of plywood, are ever exactly alike. This kind of pattern varies with the observer's position, since a change in viewing position alters the angle of reflection.

The way a log is cut influences the cell configurations seen on a piece of lumber. It may be cut to produce plain-sawed lumber or

it may be cut to produce quarter-sawed lumber. In plain sawing the log is sliced lengthwise into a number of parallel boards. In so doing the saw cuts the outermost growth rings at an angle that approximates 90 degrees. This angle diminishes as the inner rings are reached until the central ring is cut tangentially. Plain-sawed lumber is characterized by large, irregular, parabolic-shaped ring figures flanked by striped ring figures.

Quarter-sawed lumber derives its name from the fact that it was originally manufactured by sawing a log lengthwise into quarters and then cutting the board at right angles to the growth rings. This creates a figure in which the annual growth rings appear as a series of stripes because the saw is cutting them all at approximately the same angle of 90 degrees. Quarter-sawed lumber is usually more expensive because less of it can be obtained from a tree. It possesses the practical advantages of less shrinkage and warpage. Both plain and quarter-sawed wood are prized for characteristic patterning.

The rays are conspicuous in some lumber and add to the pattern interest. They appear as wavy lines at right angles to the growth-ring figure. Because of its usual light color, a ray figure is frequently called a silver flake figure.

Irregular convolutions of growth rings may account for unique patterns. The peculiar structure of the tree at the place where the wood is cut can be responsible for much variety. Stump wood that comes from where the root joins the trunk contains distorted grains that are known by such names as curly or mottle.

Tree burls are large excrescences that may occur where a tree has been injured. The twisted grain of burl wood may contain a number of dark piths that are in reality undeveloped buds. The grain in oyster burl wood shows an irregular oyster shape.

A crotch figure occurs where two large branches or parts of a tree diverge. The fibers that run in forked directions give rise to a pattern which is variously called plume, feather, or crotch.

Knots, which are the bases of limbs cut off a log, show as irregular darker areas in lumber. Although possessing decorative value, they tend to weaken wood.

One peculiar growth characteristic is that of interlocked grain. Certain trees, usually those in tropical forests, often grow in such a manner that the fibers extend in a right-slanted spiral for a certain number of years and then change to a left spiral for another span. When the lumber is quarter sawed, this interlocked grain reflects light first in one and then in another direction. This patterned reflection will look like alternate dark and light stripes that taper off into one another. Hence this type of figure is often called stripe or ribbon stripe figure.

Sometimes unusual distortions of wood grain appear in a tree for no known reason. These might be referred to as sport figures. Some of these show up in plain-sawed lumber. The bird's-eye figure that occurs in some hard maples is of this type. It is caused by sharp depressions in the growth rings that show in the lumber as a series of circlets. Some curly and blister figures are similar.

Other varieties of sport figures show up in quarter-sawed lumber. These are usually characterized by areas of light and dark that seem to roll across the grain. They are often called cross-figure or cross-roll. Mottle (which may occur in other places besides stump wood), fiddleback, raindrop, and fin-

ger roll are names given to examples of cross-figure.

Pigment infiltration may cause the second major type of figure in wood. Dark streaks in Circassian and black walnuts, English brown oak, rosewood, and red gum are caused by such coloring matter.

FURNITURE WOODS

Oak, walnut, and mahogany have been our major furniture woods. Although many other woods are used today, these three are still very important, and each is used to head a list of similarly textured woods.

Group I

Oak: American white oak, which is a light tan color, has the finest grain and is not conspicuously porous due to tyloses or filmlike cell deposits. Red oak is redder and coarser. English or pollard oak is a darker brown. Characteristics of oak:

Size of structure and density—comparatively coarse, large pores at beginning of each annual ring, dense at its end
Contour—relatively rough.
Weight—heavy.
Compressibility—very little, therefore hard.
Flexibility—not easily bent.
Firmness—firm.
Light reflection—little natural gloss except in very fine grades.
Continuity of reflection—interesting plain- and quarter-sawed figure—ray figure.
Depth of reflection—deep.

Ash: light grey brown—coarse, large summer pores, more dense winter fibers—heavy, hard, and stable—interesting plain-sawed figure—rare burl of black ash (as distinct from the more common white ash) shows curly figure used for veneers.

Beech: light reddish—no particular ornamental figure—thin growth lines, homogeneous texture, takes good finish—hard but bends easily—used generally for structural interiors of furniture—frequently found in bentwood furniture and as a substitute for walnut in European provincial furniture.

Chestnut: coarse and rough—when plain sawed has a prominent ring figure—prized for worm-eaten imperfections—excellent corewood for veneering because light, firm, and stable.

Cypress, fir, pine, cedar: soft woods of uniform fibrous structure.

Elm: light and reddish—similar to oak in texture—prominent growth ring figure—English burls prized—good bending properties.

Redwood: dark red color—natural oil—burl large and prized for figure.

Group II

Walnut: American or black walnut—early varieties a dark brown with occasional dark streaks, recent varieties light; Persian, a general name for European and Asiatic trees (primarily from England, France, and Circassian district of the Caucasus)—soft grey brown, sometimes with darker streaks (Circassian). Characteristics of walnut:

> *Size of structure and density*—comparatively large visible pores. Slightly noticeable change in size of spring and winter pores.
> *Contour*—smooth.
> *Weight*—almost as heavy as oak.
> *Compressibility*—little, of a hardness between oak and mahogany.
> *Flexibility*—good bending strength, comparable to birch.
> *Firmness*—low shrinkage, highly isotropic.
> *Light reflection*—lustrous due in part to tyloses.
> *Continuity of reflection*—changeable in highly figured crotch burl, or plume figures.
> *Depth of reflection*—medium.

Apple, pear, cherry, and fruitwoods: small pores—figure confined to plain-sawed lumber. Slightly wavy darker growth ring—these take smooth, lustrous finish—cherry has the rosiest coloring of the group—frequently used for provincial furniture.

Birch: light tan color—fine even-grain wood—finely marked wavy growth rings—takes a high polish—suitably heavy and hard for furniture.

Butternut: coarser and softer than walnut, which it resembles in plain figure.

Gum: dense, fine-grain wood—sapwood stains easily, heartwood a light reddish brown with darker infiltrations—takes smooth, satin finish.

Harewood (a species of maple sometimes called English sycamore): dyed silver grey, fades to light brown—fine smooth texture with ripple figure.

Maple (soft and hard or sugar maple): uniform texture—in good grades lustrous—curly and bird's-eye patterns prized—very hard and strong.

Sycamore: use as cabinet wood limited to veneers showing small rays—frequently used for drawer-lining veneers.

Teak: fine grain—strong—contains natural oil—yellow brown color with darker brown infiltrations—some fiddle-back figure.

Tulip: a historic wood from Brazil, known as *bois de rose* because of light color streaked with rose.

Group III

Mahogany: comes from West Indies, Central America (Honduras), upper valley of Amazon, and west coast of Africa. Characteristics of mahogany:

> *Size of structure*—fine grained.
> *Density*—pores are plainly visible, fairly uniform in size and distribution.
> *Contour*—smooth surface.
> *Weight*—a little lighter than walnut.
> *Compressibility*—hard enough for cabinet work, soft enough for carving.
> *Flexibility*—less than oak or walnut.
> *Firmness*—very stable with slight shrinkage—comparable to walnut.
> *Light reflection*—high because of close, fine grain and because pores are partially filled with tyloses.
> *Continuity of reflection*—lively and changeable—interlocked grain causing ribbon stripe figure—often has beautiful crotch and swirl figures—plain-sawed growth rings not conspicuous.
> *Depth of reflection*—medium deep reflections from visible pores.

Rosewood: a Brazilian and Indian wood—named for faint rose odor—light to almost purplish brown, pigment infiltration lines of very dark brown to black—strong and hard—medium pores, many filled with film deposits.

Prima vera: a Central American hardwood from a species of catalpa—light rosy blond color—closely resembles mahogany—ribbon stripe in quarter-sawed wood.

Satinwood: beautiful blond wood used extensively in late eighteenth-century furniture—hard, close grain—figures rival mahogany.

Unusual woods such as *almique, amaranth, avodire, bubinga, ebony, iroko, lacewood, lauaan, padouk, sabicu, snakewood, tanguile,* and *zebra wood* are used for inlays and veneers.

Reed, bamboo, rattan, cane, and *wicker* are parts of long-stemmed plants or trees—can be bent in the moist state and will become rigid when set and dry. Reed and bamboo are hollow nodular grasses. Rattan is a long vinelike stem of an Asian palm that may be split for cane. Wicker is the small twig of the willow.

BASIC WOOD MANUFACTURING PROCESS

A finished wood product is made by processes such as:

Bending: bending wood grain into a permanent shape under steam pressure in the presence of chemicals.

Carving: cutting into the surface of wood, usually for purposes of ornamentation.

Chip board: made from paper pressed into boards and given rigidity by synthetic adhesives.

Impregnation: filling the pores of soft wood with resinous material to give strength and flameproof qualities.

Inlay: fitting one or more pieces of wood into another, usually for decorative purposes.

Lamination: the resin bonding of thin slices of wood to give greater strength and dimensional stability. *Plywood* is a board made by such a process in which each layer is put down with its grain running at right angles to the previous layer.

Marquetry: veneering done with small pieces of wood to give a mosaic effect.

Sawing: described under wood figure.

Turning: producing rounded shape by bringing a blade into contact with a block of wood that is turning on a lathe.

Veneering: gluing of thin layers of wood, usually figured, to the outer face of core wood (as opposed to solid wood that is made from one piece)—if well done, veneering is strong and can provide beautiful figuring at low cost (Figure 10.2).

WOOD JOINERY

Wood joinery is the putting together or joining of two pieces of wood (Figure 10.3). In observing the joinery and bracing of a piece of furniture, an analysis of the stresses must be made to determine the strength of the resulting object. Methods of joinery include:

Dowel joints: attachment by means of a peg or dowel that fits into sockets in each piece.

Mortise-and-tenon, dovetail, or tongue-and-groove joints: fitting an extension of one piece into a socket in another. Dowel and mortise-and-tenon joints are found on well-made furniture of traditional construction.

Wedge joints: inserting one piece through another and forcing a wedge into the joint to tighten it. Sometimes used on contemporary plywood furniture where the thinness of the material makes traditional joinery impossible.

Screw joints and other methods of joinery: these were formerly thought unsatisfactory but are now frequently necessary. Epoxy resins have, in conjunction with interface materials, provided revolutionary methods of joinery.

WOOD FINISHES

The finishing of wood for preservation, dimensional stability, and appearance is an art in itself. Methods are:

Sanding: to make a smooth surface.

Staining or bleaching: to alter the color.

Filling: to put wood filler or plastic wood into the pores, holes, or cracks to level the surface.

Sealing: to put on a coating to prevent seepage of natural oils or applied stains. One sealer frequently used consists of two parts shellac to one part alcohol.

Finishing: an ideal finish should protect the wood from moisture, spotting, heat, and dirt; aesthetically, it should appear to merge with the grain rather than merely being a superimposed coating. Some finishes are:

Rubbed oil—provides a beautiful natural appearance but is not spot proof or dirt proof.

Figure 10.2. Striped, quarter-sawed figure in a fireplace panel. Residence of Mr. and Mrs. Peter J. Lloyd, Moreland Hills, Ohio.
Architect: Ernst Payer
Photograph: Bill Engdahl, Hedrich-Blessing
Veneered wood paneling makes a handsome fireplace wall in this large home.

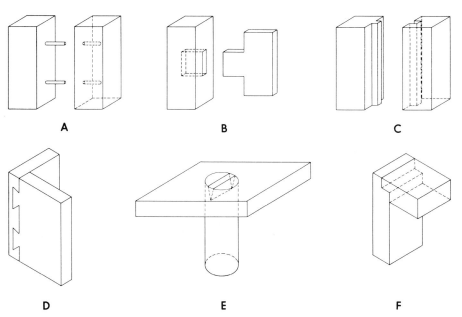

Figure 10.3. Wood joinery. (A) dowel; (B) mortise and tenon; (C) tongue and groove; (D) dovetail; (E) wedge; (F) rabbet.

Wax—provides a moisture-proof finish but is not entirely dirt proof.

French finish—many thin coats of shellac, each coat hand rubbed. Shellac may be applied in one or two coats for a less permanent finish.

Oil varnish—when applied in successive rubbed-down coatings, this is a fine finish.

Lacquer—provides one of the hardest, most economical finishes. The wood is seen through, rather than integral with, the finish.

Paint—used for an opaque finish in color.

Antique finish—a stippled application of a pigment (e.g., raw umber) in a varnish glaze, applied over paint.

WOODWORK

Wood has been a revered finish for interiors for many centuries. Because lovely veneers are available, and the contemporary style places an emphasis on natural textures, there is much use of wood within buildings today. For purposes of reference, the terms applicable to interior woodwork are:

Apron—a horizontal board set below the sill of a window or below a horizontal structural member in a piece of furniture.

Arch—a curved structural form (usually in segments of a circle) used to span an opening and support a superimposed weight. There are many kinds of arches such as the segmental, elliptical, and ogival, that take their names from their geometric forms, and others such as Tudor, Gothic, and Moorish, that take their names from the particular time or place they were used.

Architrave—in classic architecture, the lowest section of the entablature. It originally consisted of a slab or lintel that supported the frieze, cornice, and pediment. In later buildings, a flat molding surrounding any opening is known as the architrave.

Attic—the portion of an interior wall above the cornice—used in classically inspired architecture.

Baluster—a small vertical support for a handrail. A series of balusters is called a *balustrade*.

Baseboard—a board, usually with a finishing molding, that is at the bottom of a wall.

Beam—a large piece of lumber that spans a space and is used to support the superstructure.

Boss—an ornamental knob projecting from the intersection of structural members.

Bracket—a member that projects from a wall and forms a support for some weight.

Capital—the top and most ornamental portion of a column. The capitals of the classic orders were stylistically different from each other.

Casement—a window hung vertically and opening on hinges.

Chair rail—the top molding of a dado.

Clerestory—originally the upper story of a Romanesque church that was higher than the surrounding roofs. It now refers to wall space above normal room height—frequently containing windows.

Coffer—a recessed panel in a ceiling.

Column—a vertical, free-standing support for a superstructure.

Cornice—the moldings that decoratively finish the top of a wall. In classic architecture the cornice is the top portion of the entablature. It rests on the frieze and supports the pediment.

Dado—the woodwork on the lower portion of the walls of a room. It derives from the Italian word for a pedestal and originally referred to the central portion of a column's pedestal.

Dais—a raised floor in a portion of a room. Originally the word referred to the raised platform at the end of a medieval hall.

Dome—a spherical roof.

Dormer—a window projecting from a sloping roof.

Ear—the portion of a molding surrounding a door, window, or mantel that resembles an ear because it projects laterally from the rest of the molding.

Entablature—the portion of a classical building that rests on the column and supports the pediment. It consists of architrave, frieze, and cornice. In the most exact, classically inspired architecture, a complete entablature is used to finish the top portion of a wall or is used above doors and windows.

Finial—an ornamental end of a structural member.

Frieze—the central portion of an entablature resting on the architrave and supporting the cornice.

Jamb—an opening's side supports that run at right angles to the wall.

Joists—horizontal members that support a floor or ceiling.

Lintel—a horizontal piece of wood spanning an opening.

Mantel—the woodwork surrounding a fireplace. The word now refers more specifically to the shelf above a fireplace.

Molding—a narrow, shaped board used for a finish to a flat surface or to the meeting at right angles of two surfaces.

Mullion—the slender vertical bar that holds areas of window glass in position.

Newel post—the post into which the handrail of a balustrade fits.

Panel—the flat board that forms the major portion of interior woodwork. In historic work, it is held in place by vertical stiles and horizontal rails.

Parquetry—intricate patterns made from small pieces of wood, usually used for flooring.

Pediment—the triangular structure in classic architecture that is above the entablature. In interior architecture the pediment is used frequently as a decorative feature.

Pier—in interior architecture this term refers to the wall surface between windows. In architecture it is the mass of masonry, distinct from a column, that supports an arch or lintel.

Pilaster—a shallow rectangular column form semiattached to a wall.

Plinth—the lowest portion of a column, square in shape. In interior architecture it refers to the rectangular block at the base of a door trim.

Rail—the horizontal banding that holds a panel in position.

Riser—the vertical portion of a stair step.

Sash—the framing into which the glass of a window is set.

Sill—the horizontal member that forms the lowest part of a frame for a window or a door.

Soffit—the underside of a doorway, archway, window, or subordinate architectural member. Used as opposed to ceiling, which refers to the overhead lining of a room.

Stile—the vertical banding that holds a panel board in position.

Transom—the horizontal crossbar of a window or door. The term also frequently refers to a small horizontal window above a door.

Tread—the horizontal portion of a stair.

Trim—the wood finish around doors, windows, and fireplaces.

Vault—an arched covering over a corridor.

Wainscot—the name that originally referred to wood paneling completely lining a room; now it generally refers to paneling that is below the dado.

CONSTRUCTION OF WOOD FURNITURE

Much furniture and certainly almost all traditional furniture is made of wood. When made of sufficiently large pieces, most wood furniture has its members connected by means of mortise-and-tenon or dowel joinery. Laminated, metal, and plastic furniture is structured by methods appropriate to these materials.

The application of upholstery on furniture to make it more comfortable is of long-standing use, but spring construction can claim only several hundred years of existence (Figure 10.4). In upholstered furniture of traditional construction, the unexposed frame is made of thoroughly seasoned hardwood. A base of strong, interlaced webbing is tacked

Figure 10.4. Construction of upholstered furniture. *Photograph: Courtesy of Kisabeth Furniture Company, Fort Worth, Texas.*
Because upholstery covers the structure of furniture, it is essential to work with reliable companies that can be depended on to produce well-constructed pieces.

to the underside as a support for the springs. Heavy-gauge spiral springs are usual, although other shapes such as the wave form are sometimes found. Coil springs are placed close together and are attached to one another and to the frame and webbing with sturdy hemp cord.

The springs are covered with a firm fabric to prevent dust and seepage. In the past, the best upholstery padding was long curled horsehair. Other materials such as moss, palm-leaf fiber, sisal, cotton, and synthetic foam are now customary. Muslin covering is applied over the padding. After the final upholstery is fitted, it is stitched, usually with welted seams (inserted cords in a bias casing), and the whole is anchored in place by some tacking or stitching.

Cushions made with a continuous single seam are known as loose or squab construction. Cushions built up like a rectangular box are called box cushions.

There are a host of new developments used in place of spring construction. Resilient synthetic cords or webbing or spring steel bands often furnish a foundation upon which built-up cushions of plastic foam are placed. Foam rubber that can be bonded to fabric may substitute for padding and covering. Technology introduces innovations continually, often in the interest of economy and transportability.

Bed upholstery, like seating upholstery, has moved from the traditional to the simplifications found in the market today. In customary construction, steel box springs are placed on top of bed slats to form a lower layer of support. A box spring is made of a platform of wood or steel. The coiled springs are set into this frame and are attached to it and to one another. The final covering consists of padding and a firm ticking or other suitable material.

An innerspring mattress is placed on the box springs. Such a mattress is formed by units of coiled springs that are laced tightly together and covered or are individually encased in muslin pockets. A padding is then added. Mattresses should be equipped with ventilating holes to allow circulation of air within. The springs should be capable of independent action so that they can flex with the varying weights of the body.

Bed pillows are filled with down or feathers (preferably of waterfowl) or various kinds of foam or synthetic batting.

Textiles

THE IMPORTANCE OF TEXTILES

A thorough knowledge of textiles, their characteristics, their potential, and their manipulation is of paramount importance to any designer of interiors. Textiles provide the qualities of softness, resiliency, and pliancy that, along with their modification of light, color, and texture, can turn a harsh environment into a pleasant one. On the other hand, textiles can be both overdone and poorly done. Interiors today, with their great use of steel and glass, will certainly not use textiles in the manner of the past, during which inward-looking spaces were often embellished by textiles. These window treatments were themselves intended as works of art as well as adjuncts to the room design.

Textiles today have been given so many practical finishes that they can be used satisfactorily even in public places. However, the designing field is finding many ingenious substitutes for their use there. Nevertheless, we cannot entirely dismiss the need for textiles. One should be friends with them and use them with ingenuity and creativity to supply what nothing else can do so well.

HOW TEXTILES DIFFER FROM ONE ANOTHER

The large number of names traditionally associated with fine textiles can be confusing. A textile is sometimes specified by several different terms. For instance, a patterned heavy linen may be designated as a crash, a cretonne, or a textured linen. Some textile names are fairly standard, some are more recent trade names, some are current fashion terms. Although the tendency is toward greater simplification in terminology, it is advisable to preserve certain distinctions in nomenclature that lead to more careful appraisal.

It is important to know certain standard terms for decorative textiles. It is even more important to appreciate how fabrics can differ one from another and to comprehend how these differences affect performance and appearance. The basic differences occur at several stages of textile manufacture—the fiber, the yarn, the construction, the embellishment, and the finishing.

Fiber Differences

A textile fiber is the fundamental material from which a textile is made. Therefore, fiber characteristics predispose a textile toward its final and unalterable quality. Each fiber has its unique and admirable nature that makes the cloth containing it suitable for specific uses.

For thousands of years all textile fibers came from natural sources. The chief of these natural fibers are:

Cellulose Fibers—From Vegetable Sources

1. Cotton.
2. Flax—made into linen yarn.
3. Others such as hemp, jute, ramie, kapok, sisal, and coir.

Protein Fibers—From Animal Sources

1. Wool and hair.
2. Silk.

Mineral Fibers

Asbestos.

COTTON FIBER

Cotton in the boll is composed of short fuzzy fibers that form a protective covering around the seeds. The cotton thread formed from spinning is dull because of these protruding ends. Longer fibers, known as long-staple cotton, form a more lustrous yarn. Special processing and finishes can also give cotton more luster.

Cotton feels softer and more pliable than flax and it is not as heavy. Therefore, a cotton cloth will drape in softer folds than a linen cloth, but in comparable size a cotton cloth will not stand up in as straight-line folds.

Cotton is not very resilient. Therefore, a cotton cloth is apt to wrinkle. A fabric with a cotton pile should be thick so that it will not mat down.

Cotton is a firm, strong fiber. It is dimensionally stable and holds its shape well against stretching or shrinking. Moisture, heat, and cold do not easily affect it. It takes dye readily and retains it well. Therefore, although its short ends may catch dirt, it launders well.

One of cotton's biggest assets is its availability. However, it is no longer classed as an inexpensive fiber because of the lengthy process of its growth and manufacture.

FLAX FIBER (LINEN)

Flax fiber is the inner bast core of the flax plant. It has a unique feel similar to that of chamois or leather. There is a toughness about it even though it can be bent.

There are various grades of all of the natural fibers, and there are considerable differences in the qualities shown by these various grades. The finer grades of flax are the longest and the smoothest, thus reflecting the most light. As a class, however, there is a natural smoothness and luster to linen that nothing can alter.

Flax, being a good conductor of heat, is the coolest fiber to touch. Moreover, its luster makes it look cool. What an ideal fiber to weave into all manner of summer cloths!

The fineness of the best quality of flax is comparable to silk. Most manufacturers of linen cloth capitalize on the weight rather than the fineness of linen and produce cloths that can hold their own with furniture of larger scale. Linen, with its natural luster, its body and its slight irregularity, is a desirable fiber to use to express the naturalness of contemporary design (Figure 10.5).

Flax is the least resilient of the fibers. Therefore, it is seldom seen in a pile weave. Carpets made from it are of thick, matted construction. Many linens, even in furnishing fabrics, are specially treated to make them crease resistant and more resilient.

Flax is not dyed easily and does not retain color readily, facts that should be remembered when choosing linen draperies. It was for this reason that in the past these were lined. Today many beautiful linen cloths that are intended for curtains are made in a natural color and owe their interest to the texture introduced in the yarn and the weave.

Linen is not easily destroyed by heat. Because of its smoothness it does not soil readily. It absorbs moisture and dries quickly and thus is especially suitable for napery and for hospital appointments.

Flax is a very strong fiber, but irregularities in spinning may weaken it and should be guarded against.

Flax of good quality is costly to produce, and fine linen is expensive. Coarser linens are now procurable in the moderate price range.

WOOL FIBER

In addition to various quality levels of wool fiber, there are different kinds of wools that come from different varieties of sheep. The wool of each is prized for its special characteristics. Mohair, the wool of the angora goat, it strong, lustrous, and wiry. Cashmere, from the Kashmir goat, is soft and silky. Hair, which is straighter than wool, can vary from coarse horsehair to the finer camel hair. Despite these great differences, there are some qualities that wools and hairs possess in common.

Wool, in general, is not smooth to the touch. The tiny scalelike character of its structure catches the fingers and makes the fiber seem uneven.

Wool is a poor conductor of heat and therefore is the warmest fiber. It is a good insulator. Woolen draw curtains make excellent winter protection. Moreover, the wools look warm, the sleeker hairs less so.

It is not always recognized that wool is both a very light fiber and a fine fiber with

Figure 10.5. Natural fibers for use as wallcovering.
Photograph: Courtesy of the International Linen Promotion Association
These Irish, French, and Belgian linen cloths are designed to be used as wall-coverings. They provide a textural interest in contemporary interiors.

great pliability. These characteristics allow gossamer wool gauzes to fall in the loveliest of folds.

Wool is both the most elastic and the most resilient of the natural fibers. A good wool resists wrinkling, and it will spring back into position after bending. This quality accounts for its important role in the pile carpet industry.

Because the tiny wool scales become enmeshed, it is easy to spin wool evenly and the resulting yarn is firm and strong. Wool can be injured easily through excessive heat, and it may lose many of its desirable characteristics if it is not properly cared for. Since wool is similar to hair, it can be washed if handled as carefully as hair. Oriental carpets are customarily washed. Thorough rinsing is essential.

Wool is characteristically dull rather than shiny. The best-quality wool, which is cut from the most protected portions of the animal, is more lustrous. Long wool fibers, after they are sorted and given preliminary treatment, are made into the fine-quality yarns known as worsted. The luster of such yarn is very lovely. It is not too high, and it has a depth reflection that introduces myriad shadow overtones. Wool is dyed readily, and the multiple reflections soften the light from its colors. Hence there is a certain richness of color tone that wool can give to a room that is difficult to obtain from any other fiber source.

A wool of fine quality is difficult and expensive to produce. However, it is strong and should wear a long time if treated well.

SILK FIBER

Silk from the cultivated silk worm (as well as tussah silk from the wild caterpillar) is comparatively smooth to touch and lustrous to look upon. Its light reflection is always pearly and never harsh. This is because the filament is semitransparent. The entering light is undoubtedly refracted and reflected from within. Silk takes dye readily and with modern methods holds it well. Silk is the lightest, finest, and longest of the natural fibers. Woven into fine, glowing cloths, it looks cool although actually it is not a good heat conductor. The greater unevenness of the tussah yarn is due to the breaking of the silk cocoon by the moth with the consequent cutting of the filament length. Dupion silk filaments are reeled from double cocoons that have become enmeshed during formation. They make heavier and rougher yarns.

Silk is similar to wool in pliability, elasticity, and resiliency. All of its qualities make silk luxurious. It is costly to produce. However, it is one of the strongest of materials. If cared for like the other animal fibers, it is extremely durable. Wild silks are produced in the moderate price range.

HUMAN-MADE FIBERS

The manufactured fibers are called the synthetics. They are chemicals of high molecular structure that are fluids in one stage of their development and solid filaments in another. They are thus one kind of plastic. Several of the recent arrivals in the field of synthetic fibers are well known in other forms as commercial plastics.

Some of the synthetic fibers are made simply by altering the physical form of a natural substance such as wood pulp. Rayon is an example of this type. The acetates are examples of fibers made from natural substances that have undergone chemical as well as physical change. Nylon is a third type of synthetic that is actually built from more simple chemical ingredients.

There are three types of names that are given to these fibers. The most particular designation is essentially a trade name. It is assigned by a manufacturer to a particular fiber that the company manufactures. Many of these names are registered with the United States Patent Office; Celanese is an example of such a name.

Some of these particular fibers are similar in source or manufacture. A group of manufacturers making similar fibers may propose a class name for their fibers. They advance what are called fair trade practice rules for the manufacture and sale of these fibers. These they present to the Federal Trade Commission, which has the power to accept these rules and to enforce them. In that manner, for instance, the acetates were established as a class of man-made fibers. Celanese is one of the acetates.

The most inclusive group name that can be assigned to fibers returns to the natural source from which they were derived. The following classification is made primarily on this basis.[2] It is not all-inclusive. Essentially all of the names are trademarks registered by their manufacturers (the exception is nylon).

Modified Natural Polymers

A. Those derived from a cellulose base.
  1. Rayons—Bemberg, Avisco, Fortisan, Jetspun, Coloray.
  2. Acetates—Celanese, Avisco, Chromspun, Celaperm.
  3. Triacetates—Arnel.
B. Those derived from a protein base.
  1. Animal source—Caslen from milk casein.
  2. Vegetable source—Vicara from corn and Ardil from peanuts.
C. Those with a metal base—Lurex, Mylar.
D. Those with a rubber base—Lastex.

Synthesized Polymers

These are polymers synthesized from simple chemical compounds. Synthesized polymers are classified on the basis of similarities of chemical structure and thus of performance; the classification is usual to the advertising literature.

A. Acrylic fibers—Acrilan, Dynel, Orlon, Verel, Creslan.

---

[2]The major classification headings are those assigned by a committee of the American Society for Testing and Materials.

B. Polyamides—nylon, Antron.
C. Polyester—Dacron, Fortrel, Kodel.
D. Polyethylene monofilament.
E. Vinyls (not all of these are fibers, but all have decorating uses).
  1. Basically vinylidene chloride—Saran, Velon, Lumite, Naugahyde.
  2. Vinylidene chloride and acetate—Vinyon.
F. Olefins—Herculon, Vectra.

The Glasses

Fiberglass.

Each of the man-made fibers has many valuable qualities of sensuous character, performance, or price. None is suited to all purposes. Combinations of fibers known as blends are frequently made to provide more nearly universal satisfaction.

In general, the synthetics have achieved the practical advantages of strength and ease of care for a moderate price. Their textural character can be controlled within wide limits. They can provide fineness and luster with pliability. Textile technology is continually directed toward processes that will improve existing fibers.

The following list of synthetic textiles notes particular excellences in decorative use.

The rayons and acetates: suited to many decorative uses—fineness—good draping quality—controlled luster—good color range—in new developments exceptionally good color fastness, launderability, and qualities similar to synthesized polymers.

The protein-derived polymers: particularly useful in blends—soft—good moisture absorption—deterrent to static.

The metallics: useful in blends—metallic luster with launderability.

The acrylics: suited to winter bedding, felts, sturdy as well as sheer curtaining—light weight coupled with warmth and bulk—fire resistance in Dynel—dimensional stability—ease of washing with quick drying.

Polyamides: suited to carpeting, sheer fabrics—strength with great abrasion resistance—resiliency—dimensional stability—ease of washing, quick drying, and no ironing.

Polyesters: suited to light, sheer fabrics—also used for felts and fillings—strength with abrasion resistance—dimensional stability—fluffiness—ease of washing, quick drying, and no ironing.

Polyethylene monofilament: used in blends to induce pucker—high shrinkage with maximum control.

The vinyls: suited to heavy-duty upholstery—useful in blends—strength—stainproofness and color fastness.

The olefins: lightweight insulation, low cost.

The glasses: suited to curtains—fireproofness—luster—weight—ease of washing and no ironing.

YARN DIFFERENCES

Yarn is the name given to a fiber after it has been spun or thrown. Spinning consists of combining fibers, drawing them out to proper thickness, and giving them the requisite twist for strength. Silk and synthetic yarns result from the twisting together of several filaments (a variety of fiber having an extreme length). They are not drawn out. The process of making filament yarns is known as throwing.

The most distinctive character of cloth lies in its yarns. Yarns may combine several kinds of fibers or filaments. They can differ in the direction of their twists (called S or Z, according to the central stroke of these letters to the right or the left). They can vary in ply or number of ends twisted together (e.g., two ply). They can differ in the size or count of the yarns. (Size or count of yarn is based on the relation between length and weight). For continuous filaments the count is based on the relation of weight to fixed length. The unit of weight here is called the *denier*. In filament yarn, the finer the yarn the smaller the count. In yarns made of short fibers, the count is based on the length in relation to a fixed weight: the finer the yarn the higher the count. Count is also used to designate the density of the weave—the number of threads per inch in warp and weft.)

Interesting novelty yarns can be produced by variations in twist and tension. Long filaments can be cut and spun to secure controlled luster. Permanent crimping of filaments gives added strength to lessen the need for twist, thus providing lightness and added coverage, stability, and luster. Chenille yarns introduce depth and softness (notice their current use as warp binding in slat shades or blinds). Cotton yarns can be mercerized, a process of immersion in an alkali bath under tension to give added strength and luster.

Stretch yarns such as Lastex® have an elastic core covered with threads of other fibers.

CONSTRUCTION DIFFERENCES

Yarns are made into cloths (Figure 10.6). The simplest cloth construction is known as felting. Fibers (rather than yarns) are matted together to make felt. A wool fiber is customarily used since it is especially adapted to this purpose because of its natural crimp and its tendency to bend toward its roots under heat and pressure. Some new felts are constructed on a net base for added durability.

Cloths are usually made from yarns. They may be constructed from a single element or thread. Knitting, crocheting, and similar techniques are methods of looping one thread on itself to form a mesh. The use of knitting as a construction method has increased enormously in recent years. When knitting is combined with the elasticity of certain fibers, stretch fabrics of great value for upholstery are created. If properly manufactured they are dimensionally stable.

Plaiting and braiding are means of forming cloth by intertwining long lengths of multiple

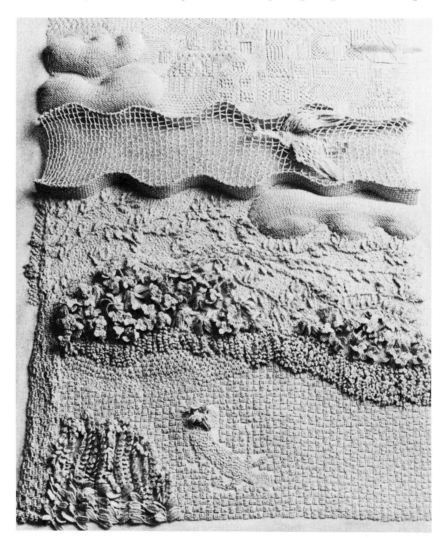

Figure 10.6. Fiberwork, "Abschied," embroidery on linen, 18″ × 26″ × 2″.
Artist: Liselotte Siegfried
Photographer: Jeremiah G. Bradstad
Fabrics can be made by many different construction processes. Some of the more unusual fabrics today, which are generally intended for decorative purposes, are called *fiberworks*. This piece, which was created by embroidery stitching on a woven fabric, illustrates well the creative texture that is possible when a textile is designed under the hand of an artist craftsman.

elements or threads. Many of the basic nets and laces are constructed of single elements or of long lengths of multiple elements by processes of interlacing. Square-meshed filet laces are made by knotting threads in the manner of making a fisherman's net. Bobbin laces are the result of interlacing bobbin-wound threads. Sometimes they are known as pillow laces because a small bolster anchors the lace as the work progresses. Nets are made by intertwining threads to form a regular mesh. These results can be machine produced by complicated mechanisms that seem miraculous in their manipulation of yarns by vertical and horizontal movements.

The major portion of the fabrics used in interior design are woven textiles made from several sets of threads on a loom (Figure 10.7). A loom is essentially a very simple artifact consisting of a rigid frame on which the lengthwise (or warp) threads of a fabric may be strung and held taut while the crosswise (or weft) threads intersect them at right angles.

The essential warp threads are wound on beams or rollers. One of these becomes the cloth beam for the finished textile. The other is called the warp beam from which the warp is fed. Sometimes a loom is equipped with more than one warp beam and can hold more than one set of warp threads. This enables the weaver to adjust the tensions of separate warp groups and to control a wider range of patterning.

Looms have equipment for raising specific warps. The smallest unit of this equipment is a heddle (called a leash on the draw loom). This consists of a loop or opening in a cord or metal bar through which one or several warp threads may be strung. A group of heddles arranged to be moved at the same time is known as a harness.

The raising of the harness is controlled by a series of cords, bars, and levers of a degree of complexity related to the particular type of loom.

When a group of warp threads is raised, it forms a shed much as the fingers of our two hands form a shed when they are placed between one another and then pivoted open. Through this shed a shuttle holding a wound length of weft thread is passed. Such a passing is known as a shot or pick of weft. A reed (so called because originally made of reed),

comb, or batten is an essential part of a loom. Its purpose is twofold: to space the warp threads and to beat or batten the weft threads into position.

There are a number of different ways to classify cloth weaves. The names derived from some of the classifications are inferior because they are not based on any real concept of how the weaving is done. For instance, it is misleading to classify a carpet as a broadloom weave since many kinds of carpets can be made on broad looms. Their weaves are no different from carpets made on narrow looms (the original width of carpet looms was 27 inches). We have seen advertisements for silk-weave or linen-weave fabrics. These terms are also ambiguous. Certain weaves are used frequently with silk yarns, but silk can and has been used in every variety of weave.

It is helpful if a classification of weaves fits both historical usage (found in museums) and current industrial usage.[3] The following is a suggested classification.

BASIC WEAVES

Plain Weave (sometimes called tabby weave)

1. A plain weave can be made on any loom that has two harnesses. One raises warp threads 1, 3, 5, 7 and the second raises 2, 4, 6, 8.
2. The regular intersecting is caused by the weft threads that go over and under adjacent warp threads and alternate this intersection every other row.
3. Variations of a plain weave are the basket (extended tabby) weave, in which the intersection is of alternate blocks of threads; and historic tapestry weave (this is not machine-made tapestry cloth), in which the weft threads carry the pattern. In historic tapestries, a weft thread goes as far as one color is needed, at which point it either interlocks with a continuing color or returns on itself.
4. The plain weave is firm and easily constructed and is therefore relatively inexpensive. Its surface is not particularly interesting, but makes a good background for printed patterns.

---

[3]The nomenclature for weaving lacks standardization. Different meanings are assigned to equivalent words in different countries and among different textile groups. The C. I. E. T. A. (an abbreviation of the French for the International Center for the Study of Ancient Textiles), which has its headquarters at Lyon, France, is an organization working for standardization.

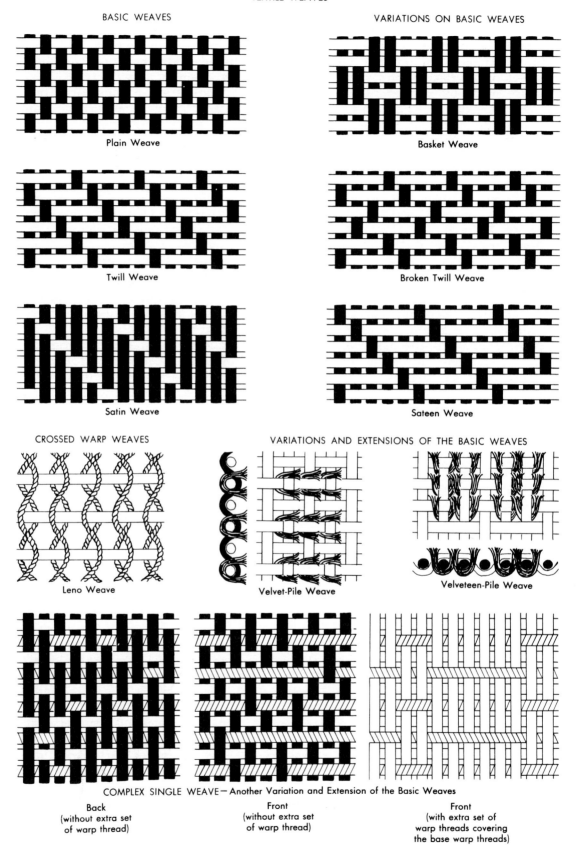

BASIC WEAVES

VARIATIONS ON BASIC WEAVES

Plain Weave

Basket Weave

Twill Weave

Broken Twill Weave

Satin Weave

Sateen Weave

CROSSED WARP WEAVES

VARIATIONS AND EXTENSIONS OF THE BASIC WEAVES

Leno Weave

Velvet-Pile Weave

Velveteen-Pile Weave

COMPLEX SINGLE WEAVE—Another Variation and Extension of the Basic Weaves

Back
(without extra set
of warp thread)

Front
(without extra set
of warp thread)

Front
(with extra set of
warp threads covering
the base warp threads)

Figure 10.7. Textile weaves.

It can be given a great deal of textural interest through varied yarn combinations.

Twill Weave

1. A twill weave can be made on any four-harness loom. Actually, a twill could be made using three sets of heddles but, because a loom will have a greater range of utility if it has an even number of sets, the four-harness loom is used. Any fabric that is woven on such a loom and takes advantage of the possibilities that it affords can be called a variation of a twill.
2. The regular intersecting is caused by a weft thread that intersects from one to three warp threads. In the next weft row it makes the same kind of intersection but progresses one warp thread to the left or right. It progresses in this manner until it returns to a repeat.
3. Some variations of a twill weave include irregular or broken twills in which the progression in successive weft shots is not regularly one thread to the left or right. Frequently the intersection in a four-heddle twill is over warp 1, 3, 4, 2, in successive shots. Patterned twills such as diaper and herringbone twills are variations produced by changing the direction of the binding rib.
4. In a regular twill a diagonal wale or rib is produced across the cloth. This will vary in sharpness and slant according to the relative thread sizes and the count (number per square inch) of the warp and weft yarns. When regular twills are made from tightly spun yarns, they have precise, regular surfaces. Patterned twills have a neat exactness. Broken twills are often used to display yarns in a more interesting way than a plain weave can do. Regular twills are intrinsically strong fabrics. The interweaving is frequent enough to be firm, and a particular warp thread takes the load in only one shot out of four.

Satin Weave

1. A satin may be woven on a loom of any number of harnesses greater than four.
2. In five-harness satin, one weft thread binds down one warp thread and then goes under the next four warps. The same binding principle extends throughout the weave, but the bound warp moves three threads to the right with each shot of weft. This makes a warp-face satin. The reverse of this process, in which the weft thread goes under one and over four warps, produces a weft-face satin. Most weft-face satins are made of mercerized cotton and are known as sateens. It is always possible to float a thread over or under a number of intersecting threads that is one less than the number of harnesses. The thread going through this last group of heddles is needed for interlocking. In a regular satin the binder always advances in regular fashion.
3. Some variations of a satin weave are irregular satins and patterned satins. Irregular satins are those in which the points of binding are spaced unequally. Patterned satins may be produced by an interruption in the regular binding system resulting in a contrast of effects and a regular pattern.
4. A satin weave results in a surface that displays long lengths or floats of yarn. It is capable of revealing the luster inherent in a fiber.

VARIATIONS AND EXTENSIONS IN THE BASIC WEAVES

When these weaves use the elaborate Jacquard loom to control the patterning, they are frequently called Jacquard weaves.

Patterned Basic Weaves

See the variations in Section 3 under each of the basic weaves just discussed.

Variations Using More Than One Set of Warps and/or Wefts

1. *COMPLEX SINGLE WEAVE.* This weave appears as one web only that can be backed or faced with an extra yarn. It may have pattern sections raised (as in piqué) or may have pattern threads brought to the surface to produce color effects (as in machine-made tapestry). *Lampas weave* is a historic variety of the complex single weave.
   a. The loom is normally equipped with ground and figure harness.
   b. The lampas weave is made by two sets of warps and two sets of wefts that are interwoven to produce a weft design effect superimposed on a ground effect. The main warp and weft combine to form the ground effect and the second warp and weft combine to form the design effect. The ground effects can be formed by any of the basic weaves or variants thereof. Pattern wefts are bound in plain or twill or are floated on the surface without any apparent binding system.

c. The lampas weave creates a thick fabric with a three-dimensional patterned effect that appears embossed.

2. *DOUBLE WEAVE.* This appears as a tubular cloth or as two separate cloths joined at intervals.

   a. Any loom with four or more heddles may be used for a double weave. Because at least two harnesses are required to perform each function in the weaving, a four-heddle loom is the simplest one that can produce a double weave. In the simplest of double-weave cloths in which two plain-weave webs are attached only at the edges, the warps for the two webs are entered alternatively through the reed. The looms required for double weaves in which the two webs are separate in some patterned portions but are interwoven in background portions are equipped with long-eyed heddles needed because the ground warp threads function in two sets of harnesses.

   b. The warps are separated into more than one series that are raised during the process of weaving one above the other and alternately woven by the wefts. Two fabrics are thus formed one above the other. They may be entirely separate or joined in parts.

   c. Patterns may be formed in double weave. This normally requires the addition of a figure harness to control the weaving of the pattern while the ground harness controls the shedding for the interweaving of the warps and wefts according to one of the defined binding systems.

   d. The double weave in its regular form has the additional bulk of a double fabric or of a two-faced cloth. It may also produce a raised effect that resembles padding or quilting (true quilting is the stitching together of two fabrics in patterns).

3. *PILE WEAVES.* In these weaves a three-dimensional effect is produced on a foundation fabric. The pile, composed of thread at right angles to the basic fabric, may be a warp or a weft thread. The foundation fabric may be formed by one of the basic weaves. Pile-weave fabrics are classified in the following manner.

   a. Warp Pile Weaves (Velvets).

      (1) The loom must contain two warp beams because of the enormous difference in the amount of warp used for ground and pile. The pile beam is above the ground warp beam. A velvet must be woven on a loom with ground and pile harness. It requires special cloth beams designed to keep the pile from being crushed. Carpet looms made on this principle are even more intricately constructed.

      (2) In a true velvet, the ground harness weaves the ground web that may be in any one of the simple weaves. This ground interlacing binds the pile yarn into the body of the cloth. Then the pile harness is raised, and a rod or wire is inserted in the shed. When the pile harness is lowered and after more ground is woven, the pile wire may be removed. If it is equipped with a sharp edge or if a cutting tool releases the wire by cutting along the loop, a cut-pile fabric results.

      (3) Patterned pile fabrics can be made by voiding the pile in the ground. It is then woven into the ground and is only brought up as a pile where the pattern dictates. Patterns can be made apparent by using piles of different height, cut and uncut piles, solid and voided pile, and by the use of different colors. Frequently a combination of several of these is used. A recent method of making patterns in pile weave has been to cut out the pile in the background (carved or sculptured pile). This is frequently done in carpets.

      (4) Pile-weave fabrics are valuable for obtaining deep reflections in textural combinations.

   b. Weft Pile Weaves. These are weaves in which an extra weft, the pile weft, is floated over several warps and is then cut to form the pile. Its decorative uses are similar to those of the warp-pile velvets. As the weft pile is usually cotton, the material is less rich in effect than the warp pile.

CROSSED-WARP WEAVE

Two crossed warps are used in making the body of the cloth.

1. Crossed warp weaves (or leno weaves) can be made on an ordinary loom with a leno attachment. This is an extra harness having U-shaped heddles. Through these the extra set of warp threads is strung. The ground warp is passed between the uprights of the doup har-

ness (from the Italian word for double) and is threaded through its own heddles. The doup yarns are shifted to one side and then to the other side of the ground yarns as the weaving progresses.

2. Regular intersecting is achieved by the alternate warp threads crossing each other between the wefts. The wefts hold the crossing in place.

3. There are no variations of the crossed-warp weave, although the leno weave is often embellished to make more interesting fabrics.

4. Gauze or leno-weave fabrics can be relatively strong and sheer.

Machinery has made weaving easier but has not assured more beautiful fabrics. The hand weaver made many intricate patterns, color changes, and texture changes by manipulating weft threads. It is less costly to set up patterns on power looms by manipulating the warp threads because, once the tie-up of the loom is made, an essentially mechanical operation can complete the process. Because the warp must be the heavier of the two threads used in weaving, the exquisite weft brocades and tapestries of the hand-loom era are largely things of the past. The general bulk of fabric that is produced is tending toward the simplest of weaves with texture introduced through yarn and with color introduced through yarn and printing.

EMBELLISHMENT OF THE BASIC FABRIC

Added Yarns

Fabrics may be enriched by the addition of yarns, integral coloration, or applied colorant pattern. Yarn can provide textural interest. One way of introducing yarns onto the body of a cloth is to use embroidery (see Figure 10.6). This is done with a needle stitch on fabric. An effect of a small embroidered figure can be machine produced by a loom attachment that contains a set of warp threads in needles. It produces a weft-wise pattern.

Some early laces were made from embroidery by cutting away the cloth background. *Point laces* (the word point is derived from an old French word for prick, hence, stitch) are made by embroidering over a skeletal network of threads sewed to a firm pattern. The pattern is then detached.

Extra yarns may be added to glorify a basic textile while the cloth is woven. Brocading is the introduction of a pattern weft inserted between the ground wefts. In many historic brocades, the movement of the brocading weft was limited to the width of the motif produced. Similar effects today are produced by patterning in a complex single weave or by special weft bobbins that produce a small weft figure.

Added Color

Color may be added to cloth through dyes and pigments. Dyeing is a complex process. Colorants and fibers interact in physical and chemical ways. In some cases dye can be applied to the fiber directly. In other instances a mordant is needed to fix the dye. The dyes known as vat dyes are insoluble and must be made soluble during the dyeing process. Often the dye is developed through several stages of treatment of the cloth.

Color can be acquired at any stage of fabric manufacture. Some of the man-made fibers are now dyed in the solution stage, a development that improves their color quality and color fastness. The use of yarns dyed in different colors can produce colored stripes, plaids, and mottled effects. A cloth can be woven of different fibers that will react differently in a dye bath. Thus one dye bath can produce several colors. Some nonabsorptive fibers cannot be dyed directly. They must have their color bonded with the aid of film-forming materials. Dispersed pigments are applied to cloth in this manner.

Color is often introduced with pattern. This can be done in the process of weaving with various colored threads. Pattern can be resist dyed on a warp before weaving (this is known as the *ikat* technique). Color and pattern can also be applied after the cloth is woven. There are many ways of accomplishing this—some as old as weaving itself. One method stems from the batik process of the East. The parts of the cloth that are not to be colored with a particular dye are treated in some manner to resist the dye. Hence this is often called resist dyeing. In batiks the surface is covered with wax to hinder impregnation. Later this wax is taken out with a solvent. Another resist dye fabric is known as tie dyeing. Pattern areas of the fabric are tied with cord so tightly that they do not take the dye into which the cloth is immersed. Both stencil and screen techniques are offshoots of the resist process.

Screen-printed fabrics have become so popular today that the designer should appreciate something of their special value. They are made by a process whereby a large frame is covered with a very fine meshed material, the screen. The parts of this screen that will hold back the dye are covered with a moisture-repellent material. Then the dye, in paste form, is forced through the open parts of the screen onto the cloth. A limited number of impressions can be made from one screen pattern. Therefore, a screen-printed fabric is comparatively exclusive. It is indeed not too expensive to have fabrics made with a unique design for the purpose of repeating motifs or colors found in other furnishings. Many firms specialize in just this sort of custom work.

Discharge printing is the reverse of resist printing. After the cloth is woven and dyed, a design is put onto the fabric by impressing parts of it with a chemical that will eradicate or discharge some of the dye.

Direct printing is different from either resist or discharge printing in that it is a direct application of colored pattern to a fabric. This process originally stemmed from wood block printing. On a wooden block the portions not intended to take the color are cut away. The paste dye is then applied to the raised portion of the block and thence to the cloth. Wood block printing of fabric is still practiced. It is possible through this technique to produce an original fabric at nominal cost. One virtue in hand-screened and hand-blocked fabrics lies in the fact that one color can be superimposed easily upon another, thereby giving depth of color tone. Such overlapping printing is rare in the machine print process because of the time necessary for the drying of one color before the next can be applied. Wallpapers as well as textiles may be printed by hand screening and by hand blocking.

The bulk of fabric printing today is done by direct printing from engraved or etched copper rollers. Each color, in the form of a dye paste or a pigmented emulsion, is applied directly from a roller. Even the background is roller printed. The preparation of these rollers is very expensive. Therefore, many impressions must be made if the finished fabric is to be reasonably priced. Because each additional color adds to the expense, the less expensive fabrics are printed in a limited color range and in one that the manufacturer expects will make volume sales.

Sometimes a design is printed on the warp threads only, giving softer colors. Warp threads of different colors used with one-color wefts produce a similar muted effect. These latter fabrics are sometimes known as jaspé or strié fabrics.

A limited number of fabrics (as well as wallpapers) are made by the photoengraving process. They are executed in the same manner as a large-volume photographic reproduction. The design is transferred to sensitized copper rollers from a photographic film. It is then etched and printed. This method can produce the most personal of fabrics because the impressions may be of favorite scenes. This need not result in a naïve pictorial representation. It can be productive of a tonal effect that is much the same as that found on the old French toiles.

Glass fibers, with their quality of being both reflective and translucent, can be printed to produce many unusual effects of pattern on ground. Reversal of tones may be accomplished when a pattern is viewed as a lustrous surface or as a diffusing screen.

TEXTILE FINISHES

The finishes applied to cloth may alter its textural character. In today's manufacturing the number of these finishes is legion and a cloth may be indebted to them for much of its visual beauty as well as for added practicality.

Some finishes make one fiber resemble another. Napping may be done to rough up cotton so that it resembles wool. Some finishes introduce the crispness of linen or the suppleness of silk. Glazing and calendering give duller materials a silk- or linenlike sheen. Moiréing is produced by embossing portions of a cloth so that it reflects light in swirling patterns. Panneing is a finish that lays pile flat so that it will reflect more light. Weighting adds tin salts to silks.

Flocking is the adhering of small pieces of fiber to a finished cloth to change its texture or to give it a raised pattern. Various processes are used to give a crinkled effect to fabrics. True crepe is produced by using tightly spun yarns of different twists. Pucker can be obtained by using various tensions during weaving. Finishes that produce three-dimensional effects may be the result of controlled shrinkage of various types of fibers used in one cloth.

Many finishes provide some practical advantage. Sizing is a well-known method of giving smoothness and body. Crease resistant, flame retardant, mildew resistant, moth repellent, water, spot, and dirt repellent—these terms suggest ways in which the usefulness of cloth is improved (e.g., Scotchgard® and Teflon® are water- and oil-resistant finishes). Continual effort is made by industry to treat cloths so that they will be dimensionally stable and will retain plaiting. Finishes are improving color fastness to sun and to gas fumes. Metallized finishes insulate cloths. When cloth is used in public buildings, it is necessary to have it treated for soil resistance. The law requires that it have a flame-retardant finish.

From the standpoint of the consumer, several questions about finishes are important: How enduring is the finish? Has the finish harmed the cloth in any way? Are the claims for its performance exaggerated? Will its cost be offset by its benefits? If special finishes are selected wisely, they may add many desirable qualities to the original textiles.

A GLOSSARY OF DECORATING FABRICS

The following listing of decorating fabrics may be helpful in making textural groupings. The general tendency today is toward a reduction in the number of fabric types and names in the interest of economy of manufacture.

*Armure**—a complex single-weave fabric characterized by heavier weft threads (rep) and a small warp pattern. Appropriate for informal, provincial-type furniture. Sometimes called a tapestry, which it superficially resembles.

Batik—a fabric in which the pattern is made by the wax-resist process. Javanese batiks are frequently used as wall hangings. Printed imitations are made today.

Batiste—a fine, sheer, soft, mercerized long-staple cotton fabric in a plain weave. Frequently embroidered or screen printed. Used for sheer curtains.

Brocade—A patterned fabric made by an extra weft yarn floated to resemble embroidery. Usually of fine silk or synthetic yarns. Appropriate for fine upholstery. Commercial brocades are often complex single-weave fabrics that give the effect of historic brocades. The name is used imprecisely today.

Brocatelle—A complex single-weave material in which the pattern is in warp-faced satin and the ground is in any simple weave. The pattern appears embossed due to manipulation of tensions. Historic brocatelles used a coarse linen or undegummed silk ground weft. Appropriate for fine upholstery on chairs of heavier scale.

Buckram—a coarse, jute, plain-weave fabric. Used as covering for upholstery springs, coarse wallcovering, or upholstery.

Calico—A plain-weave printed cotton made in imitation of an obsolete textile. Patterns are small and colors simulate those of natural dyes. Suitable for use with provincial furnishings.

Cambric—A plain-weave cotton or linen of light weight. It has many uses in linings, underflounces, and so forth.

Canvas—A heavy plain-weave cotton or linen. A sized variety is used as a support for oil paints. *Duck* is finer and lighter but similar to canvas.

Casement cloth—A name given to a group of light-weight, plain, twill, or leno-weave fabrics that may have small monotone patterns incorporated in the weave. Frequently used for draw curtains.

Chenille (the French word for caterpillar; pronounced shĕ-nēl)—The name of a yarn made by first weaving a leno fabric with widely spaced warps. Cutting between the warps provides a yarn from which a pile protrudes. Suitable for upholstery or draperies where softness and depth are needed.

Chintz—a fine, plain weave cotton usually with a printed design. Frequently glazed. Suitable for upholstery on light-scale furniture or for draperies where reflections and crisp lines are needed.

Corduroy—A cotton-weft pile fabric showing warp-wise ribs. Comes in various weights suited to upholstery or hangings. Useful to introduce a fine, soft texture for straight line pattern.

Crash—A name frequently applied to plain-weave coarse linens. Often used for upholstery of contemporary furniture.

*Cretonne**—A plain or twill-weave, unglazed printed cotton or linen fabric that is heavier

*Terms not widely used today are followed by an asterisk.

and larger in scale of pattern than chintz. Used in much the same way as chintz is but with furnishings of larger scale.

Crewel embroidery—Wool embroidery done on linen crash principally with crewel or chain stitch. Suitable for use with traditional furnishings of medium scale.

Damask—A fabric in patterned satin weave that comes in all fibers. Characterized by a flat reversible pattern. In true damask the background is warp face and the pattern is weft face. Single damask table linens are five-harness, warp-faced satin with the ground in weft satin. Double damasks are eight-harness weavings. Suitable for many uses where flat-patterned reflections are required.

Denim—A heavy cotton twill. Suitable for sturdy slipcovers, curtains, bedspreads.

Dimity—A plain-weave cotton with heavier threads introduced to make stripes or bars. Tightly spun fiber background threads result in a crisp, sheer fabric. Appropriate for curtains, especially of an informal type.

*Faille** (pronounced fil)—One of the reps, a plain weave with weft threads heavier than warp. Synthetic or silk warp is usual. Loosely spun cotton weft. Used for draperies. Lighter-weight failles are used for draw curtains.

Felt—Fabric of matted fibers sometimes on a net or foam base. A high percent of wool content is desirable. Used as pads for lamp bases, for drawer linings, and so forth. The softer felts now manufactured have more extensive uses.

Fortuny prints—Handblocked prints on basic-weave cottons. Made by Mariano Fortuny craftsmen of Venice. Color overlays give a rich textural effect. Used for hangings, draperies, and fine coverings.

Frisé (pronounced frĕ-zāy) or frieze (pronounced frēz)—Pile-weave fabric with uncut loops. Pile is frequently mohair or linen. One of the sturdiest of upholstery materials.

Gauze—A thin, open-mesh fabric, originally in leno weave. Name now applicable to plain-weave fabrics with similar characteristics. Theatrical gauze is made of linen. Used for curtains.

Gingham—Plain-weave, yarn-dyed fabric of any fiber, usually patterned in plaids. Typical ginghams are of lightweight mercerized cottons. Well suited for provincial and informal interiors.

Guimpe (pronounced gămp)—A narrow braid or

edging with a heavy cord running through it.

Haircloth—Plain or twill-weave fabric made of mohair or horsehair (often synthetic) mixtures. Nineteenth-century fabric was made of horsehair weft and used for upholstery. Contemporary mohair fabric is used for draperies.

Homespun—A loosely defined group of fabrics characterized by soft, loosely spun yarn in a plain weave.

Honeycomb or *waffleweave cloth*—A plain or twill-weave fabric with patterning in small squares.

Imitation leather—A plastic-coated fabric that resembles leather. Many varieties, each with its own trade name.

Indianhead—Trade name for a medium-weight, plain-weave cotton. Slightly heavier and less smooth than cambric. Many uses. Substantial enough for slipcovers.

Lace—An open-mesh fabric made by intertwining threads in some manner other than by intersection on the loom. Machine laces are designed to imitate the appearance of the handmade laces. The nets are classified as laces.

*Lampas**—A historically important elaborate silk fabric in a lampas weave.

Leather—Treated animal hide used as a fabric. Top grain or top cut from the hide is most desirable. Used for sturdy upholstery where sheen and depth of reflection are required.

Marquisette—A leno-weave fabric of tightly twisted yarn. Used for curtains.

Matelassé—Figured double-weave cloth with a raised design made of two webs that can be separated. Used for fine covers and upholstery where some thickness is required.

Mohair—Name given to fabric the fiber of which is largely mohair, the fleece of the angora goat. The yarn is wiry, resilient, and lustrous. Made into a pile fabric of mohair with cotton back.

Monk's cloth—Fabric made in a basketweave variation of the plain weave using loosely spun, coarse cotton yarns. Used for inexpensive hangings and covers.

Muslin—A generic name for plain-weave cottons of medium weight. Frequently refers to a sheeting material that is not as fine as percale. Many utilitarian uses.

Needlepoint—Originally referring to needle laces, the term now designates an embroidered material made by working half cross stitches on canvas. *Petit point* (little stitch) is finer than

Plate 2. Still Life with Biscuits, Pablo Picasso, 1924, oil on canvas, 32″ × 39¾″. The
Cleveland Museum of Art, Purchase, Leonard C. Hanna Jr. Bequest
Photograph: courtesy of The Cleveland Museum of Art
In this picture Picasso has demonstrated his great sense of color organization.
Much could be learned about color if one were to copy his red, blue, green,
and purple themes and his light, dark, and intermediate values, his weak
and his strong saturations, and then study their interrelations. One would
then become aware of how a great artist interlocks shapes and colors. Texture
does not play such a highly developed role in this painting.

Plate 3. Textile display at the Knoll New York showroom.
Architect: Robert Venturi
Photograph: courtesy of Knoll International
In this beautiful display of textiles there is a thematic arrangement of colors somewhat related to the one in the Picasso painting shown in Plate 2. The tall folds of the cloths introduce another element—line. Shadows, too, play their part. Cloth can be very beautiful; at its best it can scarcely be equaled for sensuous appeal.

gros point (big stitch). Name frequently applied to a plain-weave upholstery fabric in which the twist of the yarn creates a superficial resemblance to the embroidered material.

Nets—Varieties of laces characterized by regular meshes: *bobbinet*—hexagonal mesh; *filet net*—square mesh; *point d'esprit* (pronounced pwan desprē)—A bobbinet with small dotted design.

Oilcloth—A cotton material coated with linseed oil and pigments or with synthetic coatings. Used as a waterproof covering for tables and other furniture.

Organdy—Sheer, plain-weave material made of tightly spun cotton yarns. Specially processed to preserve crispness. Used for curtains.

Percale—Plain-weave, fine-quality cotton. Used for best quality sheets and pillowcases.

Piqué (pronounced pē-kā')—Cotton material characterized by a raised rib customarily running lengthwise. *Cord* is the name given to a similar but heavier fabric. Cord is made with extra warp stuffer yarns held in place by extra wefts. Useful in producing stiff, linear, tailored effects.

Pongee (pronounced pŏn-jē')—Name derived from a dress fabric of plain weave in wild (or tussah) silk. Heavier weight is known as shantung or rajah. Other names for similar cloths of varying weights are shikii silk, antique taffeta, doupion silk, and textured silk.

Quilted fabrics—Cloths in which a surface fabric, a batting interlining, and a sheer backing are stitched together in patterns for a padded effect. *Trapunto* is a decorative quilted design in high relief. Quilted fabrics are used to give thickness with fineness.

Rep—A generic name for a class of fabrics characterized by heavier weft than warp threads.

Sailcloth—Heavy plain-weave cotton material of the type originally used for sails. Sometimes called canvas or duck. Used for furniture seats and covering.

Sateen or *satine*—A weft satin-weave fabric made from mercerized cotton yarns. Natural color sateen is used for linings of draperies.

Satin—A material in a warp satin weave. Cotton, silk, and synthetics are the usual fibers. Satin is used to introduce fineness and high reflections.

Scrim—An open-mesh, plain-weave fabric made from tightly spun yarns. Coarser than a Swiss. A practical curtain material.

Seersucker—A plain-weave, medium-weight cotton with puckered warp stripes. Pucker caused by varying warp tensions. A utilitarian textile for curtains, bedspreads, and so forth.

Swiss—A sheer, crisp, plain-weave fabric made from tightly twisted cotton yarns. Usually figured with dots applied in one of several ways which affect the character and the quality of the fabric. Swisses are used for curtains, covers, and flounces.

Taffeta—A fine, light-weight, compact, plain-weave fabric in which the warp and weft are of the same size. Made of silk or synthetics. Cotton taffeta contains a percentage of cotton and synthetic fibers. Antique taffeta is made from wild silk. A lightweight silk taffeta is known today as *silk gauze*. Taffetas are used for curtains where crispness, linear draping quality, light weight, and luster are required.

Tapa cloth—A decorative cloth made in the South Sea Islands by pounding tree bark to paper thinness and applying block-printed designs. Largely used for hangings.

Tapestry—*Historical tapestry* is a ribbed material produced on a heavier warp by finer wefts. A weft of one color is carried only as far as needed in the pattern, and then another color is introduced. In the historical pictorial tapestries, the weft is usually wool and the warp linen. The weft threads hang vertically in the finest tapestries. Tapestries are intended for wall hangings and are also used for upholstery. *Machine-made tapestry* is a complex single-weave fabric designed to imitate some of the effects of the hand-loomed tapestries. The yarns are usually wool for the face with cotton or linen for the back. Used for upholstery on heavier pieces.

Terry—An uncut warp pile fabric of cotton or linen yarn with the loops extending on both sides of the fabric. Not as heavy as frisé. Appropriate for hangings.

Ticking—Closely woven cotton fabric in twill weave. Used for pillow and mattress coverings. Occasionally used for upholstery.

*Toile de Jouy** (pronounced twäl de zhoo-y)—Plain- or twill-weave cottons produced in France from 1760 to 1815 in the town of Jouy. Printed with delicately engraved monotone designs. Good imitations on today's market. Applicable for hangings and coverings on fine-scaled furniture.

Tweed—A name now given to a loosely woven, woolen twill-weave fabric. In a strict sense, a cloth of single-ply woolen yarns woven in some variation of a twill.

Velvet—A name loosely given to all pile fabrics produced by some adaptation of the velvet weave. *Velveteen* is a weft-face cotton velvet. *Corduroy* is a weft-face cotton velvet with warp wales. *Panne velvet* is a velvet with pressed pile. *Velour* is a velvet with a short, compact pile. *Plush* is a long-pile velvet. The velvets are useful for introducing deep reflections.

Voile—A plain-weave, sheer, open fabric made from tightly twisted yarns. May be of any fiber. Used for durable sheer curtains.

Floor Coverings

CARPETS

The average layman possesses very little technical knowledge of floor coverings yet spends a relatively large amount of the furnishing budget for them. This lack of information is understandable because carpet construction appears very complicated.

Over 80 percent of the carpets on the market are tufted rather than woven (Figure 10.8). This high percentage holds especially true in the contract trade (i.e., furnishings for large public contracts). In the woven class, the velvets are by far the most numerous. Axminsters and Wiltons are produced for the private domain, although even there economics favor the less expensive types. Chenilles are practically nonexistent. However, a knowledge of the traditional varieties helps materially in any appraisal of the present merchandise.

Carpet Materials

Much that has been learned about fabrics in general can be related to carpets in particular. The quality of fibers and yarns is important. If a fiber is resilient and strong it is suitable for pile carpeting. Luster is an added advantage. Softness in the blend adds a desirable textural quality. Abrasive strength is

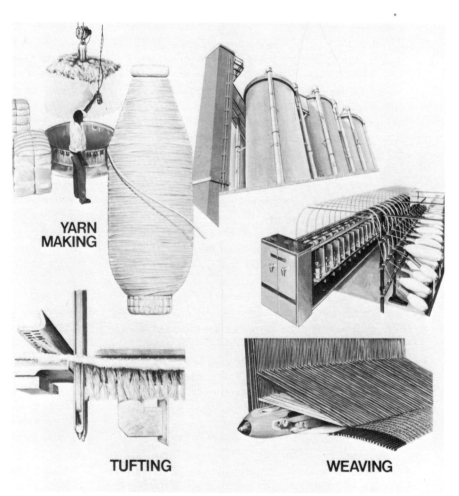

Figure 10.8. Basic carpet construction processes.
Drawing: based on an illustration provided courtesy of Bigelow-Sanford Inc.

required especially for a matte or flat-surface floor material. Backing or ground fibers should be as durable as surface yarns, and they should stand up to the same kind of cleaning.

In addition to the use of cotton, linen, wool, and synthetics, many flat weaves are made from some of the more unusual fibers such as sisal, wild grass, and rushes.

The ground or backing for carpets is of various less-expensive materials. Cotton and jute in combination are customary, although linen and wool are used. Jute is strong and stiff but not particularly pliable. It is sometimes incorporated into the backing as stuffer yarns to give extra bulk.

Carpet Construction

The quality of carpets is also related to their construction. The Eurasians make *felted rugs*. *Braided rugs* are made by sewing together braided strips of cloth. *Hooked* and *tufted rugs* are constructed by inserting loops of yarn or cloth into the body of some coarse, compact material such as burlap. *Embroidery* on a ground material produces fabrics that vary from the elegant rugs of France to coarser embroideries coming from places like Spain and Africa.

The plain weave is frequently used for floorcoverings. In the Orient it is found in the making of Khilims and Soumaks. The *Khilim* is woven in the manner of handwoven tapestries. A *Soumak* is made on a similar principle but there is a ground weft thread in addition to a pattern weft thread. The latter is manipulated like an embroidery half back-stitch, going over four warp threads and back under two. The *Aubusson* and *Beauvais* are the great tapestry carpets of France, taking their names from the places of their production. The American Indian rugs are tapestry weavings. Simple plain-weave rugs made on hand looms using strips of cotton cloth for weft are known as *rag rugs*. Tightly handwoven, wool plain-weave rugs are available from Scandinavia and many other sources.

Many carpets are made in the *pile weave* (Figure 10.9). Pile carpets were first made in that great wool-raising belt that extends from Asia Minor to the plains of China along the 35-degree north latitude. These hand-weavings are still known as Oriental rugs.

French historic handwoven pile fabrics were called *Savonnerie* from the place of their manufacture, the previous location of a soap factory. Modern handwoven and hand-tufted pile carpets come from a number of sources in addition to the Near and Far East.

Whereas all hand-loomed pile carpets are constructed on the simplest of looms, power-loom fabrics have been made on a variety of looms, each kind of which has been developed for the weaving of a particular type of carpet. The first of these was the Wilton carpet (1745). This carpet weave goes back to the days when carpet weavers in Wilton, England developed a method of obtaining a pattern pile carpet that was quicker than that of the old hand knotting. This was made feasible because of loom attachments providing pattern threads when needed. Later, Joseph-Marie Jacquard (1752-1834) of France mechanized this process.

The *Wilton carpet*, the better grades of which are always made of worsted yarn, has been called the weave with hidden value. This is because every colored yarn in the warp pile is embedded in the body of the cloth and is only brought to the surface when needed in the design. The selection of the colors for the design is accomplished today by the elaborate mechanism of the Jacquard loom. In this loom the control of the shedding is accomplished through a series of perforated cards. A highly simplified explanation of the principle is that a hole in a card will allow a warp thread to rise and come to the face of the cloth. The Jacquard machine and its tie-up is very costly. Therefore, many carpets must be woven at one time to make the effort profitable.

The colored pile yarns in a Wilton carpet are limited in number by the pile beams or frames, which are placed above the ground-warp beam. Six is the greatest number of colors usually found, although extra tones can be planted. As many as nine frames may be used in weaving special Wiltons of more durability for areas receiving much wear. Wilton looms can also produce piles of different heights and types. Wilton piles are both cut and uncut.

The chain warp is the one that intersects the weft shots to anchor the pile. In a top-quality Wilton the chain warp is usually linen or wool. In carpets of lesser quality it is cotton. Most carpets carry what are known as

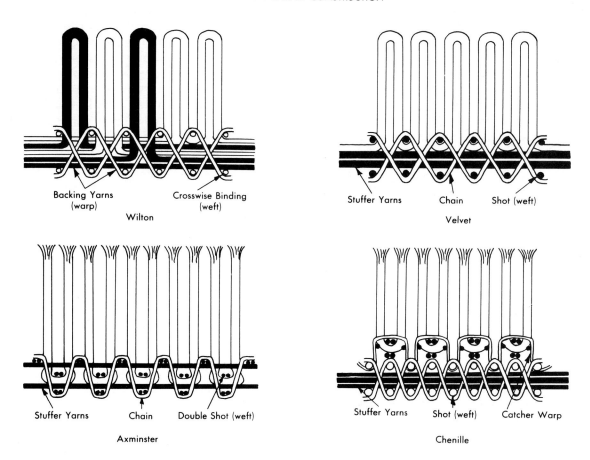

OTHER TYPES OF CARPET CONSTRUCTION

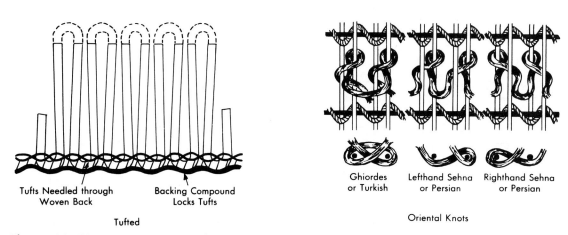

Figure 10.9. Woven carpet construction.
Drawing: based on an illustration provided courtesy of The Carpet & Rug Institute.

stuffer warps. These do not intersect with the weft but are merely carried along to give body to the cloth. In some Wiltons there may be as many as five stuffers, and in the top grades these are cotton or linen rather than jute. The number of the weft shots binding in the pile is important. A Wilton may have as many as five weft shots for each row of pile. It would then be referred to as a five-shot Wilton. A Wilton carpet provides a fine, compact texture and a deep pile.

A *velvet carpet* does not have any warp pile yarns embedded and hidden in its body. It can be woven on the simplest carpet looms, similar to those used for the weaving of un-patterned velvet fabrics. Most velvet carpets rely on textured and colored yarns to provide interest. The pile may be cut or uncut, and a profile cutting wire can produce a velvet pile of two heights. Colored pattern can be introduced into a velvet by printing. This is done by an ingenious method of printing the colors on the warp pile before it is woven into the fabric. The colors are estimated and the yarn dyed on large drums as it is needed for the pattern. It is, of course, just about impossible to get this color register perfect in alignment; therefore, a patterned velvet will frequently be stepped off just enough to resemble the diagonal steps made between adjacent colors in the hatchings of handwoven tapestries. This resemblance has given the name tapestry or tapestry velvet carpet to some printed velvet carpets. Many velvet carpets are now dye-printed after weaving.

What are some standards for a velvet carpet? It is customarily made of a heavier yarn and therefore has fewer points (pile tufts) per square inch than a Wilton. It may have a slightly higher pile than a Wilton, although many velvets do not. It will frequently have several jute stuffer yarns to give it added body. Warp chains are usually cotton. There are frequently two weft shots, although more may be found.

A velvet is a reasonably priced carpet of much worth. For a plain or yarn-textured carpet it is an excellent buy if care is taken to obtain good quality.

Axminster carpets are produced on a different principle from the Wilton or velvet carpets, and the resulting design is also very different. An Axminster weaving is one of the most economical ways to make a patterned rug.

Axminsters may contain innumerable colors and be designed to have a luxurious deep-pile look at a lower price. Therefore, the number of points is not large but the pile is high and the yarns are woolen rather than worsted to give that soft, textured look.

In an Axminster carpet the chain warp may be wool or cotton, the stuffers cotton, but the weft is jute. Therefore, this weave is clearly recognized because it results in the only carpet that can be rolled lengthwise but not crosswise. These jute weft shots are chained down by the warp. There is frequently a stuffer yarn above and below the level of the pile interlacing. One set of wefts may tie in the topmost stuffers, one set ties in the pile, and another ties in the lower set of stuffers. This makes a deep-bodied carpet that feels firm underfoot.

In weaving an Axminster, long spools the width of the rug are set up on which are wound, in order, yarn for every warp-pile color needed for a particular weft row. The winding of these spools is a very expensive process, inasmuch as it is necessary to have as many spools as there are pile rows in one warp-wise repeat of the pattern. Once the spools are wound, the weaving is relatively easy and inexpensive. When a certain spool appears in the pattern it comes down into place in the front of the loom and the necessary wool to make one tuft of pile is removed from each of its threads. Then it goes back out of use until required again by the pattern. The next spool comes into position and functions in a similar manner.

Axminster looms make up a high percentage of looms for untufted carpets today. The only rival for producing many-toned, deep-textured woolen carpets is the *tufted carpet* technique. These carpets are machine-made on the principle of handmade hooked rugs, in which a pile loop is hooked or needled into a base fabric. Such carpets are coated on the back with a plastic to prevent raveling.

One of the most expensive carpets is the *chenille carpet*. Seldom produced today, it is described here because there are old chenilles still available. The first step in its construction is just like that of a chenille fabric. A chenille yarn is woven on a separate loom. This yarn is planned so that the colors for a row of the weft pile are made on one yarn. When this yarn takes its place in the carpet, it becomes a particular weft-pile row. As many colors as desired can thus be incorporated into the rug.

The difference between a chenille fabric and a chenille carpet lies in the fact that the weaving for the latter really consists of two parts. There is first the weaving that binds down the chenille weft. In the best chenilles, this is done with fine linen yarn. At the same time that this binding is accomplished, the body of the carpet is woven. In this the chain warp is usually wool or cotton, and the stuffers may be cotton. The weft that binds in the chain warp may be wool or cotton.

It is no longer necessary to use the chenille construction for the purpose for which it was originally devised, namely for custom patterns. Chenilles have become very compact, deep-pile luxury fabrics. They are frequently embossed by cutting a design into the pile, creating a sculptured effect. These special weavings are expensive.

Carpets in which inexpensive chenille yarns are bound into plain-weave fabrics using jute binding wefts and cotton warps are called machine Smyrna rugs and are inexpensive. They should not be confused with chenille carpeting.

Because of the many new technical developments, construction alone can no longer be considered the determining factor of quality. Indeed, carpets bearing traditional weave names and woven to preserve some of the characteristics and values of the old weaves are actually produced by such modification of old techniques that they are very different products.

ORIENTAL RUGS

No study of carpets would be complete without an understanding of the hand-knotted carpets of the East known as *Oriental rugs* (Figure 10.10). There are many different ways to approach this study. The history of these carpets is interesting, since all of the conquests of the Orient have left imprints on their designs. The symbolism in their patterns tells us much about the culture of their weavers. Their manufacture, identification, market value, original use, and the great museum collections of Orientals each could be a subject for special study. We concentrate here on their current use.

Oriental carpets are woven in six geographic districts, all lying in the great wool belt of the East. They are usually called by the name of the district from which they come and are known as Turkish (from Turkey), Persian (from Iran), Caucasian (from the district in southern Russia called the Caucasus, between the Black and the Caspian Seas), Turkoman (from the district in southern Eurasia lying roughly between the Caspian Sea and the Himalaya Mountains), Indian (from northern India), and Chinese (from western China).

With the exception of a limited number of Soumaks and Khilims, most hand-loomed Orientals are also hand-knotted. A knotted pile is made with an extra weft thread that is twisted or knotted around two warp threads before being brought to the surface. There are two kinds of knots that are most commonly used. The first is the Ghiordes knot that is named for a town in Turkey (see Figure 10.9). In the Ghiordes knot a weft goes over two warps and then is brought up between them to form a pile. In a carpet woven with Ghiordes knots there is a pile tuft between every two warp threads. This makes a coarser fabric characterized by piles that are more widely spaced than those made using the Sehna knot. The Sehna knot, named after a city in Iran, is made by crossing the pile yarn under one warp and over an adjacent warp, returning under this warp to project beyond the surface (see Figure 10.9). Thus the cut pile ends are next to adjacent warps and there is a tuft between every warp. This makes a finer, more compact body.

The ground of Oriental carpets is made either of wool or of cotton, the former being customary in the great sheep-raising districts like the Caucasus and the latter being more frequent in the lower lands of Persia and China. The wool pile is softer and finer in the countries that depend on the fleece of lowland sheep. Since the lower lands lie in the path of more advanced civilizations, there is a marriage of a fine medium and a more sophisticated artistry in the work of the Persian, Indian, and Chinese weavers. The carpets woven by rugged mountaineers have strong designs like the architecture of the land. The character of Oriental carpets is variable within its unity, and their decorative uses vary as well. Such rugs as the Turkoman, Caucasian, and many of the Turkish

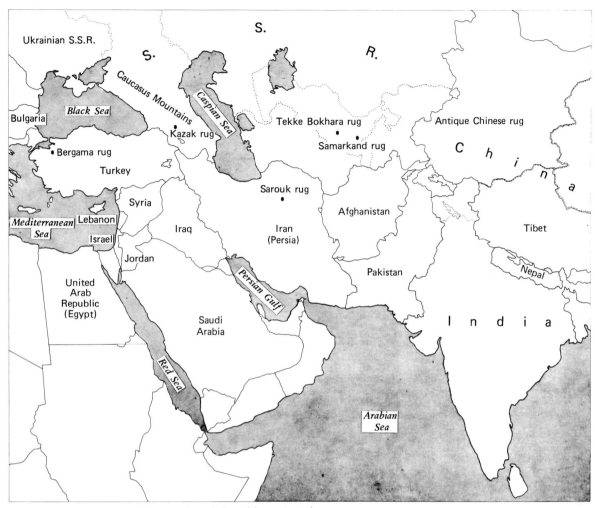

Figure 10.10. Countries that produced the older oriental carpets.

are appropriate for the interiors of large scale and coarse textures; whereas the Persian, Indian, Chinese, and many of the remaining Turkish rugs look best with finer ensembles.

Chinese Orientals are woven with the Sehna knot and have a deep, luxurious, soft woolen pile. All but the oldest have a cotton ground. Some have designs outlined with clipped pile. Many Chinese rugs are characterized by narrow border designs and symbolic central medallions. The field in some Chinese carpets is plain, unlike the customary field of other Orientals. Other fields contain small designs consisting of such Chinese symbols as the peony, the dragon, the cloud band, the wave, and the swastika. Colors are predominantly blue, ivory, and saffron yellow. A few eastern Turkoman rugs have a character that is Chinese with the inclusion of Turkoman symbols.

In contrast to the lighter tones of its eastern rugs, the real *Turkoman carpet* weaving is austere and somber. The generic name for the largest class of these rugs is Bokhara. The knot is almost always Sehna and the pile yarn is wiry and not very deep. The ground is wool, and goat's hair is used for the overcast selvedges. The ends are plain woven. Designs in Turkoman rugs are regular, prescribed, tribal designs known as guls. These are compounded of diamonds, hexagons, and octagons. The colors in these northern Turkomans are distinctive. Their reds are a subdued yellow or blood red. This is coupled with a great deal of black and some spotting of an almost white tone. Turkoman carpets are masculine in design character, yet their thinness of body renders them appropriate for use with fine furniture. They are good choices for libraries and for contemporary rooms with straight-line designs.

Situated between India and Persia, the countries of Afghanistan and Baluchistan (modern Pakistan) make carpets of small geometric designs that combine Persian blue with Turkoman reds. A deep brown is more customary than the Bokhara black in these rugs.

Indian carpets in the great tradition of Oriental rug manufacture are no longer produced. They were the weavings of the sixteenth and seventeenth centuries made during the reigns of the Moghul emperors. Indian design is frequently realistic but executed in such a light-hearted, dainty sort of way that it never seems crudely pictorial. The individual motifs may be arranged in rows or within a lattice-work design. Indian colors are far from somber. Light blue reds and yellow reds combine with other pastels to form a crisp, feminine palette. Many of today's Orientals come from India and, more especially, from Pakistan, where an extensive industry flourishes.

The *Persian rug* is frequently called the queen of the Orientals. There are many varieties of Persian carpets, and superficially they seem very different. Traveling across the south of Persia, one finds the realistic floral patterns of the Kermans contrasted with the large geometric medallions of the Shiraz. In the western mountains the tribesmen favor rows of small formal motifs such as pears, fish, or flowers. These rugs are the Saraband, Lorestan, Bakhtiari, and Kurdish carpets.

Farther north we come to towns that are in closer contact with the former capital cities of Tabriz, Herat, Ispahan, and the present capital, Teheran. The carpets woven for the court are frequently characterized by large central medallions that are masterpieces of formalized pattern. Among these are the Sarouk, Kashan, and Kermanshah (named after an alien shah from Kerman!). Larger and bolder medallions characterize the Hamadan (on a camel's hair ground) and the Gorevan, Serapi, and Herez weavings of districts adjacent to the Caspian.

The central Persian plateau, the seat of most present-day weaving, produces the Sarouk, Kashan, and Lilihan, as well as the old carpet known as the Feraghan, which bears a small stylized flower-and-leaf motif known as the herati (from the old capital of Herat) on a deep blue ground.

For all their diversity the Persian carpets stand out as being masterpieces of skillful craftsmanship and design. They show a mastery of color in relation to pattern and texture. They are fine weavings. An old Sehna (similar in pattern to a medallion Saruk) may have 400 Sehna knots to the square inch. Persian carpets are distinguished by a deep ruby red and a rich indigo blue, against which is found ivory, saffron, blue greens, and some green. It fits best into a blue-dominated scheme. The Persian motifs are frequently flower inspired, but they are formalized and admirably contrived into a flat pattern suitable for flooring.

The best *Turkish rugs* are skillfully designed. The general level of production, however, is somewhat uneven. Many of the Turkish patterns are geometric adaptations of the Persian. The prayer rug, on which Muslims kneel to pray, is characterized by a formalized niche or mihrab, which is to be turned toward Mecca, the sacred capital of the Islamic empire. The majority of Turkish carpets use the Ghiordes knot and coarse wool yarn. Colors are similar to the Persian but are somewhat more saturated. Green is more frequent. Varieties are the Ghiordes, Bergamo, Anatolian, and Oushak. Turkish carpets can be strong and beautiful accents in a room.

Caucasian carpets no longer are marketed in the West. Such names as Kazak (Cossack), Karabagh, and Daghestan suggest the wildness of the Russian steppes and the Kara Dagh Mountains. The Shirvans and Khubas come from the shores of the Caspian Sea. Persian influence is seen in some of these carpets, but in general the Caucasian carpet is at its best when allowed to be the most untamed of the Oriental weavings. The fiber and ground are of coarse wool. The knot is Ghiordes. Stylized human and animal figures, the swastika, the latchhook, and the medallion shooting tongues of flame are characteristic motifs. Colors are daring but sure, with much use of blood red and black with yellow, blue, and green.

In a true Oriental, one of the characteristics that adds charm is the small variation in pattern and color (abrash) that inevitably accompanies the hand process. In the somewhat commercialized and even industrialized production of Orientals for the modern market this particular loveliness has been lost.

If an Oriental rug is several hundred years

old, it merits being called antique. Carpets of more than fifty years of age are merely old or semiantique. Age is venerable in the East. If one studies the Oriental weavings with a discriminating eye and learns to choose between the superlative, the good, and the poor, one will find rich rewards for use today.

CARPET PADS AND FINISHES

Pads under carpets make them seem softer and protect them from abrasion and slippage. They are made from foams, both natural and synthetic, and from fibers such as felted cattle hair or jute.

The backs of carpets are frequently treated with a plastic coating intended to strengthen the fabric, to give it dimensional stability, and to keep it from raveling, thus sometimes eliminating the necessity for any separate underpadding. Carpets are often given a finish to control color and sheen. The current market should always be appraised with respect both to finishes and linings.

Ceramics

The word *ceramic* describes any object made from clay and hardened by fire. An earthen flowerpot and the finest piece of Ming china are both ceramics. What are their essential similarities and differences?

CERAMIC COMPOSITION TYPES

The basic chemicals in clay are silicon, aluminum, hydrogen, and oxygen, which combine to form a hydrous silicate of aluminum. The average clay has many impurities. These ingredients mixed in the clay account for its color, texture, and plasticity. They also determine the temperature at which it can be fired and thus set the body characteristics of the ceramic.

Pottery (Figure 10.11) is ware made from clays that cannot be fired at an intense heat (which porcelain clays can withstand). The body of pottery is opaque and porous. Unglazed pottery was used for a long time before glazes were developed to make it nonporous. The majority of pottery glazes have a composition similar to that of glass and some contain lead. Many glazes are therefore transparent. Many of these transparent glazes contain colorants that modify the color as well as the texture of the pottery on which they are placed. Some of the greatest masterpieces of the potter's art have been produced through the ceramist's mastery of glazes.

Not all glazes are transparent. Pottery clays vary in color from a red known as terra-cotta through buff to a cream color. Opaque glazes were developed to cover some of the darker clays. The introduction of tin oxide was an

Figure 10.11. Pottery tea service.
Artist: Charles Lakofsky
Photograph: Courtesy of The Cleveland Museum of Art and with the permission of the artist.

early discovery that the potters of the Near East found would make a glaze opaque.

The customary glazes on pottery clay are not fired at the temperature necessary to harden the body of the ware. Therefore a first, or so-called biscuit or bisque firing, and a second, or glost (glaze) firing, are required. When a glaze is not well fuzed to the clay body, it can chip off or craze. Unglazed pottery is known as bisque ware.

Pottery is made from the coarser red and buff clays is often called earthenware, although all ceramics are made from earth and are, strictly speaking, earthenwares. The term *faience* (from the Italian town of Faenza) became associated with colorful glazed European pottery. The term *majolica* is given to a type of faience that has metallic lusters added to a painted, tin-glazed pottery. Majolica was named for the Island of Majorca off the coast of Spain, from which it was exported. One should guard against a loose designation of any colorful, highly glazed pottery as majolica—better save the name for the real thing.

When a clay body is fired to such an intense heat that it becomes hard and stonelike and nonporous, it is said to be vitrified. *Stoneware*, which can be vitrified, is made of a clay that contains a higher percentage of aluminum silicate than the pottery clays do. Stoneware clay is often light grey or cream in color. If made very thin, it is almost translucent. True china is generally translucent.

Because stoneware does not need a glaze to make it nonporous, much stoneware is fired to a high temperature and left unglazed. Some glazes can be applied in the first firing of the stoneware. Ordinary salt is frequently added in the kiln when stoneware jugs are first fired. This produces what is known as a salt glaze, which sometimes runs down a jar in a hit or miss fashion, adding to its interesting quality.

Fine stoneware is often called ironstone china on the contemporary market. Some manufacturers call it semivitreous china. This, together with the better grades of pottery, is occasionally advertised as dinnerware. These are general terms and do not have as definite a meaning as the words pottery and stoneware.

China, or *porcelain*, is the highest refinement of ceramic manufacture. Because this fine ware first came from the Orient, it was known as china. The Italians, seeing in it a resemblance to a shell known as porcellana, gave it a name that has been translated to porcelain.

Porcelain is made of a light-colored clay known as kaolin. This clay, which is largely pure aluminum silicate, is almost infusible. To it is added petuntse or a feldspar rock that makes the kaolin fusible at an extremely high temperature. A feldspathic glaze is used with porcelain as an integral process with the biscuit firing. Sometime feldspathic glaze is placed over any applied decoration, which is then known as underglaze decoration. The high firing of body with glaze in porcelain creates a highly vitrified ware that is frequently translucent when held up to the light and which has a bell-like ring when struck (Figure 10.12).

Contemporary chinas are divided into hard-paste chinas (to differentiate them from a soft-paste china that was an early European ware attempting to duplicate the Oriental chinaware) and bone chinas. Most European chinas are hard paste and English chinas are bone. The latter are made with the addition of calcined bone, which acts like the feldspar

Figure 10.12. Contemporary Danish porcelain. "Comet," Bing & Grøndahl Copenhagen Porcelain Inc.
Designer: Henning Koppel
Photograph: Courtesy of Bing & Grøndahl Copenhagen Porcelain Inc.
This porcelain is decorated with spontaneous brush strokes in blue that emphasize the shapes. The noted ceramist Koppel designed this service in 1978 to mark Bing & Grøndahl's 125th anniversary.

to make the clay more fusible. Since it does not require as high a temperature, bone china is not as hard or vitrified as the European hard-paste china. The added materials give bone china creamier body and greater translucency than hard-paste china.

CERAMIC FORMING

There are many primitive processes by which ceramics are still being formed (see the Peter Voulkos vase in Figure 11.7 and Lisa McVey's large planter in Figure 12.11c). One ancient method involves carving or hewing out a bulk of clay to make it hollow; another derives shapes from coils or ropes of clay.

Potters learned to perfect symmetry in their work through the use of the potter's wheel, a circular revolving plate on which a lump of clay is centered and worked with the hands into the desired shapes. This technique is called wheel throwing. Many potters feel that a true pottery shape should display the roundness of wheel throwing. China pieces are also formed in molds into which clay mixed with water (slip) can be poured and from which it becomes loosened as its moisture evaporates. Molded ceramics may have their inner surfaces stamped into form. In fine mold work the potter's hand and instruments subsequently shape the thicknesses of the vessel's walls. Considerable skilled artistry can enter at this point.

CERAMIC EMBELLISHMENT

The smooth surfaces of ceramic vessels have always been a great temptation to the painter or the sculptor. Decoration can be applied both under and over the glaze. Color can be added with colored slip (moist clay), transparent glazes, enamel (low-fired glaze), and luster coats. The surface of the clay can be modeled or carved, or thick slip added to create decoration. Sgraffito or intaglio decoration is made by incising through a slip coating. The former usually consists of incised linear patterns, whereas in the latter the background is cut away around the pattern. Sometimes the artist has put decoration of superb quality on ware of inferior body, for instance, in much Persian ware. Sometimes decoration of poor quality (judged from the point of view of good decorative design) is added to wares of good body. Rarely in the total array of the world's ceramics has the artist been content merely with structural shape, color, texture, and glaze without added pattern. Yet some of the pieces so made have been the finest that the ceramist has ever produced.

CONTEMPORARY CERAMIC FACTORIES

The bulk of our utilitarian ceramics are the product of our contemporary factories. Ceramics are tied to individual factories to an extent not found in textiles. What choices are available? It is impossible to state exactly what the body and glaze of each type of ware is, because such formulas are the ceramists' secrets. An acquaintance with historical wares gives a good clue to the character of contemporary ones. In the first place, much contemporary work is the product of factories that have been in continuous existence since the eighteenth century and that today still produce wares of traditional fineness of body while using some contemporary designs. Newer factories can be compared to the old and an appraisal made.

Hard-paste china of the character of historic Dresden and Meissen (East German) china is being exported from West Germany. Some patterns are contemporary in feeling. Arzberg and Rosenthal china from Bavaria are interesting contemporary hard-paste chinas.

Fine china of the northern countries, Denmark and Finland, is available. Royal Copenhagen Danish china has long been known as a hard-paste china of excellent quality. From Finland and from various centers around the Baltic comes good pottery that is hand painted under a glaze in wares similar to the old Delft (Holland) pottery. Shapes and patterns are both traditional and modern and, as with so much northern design, are done with a light rather than a heavy hand.

The firm of Haviland at Limoges in south-central France produced some of the world's finest table china. Closed before World War I, it is now reestablished as a leading producer of hard-paste porcelain.

One center of European hand-made pottery is Vallauris. Here many Spanish and French artists such as Picasso and Chagall designed for the modern market. Italian potteries are exporting colorful wares. Their works are often marked with an individual touch; no two pieces are exactly alike. Similar pottery of traditional provincial pattern comes from France.

English bone chinas of superior quality are available. Spode, Wedgwood, Royal Worcester, Royal Doulton, Minton, Coalport, and Royal Crown Derby are factories well known for several centuries for the excellence of their products. Spode and Wedgwood also make fine quality pottery. There are many other English potteries located in and around Staffordshire that make good tableware. The shapes and applied designs of the British wares are often traditional, and frequently the patterns are delightful floral pieces or chaste classical designs. Recently, some excellent modern designing has been done.

Ireland produces a china of great translucency and of soft creamy color known as Beleek. Small wares such as tea sets are the pieces generally available.

Oriental ceramics are found in the occidental market. The Japanese ceramic tradition, like the Chinese, is in hard-paste china and in beautiful pottery. Oriental artistry combined with fine wares create lovely articles.

America's ceramic factories have gained much ground in the last seventy-five years. Lenox is known for its lustrous sheen and high translucency. The Ohio china kilns produce very good dinnerware of all types at reasonable prices. China and pottery are made in southern mountain areas. Many new California studios have come into existence that make everything from gay, colorful potteries to finer porcelains.

CHOOSING CERAMICS

What are the desirable qualities in ceramics? Practical considerations come first. Thus we note that pottery, although it is heavier than china, is more susceptible to chipping and to the crazing of the glaze. China is hard and it will shatter with a blow, but it will not chip easily. It can be subjected to great heat without harm because of the nature of its clay. Ceramics are now made that will withstand intense oven heat or go safely from freezer directly into a hot oven.

China is generally more expensive than pottery. However, a fine grade of pottery may cost more than a poor grade of china and may be a very desirable product from all points of view.

We are most concerned with the aesthetic qualities of ceramics. First, consider the usefulness of the shape. Will a pitcher hold liquids and be easy to pour from and to clean? Surfaces must be smooth for easy cleaning. Plates are frequently made without an inner rim so that there is a greater surface for serving. These, however, have no place to rest cutlery.

We notice certain things about the inner space of a vessel in relation to its volume and the walls that enclose it. Is this space beautifully designed with just that amount of variety in its concavity that will make it interesting and not enough to ruin its unity of form or its usefulness?

The walls of clay vessels may be of various thicknesses. If we observe closely, we will note that just as an interesting line varies in its thickness in an orderly fashion, so do the walls of some of the most exquisite ceramics. To observe this is a source of aesthetic pleasure. Interrelations between the space enclosed and the wall thickness are often carefully planned by the artist.

Color in ceramics can be one of its sources of appeal. To secure beautiful color, the potter needs much knowledge and skill. Ceramic colors change with kiln temperatures. For instance, a copper salt that at one temperature will produce a blue color will be green at another. Many colors, including gold, cannot be fired at the heat of the china kiln and must be added in a separate, low-temperature firing. Ceramics can be both translucent and reflective, and their color therefore varies with the nature of the ware. In the exquisite china from the Orient, color may be reflected and refracted through the application of several glazes.

Texture also contributes much to the aesthetic pleasure derived from ceramics. China responds to touch with the coolness and smoothness of quartz and the crispness of flint. Stoneware has a texture that is more like granite. Different pottery glazes possess different characteristic tactile qualities.

When the makers of china became forgetful of its pure values and loaded it with too much pattern and with heavy overglazes, modern potters turned away from porcelain to the down-to-earth beauty of earthenware. Today, ceramists are returning to stoneware and porcelain for contemporary accessories. Pattern on contemporary ceramics should be of the quality of all good decorative design of any age. It should support and contribute to the beauty of an artistic shape.

Glass

GLASS COMPOSITION TYPES

Glass is another remarkable human invention. The principal ingredient of glass is silica in the form of sand. Various alkalies, usually a combination of two or more of the following—soda, potash, lime, lead, or aluminum—are added as modifiers and act as flux. Specialized ingredients impart other desirable qualities. Glass is heated before forming. In its molten state it is referred to as the metal.

Glass is customarily classified as one of three composition types, depending on which alkalies are predominant. The commonest glass is frequently called soda or potash glass. Where color impurities remain, this is sometimes known as green glass. It does not possess great clarity, weight, or resonance. Its uses are many, with a range dependent on its refinement.

An increase in the amount of calcium in the formula results in a clearer glass that is sometimes known as lime glass. When lead oxide is added to the batch, the glass becomes heavier, more resonant, and has greater ability to refract light (or sparkle). It is of a softness that makes it easy to engrave or cut and of a high plasticity for forming. Lead glass is sometimes called flint glass, flint being a very hard, glasslike form of quartz (Figure 10.13). Fine lead and lime glass are both currently known as crystal.

Glass has entered into an era of greatly extended architectural use in addition to its age-old employment as a functional and decorative material. Some new structural uses are more acceptable because of ingredients that have been added to glass composition. For instance, it would not be practical to orient large windows to the west were it not for tinted (grey, bronze, bluish) glass. This reduces heat absorption and glare. However, it may slightly alter the appearance of interior colors.

THE FORMING OF GLASS

What the potter's wheel is to ceramics, the blowpipe (a hollow metal rod) is to glass. The shaped glass that results from the use of the blowpipe is known as blown or off-hand glass. This latter term implies that the glass has been made by hand rather than by a mechanized process.

In glass forming the craftsman takes a red hot gather of molten glass from the furnace on the end of the blowpipe and with lung power expands it to a sphere. As the glass cools or anneals, it can be further elongated or flattened. Edges can be flanged or depressed. The shape can be united with other pieces blown into handles or bases.

Glass that is called blown-molded is shaped by being blown into a mold. The mold may be of one or several parts. The latter type may leave a slight imprint on the glass along the line where the parts of the mold meet each other. One method of classifying blown-molded glass is through the number of these marks, with the glass correspondingly known as two- or three-mold glass.

A quicker and less expensive method of forming glass is by pressing. In this process the glass is poured into a forming mold that makes the outer surface. The inner is made by a plunger that presses down into the forming mold.

A newly reestablished method for shaping glass is called the plastic glass process. Bits of broken glass are fired in a refractory fire-clay mold. The glass fuses perfectly and after cooling is removed. This method is usually reserved for solid pieces and for large bas reliefs.

Another renewed method of forming is to cool the metal to plastic consistency, at which point it is modeled into a desired shape.

Heavy sheet glass of the calcium composition type is formed by several means that are basically dependent on extruding the molten glass onto a smooth surface where it is rolled between a pair of cylinders. The distinguishing feature in plate glass is that it is ground and polished on both sides to a perfectly flat pane.

A newer type of forming that accomplishes the same result is known as floating glass. In this process, molten glass is floated on a bath of molten tin where it remains until hardened. Float glass was first produced in the United States in 1963.

Large sheets of glass are on occasion given additional treatment. Some of the glass varieties that are important to the interior designer are:

Figure 10.13. Table crystal, Steuben Glass.
Designer: George Thompson
Photograph: Courtesy of Steuben Glass.
This set of table crystal has stemware design typified by a deep, rounded bowl and a spiral air-twist stem on a plain circular foot. The roundness and plainness of the ware display to best advantage the beautiful lead glass of which it is made.

Insulating glass—Two or more glass panes separated by a dehydrated air space. This allows greater indoor humidity because condensation does not occur at the inner glass surface.

Laminated glass—A composite of two or more layers of glass with a layer of plastic sandwiched between. This provides a safety factor if the glass is shattered because the plastic holds the broken pieces and prevents their escape. Such glass is variously known as safety or bullet-proof glass. The government and concerned organizations have regulations concerning the installation of such glass.

Mirror glass—Made by coating glass on one side with a thin wash of metal. Silver, copper, bronze, and chromium are the metals most frequently used, each imparting its characteristic color tone.

Reflective glass—A form of window glass coated with a thin film of chromium alloy. It allows light transmission and appears transparent on its more dimly lighted side. It has many uses, among which are applications in observation areas and wherever it is desirable to reflect solar heat without sacrificing appreciable transparency. Reflective glass acts like a mirror and thus conceals such articles as draperies as well as all daytime activity within a building. At night the reverse occurs and the exterior is blanked out, revealing the interior. Thus some form of interior shade may be required.

THE EMBELLISHMENT OF GLASS

Something may be done to glass at every stage of its manufacture to make it more attractive. Color added to the batch may emerge from the furnace transformed. A small amount of gold and tin created the famous ruby color of the old Bohemian red glass. The irridescent color that characterized the Tiffany glass of the late nineteenth century was the result of added body color. Milk glass contains an opaque white colorant. Much of the color of early American glass was the result of impurities in the metal.

Glasses of different colors can be combined in distinct patterns. Sometimes one color of glass will be contained within another. It is always intriguing to see threads of white glass within a form of colorless glass or to see a tear drop or a series of bubbles snugly ensconced within the stem of a goblet. The container and the contained shape occasionally may be of the same color, but their different thicknesses and separate walls make them appear to be different tones (dichroic). The secret of accomplishing these glasses within glasses is the same as that used by a cook in making a marble cake: the layers must be kept separate until they are set. Since glass is more viscous than cake dough, this is not difficult. Some examples are merely tours de force. Others are genuinely artistic and create an aspect of fantasy.

Color in the form of enamels or of colored glass may be added to the finished glass product. Gold and silver and other metals can be encrusted on the surface for added enrichment.

Much decoration on glass is sculptural in the sense that it affects the plane of the glass surface. Molded and pressed glass are of this nature. Sandblasting of glass produces a sculptured effect with the broadest strokes. This is done by preparing a shield for the parts of the glass to be protected and then cutting away the unprotected portions with a blast of sand.

Etched glass is eaten by acid. The entire glass is covered with a resist through which a design is cut. The glass is immersed in an acid that incises deep into the pattern. The resist is then removed. Both in sandblasting and in etching the background is sometimes the part that is cut away, leaving the design on the intact glass. Cameo glass, in which the design is in glass of one color and the background of another, may be made in this manner.

Cut or engraved glass is actually cut deeply or engraved shallowly with stone and copper wheels, respectively, revolving at great speed. Both processes require outstanding skill on the part of the craftsman.

Structural glass also may be patterned. This is usually done in the form of shallow etching or sandblasting, often with the purpose of controlling light transmission.

CONTEMPORARY GLASS FACTORIES

This century has produced glass in abundance and with merit. The Italians have followed one Venetian tradition of blowing glass into interesting plastic shapes. All Italian glass is apt to be called Venetian on today's market. Likewise, all central European glass may find itself labeled Bohemian. Bohemian glass probably comes from either Austria or Bavaria today and is remarkably clear lime glass, frequently cut or engraved.

France has made signal contributions to the contemporary glass market. The Daum Cristallerie and the Baccarat factory are famed for fluid designs essentially French in character.

The Leerdam factory in Holland and the Belgian firm Val Saint Lambert produce fine glassware. The Eda Glass Works, the Kosta factory, and the well-known Orrefors factory in Sweden manufacture contemporary glasswares. Karhula and Nötsjo glass come from Finland and have exceptional clarity. Holmegaards glass is Danish and Hadelands is Norwegian. Česká glass is from Czechoslovakia.

The English today make much fine lead glass, which they have done since the seventeenth century. They are scientists in the art of glass cutting and know just where to cut to gain the greatest brilliance from the refracted light. They make beautiful table glass that is frequently in the eighteenth-century design tradition.

America is producing much of its own glass. For perfect off-hand lead glass none can excel Steuben glass made at the Steuben Division of the Corning Glassworks, Corning, New York. The shapes are contemporary and often adhere to spherical derivations. Many of the pieces are unornamented and some have well-designed engraving.

The center of the American glass industry is in Ohio, western Pennsylvania, and West Virginia. Here in numerous factories such as the Westmoreland Glass Company, the Fostoria Company, the Libby Glass Company, the Tiffin Glass Masters, and the Blenko Glass Company, fine table glass of all types is made. The lovely colored ware of Blenko is noteworthy. Large structural glass is manufactured by the Libby-Owens-Ford Company and the Pittsburgh Plate Glass Company.

CHOOSING GLASS

Durability looms high as a consideration in the selection of glass. Any incising of the surface should be examined to determine its effect on strength. Hard calcium glass may nick, but it can be ground smooth again. It is, however, subject to fracture and will crack if struck at just the right angle.

Decorative glass is chosen largely for its aesthetic appeal. Since glass is a plastic material, we wish to sense the flowing quality in its finished form. In blown glass the curved shapes coming from the bubble seem most appropriate, although some very recent work is rectangular (see Figure 11.10). Rhythms between the masses are important. When whimsy predominates, let it be the masterful theatrics that come from the Venetian punty or from the hand of the artist engraver.

Flawless glass needs no adornment. When it is patterned, the greatest restraint is necessary to enhance rather than detract from the fluid glass quality. Cutting should be designed to aid the natural ability of glass to refract light.

The vagrant bubbles, the natural color, and the variant shapes of some glasses such as the Spanish and the Mexican have their own appeal. The sophisticated dichroism of some contemporary glass is also attractive.

The texture of glass is an indescribable thing, perhaps more appreciated through touch than through sight. The heavy thin edge of a lead crystal has a different feel (as well as a different ring) from that of other glasses. The surface of bottle glass actually seems waxy.

The Metals

GENERAL CHARACTER

The metals stand witness to human inventiveness, in both practical and artistic creations. Their extraction from the ground (mining), their smelting (refining the metal from its ore), their combination with other ingredients (alloying), and their forming all present problems that require thought and skill to solve. Metallurgy has now so advanced as a science that the twentieth century may well be called the age of metals because of our modern expertise in handling and using a large number of the over eighty metallic elements.

Metals are fusible and ductile when intensely heated. They possess great hardness and tensile strength when cooled. One of their principal aesthetic delights is their versatility in the reflection of light. They are also conductors of heat and electricity, and this gives them many operational uses.

A distinction based on rarity and therefore on cost is often made between what are termed the common metals (iron, steel, copper, bronze, brass, tin, lead, zinc, nickel, aluminum, and chromium) and the so-called noble metals (gold, silver, and platinum). Although there are many surprising crossovers, the noble metals are used primarily in fashioning art objects, whereas the common metals serve mostly utilitarian functions. Since the metals are inorganic, they do not rot or decay (although some may corrode), and thus metal artifacts tell us much about our ancestors.

THE FORMING OF METALS

The methods used to form all metals into their intended objects are similar. In the molten state metal can be extruded to any desired shape and size. In the solid state it can be cut by any tool sufficiently hard and sharp to do the job. Rolling is an industrial process that forms metal into a thin sheet. Forging is the process of forming heated metal by pounding. Hammering with a mallet over a die can be used to shape thin metal. Stamping creates forms under pressure from both upper and lower dies. Casting is the pouring of molten metal into molds of the desired shape and then cooling.

THE EMBELLISHMENT OF METALS

The visual characteristics of metals frequently are changed through manipulation of their finished surfaces. Some of these techniques are chemical processes that can produce such variations as an etched matte finish, a bright smooth one, or one designed to give the effect of a natural patina. A shiny surface also can be obtained by mechanical means such as grinding, polishing, and buffing. Burnishing is a method of polishing in which the surface is rubbed with a very hard and smooth steel or agate tool. An industrial burnishing method involves immersion and tumbling among agate or steel balls in a specific soap solution. Mechanical treatment with various wire brushes accomplishes a lined texture. Indeed, mechanical manipulation has been substituted for hand techniques in many processes.

Similar and related results are generally hand-fashioned in the noble metals. Chasing is the process whereby a surface is pounded from above with a blunted instrument. Repoussé is formed by raising a pattern from underneath. Granulation encrusts the surface with metal nodules. Engraving cuts patterns on the surface with a sharp-pointed graver. In cloisonné, thin wires are attached to a metal to form partitions for the containment of enamel. Filigree is an openwork design constructed with wires.

METAL JOINING

Because metals often show corrosive action when in contact with one another, special techniques of joining must be used. These are employed both in industrial work and in the art world (Figure 10.14).

Riveting—the bolting together of two metals—is a conspicuous and forceful method of joinery. Welding is the uniting of two pieces of like metal either by heating and allowing them to flow together or by hammering them into union. Soldering is the uniting of two metallic surfaces with the use of a metal alloy of lower melting point than the metal pieces being joined.

Figure 10.14. Sculptural metal screen. General Motors Technical Center Restaurant Building, Detroit, Michigan.
Artist: Harry Bertoia
Photographer: G. C. Ball
The steel plaques of this screen are coated with various metals that were applied in the molten state, giving rich textures and varying colors to the architectural rigidity of the framework. The wall panels in the background are Brazilian wood.

METAL TYPES

The metals used both structurally and decoratively in an interior are so numerous that they can cause some textural incompatibilities unless an effort is made to appraise their characteristics.

Aluminum is one of the latest metals to come into prominence. Of small importance before the nineteenth century, it is now in increasing use both in the structure of buildings and in furniture. Its outstanding asset is its lightness with strength. However, it must be combined with other metals for requisite hardness. Silvery in color, its soft diffusion of light adds charm to interior trims, hardware, doors, and ornamental fixtures such as grilles, railings, and lighting appliances.

Copper is a historically important metal, its use boosting civilization onto one of its earliest cultural plateaus. Copper boasts a lovely reddish brown color. Easily worked and with sufficient strength for many tasks, it has been used for bells, household facilities, and tools for at least five thousand years. Its value was greatly enhanced when metallurgists learned to combine it with tin (and later with other metals) to form the harder alloy, *bronze*, and with zinc to form the brighter one, *brass*. In addition to its practical value for weaponry, bronze was used to cast some of the world's finest sculpture. From it have been made monumental doors and large bas-relief plaques and ornaments. Brass, with less strength, has been a favorite medium for lighting fixtures, fireside equipment, interior hardware, and now for furniture.

Iron is found abundantly in nature, and has been long in use. Civilization took a big stride forward when it discovered that iron could be hardened by heating and sudden cooling and made more ductile by heating and slow cooling (annealing). Iron is characterized by a coarse, compact structure, blackish color, and considerable weight. Wrought iron contains less carbon than cast iron and being less brittle, can be forged into graceful shapes. In cast iron the artist's hand is less in evidence. Both forms of iron are found in modern furniture and in all kinds of ornamental work.

Steel is also an iron and carbon alloy, differing from cast iron in its higher percentages of carbon and lower incidence of impurities. It is finer grained and stronger than pure iron. Stainless steel, which contains 12 to 14 percent chromium, is made into contemporary cutlery as well as furniture. The structural uses of steel are discussed in Chapter 2.

Lead and *tin* are two soft metals in common use. Lead is heavy but pliable, tempting modern craftsmen to use it almost as sculptors do clay. We recognize it in its alloy with tin in the form of *pewter*, long regarded as the poor man's silver and now, with its beautiful grey color and soft patina, seen to be handsome in its own right.

FINISHES APPLIED TO METAL

One of the important innovations in modern structural and decorative metallurgy is the use of finishes bonded to the underlying metal to give protection, color, or texture. These range from the long-known process of galvanizing, the coating of iron or steel with zinc to protect it from rusting, to the anodyzing or coating of one metal with another substance by means of electrolysis. Vitreous coatings known as enamels impart a glasslike colored surface. Paints and lacquers are possible overlays.

Plated silver is the name given to silver applied to a harder metal by means of electrolytic action. The base metal is usually an alloy of copper, zinc, and nickel. The purchaser should be assured of a plate that is sufficiently thick for the use intended. Some silver-plated objects have inlaid blocks of solid sterling silver at the points that receive the hardest wear. Plated silver of comparable size is always heavier and less flexible than sterling silver. It frequently bears, along with the maker's name, some kind of indication of the quality of the plating.

SILVER AS A NOBLE METAL

We discuss silver as representative of the noble metals because the expensive gold and platinum exist beyond the orb of most interior design.

Silver must be alloyed with a harder metal to give it strength. One of the first indications of law and order in a land is the enforcement of a standard percentage of silver to alloy for legal coinage. Silversmiths seldom exceed this standard, although they might fall short of it. American silver of coinage standard is labeled *sterling*. The term solid silver means that the piece is sterling silver.

Sometimes silver is combined with gold in tableware. The fineness of gold is expressed in terms of the carat, which is a unit of weight for precious metals. Alloys of metals other than gold and having the color of gold are sometimes made into tableware. They are attractive and durable.

CONTEMPORARY SILVER

There are many firms in America that have been manufacturing sterling for over 100 years. The center of this craft is in New England and upper New York, localities that produced our famous Colonial silversmiths.

Silver is exported from Scandinavia as well as from France. This silver is heavy in weight. The designs of northern silver are typical of a long heritage of silver design. One characteristic is a large area of plain surface offset by concentrated pattern. French silver follows its national tradition, which leans toward more ornate patterns.

CHOOSING SILVERWARE

If sterling silver is all of one quality and if the quality of plated ware is reasonably assured, what then are the criteria for silver choice? In the first place, there is a practical appraisement. There may be differences in the weight of pieces even within the production of one company and of one pattern. Heavy silver will cost more than light silver. The weight selected should be practical and appropriate for its use.

Functional standards should be observed closely. Table silver pieces are tools. When buying a table knife, analyze it as a cutting and spreading tool; a fork as a skewer, a pusher, and sometimes a cutter; a spoon as a scoop, a stirrer, and a partial cutter. Examine the shape of these pieces to see if they can perform these tasks well. Take them in your hand to note how they feel. Are the weight and balance right? Is the handle shaped to suit the hand grip? Table silver is used for many years.

Silver is good to possess because of its associative value. Be on guard, however, lest a glamorous historical name that has inspired a silver pattern should blind us to the intrinsic merit of the design. Neither should family pride, associated with the possession of valuables such as silver, become of inordinate consequence.

The visual design of silver is very important. The three-dimensional shape of a piece of silver is part of its pattern (Figure 10.15). Silver should be beautiful from whatever angle it is viewed. However, we see the top surface of table silver most clearly. Therefore it should be particularly lovely when seen from this angle.

The texture of silver is important. Silver has a porous but very fine texture. It can be given a very high or low polish. Since any highly reflective surface blanks out the apparent texture of an object, contemporary silver is frequently given a satin rather than a high-gloss finish. This satin patina comes to old silver with use and is another argument in favor of constant use of household silver. If properly cared for, the patina of silver should grow more lovely with age. Many people feel that ornate silver becomes too darkly oxidized with use. Ornate patterns are usually designed with the idea that silver oxidation in the shadows contributes to a more interesting surface.

Stone

Moving backward in time, we come to the earliest humans who used stone to sustain their existence—the people of the stone age. Today's uses of stone are not as imperatively dictated, but they are not negligible. Stone is seen in walls, fireplaces, floors, furniture, statuary, and vessels. It can introduce hardness, strength, and permanence, and also can offer the aesthetic qualities of color and texture.

The lightest of the stones are the sedimentary rocks formed from sand, clay, and other substances derived from the breakdown of existing stone and settled in beds by water. Of these, limestone and sandstone are used for interior finishes and flagging. Limestone is often buff grey, and sandstone ranges from white through the greys to the reddish tones. Travertine is a noncrystalline calcium carbonate (limestone).

Marble is a metamorphic rock of hard crystalline form. Metamorphic rocks, as the name implies, have been changed by heat and pressure acting, in the case of marble, on limestone. True marbles are very hard and are found in many colors, usually local to the district from which they come. With beautiful

Figure 10.15. The noble metal: silver.
Artist: Frederick A. Miller
Photograph: Courtesy of The Cleveland Museum of Art and with the permission of the artist
Such a group of hand-crafted silver pieces really should be placed in Chapter 11 because they are so exquisitely beautiful. They are placed here because of their intended use for the embellishment of a dining service.

striations and capable of taking a polish, marble is without peer in much interior work and is the sculptor's preeminent material.

Slate results from the metamorphosis of shale or clays that have hardened into stratified rock. Formed through time, it develops layers that can be split into thin slabs. Slate is strong and durable and has many uses in interiors from counter tops and flooring slabs to blackboards. It comes in a variety of earth colors that depend on the ingredients in the local slate beds.

Granite is an igneous stone, formed by slow cooling of molten mixtures of minerals within the earth's crust. It is usually a combination of feldspar, quartz, and mica. When it is fine grained, it has a distinctive salt-and-pepper pattern. The presence of much feldspar can redden it. Crushed granite is used for terrazzo, a floor material with a matrix of portland cement or synthetic resin.

Terrazzo, if its foundation is cement, must be installed with metal or plastic dividing strips to eliminate possible cracking.

The structural installation of stones presents engineering problems that must be considered (see the Bibliography). The forms of structural stone are variously known as rubble or fieldstone (unshaped), cut stone or ashlar (dimension stone), flagstone (slabs of thin stone), and crushed or broken stone. The positioning of stone has its own vocabulary—random to regular coursing, rusticated to smooth grointing.

So beautiful and useful are the various stones that it is fortunate if an interior designer has learned to appreciate them and recognize their potential. They provide a natural hardness capable of taking polish and dispersing light to contrast with the soft fabrics that are in many instances indispensable to an interior.

The Plastics

We have used the word plastic several times in this chapter. Now it is time to take a closer look. In a broad sense a plastic is a material that can be formed in one physical state and then processed to give permanency. (Defined in this way, glass and ceramics are plastics.) The term plastic is currently used to apply to a group of synthetics that have plasticity in one state and rigidity in another. By definition in the United States, glass is an inorganic compound whereas the plastics may contain hydrocarbons and amino acids.

Classification of the plastics used in interiors roughly corresponds to that of the synthetic fibers discussed earlier in this chapter. The list below describes those most frequently encountered.

Beyond the obvious utilitarian advantages of many of the plastics, we need to appraise their aesthetic potential. The use of plastics for furniture, utensils, vessels, lighting fixtures, and even fine art forms is so new that the designer should consider both their practicality and their suitability to the particular

Figure 10.16. Furniture in plastic. Cocktail table (1966) by Neal Small, clear acrylic, H. 15½", Collection, The Museum of Modern Art, New York, Lily Auchincloss Fund; lamp (1966), Gruppo Architetti Urbanisti Città Nuova, Fiberglas with aluminum base, H. 13". Collection, The Museum of Modern Art, New York, Gift of the manufacturer.
Photograph: The Museum of Modern Art, New York

form they are given (Figure 10.16). As you learn to use plastics in your designing, you will have to set up your own criteria—for instance, does the form suggest in an artistic way the transition from plastic to solid state?

Type	Character	Some Common Trade Names	Some Uses
Acrylic	Thermoplastic (can be softened by heat)	Lucite, Plexiglas	Hardware, lighting fixtures, lampshades, furniture, tableware
Cellulose acetate	Thermoplastic	Tenite, Cellophane	Artificial leather, transparent film
Epoxy	Thermosetting (cannot be softened by heat)		Matrix for seamless and terrazo floors, surface coatings
Phenol-formaldehyde	Thermosetting	Bakelite	Baked enamels, hardware, flexible floorcovering
Melamines	Thermosetting, very hard, unaffected by strong detergents	Melamine	Tableware, laminates for surface finishes
Polyester	Thermosetting, very hard	Mylar	Floorcovering reinforcement, foams
Polystyrene	Thermoplastic	Styron, Styrofoam	Synthetic rubber (elastomers), electrical equipment, thermal insulation, panel boards
Polyurethane	Thermoplastic or thermosetting		Elastomers, thermal conductivity coatings, bristles
Polyvinyl	Thermoplastic, resistant to abrasion	Vinyls	Flooring, wallcovering, upholstery, lampshades

Paper

Most paper is made from natural cellulose fibers processed mechanically and chemically. Synthetics also play their role. Combinations of these ingredients occur. Colors, specific-use chemicals, sizing, fillers, and coatings are frequently present. When the finished product is thicker than 0.315 millimeters it is known as paperboard. Below is a partial listing.

Although paper cannot be made completely fireproof, it can be made fire resistant to meet many fire code requirements.

Papier maché is paper pulp plus a binder, making a combination that can be molded in form.

Type	Composition	Use
Acoustic fiberboard	Wood, straw, and cornstalk pulp	Acoustic treatment for walls and ceilings
Carpet felt	Waste paper and binder	Padding under carpets
Paperboard, fiber-board, chipboard	Waste paper and binder	Used where strength is not needed
Kapok	Silky fibers from seedpods of kapok tree	Thermal and sound insulation
Plasterboard	Wood pulp paper on plaster core	Dry wall interior finish
Wallpaper	Cellulose pulp	Wallcovering
Wallpaper (coated)	Wallpaper with a synthetic resin coat	Water-resistant wallcovering

Finishing Materials for Floors, Walls, and Ceilings

To complete the listing of materials usable as interior design surfaces, we give this guide, omitting those already described.

Type	Composition	Advantage	Use
Asphalt tile	A bituminous material with binder	Low cost	Utility flooring
Brick	Fired clay	Durable, textured	Floorings, fireplaces, and so forth
Ceramic tile	Glazed earthenware	Durable, easily cleaned	In areas of heavy use and where there is moisture
Cork	Spongy bark of a type of oak	Resilient, non-slip, pleasing texture	Floor and wall areas
Linoleum	Backing plus linseed oil and binders	Durable, resilient	Flooring
Rubber	Natural or synthetic	Resilient	Flooring, coves, carpet pads
Vinyls	Solid vinyl or as top layer on other materials	Many desirable qualities	Flooring

Furniture

It is now more than a half century since the first designs of modern furniture appeared on the market. First came the several pieces by Mies van der Rohe and Marcel Breuer of the famous Bauhaus school in Germany. Breuer made the first tubular metal chair in 1925. Mies, following several earlier models, designed his "Barcelona" chair in 1929 (Figure 10.17). Both are still on the market. The French architect Le Corbusier designed steel chairs that accommodated themselves to various positions of the sitter.

The Scandinavians, and in particular the Finnish architect Alvar Aalto, created chairs that have laminated bentwood frames. Some of Aalto's pieces can be ingeniously stacked in large numbers. Thonet Industries, Inc., a

Figure 10.17. The Barcelona chair.
Designer: Mies van der Rohe
Photograph: Courtesy of Knoll International
This famous chair and those that follow in this chapter illustrate some of this century's pacesetters in furniture design. Several are typical of chairs on today's market that, because of the simple excellence of their contours, indicate a trend toward furniture simplification in the interest of inconspicuous distinction and the ability to qualify a space without dominating it.

Figure 10.18. Thonet bentwood chair.
Photograph: Courtesy of Thonet Industries, Inc., York, Pennsylvania.
Steam-bent elmwood frame. Based on an original Thonet chair. Known often as the Corbusier chair because it was frequently used by that famous architect.

firm that dates back to Michael Thonet, who made bentwood furniture in the Rhineland over a century ago, pioneered in the manufacture of bent plywood and tubular steel pieces in America (Figure 10.18).

Another new-old technique in furniture design is the use of a rigid frame from which fabric is suspended or upheld for back and seat. Designer Hardoy used a removable leather support for this purpose in 1941. Architect Eero Saarinen's shell chair is designed on a variation of this principle. It is constructed of molded plastic covered with foam rubber and fabric. A separate cushion is used for back and seat. This chair is often called the leaf chair because, in its three-dimensional character, it resembles a bent leaf.

In 1940, Saarinen collaborated with Charles Eames of the faculty of the Cranbrook Academy of Art to produce the so-called organic design chair that won the Museum of Modern

Art's award for good design in modern furniture (Figure 10.19). This used a shell of laminated bent plywood shaped to fit the contours of the seated human form. Padding, when it was employed, was of foam rubber placed directly over the frame. This chair is the antecedent of the many Eames chairs on the market, all offering strength with comfort and light scale. These qualities have made them popular in the domestic market. Some of the Eames chairs have separated the design of the understructure from seat and back (Figure 10.20). This is an interesting departure that is justified solely on the grounds of function in that the lower section pivots for adaptable positioning.

In the Scandinavian handicraft tradition are chairs by the Danish designer, Hans Wegner (Figure 10.21) and the American, George Nakashima. Respect for expert craftsmanship with wood has resulted in furniture of sturdy quality, graceful form, and comparative light-

Figure 10.19. (*left*) Eames[TM] side chair.
Designer: Charles Eames
Photograph: Courtesy of Hermann Miller® Inc., Zeeland, Michigan

Figure 10.20. (*below*) Eames[TM] armchair and ottoman.
Designer: Charles Eames
Photograph: Courtesy of Hermann Miller® Inc., Zeeland, Michigan

Figure 10.21. Hans Wegner classic chair.
Designer: Hans Wegner, 1949
Construction: oak and cane, H. 30"
Collection, The Museum of Modern Art, New York,
Gift of Georg Jensen, Inc.
Photograph: The Museum of Modern Art, New York

Figure 10.22. Saarinen chair.
Designer: Eero Saarinen
Photograph: Courtesy of Knoll International

Figure 10.24. (*right*) Armchair.
Designer: A Directional Design by Jonathan Ginat
Photograph: Courtesy of Directional Industries, Inc.

Figure 10.23. (*below*) Armchair.
Designer: Warren Platner
Photograph: Courtesy of Knoll International

Figure 10.25. Chair, "Adagio."
Designer: Dennis Christiansen
Photograph: Courtesy of Dunbar

Figure 10.26. (*right*) Chair.
Designer: de Polo/Dunbar
Photograph: Courtesy of Dunbar

Figure 10.27. (*left*) Conference table chair.
Photograph: Courtesy of Baker Furniture; photographer, Bob Porth, Hedrich-Blessing

Figure 10.28. (*below*) Lounge chair.
Designer: Gae Aulenti
Photograph: Courtesy of Knoll International

Figure 10.29. Kinder furniture.
Photograph: Courtesy of Dependable Furniture Manufacturing Company
Table: H. 20", D. 33"
Chair: H. 21¾", W. 14¾", D. 13⅓"
Children need special furniture too, and this sturdy ensemble that is available in walnut or oak is just the thing for the playroom, nursery school, indeed, for any place inhabited by children.

ness of scale. This same straightforward type of design, given some modern verve with desirable structural clarity, has been produced largely in wood by designers Jens Risom and Edward Wormely.

More innovative with materials, Saarinen produced his unipedestal chair, which has a plastic frame and broadened base (Figure 10.22). Warren Platner employed metal bands to create a design that reflects beautifully the exciting, scintillating reflections of the twentieth century (Figure 10.23).

These designs are pacesetters, followed, of course, by creations from the imaginative foreign markets that, although they are procurable today, are seldom seen outside museums, architect's houses, and executive suites. By and large they are not to be seen in the furniture stores or in private homes. This is explainable. In the first place, they are slightly heavier in scale than would be suitable for use in small interiors. Second, their materials, when steel or plastic, do not mix easily with the old. Third, as chairs they are generally low slung and difficult for any but the young to use (but the young love them). Fourth, they are just too expensive for the average pocketbook. So it goes.

There is always the antique market and, despite the fact that atrocities often are committed in the name of antiquity, many antique pieces are adaptable both functionally and aesthetically to today's needs, in the domestic rather than the public domain. Reproductions might answer the same purpose were it possible to restrain the industrial manufacturers

so that they would make only good replicas from excellent designs. But the desecrating counterfeits of the Queen Anne chair, for instance, are legion.

Modern needs are different from those of a few years ago. Movability, stackability, indestructibility, as well as comfort and appearance, are criteria to be considered with various types of use. The consideration of these specifications has resulted in some very well-made, straight-line furniture that serves, as the old sofa did, for multiple seating, room dividers, and design setters (Figures 10.24, 10.25, 10.26, 10.27, and 10.28). The public market supplements these with furniture made of the new materials and suited to specific uses. The private market, it is to be hoped, will gradually produce designs suited to its many highly complex needs (Figure 10.29).

The selection and installation of materials is part of the interior designer's obligation. Therefore one must continue to extend the preliminary knowledge contained in this chapter throughout one's academic and professional career.

11

ACCESSORIES: THE SUPERNUMERARY AND THE LODESTAR

Hence it is that our artistic culture, aware that more is asked of it than the expression, however subtle, of our modern sensibility, seeks guidance from the figures, songs, and poems that are the legacy of the past under its noblest aspect— because it is today sole heir to that bequest.

André Malraux, *The Voices of Silence*[1]

If it is silver
Silver sings,
If it is song,
There is another way of shining,
And how shall one confused with stars and wings
Know why God sets His glories
Among inarticulate, inconsequential things?

Collister Hutchison, "Song for All Marys"[2]

Spend all you have for loveliness,
Buy it and never count the cost.

Sara Teasdale, "Barter"[3]

The Stage

This is the most imprudent of chapters. Its theme is how to spend money—but wisely.

Some years ago, whenever an extravaganza like *Aida* or *Julius Caesar* came to town, it was the custom to hire the supers for the mob scenes from among the local characters. There were always plenty of takers—both

among the improvident and those who enjoyed making a stage appearance. Theater

[1] Trans. Stuart Gilbert, Bollingen Series, XXIV-A. Copyright © 1978 by Princeton University Press, p. 640. Reprinted by permission of Princeton University Press.

[2] By permission of literary executors of Collister Hutchison. From *Toward Daybreak* by Collister Hutchison. Copyright © 1950 by Harper and copyright © 1978 by Archibald Hutchison.

[3] Sara Teasdale, *Love Songs*, New York: Macmillan, 1917.

techniques have changed, and now less is more. When supers are added they are trained for their role.

Theatrical performances have and always will require the star actor, one who possesses those magic qualities that a lodestar is said to have—to attract, guide, and transfigure.

In interior design the supers are called accessories such as the ashtray, the vase, the wastebasket, the fire tongs. Sometimes they perform very useful functions, sometimes they do not. Thus they can be rated indispensable or not. The lodestar, however, when it is not present or when it is represented by a weak substitute, leaves the stage character-less, its magic gone.

Procuring Accessories

These teammates may be secured from three kinds of markets: mass production, custom production, and the exclusive, one-of-a-kind establishment. Of necessity, many articles must come from the first. Since industrial firms generally employ designers for specialized products, such articles are frequently very well fashioned. The same artists may work for industry, for the custom trade, and for those who can afford to buy individually created objects. Such trichotomy frequently exists in the European market; it produces a degree of insurance against a dull trade standard on one hand and an ivory-tower approach on the other. However, adjustments are required when things are designed to be made by industrial processes. Such processes certainly favor greater regularity, but it is not necessary for them to lead to greater mediocrity. The interior designer should know all phases of the merchandising scene. Distinction is after all a matter of judgment—judgment not only about caliber but also about spending.

A word of caution in regard to this matter. It is a mistaken idea to imagine that in the industrial field every object offered for sale with a designer's name attached is necessarily well designed. Good art is only found where there is a good artist, and there certainly are motives operating in the marketplace that are not focused primarily on producing good art. This can be said as truthfully of the one-of-a-kind creation as of the many that may come from the same die.

It is good for an interior designer to know, in addition to the usual sources for functional necessities, some local or regional artists who can design and execute some accessory details that may be needed. In this section we cannot enumerate all of the excellent sources available. The uniqueness of a product is part of its charm. A sampling of work of high quality is presented here by means of a few illustrations. The reader is encouraged to enlarge on these to form an individual gallery from which to make choices.

Aesthetic Considerations

The reason for the existence of an accessory in an interior must be that it adds convenience, interest, or enrichment. Accessories can speak volumes about what a person values.

When you consider the choice of accessories, first decide on the relative attention they should attract in a room design. An accessory may be a prime accent to its immediate surroundings: for instance, a white vase with white flowers, alone on a dark glass table. Notice how such an accessory accords with and yet emphasizes the stiff and hard outlines of the ensemble.

An accessory can serve as a visual transition from one grouping to another. An oriental screen with its unfolding design may answer this description.

Or an accessory may be intended merely as an enrichment to take its place subordinate to the large room rhythms. Care should be exercised that it does not attract more attention than the object on which it is placed. I recall a lovely bronze-toned enamel ashtray that usually sat on an old walnut table. It had been made on special order with the request that it blend with the wood. It is delightful to find an accessory that may come to our attention unannounced and suddenly cause us to pause fascinated. In this sense accessories are like the stepping stones in a Japanese garden, beautifully chosen for themselves but also an enriching part of the whole.

Last, an article selected with much care may be the lodestar that can take over, mesmerize, convey its timeless message, and endow the space with character. What would Chartres be without its west window, or the Sistine Chapel without its ceiling? But one can talk on a lesser scale. One's lodestone need not be beyond the reach of funds, but it should not be purchased or placed carelessly. Give it all you have to give.

What other considerations should govern the selection of an accessory? If an accessory such as a candlestick has a practical purpose, a consideration of its suitability to perform this function is of first importance.

An accessory should be selected with great care for the quality of its medium. This is not the place to traffic with values. There can be no room for the shoddy or the fake in those objects chosen solely for their usefulness as an embroidery to the overall design of a room. If economy is necessary, consider a less expensive kind of material, or one requiring less expensive manipulation, or one in which the quality of the material is not sacrificed for added ornamentation. A good plain crystal is preferable to an inferior glass that is heavily decorated.

Careful thought should be expended on the design quality of an accessory. It need not be a definite or highly developed design. It may please simply because of its shape, color, or texture. If a complex form is incorporated in the object, it should be executed with the best possible artistry.

The expressiveness of a decorative accessory is important. It should relate to the interests of the owners and fit the meaning of the room. It is doubly expressive if it has been handcrafted. Thus accessories should be pleasant but not necessarily sentimental matters. The quality of expression in its relation to design, material, and function is a certain index to the quality of visual material that is enjoyed.

Wood Accessories

If we consider articles made largely of wood that are used more as accessories than necessities, what has our culture to offer? First there are the naturals, where the fun is in the search, as all of us know who have combed the beaches for driftwood and stones and shells.

Louise Nevelson is a greatly gifted collector of wood oddments. She transforms them through her genius into walls and wall sculptures that are the equivalent of the finest stone wall reliefs of India and the wooden ones of the Islamic countries (Figure 11.1). The resultant forms are tonal, textural, and spatial masterpieces.

A different spirit shapes the laminated freeform bowls of the artist and craftsman Tapio Wirkkala of Finland (Figure 11.2). They are precision-smooth, beautiful in grain structure, and lovely in their asymmetrical shapes.

Fabrics as Accessories

Fabrics used as art objects can provide textural relief, color, and pattern. They may come from the contemporary market, or they can have the added potential of contributing meaning when they are historic. Interest can accrue easily through the suggestion of rarity or the presence of finesse, although neither is required for a fabric to have design significance.

The weaving department of Cranbrook Academy of Art in Michigan pioneered the direction of hand weaving in this country into modern design channels. Loja Saarinen and Marianne Strengell, both from Finland, fostered a tradition of experimental work that has crystallized in the fine work of many students. Jack Lenor Larsen came from Cranbrook and today is producing, among other textiles, such specialized products as colorful textural room panels that are in effect the equivalent of the creative art of Mark Rothko or Morris Graves realized on the loom—art that is akin to minimal art.

Mechanically and industrially produced wall hangings, particularly of the sort advertised as tapestries, are often seen today. To those who enjoy historic hand-loomed tapestries, these are often very disappointing, yet the potential of tapestry technique can be exploited on the power loom. This is neither to print pictures on cloth nor to weave them by some harnessing of the double-cloth weave. This is to design with color and tonal shifts on a textural foundation (see Figure 6.7). Boris Kroll, who has always been an experimenter on the hand loom in relation to the powered one, has done particularly well in this area.

Printed fabrics can be found readily in a custom market, where they are available as wall hangings in custom colors. There are many excellent sources such as the Fortuny Company in Italy, which makes overlay prints that not only simulate historic velvets but also use some of today's patterns. The Orient provides some recent new-old types: Javanese batiks, Japanese tie dyes, Indian ikats.

Most needlework on cloth necessitates the individual artist. Mariska Karasz, a Hungar-

Figure 11.1 Wood sculpture. "Sky Cathedral," 1958, black-painted wood, 11'
3½" × 10' ¼" × 18".
Artist: Louise Nevelson
*Collection, The Museum of Modern Art, New York, Gift of Mr. and Mrs. Ben
Mildwoff*
Photograph: The Museum of Modern Art, New York
This is an environmental wall created by New York sculptor Louise Nevelson,
who assembles large constructions from separate wooden pieces. These room-
size structures project more than a textural variation to plain walls: they
play with sculptured shadows in an almost mystical way, creating something
like a forest of shades or the patterns of the dark side of a city.

Figure 11.2. Wooden serving pieces from the Collection, The Museum of Modern Art, New York. *Photograph: The Museum of Modern Art, New York Beginning upper left and moving clockwise:* James Prestini, platter (1939–40), Gift of Philip L. Goodwin; James Prestini, bowl (ca. 1939), Mexican mahogany, H. 6″, Edgar Kaufmann, Jr., Fund; Reynolds G. Dennis, beaker, "Simplicity" (1951), black walnut, oil finish, 4″ × 4″, Lemurian Crafts, Gift of the manufacturer; Tapio Wirkkala, platter (1951), laminated hand-carved plywood, L. 10½″, Gift of Georg Jensen, Inc.; and Tapio Wirkkala, platter (ca. 1950–51), leaf-shaped hand-carved plywood, L. 19″, Gift of Greta Daniel.

Figure 11.3. (*right*) Fiberwork I. "Tarzan's Rope," 472″ × 10″.
Artist: Jean Stamsta
Photograph: Courtesy of The Cleveland Museum of Art and with the permission of the artist
This woven and crocheted fiberwork was commissioned by the Cleveland Museum of Art, which invited the artist to create a work to hang in a stairwell during the 1977 exhibition titled "Fiberworks." The vibrant reds that unfortunately cannot be seen here served well to connect two levels of exhibition space.

Plate 4. Means to ends. The G. S. McKenna Gallery, Charlotte, North Carolina.
Interior designer: Peter Gluck & Associates—Gerald Allen
Photographer: Gordon Schenk, Jr.
In this lovely gallery dealing in fine antiques we see a renovation that adds much to the total charm and usefulness of the space. The long showroom proportions have been visually reduced by means of lateral divisions, giving more room for display and accentuating the short axis. This divisional emphasis has been aided by color that, while using a progression of background hues for the alcoves, accentuates the edges by means of similar hues used in a brilliant array. Attractive and suitable work in designing has increased the pleasurable review of the articles within the space.

Plate 5. A New York apartment.
Architects: Charles Gwathmey and Robert Siegel
Photograph: courtesy of Gwathmey/Siegel & Associates, Inc.; © Norman McGrath, photographer
Mr. Gwathmey's design for a New York apartment illustrates well the tendency toward the greater enrichment of interiors while at the same time preserving the clarity of the spatial order. This is to a large degree accomplished by the development of a few themes by repetition and by the grouping of several shapes into one larger ensemble—in other words, by creating a complex rather than a compound design. A sense of space is created through an open plan. The necessary structural supports are sheathed in stainless steel and demark the living area from the den or study area. The wood is white oak veneer and the walls are canvas covered. (See also Color Plate 6 and Figures 9.5 and 9.6 for other views of this apartment.)

Plate 6. Entrance floor and wall: a concentration of color and pattern. A New York apartment.
Architects: Charles Gwathmey and Robert Siegel
Photograph: courtesy of Gwathmey/Siegel & Associates, Inc.; © Norman McGrath, photographer
In a clearly defined and open entrance space, attention is directed to a painting and a superb Persian oriental carpet. The floor is of antique verde marble slabs.

ian-born American, was a leader in a renaissance of the needle. Her embroidered panels are to be seen in leading museums. Jean Lurçat did similar work in France (see Figure 10.6).

Woven, printed, and embroidered materials lead us to "fiberworks," a coined and appropriate name for those one-of-a-kind objects made from many different varieties of fibers by any of a number of methods of interwork (Figure 11.3). The production is now worldwide, with outstanding examples interestingly following the expertise of each national genius. Liselotte Siegfried's embroideries from Switzerland, Toshiko Horiuchi's knitting from Japan, Luba Krejcí's lace technique (niták) from Czechoslovakia, and Jean Stamsta's weaving from the United States are but a few examples.

Fibers, each type having its own textural appeal, are inherently decorative. Since they are flexible, they can be incorporated readily in both two- and three-dimensional design. They can fall into abstract patterns more nat-

urally, more legitimately, and even more interestingly than traditional media that require supports. There is a genuineness, a sensuousness, a warmth about the finished product that talks directly to the human experience (Figure 11.4).

The diversity found among the many nationalities now experimenting with fiberworks highlights the universality and antiquity of textiles. Because of this diversity, we can today purchase the silks of Thailand, the linens of Scandinavia, the hemps of Italy, the pounded barks of Java, and the cotton toiles of France along with some wonderful reproductions made on American looms of the historic silks of yesteryear and the new creations of today.

Floorcoverings as Accessories

Because floorcoverings are scarcely considered accessories and seldom are hand produced due to expense, they do not often ap-

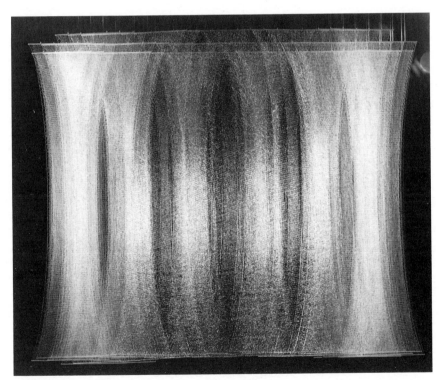

Figure 11.4. Fiberwork II. "Atmosphere of the Forest," 94" × 141" × 15".
Artist: Toshiko Horiuchi
Photograph: Courtesy of The Cleveland Museum of Art and with the permission of the artist
This beautiful knitted work is in tones of greyed mauve and brown on a dark ground. Its forty panels of knitted linen, gold, and silver filaments are hung in three shimmering layers. The changing of the colors claim attention with the viewer's changing position. This kind of abstract textile art could be used for luminous screens or wall panels.

pear in that guise in interiors. If they are chosen carefully, they can have much value in today's planning, where walls are not numerous and the floor provides some of the interior interest. Hard flooring relieved by accents of color and texture can be rewarding (see Color Plate 6).

The native weavings of many countries in the Orient, Africa, Scandinavia, and the Americas are available for choice. Techniques are both tufted and plain woven. Materials, large equipment, and requisite time makes them costly. And money alone will not buy artistry. Museum collections should be studied. Art fairs should be visited. Reliable dealers should be consulted. By examining the superlative, standards of taste can be established.

Ceramic Accessories

Ceramics, if they are to be used as accessories, should probably be obtained from few-of-a-kind productions (Figure 11.5). They can be found in the media of pottery, stoneware, and even porcelain. For example, Anne Siimes of the Arabia factory in Finland designs white porcelain bowls and vases that, with their fragility of shape and slight patterning in tone, are exquisite developments of the ceramic sculptor's art. Few are produced. Lisa McVey revives the age-old method of hewing stoneware from bulk clays (see Figure 12.11c).

Ceramic sculpture has had a well-deserved renaissance in recent years. Fantasy is shown in the work of Thelma Frazier Winter (Figure 11.6). The Italians, ever the modelers, are represented by the exuberant pieces of Lucio Fontana and the somber elegance of Guido Gambone.

And, of course, California's Peter Voulkos simply cannot be imitated (Figures 11.7 and 11.8). His work combines whimsy with the force of a dynamo.

Glass Accessories

Although glass is not considered a medium easily worked by individual artists, nevertheless private studios are increasing surprisingly. Much of the impetus for this occurred when Harvey Littleton of the University of Wisconsin introduced glass fabrication into his art studios. The work of Tapio Wirkkala, who does his own glass blowing in Finland, is

Figure 11.5. Ceramic piece.
Artist: Toshiko Takaezu
The Cleveland Museum of Art, The Mary Spedding Milliken Memorial Collection, Gift of William Mathewson Milliken
Photograph: Courtesy of The Cleveland Museum of Art
Takaezu, who is one of the most outstanding ceramic craftsmen in the United States, is of Japanese ancestry. With unmatched artistry and with the restraint of the oriental tradition, she designs works eminently suited to the ceramic medium.

significant. The work of Edris Eckhardt in gold laminated between sheets of glass (reviving lost techniques of the ancient world) adds the glories of changeable color to the translucent medium (see Figure 11.9a). Those Italians who work outside the large industries do their own blowing. The Italian glass easily forms fanciful, colorful, modern shapes that can be gracenotes to any composition.

Stained glass, which introduces color with translucency, is being revived as an art. The best artists reject the easy technique of painting pictures on glass. They exploit traditional methods and create mosaics of chromatic pieces bound by adhesives or by the traditional lead strips.

Large glass firms have loaned their facilities to artists to create unique works, many for museums (Figure 11.10).

Enamel Accessories

Enamels (glass frit low fired onto a metal base) are exceedingly important as enrichment in modern interiors. They range from the large enamel wall plaque to the many smaller pieces designed with artistry and executed with skill. Each section of the country can boast its exponents of this craft.

Metal Accessories

Metals have long been a fine medium for accessories. We find them in one-of-a-kind production, limited and unlimited editions: bowls, candelabra, beverage sets, trays, and fireside equipment. They add the aesthetic qualities of colorful reflection, beautiful shape, and distinctive texture while being practically indestructable (Figure 11.11). It is small wonder that lovely pieces command big prices and a ready market.

Because metals can be cold forged and can be washed with other metals, they have filled a need for wall screening that fits into the architectural rigidity of large spaces and helps to give textural relief. The late metalist, Harry Bertoia, may be said to have begun this trend with his designs in sculptured metal on steel (see Fig. 10.14).

Metals combined with other materials can be formed into suspended mobiles. Alexander Calder is, of course, the progenitor and leader of this art.

Figure 11.6. A grouping of prize-winners.
Textile: Dorothy Turobinski, "Parade of Rectangles"
Painting: William C. Grauer, "Moulten Sun Rising"
Ceramic Sculpture: Thelma Frazier Winter
Photographer: G. C. Ball
Good art possesses a quality alliance that, inexpressible in scientific terms, unifies such groupings as this.

Figure 11.7. (*left*) Ceramic vase: I. "Voulkos '56," slab ceramic construction, H. 37½", W. 16".
Artist: Peter H. Voulkos
The American Craft Council. Gift of Mr. and Mrs. Adam Gostomski to the Permanent Collection of the American Craft Museum of the American Craft Council
Photograph: Copyright © by the American Craft Council. All rights reserved. Not to be reproduced in any form or in any medium without the prior written consent of American Craft Council.
The inimitable imagination shown in the ceramics of Peter Voulkos is well exemplified in this vase.

Figure 11.8. (*below, left*) Ceramic vase: II (1977, H. 36").
Artist: Peter H. Voulkos
Collection: Joseph Nadel
Photograph: Courtesy, Peter H. Voulkos; Joe Schopplein, photographer
In this sturdy, well-designed vase we see another facet of the genius of Peter Voulkos. Here is a firm sculptural statement, formal in its contours byt broken by an interplay of textural eruptions.

Figure 11.9. Two glass madonnas. (A) "Vision in the Blue Grotto," laminated gold glass.
Artist: Edris Eckhardt
Photograph: Courtesy of The Cleveland Museum of Art and with the permission of the artist. (B) *Glass Madonna from the Leerdam Factory, Holland.*
Photograph: Courtesy of G. Ukmar; Milosh Ukmar, photographer
These two examples illustrate well various expressions using the same medium. The exquisite artistry of the Eckhardt glass is made by engraving and fusing silver and gold foil on ten thin laminations of glass. Other colors used are turquoise and cobalt blue with shadings of violet and rose. The Leerdam piece is blown molded. Its form is modeled by illumination both from above and from directly below.

Figure 11.10. Contemporary glass. Steuben Glass, "Passage: A Function of Eleven," H. 20", W. 16½".
Artist: Peter Aldridge
Photograph: Courtesy of Steuben Glass
This is one of a series of abstract sculptures in glass based on the idea of passage in time and space from one state of being to another. Each flight of stairs has eleven steps which, since there are nine flights, make a total of ninety-nine. Eleven has been a mystical number throughout the ages. Although each of Aldridge's designs is a frozen moment in time, it is interesting that he more often uses the rectangular than the global form, somewhat contrary to the usual expression in glass.

Figure 11.11. Copper sculpture.
Artist: Gordana P. Ukmar
Photograph: Courtesy of G. Ukmar; Milosh Ukmar, photographer
This interesting freeform sculpture in sheet copper was made as a class project when the artist was a student.

215

Figure 11.12. A table with high-fired stoneware tiles.
Furniture designer and woodworker: Robert Neudorfer, Duxbury, Vermont
Ceramist: Dorothy Olson, Brattleboro, Vermont
Photograph: Courtesy of Robert Neudorfer
The stoneware ceramic decoration on this piece represents an extension of the ancient art of stone or glass mosaic. The handcrafted table creates an artist's blend of the useful and the lovely.

Stone Accessories

Semiprecious stones are also a choice of the accessory hunter. In the upper-cost bracket, cool waxy jade can contribute its joy to the sense of touch. Bowls are made in alabaster, marble, and even the coarser limestone. "Rock hounds" treasure unshaped pieces to be finished, fondled, and viewed.

Italy may be credited with beginning a renaissance in mosaic stonework—a native craft now found in trays, tabletops, and small plaques (Figure 11.12).

Plastics as Accessories

Why not? Not only are plastics seen in trays, bowls, and practically every kind of object generally reserved for glass, but their brilliant color potential for transmitted light makes them ideal for many kinds of bibelots and bobeches.

Screens

Screens are movable partitions that play an important utilitarian and artistic role in the modern building (Figure 11.13). Many screens are made of translucent cloth or plastic. Opaque forms can be fastened between plastic layers to create shadow effects. Victoria Van Loon of the Gaillard Press is outstanding in her work with natural media sandwiched in this way.

The great painted screens of Japan are beyond most private purses. And in this genre only the best is good enough.

Antiques

The old will always rightly have its lure. It establishes continuity. It can teach appreciation for the skill of the past. It gives our imagination something to work on. It may even revive some ancestors who in this way can take part in the scene.

But, fair warning: collecting antiques is a creeping disease. Always keep in mind E. B. White's admonition: "A six-room apartment holds as much paraphernalia as an aircraft carrier. . . . To empty the place completely takes real ingenuity and great staying power."[4] And one must be certain that the values other than the aesthetic do not crowd out the latter.

Pictures

Choosing a picture (or a sculpture) is one of the most important decisions about an object of visual art that the interior designer

[4]From *Essays of E. B. White*, New York: Harper & Row, 1977, p. 3.

Figure 11.13. Living room, Windermere House. Residence of Hope L. Foote, Seattle, Washington.
Designer: Hope L. Foote
Photograph: Courtesy of Hope L. Foote
Most of the furnishings in this room were designed by Hope Foote and executed by her students, many of whom are currently active in interior design throughout the world. The large Japanese screen on the wall provides a beautiful focal point.

is called on to make. Any choice of fine art is an index of our sense of beauty. Moreover, because of their relative importance in the decorative scheme, the chosen examples disclose our sense of the worth of spiritual qualities in addition to the practical. There are many questions that must be considered in making such choices.

WHERE IS A PICTURE OR A PIECE OF SCULPTURE NEEDED?

Because art objects are in themselves focal points of aesthetic value, they are required wherever a space is barren of these values or where it needs the aesthetic emphasis that a particular picture or piece of sculpture can bring. For instance, in one house there is a corridor flanked by louvered windows that turns at a right angle at its end. The end wall was a meaningless space until it was illuminated by a fine piece of sculpture.

Sometimes a furniture grouping may be eminently useful, and the individual pieces may be well designed, but the whole grouping may not be integrated in design. The right choice of a picture may complete an aesthetic whole.

The rich contribution of a well-designed art object that can convey ideas can add immeasurably to a room.

The reverse of all this is also true. Not every blank space calls for occupancy. Blank space in proper relation to visual activity can be both restful and suggestive. It is in part a measure of the success of the hanging of pictures that their positioning serves to create such meaningful spaces.

WHAT CONSIDERATIONS AFFECT THE CHOICE OF A WORK OF ART?

In choosing art, the first decision relates to whether it should be two dimensional (pictures) or three dimensional (sculpture). When pleasure can be derived from seeing and feeling around an object, sculpture is called for. This usually negates chromatic color, although much of the great sculpture of the past used color. Pictures, however, are the great vehicle for giving joy through color, space, and texture relationships in a two-dimensional area.

The choice of the medium used in a painting or a piece of sculpture is another important consideration. The use of several media in one room is a matter of personal taste and of consideration for scale and textural attributes. The choice of design should be based on the principles discussed throughout this book.

What style is indicated? There is no dogmatic answer to this question. Good art transcends time. The people who live in a good contemporary house will probably enjoy good modern art and want it. They will be equally appreciative of the eternal qualities in art whatever its date. The artist designer should seek to harmonize all aspects of a setting, but only where strict purism prevails is it necessary to be restrictive—for instance, in a Colonial interior limiting the choice to early American paintings.

What subject matter is allowable? All subjects are transformed into beauty through great art. However, taste may eliminate some subjects from some settings, and subjects that are generally unpleasant in their suggestions might well be erased from rooms that are intended for happy social life.

WHAT MEDIUM SHOULD BE CHOSEN?

Choosing an appropriate medium requires study and a constant effort to keep up-to-date. Techniques change with time. New ones are developed and old ones are revived. The following serves merely as an introduction.

Oil Painting, Fresco, Encaustic.   These media have great visual force and are chosen for any location where the painting must carry for a distance.

Acrylic Resin.   This is a dispersed resin paint whose vehicle is water. Its performance is similar to oil. Its ease of application is considered an advantage by many. Unless covered with a varnish, the customary depth reflections from oil are absent, although its carrying power is similar.

Watercolor or Tempera.   Due to the fluidity of the solvent, the effect of a good watercolor should be spontaneous and fresh. It should not seem overworked. Watercolors can contribute a bracing quality to a room. Since their carrying power is not great, they seem best suited to smaller spaces and close viewing. Tempera paintings can be more forceful, but have a more opaque, maplike appearance.

Pastel or Crayon.   These are similar in effect and use to tempera.

Pencil, Pen and Ink, Silverpoint (made with a silver stylus), and Scratchboard Work (incised drawing made through a coating on composition board).   All of these are linear work of varying degrees of delicacy, scratchboard probably being the coarsest.

These are examples of the so-called graphic processes, to which all of the prints also belong. They are usually dependent for their effects on a linear character and achromatic tone rather than on chromatic color. They are best suited to locations where these qualities can be observed at close range.

Prints are more valuable if they are from a limited edition. Valuable prints are known as artists' proofs; the print number and the total number in the edition together with the artist's signature appear at the bottom of the print, and the block or plate is subsequently destroyed once the edition is completed.

Wood Block Printing.   Grooves are cut in a block of wood or its coating and the block is inked. The ink is then transferred to the paper from the surfaces that are not incised. Due to the difficulty of cutting, the lines are comparatively thick, and strong contrasts in tonal areas make wood block prints one of the more forceful media. Oriental artists in general use a more delicate line.

Engraving or Mezzotint.   An engraving is a print made from a copper or steel plate cut by an instrument known as a graver that makes a very even, clean line. A mezzotint is like an engraving except that the plate is pricked by the instrument. The dots make the tones.

Etching or Aquatint.   An etching plate is covered with a soft resist through which the artist draws lines with a stylus. An acid then eats out the lines. The resist is removed. The plate is inked and an impression is made. Because the resist is easily pierced, the lines of an etching can be sensitive to the artist's style of calligraphy.

An aquatint is similar to an etching in its tonal effects, with the tones accomplished through rubbing down areas of a porous ground resist before the work of the acid begins. When several plates are used, an effect similar to tempera painting can be produced.

Drypoint. A drypoint is made by pulling rather than pushing a sharp instrument over the plate. It has a line that has a soft, velvety edge. This is because the instrument leaves a burr on the plate.

Lithograph. A crayon sketch is made on a plate (originally a stone). Water is added that adheres only to the background. Ink adheres only to the crayon. A lithograph print closely resembles a charcoal drawing in its broad effects. This print is a flat reproduction that does not bear the imprint of the pressure of the plate.

Serigraphy or Silkscreen. In silkscreen stenciling, a resist is placed on a screen or mesh and paint is forced through the apertures. When several screens are used, an effect similar to a tempera painting is achieved.

Photography. Original photographic artists' proofs owe their quality to skillful handling by the artist. Many kinds of tonal effects are possible. Both color and black-and-white printing are used.

Reproductions. These are unlimited-edition prints. There are many processes available (line cuts, halftone screens, collotype, and photogravure), and they are all mechanical. Some contemporary processes can reproduce the exact texture of an original painting. Photolithography is one of these.

A copy should be judged on the basis of its accuracy of reproduction. A wide variance will be found between different facsimiles in this respect.

THE FRAME—WHY AND HOW?

The most obvious reason for framing a picture is to protect it. There are other purposes that a frame can also serve. It helps to isolate a picture from its surroundings, gives it a little world all its own, and can enhance what it borders. A frame can also merge a picture with the background on which it is hung.

Certain injunctions may be given for all good framing. The frame should complement the expressive character of the picture. This is in large part a question of textural harmony. For example, a picture that suggests an American rural scene might be set in a simple frame of oak.

The expressive character of the painting also plays a role in determining the shape of its frame. A landscape by Utrillo may be composed largely of straight lines. But it has a certain elegant and fairylike character (due to its tones and its technical handling) that seems to require some curvature in its frame.

The shape and design of a picture should be considered in choosing the shape of the frame. This generally calls for similarity in the design elements of picture and frame, but one need not demand a strict relationship— some contrast may be required for emphasis. A van Gogh picture of a countryside, because of its agitated brush strokes, would seem out of place in a smooth, straight frame. On the other hand, a curved-line painting such as Matisse's *Blue Window* seems to incorporate so many curves in its design that a straight-line frame might, by adding some straight lines, provide a suitable foil.

Many contemporary paintings are framed in elaborate, curved-line frames to provide relief from the more stark lines of the modern room.

The size of a frame is also important. Often a picture is spoiled by a frame that is too scanty or too large. However, an oil painting may be framed successfully in the simplest of narrow wood moldings usually reserved for watercolors and artist's proofs. Le Corbusier edges his paintings with a metal band that merely acts as a finish at the border of the picture. In framing an oil, such simple moldings are placed close to the picture. In media of less aesthetic force, it is customary to place a mat between the picture and the frame.

When a frame is broader than this simple edging, it should be wide enough to carry the visual weight of the picture. This forcefulness may be compounded of many things. The agitated strokes of van Gogh require a wide frame. A landscape with large, dark masses in the foreground may require a broad frame. It is a fairly safe guide to say that such a frame should be at least one sixth to one eighth the width of the picture.

The depth of a frame is another aesthetic

problem. The framer must decide whether to strengthen a flat painting by repetition of this flatness or to accentuate it by a deep, contrasting frame. Deep frames are usually preferable for pictures that represent perspectives. Such frames also break up room space more than flat ones and may thereby relieve a room that has too many flat textures and surfaces. Deep frames can cast troublesome shadows on a picture. Frames that are flat in themselves but that advance the plane of the picture or use a deeper molding adjacent to the picture are possible solutions to some of these problems.

The tone of the frame is of utmost importance. In most cases the frame should not be lighter than the lightest tone in the painting. This suggestion may be set aside in the interest of fitting the frame into the color scheme of the room or of lightening a somber painting. If a painting fades out to very light tones at the edges, a border molding in a dark tone may be placed on the frame adjacent to the painting to contain it. This border (or the entire frame) is frequently rubbed with one of the colors of the painting. A liner used with a mat achieves the same end.

SHOULD A PICTURE BE COVERED WITH GLASS?

Whether a picture should be covered with glass is a matter of common sense. Glass protects a picture from dirt and is therefore an essential covering for any picture surface that would soil easily. All pictures made on paper should be covered with glass.

Some artists prefer to cover their oils with glass. There are two objections to this practice. In the first place, glass may reflect light in a manner not intended by the artist. (Nonreflective glass, which avoids this fault, is available.) In the second place, glass detracts from the textural effects that are often present in oil paintings or original prints.

HOW SHOULD A PICTURE BE MATTED?

A mat is a flat piece of material, usually cardboard, which has an opening (very carefully cut with a beveled edge) for the picture. It is advisable to use a mat on any picture that requires greater importance in its position.

A picture finished with a mat usually needs little else in the way of a frame. An unobtrusive molding or corner brackets may be sufficient.

Some mats are integral with the frame of the picture. They are merely flat extensions of the picture frame and are made of the same or similar material. This is a favorite method of framing opaque watercolors and occasionally oil paintings.

The shape of the picture, its design, its expressive character, and the nature of the surroundings are all important in determining the nature of the mat. Only a few guideposts can be given.

The first suggestion is that the shape of the mat should correspond to the shape of the picture but that, for the sake of interest, it may vary from it slightly (Figure 11.14). For example, a root 3 horizontal rectangular picture might be placed in a root 2 mat (see Chapter 5). The mat is frequently less elongated than the picture.

The absolute size of a mat should be large enough to accomplish its purpose of isolating and dignifying the picture. The marginal areas frequently bear a rhythmic relation to the picture size and thus determine the absolute size of the mat. Very small prints occasionally are placed in very large mats. The mats of a group of pictures of various sizes can be planned to be uniform in outside measurements.

The standard American museum mat for artist's proofs is a hinged mat measuring 14½ by 19½ inches. An artist's proof should never be pasted down solidly to the back mat. The print should be loose so that the texture of the paper, the identification, and the plate mark can be examined. This plate mark is the depression made in the paper by the metal plate from which the print is taken. These are all of interest to the connoisseur.

The relation of the marginal sizes surrounding a picture is decided by the artist's understanding of their purpose. If visual stability is desired, the bottom margin is frequently the widest. In a vertical picture, the top margin may be next in size and the side margins the narrowest. They may decrease in accordance with dynamic ratios. In horizontal pictures, if width is to be stressed, the side margins may be larger than the top. If a more static effect is desired, these three or possibly all four margins may be the same (Figure 11.15).

The tone of a picture mat should be selected carefully. As a general rule, it should

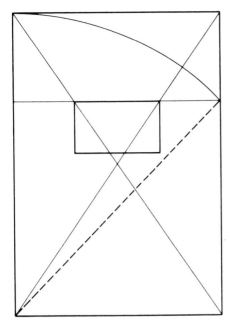

Figure 11.14. A root 3 horizontal rectangle in a root 2 vertical.

Figure 11.15. Mats on pictures. The problem of choosing proportions for mats on pictures is not always best solved by a rigid adherence to a proportional system. Many complicating factors such as linear or tonal movements that create new relations may suggest that proportions need to be adjusted by the eye—a most sensitive instrument.

not be more saturated than the background of the picture nor lighter than its highlights. The tone of a mat is frequently one of the cooler, lighter, duller tones of the painting. Occasionally one of the darker tones will create greater enrichment. A warmer tone may accord well with a symphony of warm hues.

The French, in framing graphic prints, frequently use a dull blue mat of medium tone. This blue seems to bring out the richness of the velvetlike black tones, and its middle lightness seems closely related to the middle tones of the picture. Such a mat is often surrounded with a narrow gold frame. Frequently a few color lines are drawn close to the opening of the mat, and a wash of harmonious color is placed between the lines. This is known as a French-lined mat.

The opening in a mat for artist's proofs is usually cut to show a margin from the plate mark of about one quarter of an inch on the sides and one half of an inch at the bottom. This bottom margin should provide space for the numbering of the proof and for the signature of the artist. The edge of the opening of the mat forms an additional line around the plate mark that emphasizes it.

A reproduction of a painting may be framed with or without a mat. If the reproduction is made by a process that simulates the texture of an original oil and if no glass covering is required, it would be better not to use a mat. Even though a facsimile is done on paper so that it requires a glass covering, it may be framed close and without a mat. This close framing is possible to the degree that the forcefulness of the painting can compete successfully with a close frame. When such a facsimile is framed close, the frame probably should not be as heavy or as large as that placed on the original painting. If a mat is used around a facsimile of an oil, its texture may be heavier than that of a mat for a watercolor or graphic print.

HOW AND WHERE TO HANG PICTURES

Perhaps the most troublesome problem in interior designing is the problem of how and exactly where to hang pictures. Pictures are chosen for many different reasons, but the one common denominator to all of these is that a picture is meant to be a focal point of attention. Therefore, viewing conditions should be arranged with this in mind. If the picture has something to say, it should be allowed to say it.

This will rule out all tricky plans where the machinery of hanging becomes more important than the picture. The usual position for a picture is flat on a wall. Experimental setups on freestanding supports are only reasonable when the two-dimensional character of a picture is not violated.

A picture should be hung so that the wires and hooks that give it support are inconspicuous. Occasionally there may be a decorative reason for showing these mountings. The French traditionally hang their oval pictures with elaborate silk cords from which tassels are appended. This gives verticality, which fits the picture into the room panel.

Were there no other consideration to alter the case, a picture should be hung at the best eye level for viewing while standing (Figure 11.16). That means that the center of interest of the picture should come about 5 feet 5 inches above the floor. Deviation from this should be down rather than up, because it is easier to look down than up. Moreover, pictures frequently are viewed from a seated position (Figure 11.17).

The design of a room may place its demands on the positioning of a picture. The furniture near a picture becomes of great importance in determining placement. Greater coordination of spaces is accomplished when isolated objects such as pictures are rhythmically grouped with other objects such as furniture to make a larger whole. With a little careful planning, this usually can be accomplished without hiding the picture or making it too low for viewing. If the furniture is extremely high, it is best not to hang pictures above it.

The entire wall plan of a space enters into

Figure 11.16. Where to hang a picture: I. An office in the Seagram Building, New York.
Architects: Mies van der Rohe and Philip C. Johnson.
Photograph: Ezra Stoller © ESTO
The pictures in this suite of offices are placed with the center of attraction of the painting at the eye level of a person standing. Note the simplicity of the frames, in which a narrow wood or metal molding is all that separates the picture from the wall.

Figure 11.17. Where to hang a picture: II. Former residence of George E. Danforth, Cleveland, Ohio.
Photograph: Courtesy of George E. Danforth
Sometimes a painting is hung so that it can be seen best by a person who is seated.

a decision about where to hang a picture. If walls are well defined in panels, the picture placement should be considered in relation to the panel on which it is hung. It will ordinarily please if the picture proportions vary slightly from those of the panel but are related to them. In placing a picture in a panel, the margin of space below the picture generally should be smaller than above the picture, but many factors can alter this precept.

Few walls are broken into panels today. An attempt is made to treat the entire wall as one unbroken plane surface that may even project beyond the boundaries of the room. Thus walls are given a horizontal emphasis and are connected rhythmically with all the other wall surfaces in view. In such a situation an art work should be placed to aid the

kind of rhythm and balance that has been planned for the area (Figure 11.18).

One occasionally sees unique arrangements. For instance, several pictures might be hung as a group. This is sometimes done when one is not sufficiently large for a position. Pictures should be hung very close together if they are to be seen as a group. The space between the pictures should be narrower than the width of an individual picture. In grouping them in this manner, the expressions of the individual pictures are often lost in the expression of the group. Therefore, pictures so hung should be similar in character, and the import of the picture will be less obscured if its character is more decorative than meaningful.

Sometimes pictures are arranged in a verti-

Figure 11.18. A wall hanging. A private residence, New York State.
Architects: Crissman & Solomon
Photograph: © Steve Rosenthal
Here the room dictates the placement of the tapestry wall hanging. It is hung
loosely and relates to the wall space, the upper window, and the dark room
accents rather than to any low level of furniture, or indeed to the most advantageous level for viewing.

cal or a horizontal row. In such an arrangement the value of any individual picture falling outside the range of vision is practically
nullified. The whole arrangement must gain
in pattern decorativeness if this loss is to be
justified.

A stepladder arrangement of pictures
should be handled with extreme caution. The
pictures are apt to become stepping stones
to carry the eye toward the ceiling. If a larger
picture is placed in the center and a step-down
as well as a step-up arrangement is planned,
the eye may be kept where it belongs. Pictures placed on the wall adjacent to a stairway
are, for obvious reasons, an understandable
exception to this guideline.

Some very good pictures may prove difficult to hang because they are too small for
the space to be filled. To make such a small

picture seem more appropriate for a space, it
may be hung on a cloth wall hanging of larger
size. (Hangings can also make good backdrops
for sculpture.) Sometimes a wall stencil can
be used to frame a group of small pictures.

Sculpture

The original meaning of the word sculpture
implied something cut away, as in the chisel-
ing of stone (Figure 11.19). Indeed, the great
French workers in brass and bronze cut away
the metal after the original form was molded,
so that they were known as *chiseleurs*. Sculpturing of this nature is done today in many
materials (Figure 11.20). The purpose is not
only to create a form that has its mass and
space organized into a good three-dimensional design, but also to bring out the natural

Figure 11.19. Marble sculpture I. "Rumination."
Artist: William M. McVey
The Cleveland Museum of Art, Norman O. Stone and Ella A. Stone Memorial Fund
Photograph: Courtesy of The Cleveland Museum of Art
This figure shows not only masses but shadows and highlights in rhythmic forms consistent with the hard white marble from which the sculpture was chiseled.

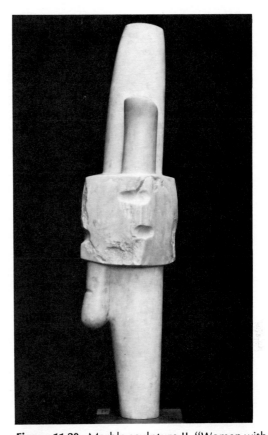

Figure 11.20. Marble sculpture II. "Woman with Child," H. 44".
Artist: Isamu Noguchi
The Cleveland Museum of Art, Contemporary Collection of the Cleveland Museum of Art
Photograph: Courtesy of The Cleveland Museum of Art
Despite its hardness and high polish, this is marble you want to touch. Its subject, form, and material are exquisitely blended to make a whole—a master work.

Figure 11.21. Wood sculpture. "Reclining Figure," elm wood, 1935–36.
Artist: Henry Moore
Albright-Knox Art Gallery, Buffalo, New York, Room of Contemporary Art Fund

Photograph: Albright-Knox Art Gallery, Buffalo
Here not only masses but also voids together with highlights and shadows create rhythmic forms that are consistent with the wood grain. Moore's sculpture suggest the growth and the positive-negative that is in all nature.

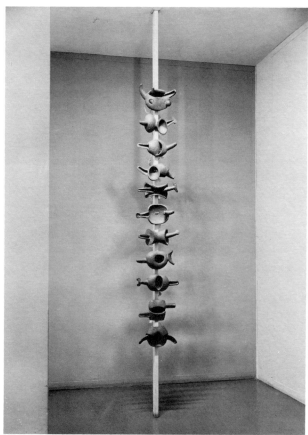

Figure 11.22. Ceramic sculpture. "Even the Centipede" (1952).
Artist: Isamu Noguchi
Collection, The Museum of Modern Art, New York, A. Conger Goodyear Fund
Photograph: The Museum of Modern Art, New York
This type of sculpture, sometimes called agglutinated sculpture because it is made of many small pieces comprising a whole, is of Japanese *kasama* ware, a high-fired earthenware. In this sculpture, each of the eleven pieces is about 18 inches long. They are mounted on a wooden pole 14 feet high. An extremely interesting unity is made from diversity.

structure of the material through the design. Wood sculpture has forms that seem to grow from the grain of the wood (Figure 11.21).

Plastic sculpture or modeling creates forms that show the hand-forming rather than the hand-cutting process. Such objects are first made in clay or some similar plastic material (Figure 11.22). They are then given permanent form by either firing or casting replicas from a mold. Since several copies can be made by the latter method, such pieces are similar to artists' proofs in prints. The design might well indicate the original plasticity of the medium.

Three-dimensional design is now created with many new materials and processes. some sculpturing is done with a blowtorch on metal. Wire and plastics are used. Unlimited reproductions of sculptured pieces are also produced. These are divorced from the artist's supervision, just as the unlimited reproductions of two-dimensional art are. Many artists, however, will not allow duplicates to be made without their final approval of the result. The work of many firms includes such a quality guarantee.

How to Develop Appreciation

It is possible to give some suggestions and guidelines that may lead toward the growth and development of appreciation. Fine art can have various kinds of appeal. For instance, a craftsman is frequently more interested in the material or its handling than in its statement. The consistency of a technique in any artifact indicates deliberation and skill that can initiate our admiration. One approach to appreciation is through attempting to create. It is soon seen that much modern art revolves around technique experimentation.

Then, too, while experimenting and learning about technical matters, try to set down sensuous material in various kinds of order. The order may not be analyzed, but colors (Figure 11.23), linear tracks, spaces, imitated textures—all of these in juxtaposition may provide interest. Doodling is fun, and some artists seem able to preserve this simple expression of joy through free rendering. Does something of the excitement of creation come across to us from their work (Figure 11.24)?

Figure 11.23. Color changes. "Red Maroons," oil on canvas, 79" × 81".
Artist: Mark Rothko
The Cleveland Museum of Art, Contemporary Collection, and Friends of The
Cleveland Museum of Art.
Photograph: Courtesy of The Cleveland Museum of Art
Sometimes the artist educates our eye to see subtle shifts of color in relation
to shape; such an artist is Mark Rothko.

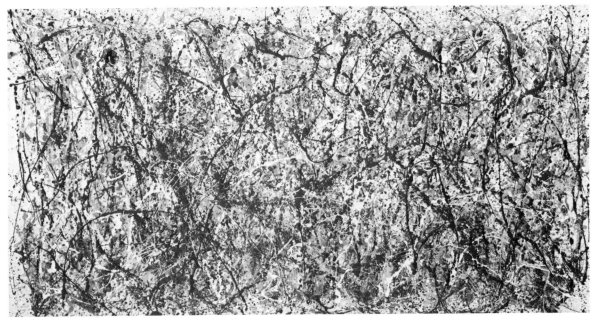

Figure 11.24. Doodling? "One" (Number 31, 1950), oil and enamel paint, on
canvas, 8' 10" × 17' 5⅝".
Artist: Jackson Pollock
Collection, The Museum of Modern Art, New York, Gift of Sidney Janis
Photograph: The Museum of Modern Art, New York
Why should a creation that some might consider pure doodling be elevated
to the status of fine art? For several reasons. Look closely and you will discover that this is not ordinary free play. Complex and involved pattern tracks
emerge as one steadily gazes at the canvas. Visible accents punctuate the
rhythms of performance. Such subtleties provide a textural interest that can
often give needed relief in interiors done in steel, glass, and plaster.

Figure 11.25. Concentration on a limited number of components. "Accent Grave," oil on canvas, 75¼" × 51¾".
Artist: Franz Kline
The Cleveland Museum of Art, Anonymous Gift
Photograph: Courtesy of The Cleveland Museum of Art
Many observers want to translate this painting into the head of a horse. It is not. It is an isolation of spatial arrangements that evokes a powerful feeling of strength. In this and the foregoing paintings, the artist has made us more keenly aware of color, texture, and shape as the underlying factors of all visual art.

On the other hand, our approach of experimentation with order may create an interest in art that has been done with meticulous care, with isolation, and with concentration on the potentialities of one or two components (Figure 11.25). This sort of art may intrigue a scientific-minded person, one who wishes to find the perfect solution to a problem of limited range.

We may find ourselves sitting before a painting and following the routes of its more complex thematic relations (Figure 11.26; see also Color Plate 2). Many realignments of the visual material are possible and are interesting to trace. We may find ourselves appreciating what the critic often calls plastic organization, which is our familiar design precept of "several alignments."

Because most contemporary art emphasizes sensuous design, it is desirable that an appreciation of its other qualities, when they are present, should come through this doorway. This is not to denigrate realism in art. Today's art seems to be giving us a much-needed lesson—it teaches that the basic value in art is found in its design, but its richest value lies in something incorporated with sensuousness. It is a stodgy onlooker who cannot sense that the expressive power of the shapes, colors, and textures tell us about

Figure 11.26. A magnificent design. "Fan, Saltbox, Melon," oil on canvas, 32" × 25¼".
Artist: Pablo Picasso
The Cleveland Museum of Art, Purchase, Leonard C. Hanna Jr. bequest
Photograph: Courtesy of The Cleveland Museum of Art
Picasso puts it all together—color, texture, and shape—a truly wonderful design! Moreover, there is a great deal of meaning packed into this canvas—meaning conveyed through design.

Figure 11.27. How much realism? How much expression? "Bird Singing in the Moonlight," gouache, 26¾" × 30⅛".
Artist: Morris Graves
Collection, The Museum of Modern Art, New York, Purchase
Photograph: The Museum of Modern Art
This realism, this expression is enough. It is realism for the sake of expression. Design, although not complex, is not absent.

the artist's world today (Figure 11.27). When this communication is succinct and unlabored, we often find in it a delightful form of wit.

The leaders in the scientific world appreciate another sort of imagery. Scientists deal in concrete symbols for abstract relations. The symbols of visual art derive from the basic matter of experience, the components of sensation, and are used to make an idea understandable. Let the physicist and the chemist attempt to explain the taut explosiveness of the atom; let the engineer try to show the motion that has conquered the air; let the sociologist draft a conception of the majesty of our cities, and let the psychologist chart their nervous energy. They should then find in the works of Feininger, Brancusi, Sheeler, and Marsh a creativity that reflects their own. If one still likes a picture only as an ex-

act representation of something, the concentration can be on the variety of ways of portraying a subject. It is sometimes a good idea to see how an interesting topic has been depicted by different artists. Thus if a person likes the sea, he or she might like the oils of Waugh. A completely different treatment is found in a Marin watercolor. What of the mood of the sea in a painting by Mattson, and how different is the work of Ryder? Which would be chosen to use in a design situation, and why?

Out of such a study of one subject treated in different ways by different artists comes the idea that there is more than one way to show the same subject and still get the idea across in a very likeable manner. Every camera enthusiast knows how to vary the representation by varying the lens or station point.

Figure 11.28. Visual art, literature, music. Interior, private residence.
Interior design: George Nelson Associates
Photographer: Scott Hyde
Rudders to steer by: literature, music, and art. This apartment, designed by
George Nelson, who in his writing has done so much to clarify our thinking
about the place of art in today's world, becomes a symbol of what he has
meant and has stood for.

The painter has more freedom than the photographer in his representation and has used this freedom imaginatively since the beginning of art. The idea of relative importance of objects can be communicated by their size and position in space. We accept this idea very easily in advertising art. The artist can convey the idea of motion or mobility of objects by representing one object as seen through another object, which conceivably has just taken up its position in front of the first object. A montage lets us see two scenes at once. This is a favorite technique of the motion picture. In short, the painter can tell us many things about objects sign language, and it is enlivening to discover them.

The subject matter of today's art is as varied as our world; the interpretation of this subject matter is as varied as human experience. The artist worthy of the name will employ the medium to give a message of the joy that the eyes can bring, to show the order that can be found in the visual world, and to convey something of the human struggle. The contemporary artist is apt to consider these accomplishments in this relative order. But the meaning that is asked for in a work of art is indivisible.

The artist is the perpetual foe of regimented unity—a fact for which our syndicated culture should give thanks. The artist is also forever conscious of the links that bind experience (Figure 11.28). Our specialized civilization has lost these links. When they are found again, art will be different.

The Trial Run

The best way to test any work of art is to live with it for a time. Most dealers will permit one to take a picture out for a short period on loan. Some art clubs allow their members to borrow works of art on yearly loans. Membership in such clubs is for a fee, but it is a very good way to gain the message of a work of art and to see which art is the wisest personal choice. Many libraries also have framed reproductions of art works to lend.

Should a work of art be left in the same position forever? Sometimes the answer is yes, sometimes no. A happy change of scene makes one the more eager to return. In the oriental home, pictures are placed like flowers, in a varying order. This enables the family and friends to look with a fresh eye.

If well-placed art objects seem to lift rooms out of the impersonal, ordinary class and to give them that vitality that some personalities give to a gathering, the expenditure in time and money that went into their purchase is warranted. If art continues to do this over the years, it is worth more than stocks and bonds, on which we collect a dividend only every quarter, whereas our art dividend comes daily.

12

THE TOTAL ART FORM: PUTTING IT ALL TOGETHER

*and I know not if, save in this, such a gift be allowed to man,
—That out of three sounds he frame, not a fourth sound,
but a star.*

Robert Browning, "Abt Vogler"[1]

*One technical definition of a system is as follows: a system is
a structure of interacting, intercommunicating components
that, as a group, act or operate individually and jointly to
achieve a common goal through the concerted activity of the
individual parts. This is, of course, a completely satisfactory
definition of the earth, except maybe for that last part about a
common goal. What on earth is* our *common goal? How
did we ever get mixed up in a place like this?*

Lewis Thomas, Note from a Universe Watcher[2]

*Monsieur Clopet asked: "And what are the books you have
under your arm?" Louis replied: "Books I was told at the
American legation I would need." "Ah, yes, let me see them."
He took the books, selected a large work on Descriptive
Geometry, and began to turn the pages. "Now observe: Here
is a problem with five exceptions or special cases; here a
theorem, three special cases; another nine, and so on and on,
a procession of exceptions and special cases. I suggest you
place the book in the waste basket; we shall not need it here; for
here our* demonstrations shall be so broad as to
admit of *NO EXCEPTIONS."*

Louis Sullivan, The Autobiography of an Idea[3]

The Method

If you consider the three quotations that begin this chapter, you will see that a poet, a biologist, and a teacher have expressed similar ideas over the last century. All tell of a hope, a goal, a question, and a belief that to see the universe whole and to create in similar manner requires planning, interrelating, and summarizing, and it necessitates flexibility and breadth of viewpoint. Conceptions that are too narrow will not avail. Rules and exceptions—no. Goals and means in relation to them—yes. Questioning, eternal questioning—absolutely necessary.

Much of this chapter, therefore, merely illustrates methods of inquiry. The illustrations given will only be valid for a particular set of conditions; other ones must be found to provide the best answer for other conditions.

In the sections of this chapter, design considerations are discussed in relation to floors, walls, windows, and upholstery. Very little will be said about color because this subject has already been discussed in detail in Chapters 7 and 8. Any good designer must, of course, always keep color in mind and must also always consider how it interacts with everything else.

Integrating: Floor Coverings

HOW ARE FLOOR COVERINGS AND DESIGN RELATED?

What is the general character of the floor in relation to the whole art form? How limiting are functional considerations? Although the total art form must be kept in mind, the practical and meaningful considerations of floor coverings must always come first and must, in a sense, dictate the special sensuous solution.

WHAT ARE THE TEXTURAL CONSIDERATIONS?

Texture should be the first consideration in any solution to floor covering. Should there

be any hard texture evident, or should the entire floor be covered with a soft fabric? Hard surfacing may contribute greatly not only to an illusion of space but also to a harmony with architectural concepts. Where carpeting is required (sometimes by law), select a tightly twisted uncut pile wherever throw rugs are going to be used as well. A relatively close, evenly textured carpet will increase the sense of space. Shaggy pile will always diminish space. Advancing and receding movement will be created by carpets with various depths of pile. This should be related to the overall room movement.

TO WHAT EXTENT SHOULD A FLOOR BE COVERED?

A room is enlarged by uniform wall-to-wall treatment or by the coordination of floor covering with room shape. However, extensive carpeting has two pitfalls—monotony and overinsistence.

FLOOR COVERING—PLAIN OR PATTERNED?

Absence of pattern enlarges space. Plain covering aids the concept of designing in flat surfaces. Pattern relieves the monotony of the floor expanse. Accent rugs can be centers of interest (see Color Plate 6). The force of floor pattern can balance wall pattern or texture. Pattern can be practical in concealing wear, dirt, and uneven floors.

HOW SHOULD A PATTERN FOR FLOORS BE CHOSEN?

Floor pattern should first be good design and should relate to the room design. Because a floor pattern is to be walked on, it should be preferably a nonrealistic, nondirectional, stylized, flat pattern (for explanation of these terms, see the next section). If pattern and background are similar in tone, forward and backward movement will be minimal. In special cases such as in the use of oriental prayer rugs, directional pattern can be appropriate for directed emphasis.

Integrating: Wall Treatments

WALLCOVERING—PLAIN OR PATTERNED?

Walls without pattern enlarge space. They keep the wall planes intact and indeed are the only solution when the architecture is planned as the principal design statement. They are

[1]Reprinted from *The Complete Poetic and Dramatic Works of Robert Browning*, Houghton Mifflin, 1895.

[2]*The New York Times*, July 2, 1978 © 1978 by The New York Times Company. Reprinted by permission.

[3]New York: Press of the American Institute of Architects, 1924, pp. 220–221.

Figure 12.1. A corporate office.
Architects: Schmidt, Garden & Erickson
Interior designer: Beverly Jablonski
Photographer: James R. Norris
The carpeting in this handsome office is deep and luxurious, but it keeps its
place in the total room scheme because its tonal values are close to each other.
A very light pattern against a dark body would have called undue attention
to the floor and would have destroyed the desired effect of the whole.

the appropriate choice where pictures are to be hung. On the other hand, a room with a prominent traditional architectural feature (such as paneling to a dado) may need pattern on the plain surfaces for balance. A room with irregular wall areas (such as a recess) may use pattern for disguise or, conversely, to set the irregularities apart. Pattern can camouflage poor walls. It can balance a busy floor. Mural decoration can be an interesting substitute for a movable picture or a screen. A *trompe l'oeil* mural may be the only way to give spaciousness to a confined area.

CHOOSING THE PATTERN OF A WALLCOVERING

Wall pattern (including wallpaper) must be of good design by all standards. Because a large mural pattern is constantly in view, it is important that its design possess a degree of complexity so that the eye may find several paths along which to travel. However, the pattern should not be as intricate as that of a painting, because it would then present too much busywork for the attention.

A good mural design should contain rest positions (Figure 12.2). These are especially necessary because a wall design is usually repetitious. Without these quiet centers, a wall becomes disturbingly active.

Some persons make the mistake of thinking that a good wall pattern should always be inconspicuous. The degree of insistence of the pattern depends on its function in the total design and bears no particular relation

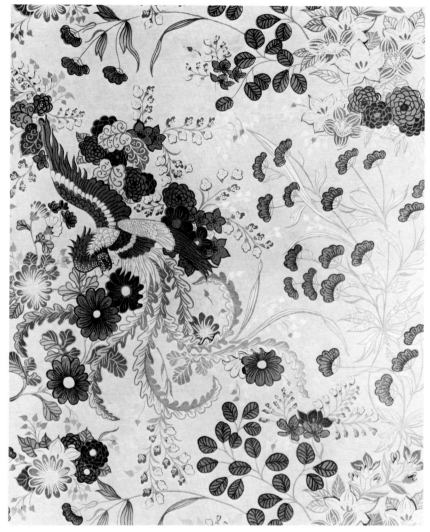

Figure 12.2. Wall pattern. "Imari," Albert van Luit & Co.
Photograph: Courtesy of Albert van Luit & Co.
The flowers in this wall design are represented as areas, and the design is
basically flat because there is no shading to indicate volume. The restful principal motif is well designed, although the supporting smaller accents
possibly become too busy in this color scheme because of the value contrasts
that accentuate the many small spots. Some of this contrast may derive
from the translation here into a black and white print.

to its intrinsic merit. Since wall patterns can
be bought in papers in several different color
combinations, it is often a good practice to
examine a particular design in its most contrasting color relationship. If it stands up under this kind of examination, it can be used
safely in the tones that would give just the
right amount of emphasis for a particular
area.

In general, wall patterns should be scaled
to the size of the space. However, this is
not a blanket rule. In the first place, a pattern
that is too diminutive, especially if it is a
design that would be better suited to a larger

scale, may merely appear trivial. Again, the
compressed size of a pattern may result in
an exaggerated and quick movement that will
make a room seem smaller than a larger pattern having a more restrained movement
would. Other factors such as the pattern design quality, its insistence, and its flatness,
will modify its scale potential.

There are the flat designs, in which there
is no three-dimensional modeling. Most linear designs fall into this category, although
area designs may also be flat. Flat designs fit
best in the treatment of any wall as a plane
because they hold their place well in the

plane. Since they do not advance noticeably from the wall surface, they can be used to great advantage in a small room. A flat design can be larger in scale than one with depth without reducing the apparent room size.

Many designs have three-dimensional modeling on a flat background. Here the design stands out and is used best in a space that would benefit from some reduction in size.

Last, the depth treatment in a design may be one that uses all the known laws of perspective to create the illusion of the recession into distance. This kind of design may be used effectively to enlarge space. One must be very careful, however, that the force of pattern activity on a wall does not bring it forward more than the perspective vista pushes it outward.

Closely related to a consideration of depth treatment in wall patterning is the study of the degree of stylization in the pattern. A highly realistic pattern is one in which a sense of reality is accomplished by the use of many devices known to the painter. The colors that appear in nature are duplicated; the lights and darks that simulate the three-dimensional modeling of nature are depicted; linear perspective is used to reproduce the natural positioning of objects in space. From this representation of reality the artist-designer may depart as far as he or she wishes.

A pattern that deviates from nature but uses a natural subject as its point of departure is frequently called a stylized pattern. The artist does not alter nature merely for the sake of being different but to create a more developed design relationship.

When a pattern deviates markedly from nature to the extent that nature becomes merely an inspiration for the design, it is frequently called an abstract design. A step further on this path away from realism is nonobjective or nonrepresentational design, in which no reference to any natural object can be observed. Because there is a relation between this kind of design and the impersonal character of today's world, nonobjective design often seems appropriate to modern buildings.

There are other ways to depart from nature in making a design. Realistic motifs can be arranged into a larger designed composition.

Here it is the arrangement that deviates from reality. Represented objects may be altered in scale, some large, some small. They may be changed in position, some upright, some upside down. They may be unrealistically colored or textured. They may be enclosed within a designed frame.

The subject matter produced and enjoyed in art is closely related to the culture (including the technical processes) of a people. For instance, folk pattern is liable to be composed of many somewhat unrelated motifs, each individually stylized. It resembles children's art in this respect. Early American wallpaper pattern, although it stems from European work, is influenced by the simple stencil and block processes that were used. These processes did not lend themselves readily to the nuances of realistic portrayal. The most characteristic contemporary design, for all of its abstraction, is marked by a strong rhythm. More conventional or more formal period designs frequently use bisymmetry or enclosure within a restricting framework.

Several suggestions seem to come from these observations about design types. There is no direct correlation between a type of design and its intrinsic excellence. The character of the design should be chosen with great sensitivity to the character of the room and the personalities of its occupants. In a group of closely associated spaces, there is greater unity when one type of design character predominates.

In general, the sense of a wall is best preserved by a flat design that is at least stylized to the degree that is necessary to support the room structure. There may be times for deviation from this. If the planes are complicated, for instance, in slanting ceilings and dormer niches, the wall designs may have to be nondirectional and even realistic.

WHAT TEXTURES ARE APPROPRIATE FOR WALLS?

Smooth, matte textures will increase apparent size. Highly reflective textures may cause brightness glare. Imitative textures used on walls are a matter of taste. Natural textures such as wood veneer and grass cloth seem appropriate for architecture that is closely related to natural settings. Three-dimensional textures present some cleaning problems.

Integrating: Window Treatments

WHY TREAT WINDOWS?

Window treatment is a major problem in interior design. Windows are generally functional as well as decorative. Both their utility and their enjoyable qualities should be increased by proper handling. Treatment is for the purpose of modifying the light, softening the window edge, gracing the window shape, and adding privacy.

HOW IS WINDOW TREATMENT RELATED TO ROOM DESIGN?

The answer to the question of the relationship between window treatment and room design varies. When the window is a focal point, visual forces should be arranged to carry the eye to the window. Then the consideration is one of relative emphasis. If the view from the window is desirable, the window treatment should be unobtrusive. If there is only modest interest in the view, the decorative treatment should not obstruct vision outward, but it may at the same time claim more attention. If the view is poor, it is best to shut it out and concentrate interest on the window location. Questions of lighting must also be considered carefully.

When the window is not a focal point, give it a treatment that will make it less forceful than other centers of interest.

Figure 12.3. Window treatment: I. A traditional Fifth Avenue apartment.
Interior designer: Robert K. Lewis Associates, Inc., New York, New York
Photograph: © Mark Ross
Most of the furnishings of this Fifth Avenue apartment are traditional. A light, warm color scheme unifies the ensemble and creates the appearance of space. The curtaining in the living room is silk hung in lines that repeat the architectural surround. In the adjoining room, vertical blinds carried only to the base of the window apron create a greater informality of treatment while retaining the modern uplift of the total design.

Figure 12.4. Window treatment: II. A Manhattan residence.
Interior designers: Barbara Ross and Barbara Schwartz of Dexter Design
Photograph: © Jaime Ardiles-Arce
This is a very interesting solution to requirements that no architectural changes
be made in the existing apartment and that the finished result should be
contemporary and not appear ostentatious. Light wood tones predominate
and are relieved by the greyed green of plants and leather upholstery. Tables
can seat four to eight. Attention here is called to the matchstick blinds at
the windows, which allow a pleasant filtering of the outside light without de-
tracting from the airy feeling of space within. The walls have a textured linen
covering. The painting above the buffet is by Susumu Saguchi, illustrating
minimal coloring that causes the eye to move through slight variations in tones.
The painting on the far wall is by Ed Baynard.

PLAIN OR PATTERNED WINDOW TREATMENT?

Plain material, except when it is greatly
contrasted with its surroundings, is less emphatic than patterned. It may provide an opportunity for textural interest. It can provide
an interesting play of light and shade through
the relative compactness or openness of the
weave. It can provide the contemporary feeling of wall-plane designing.

Pattern, on the other hand, provides interest. It can supplement room design. When
helped by color, it can unite a number of unrelated factors into one large pivotal detail.

WHAT KIND OF PATTERNS SHOULD BE CHOSEN FOR WINDOWS?

Any pattern at a window should be of good
design by all standards. If the window treatment is accomplished through a taut material
such as screening, the principles of wall patterning are relevant. If the treatment introduces folds of textiles, the following considerations are very important: The pattern
should be closely related to the texture and
the processes of production evident in a textile. Some textures will hang in stiff folds,
which seem to require bolder linear patterns

made by such processes as weaving or block printing. Some fabrics fall in soft folds and seem suited to fragile designs made possible through roller printing or photoengraving.

The pattern should be effective when hanging. Its rhythms should be observed in this position. At a window where patterned draw curtains are used, the material must be considered in two positions—first when the curtains cover the window and again when the draperies are pulled open and are concentrated at the sides of the window. The conspicuousness of the pattern in these two situations should be noted.

Textile patterns may simulate texture or may impose a tapestry effect by means of color. Both these kinds of pattern give an illusion of added fabric weight.

WHAT TEXTURAL CONSIDERATIONS ARE IMPORTANT?

Texture in relation to windows introduces a problem that is a counterpart to the one encountered in the treatment of floors. Should any treatment accorded windows be of a hard material or a soft one (e.g., wood shades or cloth draperies)? Because the vast bulk of interior design work is now done in public buildings, the former has come to dominate the latter, although for use in private areas cloth still holds sway.

That aspect of fabric texture commonly known as the hand or the handle is exceedingly important to the linear treatment of draperies. The fabric cannot be sleazy or the weight of abundant folds will drag it down. If the fabric is intended to support a straight-line theme, it must have the backbone to do so. If it is intended to drape into soft curves, it should have the necessary pliancy for the purpose.

Many a drapery treatment has been spoiled because there was not enough of the material used either in length or in fullness. Window treatment in cloth is designed to display the sensuous character of the cloth—its texture and color as they relate to line. For this a liberal expanse is required.

Any textural play of opaque and translucent areas should be considered carefully both in taut and in loose treatments. If the purpose of a window covering is to modify the light, its patterning should not create blotchy shadows or attract undue attention.

In treatments using any variety of slat blinds, the textural relation between the body material and the draw tapes and cords is important. One designer is careful to see that the warp threads of lattice-wood shades are of a soft, nubby material. Plastic slats, on the other hand, would seem more related to a hard, twisted cord.

THE POSITIONING OF WINDOW COVERINGS

Contemporary windows have a minimum of architectural framing. The apron has virtually disappeared along with the elaborate entablatures of classically inspired periods. The customary precepts about how to hang shades and curtains must be modified to suit the new simplicity.

Glass curtains were planned originally to modify light and to aid privacy. Their original use dictated a simple treatment. They were gathered onto rods that were attached to the upper sash and they extended to the sill. At times they were stretched on frames that covered glazed areas. Glass curtains today, however, are frequently related to the drapery treatment and derive their positioning from the latter.

Draperies are curtains that are hung at the side of the window for the purpose of softening the sharp edge of light made between the window and wall. Although draperies are frequently of an opaque material, the new treatment of combining drapery and glass curtaining in one fabric has led designers to create a number of translucent materials for this purpose. It is not intended that these be lined. The usual drapery material, however, looks better if it is lined. Some new drapery textiles are complex single-weave cloths designed not to require lining. They should be handled like lined fabrics.

A lined drapery must be hung in firm pleats (French pleats are one variety) or looped up onto a rod. Such a drapery is usually too thick to be gathered on the rod. Unlined curtains of an informal character can be gathered. The use of a heading or a fold of cloth above the rod casing depends on the character of the fabric and the position on the rod. Very soft fabrics may look better without a heading.

When the window trim possesses an elaborate architectural character, the draperies may be hung entirely within the frame or be designed to cover only a portion of the trim.

On most wood-framed windows the rods are placed so that the top of the curtain will come to the top of the trim and the side framing will be covered. The rods may extend out onto the wall to convey an impression of added width. Often the rods are placed close to the ceiling. Proportional relations influence placement.

Many curtains today are hung from an inconspicuous track placed close to or on the ceiling. This positioning is frequently used even though the window itself does not have that height. The length of contemporary curtaining should be related to the character of the room design, the positioning of the upper rods, the fabric, and the window. Curtains usually extend to the sill, just below the sill, or to the floor.

Traverse or draw curtains can be pulled back or drawn over a window. Such curtains were originally suspended behind draperies and were only pulled across the window for privacy. They were frequently made of a plain casement cloth. With the greater simplification of modern window treatment, the functions of drapery, traverse curtain, and glass curtaining are often combined in one hanging. If a traverse curtain is drawn by pulley cords, it must be pleated or looped onto the traverse fixtures. If there is a great expanse of window to be covered, a pocket should be planned in the wall to take care of the voluminous material when the curtain is drawn back.

The simplification of window treatments has generally eliminated the use of valances. The purpose of a valance is to conceal the mechanism from which curtains are hung, to make an ornamental finish for the top of the window, and to harbor light fixtures. It also shortens the apparent height of windows. Valances may be designed as tailored coverings for a valance board or cornice board (a wooden frame), or they may be of elaborately draped material. The latter type are often called swags or lambrequins. They were used traditionally in many window treatments of the past. If valances are used today, they should be carefully considered in relation to the rest of the window and room design. It would seem undesirable to design them of any shape, color, or texture that would call undue attention to the upper part of a room.

The process of simplification has also removed many other parts of window treatments such as curtain knobs, tiebacks, and floor hooks (placed in the floor to fasten curtains in place). All of these additions may be desirable for specific window treatments.

Curtains are frequently divided horizontally into two sections, creating what is frequently called cottage or café curtains. This is a current modification of a very old device. It is a useful scheme, because it enables one to secure privacy without completely blocking out the upper light, or to modify the upper light without obstructing the lower view. Such curtains are usually of an informal character. They break a window height into two parts and are thus more visually busy.

The placement of shutters, roller shades, Venetian blinds, vertical slat blinds, and screens must be dictated by the design of the window in relation to the room. Both for practical reasons and because they echo architectural lines, hard materials are predominantly used for public buildings.

Upholstery

In the upholstery of furniture, there is a very close relation between the basic object and the added material. A piece of furniture has a shape and a color and a texture, each of which should harmonize with its chosen upholstery.

WHAT TEXTURES SHOULD BE CHOSEN FOR UPHOLSTERY?

In a consideration of upholstery material, texture seems more important than pattern. In addition to the fundamental textural affinities of structure, apparent weight, and amount and depth of light reflection, the following textural qualities are especially important:

The compactness and precision of grain, the surface contour, and the changeable character of the light on materials all influence upholstery selection. A trim, sleek frame requires a taut-appearing fabric. It may possess a directional grain such as is found in a twill or a rep. Surface contour and light breakup should be relatively even so that there will not be too much activity in the reflections.

On the other hand, a piece that is informal in shape and thick in its contours will require

Figure 12.5. Upholstery: I.
Fabric: moiré silk damask by Brunschwig et Fils, Inc.
Photograph: © Brunschwig et Fils, 1981
This lovely silk and cotton damask in a pattern that suggests moiré or watered silk is most appropriate for the upholstery of a traditional Louis XVI chair. The chair itself is so exquisitely carved that the carving should not be upstaged by pattern in the upholstery. This fabric with a fine texture and an unobtrusive variation in its tones is an ideal covering and makes the entire piece compatible with a contemporary interior.

Figure 12.6. *(top right)* Upholstery: II.
Fabric: wool damask by Brunschwig et Fils, Inc.
Photograph: © Brunschwig et Fils, Inc., 1981
This wool damask is exactly suited to the eighteenth-century wing chair. The bisymmetrical fabric design corresponds to the relative formality of the chair. Its large scale makes it compatible and yet its unobtrusiveness and fine linear character create a finesse that agrees with the quality of the furniture. Its monochromatic scheme allows the beautiful lines of the chair to predominate.

Figure 12.7. *(right)* Upholstery: III.
Fabric: textured wool, Brunschwig et Fils, Inc.
Photograph: © Brunschwig et Fils, Inc., 1981
A large piece of upholstered furniture is covered best in a fabric that has no definite pattern. Here the pattern is small enough to suggest texture, and its slightly raised motifs serve to break the large bulk of the piece.

Plate 7. An inflow of light. Residence of Peter Kurt Woerner, Guilford, Connecticut.
Architect: Peter Kurt Woerner
Photograph: © Robert Perron 1976
This house (the exterior of which is seen in Figure 2.9) is built to capture the utmost daylight in its dining area, which could be called a greenhouse dining room. In keeping with the marshland of the exterior, the furnishings echo a somewhat rugged and simple character. The rush-seated chairs, the colorful linen cloth, and the pottery accoutrements together with the tile floor create a harmonious textural interest.

Plate 8. The Ming furniture room, Astor Court, The Metropolitan Museum of Art, New York, Gift of the Vincent Astor Foundation, 1980.
Photograph: © 1980 by The Metropolitan Museum of Art, all rights reserved
Here is exemplified architectonic thinking in its essential form. The space itself is considered primarily in determining arrangements within. Only after this rapport is clearly and rigorously established can the embellishment that makes the work more rich and complex be used.

a firm material but one that does not possess a right or left directional character in its weave. A certain unevenness of contour is desirable for correspondence with the lack of definition in the frame. A firm, plain-weave fabric with nubby yarn may be suitable.

All chairs that are designed in three dimensions, meaning that their backs, seats, and arms deviate considerably from their respective planes, also require nondirectional weaves. The surface contour of the material depends on the thinness and general attenuation of the furniture's structural members as well as on the amount and quickness of their curvature. A finely etched damask might be suitable for one wing chair, and another would require a puffier matelassé. If the breakup of light in any material causes quick visual motion, the material may prove too active and forceful for a small chair and too busy for a large one.

WHAT ABOUT PATTERN IN UPHOLSTERY?

In upholstery, it is the scale of every part of a pattern that is important. Scale in relation to linear character should be noted. A fine line drawn with grace may be used on smaller chairs even though the complete fabric pattern is large in scale. A pattern with a quick, nervous line movement may prove more forceful than a larger pattern with more poise. A large chair may require a pattern composed of area relations rather than linear ones.

The arrangement of the patterning is also an important consideration. As in wall patterning, a compact, compartmentalized pattern is more formal than one that bursts its bounds. If such a compact pattern is small in relation to the texture scale, it is liable to suggest a conventional, even a smug kind of character. Thus a small chair of provincial feeling looks right in a neat, diamond pattern. A large, formal, Chippendale cabriole-leg chair might require a bisymmetrical, formalized pattern, where an informal Queen Anne chair of similar curvature would look better with a sprawling pattern.

HOW DOES COLOR RELATE TO UPHOLSTERY?

The principal aspects of this problem were considered in Chapters 7 and 8. The implied relations between color and shape may impose lighter colors on fragile shapes and darker colors on heavy pieces.

Tonal changes in upholstery should be considered carefully. Great contrast in tone accentuates pattern activity. It is seldom wise to break up a furniture shape by using several tones in the upholstery. When this is done, divide the furniture at its structural points. These suggestions may be nullified if the furniture is so huge and architectural in character that it is necessary to camouflage its extent.

Review and Summary

INTERWEAVING THE DESIGN COMPONENTS: THE RESULTANT FORM

Having considered the small parts (e.g., carpets related to floors, curtains to windows), we now reverse the process to look at the large in relation to the little. This is by way of review and summary. Here we focus on the design components and notice their interweaving. The following ordered list should be an aid to our troubleshooting as we ask ourselves questions about just what we have or have not accomplished.

1. Have we gained the effects desired?
   a. Some colors are harsh in a shiny texture, pleasant in a soft texture.
   b. Some textures seem functional in one color, impractical in another.
2. Have we chosen the best shape, color, and texture qualities to gain the effects desired? These must support one another. For example:
   a. A curved line with a pink color may suggest femininity.
   b. The combination of some bold curves with pink may prove inharmonious.
3. Have we considered the development of basic qualities for the purpose of intensification?
   a. Which qualities have been most emphasized?
      (1) A contemporary house in a natural setting might demand that color development be curbed in the interest of texture.
      (2) An old, nondescript city building could play up color.
      (3) A great architectural concept might emphasize shapes.
   b. How has the enhancement of a quality been accomplished?
      (1) Through its original importance (using a large amount of the quality either alone or in repeated units)?
         (i) A stone fireplace wall speaks of natural textures in no uncertain terms.

(ii) The dominance of natural colors makes the textures more noticeable.

(2) Through an importance gained by a variety of expressions of the quality?

(i) Straight-line planes become dramatic when horizontal, vertical, and even diagonal directions are counterposed. Color can aid this drama.

(3) Through an importance gained by contrasting different qualities?

(i) A three-dimensional curved frame can foil a straight-line, flat-designed painting. It also can correspond in color to other notes in a room.

4. Have we planned the arrangement (the alignment of forces) of the various visual themes (the larger groupings) to create desired movement and rest? For example:

a. Simple activity.

A curved line may call attention in one direction and a flash of red may pull in another.

b. Directed movement or rhythm.

(1) Masses of grey contrasted with shapes of bright colors may create background-to-foreground interest.

(2) Compactly arranged furniture groups may be integrated further through repetitive color.

(3) Climaxes to centers of interest may be built up in one direction through progressions of color, in another through shapes. Interesting tensions are thus created that make the ultimate resolutions more vital.

c. Choices of various alignments through interlockings (the complexity of the design).

A piece of furniture may figure in a straight-line theme, a blue color theme, and a texture progression, sending the attention wandering down any of these quality paths.

d. Rest or stability (equalizing forces and tensions around visual centers or axes).

A dark wall can balance an expanse of nature seen through a large window.

5. Has integration (interweaving, a unifying of coordinated forces) resulted?

TWO CONTRASTING EXAMPLES OF DESIGN ORGANIZATION

Let us consider the realization of two rather different designs for a room. In both cases the room is identical: the floor plan and the details are simple and the architecture is contemporary. The design qualities and their development are responsible for the great divergence of the resulting designs, although each room is well designed from the standpoint of presenting a unified whole that enhances the effect of the chosen qualities in an interesting way.

1. Shape

Room A: active shapes important; graceful curves dominant (see Figure 12.3).

Room B: straight lines dominant; strong curves for contrast (see Figure 5.14).

2. Color

Room A: quiet tones; light values; small intervals.

Room B: achromatic tones; large intervals.

3. Texture

Room A: small intervals; medium weight; luster of fruitwood dominant, accompanied by that of linen, pewter; softness in carpet.

Room B: large intervals; medium weight; wood without pronounced luster; nonreflective upholstery contrasted with reflective metal; sleekness of slate; concentrated depth and resiliency in the rug.

4. Alignment

a. Background-to-foreground movement.

Room A: subdued background; shape activity in foreground.

Room B: more active background because of bold shape in accessories.

b. Lateral movement to centers of interest.

Room A: accomplished through interwoven shape, color, and textural rhythm.

Room B: accomplished through space relations, tonal rhythms.

c. Choices:

Room A: color interlocking with various shapes and textures.

Room B: dark tones an interlocking force.

d. Stability.

Room A: established by equality of tensions around a central axis.

Room B: established around axes crossing at acute angles.

The Art of Interior Design Today

In 1931, the first American organization of professional interior designers was established. Since then, the entire world has seen far-reaching changes, which have altered the scope, the practice, and the character of even so small a segment of global activity as interior design. Although much early work has lived to influence today's norm, nevertheless the close observer notes conspicuous differences when comparing past designing with today's.

The intent of this volume is to show not only interiors that have pleased people but also those that possess ordered internal visual relationships—in other words, good design. Some of these may seem extreme to readers who have not been following the developments in this art. However, the designs illustrated were chosen because they were judged among the best of current production and because they possess qualities that will make some of them the pacesetters of the future.

Many examples seen here are not for the average purse. Today we are fortunate that the public purse—whether civic or commercial—is sometimes able to foot the bill for creativity that is expensive. In costly undertakings, the new is often introduced to be modified later in terms of greater practicality.

Interior design has just begun to realize that it has a wealth of scientific and industrial tools at command for its performance. These tools enable it to give physical reality to aesthetic ideas that the late twentieth century is now viewing with understanding and appreciation. I believe, with some possibly arrogant surety, that only recently has a twentieth-century style using twentieth-century means and supported by twentieth-century culture come into existence.

SPACE AND MOVEMENT

Designs today tend to be more complex than compound. This means that few rather than many visual traits are developed—for example, shapes and color are made prominent through repetition and contrast rather than through variation. In the best work this leads to greater simplicity and often to heightened drama. True, in the leveling world of the marketplace, design has often lost the knack of equating drama with simplicity. Simplicity, if it is not vacuity, must exploit formal relations.

Architectural shapes today incorporate full curves to oppose straight lines. Seldom, except in domestic interiors, is the biomorphic curve in evidence. This is in keeping with the dynamic character and mechanical methods of our present century.

Space is still the flaunted touchstone. It is now more frequently attained by grouping similar shapes rather than by scattering dissimilar ones. The lone rocking chair calling attention to unoccupied space, the chairs too far apart for civilized conversation, the many small articles confusing communication routes—all have been eliminated, and the resulting form benefits by being infinitely more architectonic.

Grouping of shapes has brought back the long piece of seating furniture (see Color Plate 5). In placing furniture today into workable relationships, both the large expanse and the intimate space are better served than they were in the past. The furniture ensemble usually is designed with straight lines and in an appropriate scale. Some examples unfortunately lean toward buxomness rather than muscularity. This tendency is just one of the manifestations of the fact that industry often caters to popular taste. And popular taste deserves some consideration—great design must be good, but good within the framework of a culture.

Interior architectural planning has moved from emphasis on complete open planning to that of a more plastic organization in space. There is an ingenious use of divisional walls, partial-height walls, and see-through and screen walls (Figure 12.8). These break up space interestingly yet functionally, and leave a suggestion of distance beyond. This development certainly is in the interest of serving human psychological needs.

It is noticeable that the paths directing physical movement through interior space are now often planned to be at variance with the architectural framework. At face value, this seems questionable. It has been justified by designers on the grounds of functional considerations, and it generally does create more interesting as well as more purposeful journeys. It is, however, not new to architecture. Mies van der Rohe, who had the good fortune to work with large spaces, made such a circuitous path in the interior of the Tugendhat house, with no violence done to the straight-line architectural form. But Mies was both artist and engineer. How to direct

Figure 12.8. Plastic space organization. Offices of The Doody Company, Columbus, Ohio.
Interior design: Design Collective, Columbus, Ohio
Photograph: Hedrich-Blessing
In this portion of a suite in a corporate office, we see a pleasant modification of the open plan. Provision is made for functionally required partial isolation and for views into spaces and the activities contained therein that provide psychological relief.

traffic flow in a route adverse to architecture and yet preserve architectonic thinking? This presents a challenge.

It seems true that many routes planned within buildings are associated with bizarre and impractical placements of volumes. The difficulty of bringing the total environmental design into a fluid and unified organization without denying the clarity taught by the masterworks often seems to have eluded both architect and interior designer. There is cause here for straighter thinking.

In addition to diagonal and circuitous paths through space, the fourth-dimensional route (so called because traversing a space requires time—the fourth dimension) is increasingly in evidence (Figure 12.9). In architecture the

effect is maneuvered through such details as high ceilings, open stairs, slanting and tall windows, and batteries of directional lights. Interior design uses mobiles, plants and pictures hung high, books and ornaments that reach far above eye level. Although practicality hardly can be argued as the essence of all this, it does incorporate a new way of looking. And, just possibly, it is one answer to the cramped conditions of modern life. Better to have even the merest glimpse of sun and sky than of a neighbor's kitchen across a narrow space.

Possibly bearing some relation to this upward, fourth-dimensional vision, a new kind of line—a linear track—has appeared. Line remains the swiftest and surest embodiment of symbolism. As modernity is so closely allied to movement, a moving line epitomizes its essence. This line is occasionally tenuous, like that in a Klee painting. But don't expect suppleness, except in the occurrence of the ubiquitous trailing plant. Contemporary line is more often drawn taut into a three-dimensional grid, with thrust and counterthrust clearly defined like the exposed sinews of great steel trusses (Figure 12.10).

COLOR AND LIGHT

The sensuous qualities of color and light have taken over the interior designing arena with surprising swiftness. Industries have learned to systematize offerings so that package deals can be secured readily. An attempt has been made to eliminate the quality of trial and error. Color and light only recently have acquired their rightful importance in the designing of public as well as of private buildings.

It is not the use of brilliant color, dramatic black and white contrasts, and flooding intensities of light casting dark shadows that are currently in evidence. Rather, light and color in partnership seem to diffuse space, making its volumes appear somewhat nebulous. From a functional viewpoint light in today's interiors is localized where it is

Figure 12.9. A three- and four-dimensional view. Lewis Dowell House, Seattle, Washington.
Architect: Paul Kirk
Photographer: Dearborn-Massar
This charming home built a few years ago demonstrates some advanced architectural conceptions. From the various stations there is always an interesting spatial view that is often focused obliquely up or down. This kind of view is termed fourth dimensional because it requires a visual journey in space, thereby evoking time—the fourth dimension.

Figure 12.10. Taut lines and fractionated light. Lobby, the Grand Hyatt Hotel,
New York.
Architects: Gruzen & Partners
Interior Designers: GKR, Inc., Barbara Green, President, and Dale Keller &
Associates
Lighting: Jules Fisher & Paul Marantz Inc.
Photograph: © Mark Ross
Peter Lobello's brass sculpture suspended over a marble fountain in the lobby
of one of midtown Manhattan's newest hotels expresses the excitement of
contemporary urban existence along with a little of its tension. Although the
lobby is lighted with natural light from three sides, artificial lighting supplements this. The major source is backed with brass strips that sparkle. In addition,
theatrical spots reflect light off the bronze-mirrored trusses. An overall
wash of down light was avoided since it was unnecessary during the day and
not suitably dramatic at night. Although the planning here was for highly
specialized requirements, the results nevertheless seem characteristic of a
large range of contemporary designs that might be a vanguard exposition of the
nervous energy that characterizes our times.

needed. Where possible, natural light is designed to travel across rooms. In the new
aesthetics, light played against color is often
used for mood creation. Light appears in
soft pools broken by brittle fractionations,
like the diamond or the star that vibrates
most effectively when played against dark or
shade.

As early as 1922, Mies van der Rohe said
that he had discovered in his work with glass
models that the play of reflections in glass-
enclosed spaces was more important than the
usual effect of light and shadow.[4] This is an

[4]Philip C. Johnson, *Mies van der Rohe*, New York: The Museum of Modern Art, 1947, p. 182.

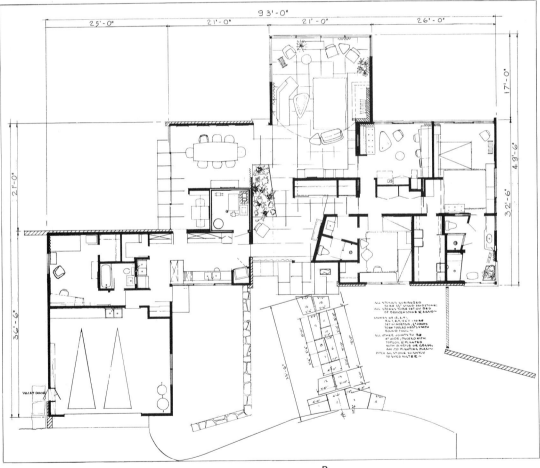

B

Figure 12.11. The old with the new: a lovely and livable home. Residence of Mr. and Mrs. Ernst Payer, Moreland Hills, Ohio.
Architect: Ernst Payer. (a) Exterior. Photographer: C. W. Ackerman. (b) Plan. This house has a handsome contemporary exterior and a particularly good circulation pattern.

Figure 12.11. (*Continued*). Photographer: Charles Hudson. (c) The living room, an exceptionally beautiful interior space, has an inviting atmosphere at all seasons. It is enriched with sixteenth-century Nepalese sculptures, three Rhenish Gothic figures, a Moroccan rug, and a ceramic plant container by sculptor Lisa McVey. The floor is dark green slate, the fireplace wall is cork, and the table is designed by the architect.

observation that is now bearing fruit. It presents yet another challenge to keep the phenomenon of reflection within formal control, to harness it so that it does no functional damage to an interior space, and yet to preserve its wonderful aesthetic potential.

Today's colorist uses saturations in the weak range to hold ensembles together. Color values are lower, and thus they anchor space

more closely to the earth. This appears to be more important psychologically the higher the elevator ascends into a skyscraper apartment or executive suite.

TEXTURE

How long has it taken designers working with steel and glass (the hard materials) and with synthetic finishes (from which light comes harshly off the surface) to learn that the combination of these substances is not only unpleasant but is frequently irritating and painful! Mies knew this. His steel chairs are covered with leather, which reflects light from deep in its pores; his floors have high-pile wool rugs; his partitions are striated wood and diffusing onyx; his hangings are silks in plain and pile weave.

These materials, however, are either too expensive or too impractical for most occasions. And it has taken the design industry much time to learn how to give soft and changing lights to hard textures. A Pollock painting would serve this purpose, but how many can afford such art work? Many new products to suit this purpose are now available—synthetic leather with variegated shifts of color, wickerwork that disperses light with its open weaving, shaggy rugs, textiles with raised patterns or with designs that break up light, plants (real ones, of course), sculptured metal, natural fiber wallcoverings, ombre wall finishes. Thank you, industry!

OLD AND NEW

The use in interior design of the new with the old is fortunately of frequent occurrence

today, and this is indeed a notable sphere of cooperation between architecture and interiors (Figures 12.11a, b, and c). This is not a phenomenon restricted to the private dwelling, where it is often the result of necessity rather than choice. It is seen frequently in public places, where it could be credited to an awareness awakened by the presence of the historic preservationist on the scene. The many restorations of historic landmarks for today's uses have called into being the specialist, the architect, the interior designer, the consultant, each of whom is versed in an understanding of this sort of endeavor.

It is not possible for the old to be exactly like the new, and such verity should not be attempted except where restoration is literal in its purpose (Figures 12.12a, b, and c). Therefore, where a modern focus is intended, modernity should predominate. The genuinely old frequently can fit into a present-day scheme with no greater change than is demanded by scrupulous renovation. Fine work of the past (even provincial work) has its integrity and will grace contemporary locations (Figure 12.13), but poor design from the past and poorly designed copies of the past—no.

Figure 12.12. Careful restoration of the old for the new. The Providence Athenaeum, Providence, Rhode Island. Restoration, architecture of addition, landscape architecture, and interior design: Warren Platner Associates
Photographer: Ezra Stoller © ESTO. (a) Exterior. The best of restoration work combines change with great respect for the fine qualities of the old. The Providence Athenaeum is a library built in 1836 that today houses a collection of nineteenth-century literature. It is situated on a street of historic Greek-revival townhouses. The restoration program called for a library addition plus a reasonably priced renovation of the old quarters. The facade of the original has been left intact and a corresponding granite masonry block has been appended to it.

12-12b

12-12c

Figure 12.12 (*Continued*). In the reading room (*b*) and (*c*) of the Providence Athenaeum library space has been opened up and bookshelves, which are mechanized roll-outs in pavilion form echoing some of the spirit of the old building, have been installed. The chief librarian's office and rare book room are housed in a glass-enclosed space that overlooks the entrance court. Furnishings, which are in many instances old, have been chosen for their sturdy simplicity. Finishes are inexpensive but have the elegance that comes from restraint, appropriateness, and good design.

252

Figure 12.13. Richness with restraint. The Astor Court viewed through the Moon Gate, The Metropolitan Museum of Art, New York, Gift of the Vincent Astor Foundation, 1980.
Photograph: © 1980 By The Metropolitan Museum of Art, all rights reserved
The main entrance to the Astor Court is the moon gate in the south wall. Looking through the moon gate to the north, one sees only parts of the garden and primarily zones of darkness and brightness, a manifestation of the complementary pairs of Ying and Yang. The eye moves from the white wall to the dark vestibule, to the sunlit garden, to the dark Ming Room, and on to the bright windows at the far end. The contrasts create a sense of rhythm, distance, and space (quoted from the Metroplitan Museum of Art *Bulletin*, Vol. 38, No. 3, Winter 1980/81, p. 30).

Conclusion

The formula

$$World \rightarrow Stimulus \dashrightarrow Organism \rightarrow Response \rightarrow World$$

is now complete. From the world of experience we have found the stimulus to produce the conscious response of beauty. In the process, a force has been created that will have its countereffect on the world. Beauty is a dynamo that can transmit a spiritual power to many who are in its field.

Good designing is so simple that it is nothing more than inspired common sense. But it is so difficult that to learn all there is to learn about it would take the dedication of a lifetime.

Loving concern takes no account of years

and effort. From such devotion alone is created beauty. Wherever beauty is created, it stands as eternal witness to the fact that, from the material of life, we can make that which is of the spirit.

This book proposes one method of working through to this result. Certainly there are many more. As the late ornithologist Edward Howe Forbush, in his *Birds of Massachusetts*, said of the barn owl, "When divested by sci-ence of its atmosphere of malign mystery, this owl is seen to be not only harmless, but a benefactor to mankind and a very interesting fowl that will repay close study."[5]

So it is with the art of interior design.

[5]From "Mr. Forbush's Friend," *Essays of E. B. White*, by E. B. White. Copyright © 1966 by E. B. White. Originally appeared in *The New Yorker* and reprinted by permission of Harper & Row, Publishers, Inc.

Figure 12.14. And a light touch with heavy things. Steuben Glass figure, "Hippopotamus," L. 6¼"
Designer: Lloyd Atkins
Photograph: Courtesy of Steuben Glass
According to Leonardo da Vinci, "The hippopotamus feeds on plants and goes into them backwards so that it may seem as though he had come out." Now, having finished and emerged, try going through again, and this time make your own collection of illustrations!

SUGGESTIONS FOR THE FURTHER USE OF THESE CHAPTERS

Chapter 1. Good Art: The Problems We Face

1. Secure a picture of some interior that you think is beautiful. Ask someone else's opinion about this. Record where your two views diverge, if they do.
2. Secure a copy of some famous picture. Why do you like or dislike this painting?
3. Name some instances where the interior designer might make use of science.
4. Of what specific benefit is science in the production of art?
5. In thinking about designing an interior space such as a schoolroom, list some of the various specific considerations to which you might give attention.
6. Under what broad categories—function, expression, or design—would each of the considerations you listed in exercise 5 be classed?
7. Does popular writing today make any use of the terms good taste or poor taste?
8. Do you think you could ever change someone's mind about what that person considers beautiful? How would you attempt to do so?
9. Can you remember anything that in the past you considered beautiful but do not now? Can you give any reason for your change of mind?
10. Read or scan one of the reference books given for this chapter. What is its main thesis? Do you agree or disagree? Give reasons.

Chapter 2. Coordinating Interior Design with Building Structure

1. What, in your opinion, are five of the most beautiful buildings in the world? Can you give reasons for your choice?
2. To what groups of professionals is the work of the interior designer closely related?

3. If you were setting up a school curriculum for the training of any of these professionals, how would you interrelate the courses of study?
4. Observe and begin to record buildings with respect to their structures (probably in a notebook with photographs and accompanying explanations).
5. In your collected illustrations, have you any criticism to offer about the kind and placement of the windows and doors? Would you agree about their placement, and if not, what alternatives would you suggest?
6. Have you any judgment to offer about design treatment in relation to the structure observed in your collected pictures?
7. Locate two illustrations, one of an interior that has in your judgment been accorded an architectonic treatment and one that has not (architectonic: resembling architecture in structure and organization).
8. Do you think that a public enlightened on such matters is desirable or not?
9. The relation between structure and design, because it is a controversial subject, is a good one for debate. There is no better whetstone than a good argument, provided all the rules of proper debating are adhered to—rationality, open-mindedness, objectivity, plus an informed background.
10. Read or at least interest yourself in one of the reference books given for this chapter. What is its main thesis? Do you agree or disagree? Give reasons.

Chapter 3. Functional Planning of Interiors

1. Name twenty-five types of building with respect to their uses (e.g., schools).
2. List various interior design systems that you have found advertised. Give name, advertiser, address, and name of the magazine where found.

3. Review some book or magazine article concerned with the planning of some type of building other than a house. Give the correct bibliographical reference.

4. Investigate the zoning laws in your community and state your opinion of them.

5. Make or select a house plan. Analyze it with respect to one of the areas detailed in this chapter.

6. Analyze the psychological benefits that you would like to find in a dwelling planned for your own use.

7. Analyze a plan of some building other than a house with respect to its circulation pattern.

8. Make a plan of some building area, placing functional equipment in it. For sizes and needs consult a source for equipment (see the Bibliography). This sort of problem may start a specialized career for you.

9. Write a paper on your solution to problem 8, justifying it.

10. Draw an elevation of one wall of your plan.

11. Draw a perspective grid of this area.

12. On an overlay of your grid, draw a perspective of some view of the room.

Chapter 4. Design Organization

1. Select a picture of a room. Apply each of the tests of a good design as stated in this chapter. How does your room register?

2. Can you name the factor that you think has made it good or poor?

3. Make a list or two of qualities you would organize into one of the following: a living room; an office; an expensive restaurant; a diner.

4. Under which of these phrases—a physical state, an emotional state, a mental state—would you classify each of the qualities listed in exercise 3?

5. Sketch two walls of a room (you will only learn to do this by practice). Designate, by means of objects placed on or near it, the center of attention on one wall.

6. Sketch three walls of the same or a different room, and balance the wall forces.

7. Select an illustration of an interior design of some area that does not lend itself to comprehension in one view (e.g., a restaurant or an office). Suggest how the principles outlined in this chapter have some validity for appraising its design. Suggest some ways in which so rigid an appraisal would be an unrewarding exercise. Are there any guideposts you see that pertain to this sort of design? Write about them.

8. Select a copy of a masterpiece picture and trace several choices of visual paths through it.

9. In what ways does an interior design differ from a painting in terms of design?

10. Examine some interior design that has been widely acclaimed. Criticize it in respect to its value in our culture, its value judged solely as design, and its

value as you would judge it by your overall standards. If it fails in one of these classifications, try to find a similar example that succeeds.

11. Read and comment on, in terms of this chapter, one of the books suggested in the Bibliography.

Chapter 5. Space and Shape in Interiors

1. Find illustrations, preferably of a room interior, that incorporate static proportions.

2. Find illustrations of some room that seems significant when perceived as space.

3. Make a scaled root triangle in lightweight cardboard to use in testing proportional relations.

4. Locate or draw some furniture that has good geometric curves; organic curves.

5. Locate an object that, in your opinion, has good (or poor) structural and decorative design.

6. Locate several illustrations of poorly designed furniture.

7. Do you think that designers are improving or retrograding in respect to furniture design? Substantiate your opinion.

8. Locate an interior that, in your opinion, has good architectonic design; locate one that does not.

9. Take some small space and carry on its design from the standpoint of spatial organization. Make a sketch.

10. Read and comment on, in terms of this chapter, one of the suggested readings in the Bibliography.

Chapter 6. Light as an Aesthetic Factor in Interior Design

1. If you can locate a photometer that is calibrated in footcandles, or lux, take readings at crucial locations in a given space. Measure the light found in the immediate surround and in the general environment. Make a chart of these findings.

2. Suggest any corrections that you think are necessary to improve the lighting situation measured in exercise 1.

3. Mount some materials that have a matte surface and others that have a glossy surface. Look at them under intense light. Describe what you see.

4. Name several examples where directional and nondirectional light are called for.

5. Mount some illustrations of lighting. Discuss them from the point of view of functional, expressive, and design purposes.

6. Write a paragraph about the latest theories of lighting of paintings, sculpture, or glass. Give bibliographic references.

7. Mount or draw some illustrations of window treatments for light control.

8. Send for pamphlets from a large lamp manufacturer indicating the various bulbs it makes. Tabulate them with respect to their control of light.

9. Create a lighting plan for the space you have been designing.
10. Read and comment on, in terms of this chapter, one of the suggested readings in the Bibliography.

Chapter 7. Understanding Color

1. Read the labels on some commercial paints and determine:
   The name of the colorants used, if given.
   The name of the vehicle, if given.
   Whether these should be called oil based or water based.
2. Read the labels on a commercial varnish, shellac, lacquer, and enamel. What have you learned about their composition and use?
3. Name several expensive and several less expensive colorants.
4. Which will cost more, a dark or a light paint? Why?
5. Test and record your color vision.
6. Find two color examples in which two attributes are the same, forcing contrast in the third attribute.
7. Find a good example of additive mixture by the eye in some commercial sample (textile, carpet, or wallpaper).
8. Find a color print of some famous painting and analyze the highlights and shadows in it with respect to color.
9. Read and comment on, in terms of this chapter, one of the articles suggested in the Bibliography.

Chapter 8. Using Color in Interiors

1. Use the plan adopted in Chapter 3 and place colors in it. A watercolor or tempera rendering may substitute.
2. Paint (or find and label) an illustration of one of the visual color paths as used in a room.
3. Paint (or find and label) an example of a close hue harmony used in a room.
4. Paint (or find and label) an example of a divergent hue harmony found in a room.
5. Paint (or find and label) an example of a room color plan of low saturation.
6. Paint (or find and label) an example of a room color plan of high saturation.
7. Paint (or find and label) an example of an unusual lightness–darkness harmony found in a room.
8. Write a paragraph of criticism of some room color scheme in respect to the factors mentioned in this chapter.
9. Try to create a color plan for someone whose color sense differs from yours.
10. Read and comment on one of the articles suggested in the Bibliography.

Chapter 9. Understanding Texture

1. Find and analyze an example of a good textural design.
2. Find an example of a poor textural design.
3. Collect a list of words from your current reading that you think are texture-connected.
4. Analyze some current materials with respect to their textural attributes.
5. Select a wall pattern that gives the effect of texture.
6. Select a carpet or an illustration of one that is quiet in its total effect and yet has textural contrasts incorporated into it.
7. Find an illustration in which a fine-scaled texture has been made to appear heavier through pattern.
8. Describe in detail some textures that will combine well with steel and glass. Justify your choices (this will take considerable thinking, and such thinking about texture should continue throughout your study of the rest of this text).
9. Describe some textures that will combine well with pine. Justify your choices.
10. Read and comment on one of the articles suggested in the Bibliography.

Chapter 10. The Materials of Interior Design

1. Start a collection of wood samples that represent woods useful in interiors. Detail them with respect to species, habitat, character, and uses.
2. Secure an illustration of a currently advertised piece of furniture and analyze the information about it given in the advertisement.
3. Secure a sample or an illustration of a currently advertised textile. Analyze the information about it with respect to basic textile characteristics.
4. Secure an illlustration of a currently advertised carpet or rug. Analyze the information about it in relation to your knowledge of the subject.
5. Secure an illustration of a currently advertised ceramic. Analyze the information about it in relation to your knowledge of the subject.
6. Secure an illustration of a currently advertised glass. Analyze the information about it in relation to your knowledge of the subject.
7. Secure an illustration of a metal interior artifact. Analyze the information about it provided in the advertisement in relation to your knowledge of the subject.
8. Secure an illustration of some hard surfacing material. Analyze the information about it provided in the advertisement in relation to your knowledge of the subject.
9. Make a scrapbook of currently advertised furniture giving the following information about each example: firm name and address; material and fabrication; your analysis of its design.

10. Give a brief synopsis of some article listed in the Bibliography.

Chapter 11. Accessories: The Supernumerary and the Lodestar

1. Find an illustration of a fabric used as an accessory to a decorative scheme. Document its character and source.
2. Find an illustration of a ceramic used as an accessory to a decorative scheme. Document its character and source.
3. Find an illustration of a glass object used as an accessory to a decorative scheme. Document its character and source.
4. Find an illustration of an enamel used as an accessory to a decorative scheme. Document its character and source.
5. Find an illustration of a metal object used as an accessory to a decorative scheme. Document its character and source.
6. Find an illustration of a stone object used as an accessory to a decorative scheme. Document its character and source.
7. Find an illustration of an antique used as an accessory to a decorative scheme. Document its character and source.
8. Sketch or find an illustration of an interior that emphasizes a work of fine art.
9. Sketch or find an illustration of an interior that emphasizes several works of fine art.

10. Read and comment on some article in the Bibliography.

Chapter 12. The Total Art Form: Putting It All Together

1. Locate an illustration of a recent interior and criticize its floor treatment constructively.
2. Locate an illustration of a recent interior and criticize its wall treatment constructively.
3. Locate an illustration of a recent interior and criticize its window treatment constructively.
4. Select illustrations of seating furniture and provide samples of suitable upholstery material for these pieces. Detail the name, fiber, construction, and your reason for the selection.
5. Complete the project that you commenced earlier (Chapter 3, Problem 8), placing colors on the various articles.
6. Make a texture scheme detailing the textures used.
7. Describe some section of the ensemble in as detailed a manner as possible. Later it will be found that the commercial world of designing has its specific terminology for this process, known as the giving of specifications, or *specs* for short.
8. Using the outline of aesthetic qualities and their development, fill it in with respect to your project.
9. Select an illustration of a recent interior and comment on it as representative of our culture.
10. Select some article from the Bibliography and comment on it.

BIBLIOGRAPHY

This bibliography has been compiled with the intent of providing a core list of the best recent material applicable to the subject at hand. It certainly is not all-inclusive, and it is deliberately not extensive. Its aim is to supplement the text in a necessary and intelligible way. Some books listed are not of recent vintage. They are fundamental.

Books noted under one chapter heading are frequently applicable to another.

General

Alexander, Mary Jean, *Designing Interior Environment*, New York: Harcourt Brace Jovanovich, 1972.

Ball, Victoria Kloss, *Architecture and Interior Design: A Basic History through the Seventeenth Century*, New York: Wiley, 1980.

———, *Architecture and Interior Design: Europe and America from the Colonial Era to Today*, New York: Wiley, 1980.

Bevlin, Marjorie Elliott, *Design Through Discovery*, New York: Holt, Rinehart & Winston, 1980.

Brett, Lionel, *Architecture in a Crowded World: Vision and Reality in Planning*, New York: Schocken, 1972.

Corbin, Patricia, and **Ernst Beadle,** *Designers Design for Themselves*, New York: Dutton, 1980.

Cornell, Jane, *Successful Custom Interiors*, Farmington, MI: Structures Publishing Co., 1979.

Crane, Catherine C., Ed., *Residential Interiors Today*, New York: Whitney, 1977.

Faulkner, R., and **S. Faulkner,** *Inside Today's Home*, 34th ed., New York: Holt, Rinehart & Winston, 1968.

Faulkner, R., and **E. Ziegfeld,** *Art Today*, 5th ed., New York: Holt, Rinehart & Winston, 1969.

Faulkner, Sarah, *Planning a Home: A Practical Guide to Interior Design*, New York: Holt, Rinehart & Winston, 1979.

Friedmann, Arnold, John Pile, and **Wilson Forest,** *Interior Design: An Introduction to Architectural Interiors*, 2nd ed., New York: American Elsevier, 1976.

Fuller, R. Buckminster, *Synergetics*, New York: Wittenborn, 1975.

Hatje, Gerd, and **Ursula Hatje,** *Design for Modern Living*, New York: Abrams, 1962.

Hunt, William Dudley, Jr., *Encyclopedia of American Architecture*, New York: McGraw-Hill, 1980.

Huxtable, Ada L., *Kicked a Building Lately?* New York: Times Books, 1978.

Magnani, Franco, *Interiors for Today*, New York: Wittenborn, 1975.

Nelson, George, *Problems of Design*, New York: Watson-Guptill, 1979.

Papanek, Victor, *Designing for the Real World*, Des Plaines, IL: Bantam, 1976.

Rogers, K. E., *The Modern House, U.S.A., Design and Decoration*, New York: Harper, 1962.

Whiton, Sherrill, *Interior Design and Decoration*, 4th ed., New York: Harper & Row, 1974.

Chapter 1. Good Art: The Problems We Face

Bennet, Corwin, *Spaces for People: Human Factors in Design*, Englewood Cliffs, NJ: Prentice-Hall, 1977.

Chandler, Albert R., *Beauty and Human Nature*, New York: Appleton-Century-Crofts, 1934, pp. 3–33.

Dewey, John, *Art as Experience*, New York: Minton, Balch, 1934.

Gilbert, Katherine, *Aesthetic Studies*, Durham, NC: Duke University Press, 1952, pp. 3–22.

Munro, Thomas, *The Arts and Their Interrelations*, New York: Liberal Arts Press, 1949.

Perry, Ralph Barton, *Realms of Value*, Cambridge: Harvard University Press, 1954.

Pile, John, *Design: Purpose, Form and Meaning*, Amherst: University of Massachusetts Press, 1979.

Santayana, George, *The Sense of Beauty*, New York: Scribner's, 1896.

Chapter 2. Coordinating Interior Design with Building Structure

Allen, Edward, *How Buildings Work*, New York: Oxford University Press, 1980.

Cowan, Henry J., *Architectural Structures: An Introduction to Structural Mechanics*, New York: American Elsevier, 1971.

Debaights, Jacques, *The Modern Fireplace*, New York: Van Nostrand Reinhold, 1975.

Dietz, Albert G. H., *Dwelling House Construction*, Cambridge: M.I.T. Press, 1971.

Egan, M. David, *Concepts in Architectural Acoustics*, New York: McGraw-Hill, 1972.

Flynn, John E., and Arthur W. Segil, *Architectural Interior Systems: Lighting, Air Conditioning, Acoustics*, New York: Van Nostrand Reinhold, 1970.

Franta, Gregory, and Kenneth R. Olson, Eds., *Solar Architecture*, Ann Arbor, MI: Ann Arbor Science Publishers, 1978.

Heschong, Lisa, *Thermal Delight in Architecture*, Cambridge: M.I.T. Press, 1979.

Hohauser, Sanford, *Architectural and Interior Models*, New York: Van Nostrand Reinhold, 1970.

Hornbostel, Caleb, *Construction Materials*, New York: Wiley, 1978.

Negnoponte, Nicholas, *The Architecture Machine*, Cambridge: M.I.T. Press, 1970.

Ormerod, Milton B., *Architecture and Properties of Matter: An Approach Through Models*, New York: Crane-Russak, 1970.

Otto, Fred, *Tensile Structures*, Cambridge: M.I.T. Press, 1972.

Propst, Robert, and Michael Wodka, *The Action Office Acoustic Handbook*, Zeeland, MI: Herman Miller Marketing Resource Group, 1976.

Quarmby, Arthur, *Plastics in Architecture*, New York: Praeger, 1973.

Salvadori, Mario, *Why Buildings Stand Up*, New York: Norton, 1980.

Shurcliff, William A., *Thermal Shutters and Shades*, Andover, MA: Brick House Publishing Co., 1980.

Torroja, Eduardo, *Philosophy of Structures*, translated by J. J. and Milos Polivka, Berkeley: University of California Press, 1958.

Watson, Donald, *Energy Conservation Through Building Design*, New York: McGraw-Hill, 1978.

Wright, David, *Natural Solar Architecture*, New York: Van Nostrand Reinhold, 1978.

Chapter 3. Functional Planning of Interiors

Brett, James, *The Kitchen*, New York: Watson-Guptill, 1977.

Clurman, David, and Edna L. Hebard, *Condominiums and Cooperatives*, New York: Wiley, 1970.

Conran, Terence, *The Bed and Bath Book*, New York: Crown, 1977.

———, *The Kitchen Book*, New York: Crown, 1977.

Curran, Jane, *Drawing Plans for Your Own Home*, New York: McGraw-Hill, 1976.

Dalzell, James Ralph, *Plan Reading for Home Builders*, New York: McGraw-Hill, 1972.

De Chiara, Joseph, and John Callender, *Time-Saver Standards for Building Types*, 2nd ed., New York: McGraw-Hill, 1980.

Fengler, Max, *Restaurant Architecture and Design*, New York: Wittenborn, 1971.

Gaines, Richard L., *Interior Plantscaping: Building Design for Interior Foliage Plants*, New York: McGraw-Hill, 1977.

Goldsmith, Selwyn, *Designing for the Disabled*, Forest Grove, OR: International School Book Service, 1977.

Gosling, David, and Barry Maitland, *Design and Planning of Retail Systems*, New York: Watson-Guptill, 1976.

Halse, Albert O., *Architectural Rendering: The Techniques of Contemporary Presentation*, 2nd ed., New York: McGraw-Hill, 1972.

Hanks, Kurt, and Larry Belliston, *Rapid Viz*, Los Altos, CA: Kaufmann, 1980.

Herman Miller Design Resource Service, *The Dormitory Experiment*, Zeeland, MI: Herman Miller Marketing Resource Group, 1975.

Izenour, G. C., *Theater Design*, New York: McGraw-Hill, 1977.

Jewell, Don, *Public Assembly Facilities: Planning and Management*, New York: Wiley, 1978.

Lawson, Fred, *Designing Commercial Food Service Facilities*, New York: Watson-Guptill, 1975.

Leach, S. D., *Techniques of Interior Design: Rendering and Presentation*, Hightstown, NJ: Architectural Record Books, 1978.

Leggett, S., C. W. Brubaker, A. Cohodes, and A. S. Shapiro, *Planning Flexible Learning Places*, New York: McGraw-Hill, 1977.

Lynn, Edwin C., *Tired Dragons: Adapting Church Architecture to Changing Needs*, Boston: Beacon Press, 1972.

Mulvey, Frances R., *Graphic Perception of Space*, New York: Van Nostrand Reinhold, 1969.

Panero, Julius, *Anatomy for Interior Designers*, 3rd ed., New York: Whitney Library of Design, 1962.

Panero, Julius, and Martin Zelnik, *Human Dimensions and Interior Space*, New York: Watson-Guptill, 1979.

Pile, John, *Open Office Planning: A Handbook for Interior Designers and Architects*, New York: Watson-Guptill, 1978.

Ramsey, C., and H. R. Sleeper, *Architectural Graphic Standards*, 7th ed., Robert T. Packard, A.I.A., Ed., New York: Wiley-Interscience, 1981.

Rosenfield, Isadore, *Hospital Architecture*, New York: Van Nostrand Reinhold, 1971.

Safdie, Moshe, *For Everyone a Garden*, Cambridge: M.I.T. Press, 1973.

Saphier, Michael, *Office Planning and Design*, New York: McGraw-Hill, 1968.

Schubert, Hannelore, *The Modern Theatre: Architecture, Stage Design, Lighting*, New York: Praeger, 1971.

Sorenson, Robert, *Design for Accessibility*, New York: McGraw-Hill, 1979.

Weiss, Joseph Douglas, *Better Buildings for the Aged*, New York: McGraw-Hill, 1971.

Chapter 4. Design Organization

Arnheim, Rudolf, *Visual Thinking*, Berkeley: University of California Press, 1980.

Garrett, Lucian, *Visual Design: A Problem Solving Approach*, New York: Reinhold, 1966.

Itten, Johannes, *Design and Form: The Basic Course at the Bauhaus*, 2nd rev. ed., New York: Van Nostrand Reinhold, 1976.

Kepes, Gyorgy, *The Language of Vision*, Chicago: Theobold, 1948.

_____, *The Module, Proportion, Symmetry, Rhythm*, New York: Braziller, 1966.

Sommer, Robert, *Personal Space: The Behavioral Basis of Design*, New York: Prentice-Hall, 1969.

Chapter 5. Space and Shape in Interiors

Albers, Josef, and Francois Bucher, *Despite Straight Lines*, Cambridge: M.I.T. Press, 1977.

Arnheim, Rudolph, *Art and Visual Perception*, Berkeley: University of California Press, 1954.

Baillie, Sheila, and Mabel R. Skjelver, *Graphics for Interior Space*, Lincoln: University of Nebraska Press, 1979.

Bloimer, Carolyn M., *Principles of Visual Perception*, New York: Van Nostrand Reinhold, 1976.

Hambidge, Jay, *Dynamic Symmetry: The Greek Vase*, New Haven, CT: Yale University Press, 1920.

Liman, Ellen, *The Spacemaker Book*, New York: Viking, 1977.

March, Lionel, and Philip Steadman, *Geometry of Environment: An Introduction to Spatial Organization in Design*, Cambridge: M.I.T. Press, 1975.

Sommer, Robert, *Personal Space: The Behavioral Basis of Design*, New York: Prentice-Hall, 1969.

Zevi, Bruno, *Architecture as Space*, New York: Horizons, 1975.

Chapter 6. Light As an Aesthetic Factor in Interior Design

Evans, Benjamin H., *Daylight in Architecture*, Hightstown, NJ: Record Books, 1980.

Flynn, John E., and Samuel M. Mills, *Architectural Lighting Graphics*, New York: Reinhold, 1962.

Gilliatt, Mary, and Douglas Baker, *Lighting Your Home: A Practical Guide*, New York: Pantheon Books, 1979.

Hopkinson, R. G., and J. D. Kay, *The Lighting of Buildings*, New York: Wittenborn, 1969.

Illuminating Engineering Society of North America, *IES Lighting Handbook: 1981 Reference Volume*, John E. Kaufman, Ed.; Howard Haynes, Asso. Ed., New York: Illuminating Engineering Society, 1981.

_____, *IES Lighting Handbook: 1981 Application Volume*, John E. Kaufman, Ed.; Howard Haynes, Asso. Ed., New York: Illuminating Engineering Society, 1981.

Kalff, Louis C., *Creative Light*, New York: Whitney, 1971.

Larson, Leslie, *Lighting and Its Design*, New York: Whitney, 1964.

Mullin, Ray C., *Electrical Wiring—Residential*, 5th ed., New York: Van Nostrand Reinhold, 1975.

Nuckolls, James, *Interior Lighting for Environmental Designers*, New York: Wiley, 1976.

Phillips, Derek, *Lighting in Architectural Design*, New York: McGraw-Hill, 1964.

Staley, Karl A., *Fundamentals of Light and Lighting*, Cleveland: General Electric Company, 1960.

United States Department of Energy, *Lighting*, DOE/CS-0006, Washington, DC: United States Government Printing Office, 1980.

Chapters 7 and 8. Understanding Color; Using Color in Interiors

Albers, Josef, *Interaction of Color*, New Haven, CT: Yale University Press, 1963.

Birren, Faber, *Color and Human Response*, New York: Van Nostrand Reinhold, 1978.

Burnham, Robert W., R. M. Haines, and C. James Bartleson, *Color: A Guide to Basic Facts and Concepts*, New York: Wiley, 1963.

Carpenter, H. Barrett, *Colour*, New York: Scribner's, 1932.

Color Association of the United States, *The Standard Color Reference of America*, 10th ed., New York: Color Association of the United States, 1981.

Evans, R. M., *An Introduction to Color*, New York: Wiley, 1959.

Gerritsen, Frank J., *Theory and Practice of Color*, New York: Van Nostrand Reinhold, 1974.

Halse, S. O., *The Use of Color in Interiors*, 2nd ed., New York: McGraw-Hill, 1978.

Inter-Society Color Council, *ISCC Comparative List of Color Terms*, Washington, DC: Inter-Society Color Council, 1949.

Itten, Johannes, *The Art of Color*, New York: Reinhold, 1961.

Mayer, Ralph, *The Artist's Handbook of Materials and Techniques*, New York: Viking, 1940.

Optical Society of America, Committee of Colorimetry, *The Science of Color*, New York: Crowell, 1953.

Verity, Enid, *Color Observed*, New York: Van Nostrand Reinhold, 1980.

Chapters 9 and 10. Understanding Texture; The Materials of Interior Design

Beard, Geoffrey, *International Modern Glass*, New York: Scribner's, 1978.

Burnham, Dorothy K., *Warp and Weft: A Textile Terminology*, Toronto: Royal Ontario Museum, 1980.

Caplan, Ralph, *The Design Impact of Herman Miller*, New York: Watson-Guptill, 1976.

Clark, Garth R., and Margie Hughto, *A Century of Ceramics in the United States*, New York: Dutton, 1979.

Edlin, Herbert L., *What Wood Is That? A Manual of Wood Identification*, New York: Viking, 1977.

Ellsworth, Robert Halfield, *Chinese Furniture*, New York: Random House, 1971.

Garner, Philippe, *Twentieth Century Furniture*, New York: Van Nostrand Reinhold, 1980.

Gregorian, Arthur T., *Oriental Rugs and the Stories They Tell*, New York: Scribner's, 1978.

Hackmack, Adolf, *Chinese Carpets and Rugs*, Rutland, VT: Charles E. Tuttle, 1979.

Hall, A. J., *Standard Handbook of Textiles*, New York: Chemical Publishing Co., 1969.

Hamer, Frank, *The Potter's Dictionary of Materials and Techniques*, New York: Watson-Guptill, 1975.

Hartung, Paul, *Creative Textile Design: Thread and Fabric*, New York: Reinhold, 1964.

———, *More Creative Textile Design: Color and Texture*, New York: Reinhold, 1965.

Hawley, Walter A., *Oriental Rugs Antique and Modern*, New York: Dover, 1970.

Herbert, Janice S., *Oriental Rugs: The Illustrated Buyers Guide*, New York: Macmillan, 1978.

Hogben, Carol, Ed., *The Work of Bernard Leach*, New York: Watson-Guptill, 1978.

Hughes, Graham, *Modern Silver*, New York: Wittenborn, 1967.

Jacobson, Charles W., *Check Points on How to Buy Oriental Rugs*, New York: Wittenborn, 1970.

Johnson, David, *The Craft of Furniture Making*, New York: Scribner's, 1979.

Joseph, Marjory, *Introductory Textile Science*, New York: Holt, Rinehart & Winston, 1977.

Kribs, David A., *Commercial Foreign Woods on the American Market*, New York: Dover, 1968.

Kuhn, Fritz, *Decorative Work in Wrought Iron and Other Metals*, New York: Crown, 1977.

Laging, Barbara, *Furniture Design for the Elderly*, Chicago: National Society for Crippled Children and Adults, 1966.

Larsen, Jack L., and Jeanne Weeks, *Fabrics for Interiors*, New York: Van Nostrand Reinhold, 1975.

Meilach, Dona Z., *Decorative and Sculptural Ironwork*, New York: Crown, 1977.

Nelson, Glenn C., *Ceramics: A Potter's Handbook*, 4th ed., New York: Rinehart & Winston, 1978.

Newman, Thelma R., *Plastics As Design Form*, Radnor, PA: Chilton, 1972.

Pile, John, *Modern Furniture*, New York: Wiley, 1978.

Reed, Christopher Dunham, *Turkoman Rugs*, Cambridge: Harvard University Press, 1966.

Reznikoff, S. C., *Specifications for Commercial Interiors*, New York: Whitney, 1979.

Scharff, Robert, *Complete Book of Wood Finishing*, 2nd ed., New York: McGraw-Hill, 1974.

Seiber, Roy, *African Textiles and Decorative Arts*, New York: Museum of Modern Art, 1972.

Shea, John G., *Anatomy of Contemporary Furniture*, New York: Van Nostrand Reinhold, 1973.

Sherwood, Malcolm H., *From Forest to Furniture*, New York: Norton, 1936.

Shoskes, Lila, *Contract Carpeting*, New York: Watson-Guptill, 1976.

Stuart, Azalea, and Jack Lenor Larsen, *Elements of Weaving*, New York: Doubleday, 1967.

Taylor, Lucy, *Know Your Fabrics*, New York: Wiley, 1951.

Weeks, Jeanne G., and Donald Treganowen, *Rugs and Carpets of Europe and the Western World*, Radnor, PA: Chilton, 1970.

Wingate, Gillespie Addison, *Know Your Merchandise*, New York: McGraw-Hill, 1964.

Zahle, Erik, Ed., *A Treasury of Scandinavian Design*, New York: Golden, 1961.

Chapter 11. Accessories: The Supernumerary and the Lodestar

Albers, Josef, *Search Versus Re-Search*, New York: Wittenborn, 1970.

Clarke, Brian, Ed., *Architectural Stained Glass*, New York: McGraw-Hill, 1979.

Gaines, Richard L., *Interior Plantscaping: Building Design for Interior Foliage Plants*, New York: McGraw-Hill, 1977.

Heydenryk, Henry, *The Right Frame*, New York: Heineman, 1964.

Insall, Donald, *The Care of Old Buildings Today*, New York: Watson-Guptill, 1975.

Macnaghten, Patrick, *Furnishing with Antiques*, New York: Hippocrene Books, 1976.

Reif, Rita, *Living with Books*, New York: Quadrangle, 1973.

Wallach, Carlo, *Interior Decorating with Plants*, New York: Macmillan, 1976.

Chapter 12. The Total Art Form: Putting It All Together

Architectural Record, *Recycling Buildings: Renovations, Remodelings, Restorations, and Reuses*, Elisabeth K. Thompson, Ed., New York: McGraw-Hill, 1977.

Davern, Jeanne E., Ed., *Architecture 1970–1980: A Decade of Change*, New York: McGraw-Hill, 1980.

Magnani, Franco, *Interiors for Today*, New York: Wittenborn, 1975.

Zevi, Bruno, *The Modern Language of Architecture*, Seattle: University of Washington Press, 1977.

INDEX